Readings in Electronic Commerce

Readings in Electronic Commerce

Edited by

Ravi Kalakota
University of Rochester

Andrew B. Whinston
University of Texas, Austin

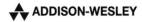
ADDISON-WESLEY

An imprint of Addison Wesley Longman, Inc.

Reading, Massachusetts • Harlow, England • Menlo Park, California
Berkeley, California • Don Mills, Ontario • Sydney • Bonn • Amsterdam
Tokyo • Mexico City

Acquisitions Editor: Thomas E. Stone
Associate Editor: Deborah Lafferty
Production: Editorial Services of New England
Project Manager: Jane Judge Bonassar, Editorial Services of New England
Cover Designer: Loren Hilgenhurst Stevens
Illustrations: Scientific Illustrators
Composition: Compset Inc.

Library of Congress Cataloging-in-Publication Data

Readings in electronic commerce / edited by Ravi Kalakota, Andrew
    Whinston.
        p.   cm.
    Papers presented at the sixth Organizational Computing,
Coordination, and Collaboration Conference, held in Austin, Texas in
October of 1995.
Includes bibliographical references and index.
    ISBN 0-201-88060-1
    1. Electronic commerce—Congresses.   I. Kalakota, Ravi.
II. Whinston, Andrew B.   III. Organizational Computing,
Coordination, and Collaboration Conference (6th : 1995 : Austin,
Texas)
HF5548.3.R43   1997
658.8'00285' 467—dc20   96-27588
                                                                 CIP

Access the latest information about Addison-Wesley titles from our World Wide Web site:
http://www.aw.com/cseng/

1 2 3 4 5 6 7 8 9 10-MA-0099989796

Contents

PART 1:   Introductory Overview

PART 2:   General Business and Policy

Preface

The majority of the chapters in this book are based on papers presented at the Sixth Organizational Computing, Coordination, and Collaboration Conference held at the IC² Institute in Austin, Texas, in October 1995. The purpose of this conference was to address research issues facing academia and industry in the age of electronic commerce. Experts in the field of electronic commerce came together with the goal of helping companies to better understand the shape, structure, and operation of business in the coming millennium.

As the fastest-growing facet of the Internet, electronic commerce offers functionality and new ways of doing business that no company can afford to ignore. The basis for moving to an electronic commerce is a belief that electronic markets have the potential to be more efficient in developing new information goods and services. In addition, electronic commerce also offers companies new ways of finding global customers and trading partners. The Sixth Organizational Computing, Coordination, and Collaboration Conference was aimed at promoting electronic commerce research and practice. Electronic commerce is expected to make obsolete much of the accumulated research in business and to create and demand radical changes in the process, product, and promotion to better exploit the digital platform.

This emerging electronic marketplace is an uncharted frontier, and, much like the "Wild West" of the past, needs to be tamed. The challenge is simple: using emerging technology, how do we create a business environment or infrastructure that will ensure efficient electronic markets? What does it take in terms of new organizational structures like the network structures facilitated by smart and wireless messaging; new electronic institutions such as brokerages staffed by electronic brokers or agents; new business processes better suited for mass customization, global sourcing, and logistics; and new financial payment mechanisms and mercantile protocols?

To explore and exploit new frontiers, we need to integrate business concerns with the changing technology. This conference sought to provide this integration by bringing together leading business researchers who specialize in the various facets of electronic markets—namely, economics, finance, marketing, production, and operations management—and technology experts in the industry who are creating the electronic commerce infrastructure. In addition, experts who specialize in the WWW browsers, electronic cash, encryption, software agents, MIME-based messaging, EDI, and structured documents made presentations.

It is no longer sufficient for electronic commerce to be viewed as a path-breaking technology. Electronic commerce is already playing a significant role in determining the strategy of today's companies in providing value to external and internal customers. The challenge facing companies is to increase the effectiveness of electronic commerce activities in order to achieve business performance. As successful organizations have taken a process-oriented view of their business, they will have to reevaluate the role of electronic commerce in terms of alignment with corporate goals.

This book is divided into five parts. Part One, an introductory overview of electronic commerce, includes three chapters. The first, "An Unaffiliated View of Electronic Commerce," by David H. Crocker, discusses the reasons that the Internet will serve as the global conveyor of transactions for on-line commerce. It also discusses the nature of the technical and operational concerns of electronic commerce and offers solutions to these problems. Chapter 2 by Donna L. Hoffman, Thomas P. Novak, and Patrali Chatterjee explores three main issues associated with the explosion of commercial activity on the Web. Dr. Hoffman explores the role of the Web as a distribution channel and a medium for marketing communications, the factors that have led to the development of the Web as a commercial medium, and finally, the barriers to commercial growth of the Web from both the supply and demand side perspectives. Chapter 3, "An Evaluation of the World Wide Web as a Platform for Electronic Commerce," by Daniel W. Connolly, evaluates the Web with respect to each of Douglas Englebart's twelve requirements for an open hyperdocument system. Englebart's requirements are derived from experience in using computer-supported collaborative work (CSCW) to support large-scale electronic commerce.

Part Two is entitled "General Business and Policy." The first of three chapters in this section is entitled "Electronic Commerce: A Washington Perspective." Its author, James B. Rapp, seeks to make those involved in electronic commerce aware that public policy issues need to be on their "radar screens" when making business decisions, as they will impact pricing, service/product offerings, and marketing approaches.

One of the most politically controversial areas in electronic commerce is the right of governments under certain legally defined conditions to get access to private information. In Chapter 5, Dorothy E. Denning outlines the issues of establishing worldwide standards for creating and managing key escrows by trusted third parties that recognize the competing needs for privacy and governmental disclosure.

"The Essential Role of Trusted Third Parties in Electronic Commerce" by A. Michael Froomkin is the title of Chapter 6. In this chapter, Froomkin discusses the idea that cryptographic protocols for secure electronic transactions require that there be at least one trusted third party to the transaction, such as a bank or a "certification authority" (CA). These partly cryptographic, partly social protocols require new entities, or new relationships with existing entities, but the duties and liabilities of these entities are uncertain. Until these uncertainties are resolved, they risk inhibiting the spread of the most interesting forms of electronic commerce and causing unnecessary litigation. CAs do explain why these entities are important to electronic commerce and suggest that these entities are likely to provoke some interesting legal problems.

Part Three, "Pricing and Electronic Transactions," contains three chapters. Chapter 7, by Nathaniel S. Borenstein and coauthors, discusses the lessons First Virtual learned from a year's experience with the actual operation of its Internet Payment System, as well as the company's views on the future of First Virtual's Internet Payment System in particular, and on Internet commerce in general. Alok Gupta, Dale O. Stahl, and Andrew B. Whinston discuss "Economic Issues in Electronic Commerce" in Chapter 8. They focus on the economic challenges in this market and present some simulation results from the point of view of social welfare and optimal resource management. They also describe the difficulties of sustaining the socially optimal behavior because of the private market competition and the lack of property rights. Finally, Chapter 9, by B. Clifford Neuman, discusses the design of a flexible framework for network payment. Several payment models, including the NetCheque® and NetCash systems, are presented and their characteristics discussed. These two systems, developed at the University of Southern California, show how the design of a payment system can influence its flexibility by minimizing system-imposed constraints on the policies implemented by servers.

Part Four, entitled "Document Management and Digital Libraries," includes two chapters. Chapter 10 by Larry Masinter discusses electronic document management, reviews assumptions for future networking capabilities and electronic commerce, and presents an overview of four kinds of document management applications. It also explores the ways in which the network will change the nature of document management for each of those applications. In Chapter 11, "Smart Catalogs and Virtual Catalogs," Arthur M. Keller presents an architecture for electronic catalogs.

Business applications of electronic commerce are discussed in Part Five. The purpose of Chapter 12, by Aimo Hinkkanen and colleagues, is to describe an information system used in a real-time environment which can be employed to manage and control all activities in the supply chain. In Chapter 13, entitled "Electronic Markets," R. Preston McAfee and John McMillan present a radical new way of conducting auctions in the electronic environment. This chapter explains how electronic markets may function in creating allocations of goods and services where traditional supply and demand work poorly.

In Chapter 14, Ramnath Chellappa, Anitesh Barua, and Andrew B. Whinston discuss one of the industry's fastest-growing segments: corporate Intranets. Finally, Chapter 15, "Electronic Publishing versus Publishing Electronically," by Ramnath Chellappa, Anitesh Barua, Jennifer Oetzel, and Andrew B. Whinston, presents a revolutionary new way of utilizing Internet technology. The chapter shows how Marshall McLuhan was right when he said "The medium is the message."

In summary, investments in electronic commerce, whether in time or money, typically introduce far-reaching organizational and technological issues. It is no longer sufficient for electronic commerce to be viewed as a path-breaking technology. Electronic commerce is already playing a significant role in determining the strategy of today's companies in providing value to external and internal customers. The challenge facing companies is to increase the effectiveness of electronic commerce activities in order to achieve business performance. As successful organizations have taken a process-oriented view of their business, they will have to reevaluate the role of electronic commerce in terms of alignment with corporate goals.

Acknowledgments

We are deeply indebted to George Kozmetsky and the RGK Foundation for their financial support of the Sixth Organizational Computing, Coordination, and Collaboration Conference. Without their support, the conference would not have been possible. Cynthia Smith, Melissa Brown, and Jami Hampton, RGK Foundation staff, deserve special thanks for their flawless organization and execution of the conference. In addition, financial support from the Information Technology and Organizations program at the National Science Foundation helped make this a first-class conference and an international event. We especially wish to thank the program managers, Drs. Su Shing Chen and Les Gasser.

We would also like to thank Robert Sullivan, the Director of IC^2, for his support and for allowing us to use IC^2's conference facilities. We felt particularly fortunate because the acoustics and architecture of the IC^2 complex make it uniquely suited to facilitating a lively exchange of ideas in an attractive environment. Debbie Lafferty, associate editor at Addison Wesley Longman, was amazingly patient from beginning to end, and her guidance along the way was invaluable. Finally, thanks goes to Jennifer Oetzel for her superb editorial work. She deserves our sincere gratitude for efficiently assembling the conference papers.

Ravi Kalakota
University of Rochester
kalakota@uhura.cc.rochester.edu

Andrew B. Whinston
University of Texas at Austin
abw@uts.cc.utexas.edu

List of Contributors

Anitesh Barua
Graduate School of Business, University of Texas at Austin, Texas

Nathaniel S. Borenstein
First Virtual Holdings, Incorporated, San Diego, California

Patrali Chatterjee
Owen Graduate School of Management, Vanderbilt University, Nashville, Tennessee

Ramnath Chellappa
Graduate School of Business, University of Texas at Austin, Texas

Daniel W. Connolly
W3 Consortium at the Massachusetts Institute of Technology, Cambridge, Massachusetts

David H. Crocker
Brandenburg Consulting, Sunnyvale, California

Dorothy E. Denning
Georgetown University, Washington, DC

John Ferguson
First Virtual Holdings, Incorporated, San Diego, California

A. Michael Froomkin
University of Miami School of Law, Coral Gables, Florida

Alok Gupta
Graduate School of Business, University of Texas at Austin, Texas

Gerald Hall
First Virtual Holdings, Incorporated, San Diego, California

Aimo Hinkkanen
University of Illinois, Urbana-Champaign, Illinois

Donna L. Hoffman
Owen Graduate School of Management, Vanderbilt University, Nashville, Tennessee

Ravi Kalakota
Simon Graduate School of Business, University of Rochester, Rochester, New York

Arthur M. Keller
Stanford University, Palo Alto, California

Carlyn Lowery
First Virtual Holdings, Incorporated, San Diego, California

Larry Masinter
Xerox Palo Alto Research Center, Palo Alto, California

R. Preston McAfee
Department of Economics, University of Texas at Austin, Texas

John McMillan
Graduate School of International Relations and Pacific Studies, University of California, San Diego, California

Richard Mintz
First Virtual Holdings, Incorporated, San Diego, California

B. Clifford Neuman
The Information Sciences Institute, University of Southern California, Los Angeles, California

Darren New
First Virtual Holdings, Incorporated, San Diego, California

Thomas P. Novak
Owen Graduate School of Management, Vanderbilt University, Nashville, Tennessee

Jennifer Oetzel
Consultant, Global Technology Consultants, Austin, Texas

Beverly Parenti
First Virtual Holdings, Incorporated, San Diego, California

James B. Rapp
CyberStrategies, Alexandria, Virginia

Marshall T. Rose
First Virtual Holdings, Incorporated, San Diego, California

Porama Saengcharoenrat
Department of Mathematics, University of Illinois, Urbana-Champaign,
Illinois

Dale O. Stahl
Department of Economics, University of Texas at Austin, Texas

Jan Stallaert
Graduate School of Business, University of Texas at Austin, Texas

Einar Stefferud
First Virtual Holdings, Incorporated, San Diego, California

Lee Stein
First Virtual Holdings, Incorporated, San Diego, California

Carey Storm
First Virtual Holdings, Incorporated, San Diego, California

Ed Vielmetti
First Virtual Holdings, Incorporated, San Diego, California

Marc Weiser
First Virtual Holdings, Incorporated, San Diego, California

Andrew B. Whinston
IC^2, Graduate School of Business, University of Texas at Austin,
Texas

Pierre-R. Wolff
First Virtual Holdings, Incorporated, San Diego, California

Biographical Sketches of the Authors

Anitesh Barua

Anitesh Barua is an assistant professor of information systems and associate director of the Center for Information Systems Management in the Department of Management Science and Information Systems, Graduate School of Business, University of Texas at Austin. He received his Ph.D in information systems from Carnegie Mellon University in 1991. His research interests include IT productivity and business value, complementarity between IT and organizational design, trading partner selection over electronic networks, and the design of Internet- and Intranet-based collaborative systems. Dr. Barua has received several awards for his research and teaching, including the William W. Cooper Doctoral Dissertation Award in Management and Management Science from Carnegie Mellon University, and the CBA Foundation Teaching Award for Assistant Professors from the University of Texas at Austin. His research papers have been published (or are scheduled to appear) in leading journals and conferences, including *Decision Support Systems; IEEE Transactions on Systems, Man and Cybernetics; International Journal of Flexible Manufacturing Systems; Information Systems Research; Journal of Organizational Computing; MIS Quarterly;* and *Organization Science.*

Nathaniel S. Borenstein

Nathaniel S. Borenstein is a founder and chief scientist of First Virtual Holdings, Incorporated. Previously a researcher at Bellcore and Carnegie Mellon University, he is a primary author of MIME, the Internet standard format for interoperable multimedia data, and the author of various widely used software packages, including metamail™, Safe-Tcl™, ATOMICMAIL™, and the Andrew Message System™. He specializes in end-user interfaces and is the author of the book *Programming as If People Mattered.*

Patrali Chatterjee

Patrali Chatterjee is a doctoral candidate in management (marketing) at the Owen Graduate School of Management, Vanderbilt University. She received her M. Sc. in physics and her M.B.A. from J. B. I. M. S., University of Bombay,

India. Her current research interests involve modeling consumer behavior, information search and decision making in computer-mediated environments, consumer response to advertising, and strategic use of consumer transaction information.

Ramnath Chellappa

Ramnath Chellappa is a doctoral candidate and assistant instructor in the Department of Management Science and Information Systems at the University of Texas at Austin. He is also a research associate at the Center for Information Systems Management, where he conducts research in the areas of client/server architecture, data communication, electronic commerce, and Internet and Intranet technologies. He is also the architect of *EC World,* an on-line electronic journal on the Internet. Mr. Chellappa, who has a background in mining and petroleum engineering, worked as a UNIX systems analyst before entering the doctoral program at the University of Texas. His research papers have appeared in the *Journal of Organizational Computing* and the *Handbook of Human Factors and Ergonomics,* among others. Mr. Chellappa expects to graduate in May 1997.

Daniel W. Connolly

Daniel W. Connolly, a research associate at the Massachusetts Institute of Technology/W3C, discovered the Web project soon after graduating from the University of Texas at Austin in 1990. His industry experience in on-line documentation tools, distributed computing, and information delivery kept him in touch with the project while he was at Dazel and HaLSoft. His background in formal systems led him to work on the specification of HTML and other parts of the Web.

David H. Crocker

David H. Crocker is a principal with Brandenburg Consulting, providing strategic business, marketing, and technical planning and design for networked applications. Mr. Crocker assists clients in developing and using Internet products and services. He has participated in the development of internetworking capabilities since 1972, first as part of the Arpanet research community and more recently in the commercial sector. Mr. Crocker has been a key contributor in the development of Internet Mail, as well as developing MCI Mail. He has worked at a number of Silicon Valley companies, producing a wide range of TCP/IP, OSI, and network management products. He is a founder of the Internet Mail Consortium and continues technical involvement in Internet standards activities for transport services, electronic mail, and electronic commerce.

Dorothy E. Denning

Dorothy E. Denning is a professor of computer science at Georgetown University. Address: Georgetown University, Computer Science Department, Reiss 225, Washington, DC 20057; 202-687-5703; denning@cs.georgetown.edu; http://www.cosc.georgetown.edu/~denning.

John Ferguson

Customer support team member, First Virtual Holdings, Incorporated.

A. Michael Froomkin

A. Michael Froomkin is an associate professor at the University of Miami School of Law in Coral Gables, Florida, specializing in Internet law and administrative law. Recent publications include *The Metaphor Is the Key: Cryptography, the Clipper Chip, and the Constitution*, 143 U. Penn. L. Rev. 709 (1995) and *Reinventing the Government Corporation*, 1995 Ill. L. Rev. 543. Before entering teaching, Professor Froomkin practiced international arbitration law in the London office of Wilmer, Cutler & Pickering. He clerked for Judge Stephen F. Williams of the U.S. Court of Appeals, D.C. Circuit, and Chief Judge John F. Grady of the U.S. District Court, Northern District of Illinois. Professor Froomkin is a graduate of the Yale Law School, where he served as articles editor of both the *Yale Law Journal* and the *Yale Journal of International Law*. He has an M.Phil. degree in history of international relations from Cambridge University in England, which he obtained while on a Mellon Fellowship. He is a foreign associate of the Royal Institute of International Affairs and a fellow of the Cyberspace Law Institute. Professor Froomkin's idiosyncratic home page can be found at http://www.law.miami.edu/~froomkin.

Alok Gupta

Alok Gupta is a doctoral candidate in the Department of Management Science and Information Systems at the University of Texas at Austin. He has a bachelor's and a master's degree in engineering from the Institute of Technology in India and Pennsylvania State University, respectively. His academic background is in the areas of information systems, operations research, economics, and statistics. His current research is concerned with the potential of prices in engineering and improvement in the performance of the Internet. In collaboration with Andrew Whinston and Dale Stahl, he has proposed price adjustment mechanisms and has studied a simulated behavior of the Internet as an economy. Another ongoing research topic is the development of Intranet resource management applications and the role of pricing in managing real-time databases using electronic commerce principles. In general, Gupta is pursuing several topics that involve the economics of electronic commerce.

Gerald Hall

Senior UNIX systems administrator, First Virtual Holdings, Incorporated.

Aimo Hinkkanen

Aimo Hinkkanen studied mathematics at the University of Helsinki, Finland, and received a Ph.D. in 1980. He has held faculty positions at the University of Michigan and the University of Texas at Austin. Currently he is professor of mathematics at the University of Illinois at Urbana-Champaign. He has been an Alfred P. Sloan Research Fellow. Dr. Hinkkanen's principal research interests are in complex analysis, particularly complex dynamical systems and quasiconformal analysis.

Donna L. Hoffman

Donna L. Hoffman is an associate professor of marketing at the Owen Graduate School of Management at Vanderbilt University. She jointly directs Project 2000, a research program in computer-mediated marketing environment, which is devoted to studying the marketing implications of commercializing the World Wide Web. Examples of current projects include (1) developing the strategic marketing implications of commercial scenarios of the Web; (2) modeling consumer response to advertising and consumer search and purchase behavior in on-line commercial environments; (3) survey research on Internet usage; and (4) consumer behavior implications of computer-mediated communications.

Ravi Kalakota

Ravi Kalakota is the Xerox Assistant Professor of Information Systems at the University of Rochester's Simon Graduate School of Business. He has been working in the area of electronic commerce since 1992 and is coauthor, with Andrew B. Whinston, of *The Frontiers of Electronic Commerce* (Addison-Wesley).

Arthur M. Keller

Arthur M. Keller is a senior research scientist at Stanford University. He is project manager of Stanford University's participation in CommerceNet, which is doing the first large-scale market trial of electronic commerce on the Internet. He leads the effort on smart catalogs and virtual catalogs. He was manager of the Penguin Project, to provide sharing of persistent object data among multiple applications. He is also working on managing inconsistency in federated, autonomous database systems. His publications include work on database security, databases on parallel computers, incomplete information in databases, database system implementation, hypertext databases, and computerized typesetting.

Carlyn Lowery

Director of development, First Virtual Holdings, Incorporated.

Larry Masinter

Larry Masinter is a principal scientist at the Xerox Palo Alto Research Center. His interests focus on document management, digital libraries, and Internet information systems, through development of systems architectures for document management, coordination of research in technologies useful in digital libraries, and development of Internet standards for the World Wide Web. He received a Ph.D. in computer science from Stanford University and in 1992 received the ACM Software System Award.

R. Preston McAfee

R. Preston McAfee, professor of economics at the University of Texas at Austin, is a leading expert on electronic auctions. He has been retained as the principal consultant by the Federal Communications Commission to devise mechanisms for allocating wireless frequencies. He is also coeditor of the prestigious *American Economic Review* and recently was a visiting professor at the Massachusetts Institute of Technology.

John McMillan

John McMillan is professor of economics in the Graduate School of International Relations and Pacific Studies at the University of California, San Diego. He has authored four books, including *Games, Strategies, and Managers,* which explores the practical content of game theory for managerial decision making, as well as more than fifty articles on economic theory, applied microeconomics, and international trade. His current research is on the transition of the formerly planned economies, and on the design of market institutions. He has acted as a consultant for governments and firms in the United States, Mexico, Canada, Australia, and New Zealand, including advising various governments on the design and implementation of spectrum-license auctions.

Richard Mintz

Documentation writer, First Virtual Holdings, Incorporated.

B. Clifford Neuman

B. Clifford Neuman is a scientist at the Information Sciences Institute of the University of Southern California and holds a research faculty appointment in the Department of Computer Science. After receiving a B.S. degree from the Massachusetts Institute of Technology in 1985, he spent a year working for Project Athena, where he was one of the principal designers of the Kerberos authentification system. Dr. Neuman received M.S. and Ph.D. degrees from the University of Washington, where he designed the Prospero Directory Service, which is widely used to locate information from Internet archive sites. His recent work includes the development of a security infrastructure supporting authorization, accounting, and electronic payment mechanisms. Dr. Neuman leads the design and implementation of the NetCheque™ and NetCash™ payment systems.

Darren New

Author of First Virtual's InfoHaus software, First Virtual Holdings, Incorporated.

Thomas P. Novak

Thomas P. Novak (A.B. Oberlin College; M.A., Ph.D., L.L. Thurstone Psychometric Laboratory, University of North Carolina, Chapel Hill) is an associate professor of management and co-director of Project 2000 at the Owen Graduate School of Management, Vanderbilt University (/www2000.ogsm.vanderbilt.edu/.). Novak and his colleague Professor Donna L. Hoffman started Project 2000 in 1994 to study the marketing implications of commercializing computer-mediated environments like the World Wide Web on the Internet. In the summer of 1995, Novak was a visiting scholar at Interval Research Corporation. Novak brings five years of professional experience in the advertising industry to academics. He sits on the editorial board of the *Journal of Electronic Commerce* and reviews for all the major marketing and electronic commerce journals. Novak is a noted Internet marketing expert, has published numerous scholarly articles in the major U.S. and European marketing journals, and is a contributing writer to both *Wired* and *HotWired*. During the summer of 1995, Novak helped to debunk the Rimm study on marketing pornography on the Internet and the *Time* magazine cyberporn cover story. *Internet World* has named him an Internet Hero for 1995. In April 1996 Novak received the TLA/SIRS Intellectual Freedom Award for his work.

Jennifer Oetzel

Jennifer Oetzel is a consultant at Global Technology Consultants based in Austin, Texas. She has a B.A. in economics and an M.S. in community and regional planning, both from the University of Texas at Austin. In 1995 Ms. Oetzel was awarded the Wolf E. Jessen Endowed Presidential Scholarship for her evaluation of the U.S. Agency for International Development (USAID)/Tunisia Technology Transfer Project. For the past two years, Ms. Oetzel has been associated with the European Mediterranean Network (EUMEDNET), a research project based in Malaga, Spain, established for the purpose of promoting electronic commerce throughout Europe and North Africa. Ms. Oetzel was the managing coordinator of *EC World*, an electronic journal focusing on issues in electronic commerce on the Internet. She was a consultant at the Center for Information Systems Management in the Graduate School of Business at the University of Texas at Austin.

Beverly Parenti

Managing director, First Virtual Holdings, Incorporated.

James B. Rapp

James B. Rapp, president of CyberStrategies in Alexandria, Virginia, is a longtime user of the Internet services and commercial on-line services. He has been a formal beta tester of three national Internet services and one on-line service. Mr. Rapp has assisted numerous business people in awareness, access, and business utilization of the Internet through introductory electronic commerce sessions taught on behalf of the George Washington University, on a one-to-one basis, and by addressing audiences at events such as Internet '95, and InterAct '96. He possesses a unique combination of public (U.S. House of Representatives, Export-Import Bank of the United States, Department of Defense, Department of Housing and Urban Development) and private sector (Global Resource Group, the American Council for Capital Formation, Pierce Investment Bank) experience, which when combined with his extensive Internet background enables him to develop unique electronic commerce/public policy strategies.

Marshall T. Rose

Principal, First Virtual Holdings, Incorporated.

Porama Saengcharoenrat

Porama Saengcharoenrat received her Ph.D. from the Department of Electrical Engineering at Imperial College, University of London, in 1982. She has held faculty positions at the Prince of Songkla University and the University of Texas at Austin. Currently she is a research associate in the Department of Mathematics at the University of Illinois at Urbana-Champaign. Dr. Saengcharoenrat's principal research interests are in enterprise modeling and computer simulation.

Dale O. Stahl

Dale O. Stahl received B.S, M.S., and engineering degrees from the Massachusetts Institute of Technology in electrical engineering, with research experience in computer science and neural nets. He received his Ph.D. from the University of California at Berkeley, with a focus on mathematical economics. He has held positions at Duke University, MIT, Boston University, and Tillburg University in the Netherlands, and is currently with the University of Texas, Austin. He has published more than thirty articles in the top economics journals in general equilibrium theory, dynamics and stability theory, game-theoretic approaches to price determination, network pricing, and experimental game theory.

Jan Stallaert

Jan Stallaert received his Ph.D. from the Anderson School of Management at UCLA, where he was a visiting assistant professor between 1992 and 1994. He is now an assistant professor in the Graduate School of Business at the University of Texas at Austin. His research interests are large-scale optimization problems for supply chain management and financial engineering. Dr. Stallaert is also a consultant for several Fortune 500 companies.

Einar Stefferud

Co-founder, First Virtual Holdings, Incorporated.

Lee Stein

Chairman and CEO, First Virtual Holdings, Incorporated.

Carey Storm

Managing director of corporate development, First Virtual Holdings, Incorporated.

Ed Vielmetti

Research engineer, First Virtual Holdings, Incorporated.

Marc Weiser

Internet commerce administrator, First Virtual Holdings, Incorporated.

Andrew B. Whinston

Andrew B. Whinston is the Hugh Roy Cullen Centennial Chair in Business Administration; professor of information systems, computer science, and economics; Jon Newton Centennial IC Fellow; and director of the Center for Information Systems Management in the Graduate School of Business at the University of Texas at Austin. He is the coauthor, with Ravi Kalakota, of *The Frontiers of Electronic Commerce* (Addison-Wesley). Dr. Whinston is also the editor of the journals *Decision Support Systems* and *Organizational Computing and Electronic Commerce* and coauthor or coeditor of fifteen books and over 250 articles. Recent research interests are Internet pricing and application of client-server computing, especially to support groups working collaboratively.

Pierre-R. Wolff

Pierre-R. Wolff is director of strategic planning for First Virtual Holdings Incorporated (FVH), based in San Diego, California. FVH has developed a safe and convenient system of payment for goods and services on the Internet, a payment system created to enable the safe global buying and selling of information by anyone with access to the Internet. Wolff's experience includes serving as business development manager for Reuters NewMedia, a wholly owned subsidiary of Reuters Holdings, Inc. While at Reuters, he was involved in the evaluation of acquisition and investment candidates, exploration of business opportunities outside Reuters's core markets on the Internet, and development of new information-based products. In addition, he served as a general resource on Internet issues throughout the company. Pierre obtained his M.B.A. in strategy, innovation, and information technology, from Theseus Institute in Sophia Antipolis, France, and conducted his undergraduate studies at Carnegie Mellon University in Pittsburgh, Pennsylvania.

PART 1

Introductory Overview

Part One contains essays that present an overview of the field of electronic commerce. Chapter 1, by David H. Crocker, is an overview of the technology as a foundation for electronic commerce. He lists the necessary requirements for the development of commerce, such as reliability, speed, security, and pervasive connectivity. As he points out, not all the issues have been resolved. As examples, he refers to security, the need for third-party certification, the diverse ownership of the global network, and the need to establish who is responsible for the overall performance of the network.

In Chapter 2, Donna L. Hoffman, Thomas P. Novak, and Patrali Chatterjee address issues of electronic marketing and sales. In their opinion, electronic commerce has the potential to revolutionize marketing. For example, they point out that with electronic commerce consumers have potentially much more choice, more ability to try out the product, and greater interaction with the sellers. Another issue is the size of the overall market, that is, how many users are connected to the Internet. The authors argue that developing reliable marketing research methods, although challenging and often controversial, is crucial to maintaining advertiser support on the Internet.

In Chapter 3, Daniel W. Connolly discusses each of Douglas Englebart's essential elements for an open hyperdocument system and evaluates them with respect to the World Wide Web. Specifically, Connolly discusses whether or not each of the requirements has been met. He also considers the likelihood that they will be met in the future if they are not already, as well as the obstacles to the adoption of each of the requirements. Connolly ends his discussion by arguing that eventually each of Englebart's requirements will be met and will become part of the World Wide Web infrastructure.

1

Chapter 1

An Unaffiliated View of Internet Commerce

David H. Crocker

ABSTRACT

The Internet is quickly becoming the global data communications infrastructure. Whatever underlying changes are made to its technologies, the result will be called the Internet. Until recently the business community did not view the Internet as a viable option for wide area communications. Changes are afoot, but they raise basic questions about reliability, efficiency, and security of the transactions that are the essence of commerce. Although millions of people today use the Internet, broad-based acceptance of its role for formal and even legal transactions is lacking.

This paper discusses the reasons the Internet will serve the role as global conveyor of transactions for on-line commerce and the nature of the technical and operational concerns, as well as their resolution. A summary of the approaches for doing on-line account-card services is also given, along with a description of the relevant standards work that is under way. As a bonus, the paper suggests various architectural issues that the technical community should consider as it continues to enhance this global infrastructure.

INTERNET FOR COMMERCE

Today, data communications among businesses use private services called value added networks (VANs), private telecommunication links between individual trading partners, global commercial e-mail services, usually based on the X.400 standard, and off-line techniques such as mailing each other tapes of data. These techniques tend to be slow, expensive, or both.

However, their use is well understood by the business community, especially with regard to safety. When one company is sending another an order for critical manufacturing components or is sending authorization for payment of millions of dollars, they want to be sure it will arrive at the correct destination, in a timely manner, and without having been reviewed by competitors. The recipient also wants assurances that the communication is really from its purported author. Reliability, speed, and security are fundamental requirements, and company auditors will not allow them to be treated lightly.

Besides satisfying all the technical concerns, a service claiming to be an "infrastructure" needs to ensure that all the "right" people and organizations use it. If one organization wants to communicate with another, the infrastructure is useless unless both are attached to it. The Internet has grown to the point that a company's "trading partners" are likely to be attached to the Internet. This is especially true in some industry sectors today and is becoming more so for others. Marketing and collaboration opportunities deriving from the combined mechanisms of the World Wide Web and e-mail are a powerful draw for companies. A short time ago, companies were attaching to the Internet simply so they could say they had done so, but they expected real commercial benefit from *use* to come later. That "later" has already arrived.

Once a company acquires its link to the Internet, concerns about cost, convenience, and its global "reach" prompt management to ask whether the link can also be used for services currently being obtained through other mechanisms. When enough companies ask such questions, there's considerable pressure to make the answers be yes. Apart from the excitement engendered by media enthusiasm, the real utility of Internet access is moving companies to find ways to satisfy this requirement. The question is whether they will succeed.

A Global Internet

The history of the Internet is well documented [LYNRO93]. It began as a research project, the Arpanet, to explore a technology called packet switching, intended to permit robust communications.[1] From its start this research activity had to grapple with the success problem of being massively useful. Researchers quickly came to rely on the network's availability for working with each other, but the nature of networking research requires doing things *to*

---

[1] The original reference was to surviving hostile, battlefield conditions. This was, after all, an experiment funded by the military. Few people realized that another venue with a "hostile" infrastructure for which packet switching would be essential was the world of *commercial* telecommunications.

the network itself, which can affect its functionality or break it completely. Since the community comprised only a few hundred researchers, most with U.S. Department of Defense funding, working through these and other operational issues was not difficult. The community was small, homogeneous, casual, and extremely open. Many sites on the Net did not even have login (password) security!

Even though the Arpanet became the Internet, incorporated a much broader range of participants, moved from single, central management into a fully distributed model with many independent operators providing Internet access, and grew to many tens and even hundreds of thousands of users, this basic tone of open and casual trust did not change for more than twenty years! Only when the population of users started being counted in the millions did user misbehavior become a significant issue. Only when business started considering the Internet for financial and contractual transactions was there serious focus on service guarantees and security.

The challenge is to add facilities that satisfy these concerns without losing the ability to use the Internet in its long-standing style. People and organizations need both casual and formal, open and restricted, friendly and competitive styles of interaction. The communication infrastructure for these interactions needs to be compatible with the full range of human requirements. A network with no ability to authenticate the source of data cannot be used for signing credit card transactions. Yet a network that has onerous requirements for following careful, formal procedures before sending each and every piece of data cannot be used for casual conversation among friends. The Internet faces the challenge of supporting both styles of use.

Requirements for expanding the Internet into its additional roles encounter three categories of technical effort: scaling, security, and management. Can the Internet grow two or three orders of magnitude and still be made to work? Can requirements for signing, sealing, and certifying data be added to the functional mix? Can the complex array of independent Internet service providers collaborate and coordinate with each other well enough to ensure required levels of reliability and performance?

Scaling

None of today's Internet existed when the Arpanet first operated. Every hardware and software component has been replaced, with most going through multiple rounds of evolution. All of this has been done while the Net itself operated continuously. From a few hundred original users to tens of millions today, that operation has sometimes been problematic, but it has continued nonetheless. The Internet's track record for moving through *five* orders of magnitude of growth should be reassuring. It does not make the next two orders of magnitude of growth less daunting, but it does suggest that the technical community has a good basis for success. Moving from use by a few, expert users up to a level that includes every single person on the globe is quite a change, but the skeptical need to be cognizant of this track record.

Security

It seems odd that a research project funded by the military should have so little technology or operational history with secure use. In reality it has a great deal, but that work was done separately by other communities in the military and national security organizations and, as is typical, was not shared more broadly. In reality the development and deployment of basic security services on the Internet has been highly problematic. Besides difficulties accruing from legal and political concerns, there has also been an issue with mind-set. Military and national security requirements are quite strict. Costs to satisfy them can be quite high. The risks of having inadequate security, as well as the skills of potential attackers, make it essential that technical efforts be stringent and complete.

The commercial world is different. Its technical requirements are far less onerous, and it must be much more cost-sensitive. Security services need to be real and sufficient, but small amounts of failure can be tolerated as the "cost of doing business." This is a very different way of thinking, and most of the security technical community grew up doing work for the military. It is taking time for that community to adjust its design goals to accommodate this different world.

From the technical side, there are a variety of underlying technologies that can be used for the classic requirements of signing (authentication) and sealing (privacy). They have existed for some years and are relatively well understood. The challenge is their deployment. Barriers, here, are the management of encryption keys and the management of legal constraints. Key management refers to methods for creating and exchanging security keys so that their users can trust them. If a recipient uses a particular key to authenticate the originator of a document, how can that recipient be certain that the key belongs to the purported originator? Public key technology makes this problem tractable but does not inherently solve it. Legal difficulties pertain to export restrictions on security technology. Their premise is that matters of national security require the ability to monitor (decrypt) trans-national data flows. While this issue can largely be ignored for communications within a given country, business is global; it needs to communicate across borders, often with authentication and privacy for the data.

An additional functional requirement is nonrepudiation, which certifies the event of origination or reception. Here the technical picture is fuzzier. On-line techniques for providing this service today entail the use of trusted, independent third parties. Transactions between trading partners are sent through a third party who logs them. Dispute resolution is accomplished by inspecting the logs of the intermediary to see whether a transmission was sent and received. Techniques for performing this function in an automated fashion, without passing the message through an intermediary are new, have received little general review, and have essentially no operational history. While the techniques are appealing and seem likely to be adequate, their application to matters involving contracts and finance requires development of appropriate case law. This will take some time. In the interim, there is nothing to prevent the use of trusted, independent third-party logging services via the Internet.

Management

One of the frustrations about the Internet is that no one agency owns it; there is no sole responsible authority. Problem resolution is therefore like much of the rest of the world, requiring discussion and debate among a collection of vendors (providers), each of whom is independent of the others. In most of the telecommunications world, there is a long history of strict standards, tight regulation, and international treaties to account for the high level of quality control in inter-provider operation. The Internet has tended to achieve similar results through goodwill among its operators. Unfortunately, goodwill has its limitations, especially when those operators are pushing for aggressive growth of their own network services and therefore must focus primarily on internal operations.

As a consequence, the performance for data traffic between Internet provider networks is not nearly as good as within. Connection points—variously called interchanges or exchanges—are sometimes inadequate for current requirements. Providers are aware of this and assure their customers that matters will be fixed through the development of additional and larger exchanges facilities. In the meantime, customers often need to make connections to multiple providers or to use providers who themselves have multiple "upstream" paths in order to obtain required levels of throughput and reliability.

A different issue is problem reporting and resolution. When a user on one provider's network has difficulty communicating with a user on another provider's network, how is the problem resolved? There are a number of umbrella organizations run by providers to assist in these matters, but it is generally not possible for a customer to obtain specific guarantees about reliability, performance, or problem handling. For some business activities, these guarantees are essential. It is unclear how the providers will respond to this requirement. For the current third-party services that do provide (non-Internet) guarantees of service, the guarantees apply *only* when both trading partners are connected to that *one* network. When traffic transits multiple third-party (non-Internet) networks, no guarantees are supplied. In this regard the Internet is not at a disadvantage.

What Is Business?

This section is intended to provide a caveat to the reader and a context for evaluating Internet usability. Much is made about using the Internet for commerce and about its (in)adequacy for the task. Usually the focus is only on the most stringent business requirements. This section is intended as a reminder that business is a multifaceted activity, with a broad range of requirements. Not every document needs a notary public or an armed escort. The discussion is divided among the typical business groups responsible for the life cycle of a product.

Research and Development

Developers who create products must peruse the international community of ideas and otherwise interact with the outside world. This was exactly the playground for the early Arpanet, and the modern Internet continues to be a rich source of opportunities and capabilities for acquiring and sharing ideas. Electronic mail and the recent addition of the World Wide Web greatly facilitate exchange of ideas among geographically distributed communities. In fact, these two services provide a common theme for many collaborative activities throughout the business cycle. Within the research and development world, their other major application is for distributed development teams. Work is facilitated even when the distribution of the group is only across the street or even next door; it doesn't have to be across the globe. Security and reliability requirements for these activities are modest and are well met by the current Internet.

The other major research and development activity to be helped by the Internet is product testing, especially when the product can be digitized, such as software or documents. Getting the product out to test customers and getting their responses back is made fundamentally easier when a high-speed infrastructure connects the participants. The Internet can often be used for these functions today. When participants are attached to competent

Internet service providers, high reliability is the norm. Only when communications need special levels of reliability or substantive privacy does the current Internet become problematic for standards and off-the-shelf solutions. Even then special alternatives are available; they may be somewhat costly and require extra effort, but they work.

Support

Product support is based on customer interaction. In many ways it is the testing activity made public. Support staff must be able to receive questions and problem reports and to return answers and product updates. The Internet permits highly timely interaction, without the burden of being kept on hold. When the product is digital, it also permits distribution—the "push" of product modifications—out to customers far more easily than is otherwise possible. Here, security and reliability requirements are sometimes, but not always, more stringent. Today's Internet can be used comfortably in many support situations, as it has been for at least ten years.

Marketing

Marketing involves research and education. The research function here is facilitated in the same way for product development. Potential customers can be contacted and involved in ongoing dialogue about requirements and preferences. Education requires informing potential customers about the product, both by "pushing" literature and advertising to them, such as by targeted mailings, and by making it available to them for voluntary "pulling," such as by accessing Web pages. A cautionary note: Pushing unsolicited marketing literature, called "spam," to Internet users is a more serious matter than in the paper world.

Sales

As with marketing, sales requires educating the customer. It then requires negotiation, purchase processing, and, of course, product delivery. While face-to-face and telephone interaction remains essential for some parts of these activities, many can be conducted over the Net.

It is important to note that many of these activities are well established on the Internet. Although academia and research are often viewed as being worlds apart from the requirements of business commerce, the reality is that product development is very much like engineering research, although with rather more constrained delivery goals and schedules—and researchers negotiate their contracts. In fact, support of Arpanet/Internet customers by commercial vendors has been explicitly permitted for most of the life of the Internet.

What has changed? First, the current world requires formal performance and security assurances that the previous world did not. Second, there really are some applications for which stronger mechanisms—especially for security—are required. However, much of commerce involves informal communication modes, and for these circumstances the Internet works just fine today, as it has for twenty years.

TECHNICAL PERSPECTIVES

What is wonderful about the Internet is that there are so many ways to use it. The problem with the Internet is that different modes of use have very different capabilities and limitations. A basic question, then, is the means by which a user can access the Internet. Much of the debate about the number of users on the Internet is the result of using different criteria for access.

To Be "On" the Internet

A simple distinction is between the portion of the Internet that is the "core," offering the services that others access, and the "consumer" modes of access to those services.[2] This section considers the choices in more detail [CROC95b].

Full

Full Internet access means that the user's system is attached full-time, runs the "native" stack of Internet technologies, and offers at least some of the services for others to access. Full-time access means that users from the Net can access the system at any time. This mode is used by the Internet core. The remaining modes of access are employed by users, the Internet's consumers.

[2] The core/consumer distinction was coined by John Quarterman and Smoot Carl-Mitchell <http://www.tic.com>.

Direct

Eventually users will all have their own computers running their own stacks of Internet technology. Their access will be technically identical to those with "full" access except that their machines will not always be attached and they run client software, not server. A typical example today is home users who dial up their local Internet service provider and use the SLIP or PPP services to obtain "native" Internet access. This is the highest-quality user access, with all user data and choice of applications sitting at the user's own machine. It is more cumbersome today than is reasonable for a truly mass market, but this is being remedied.

Client

Direct access is a special case of the Client mode of access. For Client access, the user runs an Internet application on their own computer but may have different (non-Internet) technology underneath or may have various barriers, such as firewalls, which limit that access.

Mediated

The simplest style of interactive access is to treat the user's computer like a simple terminal and let a third-party, on-line service run the applications that access the rest of the Internet. This mode allows the on-line service to mediate the user's view and relieves the user from many complexities. It also limits the user's choice of applications to those provided by the on-line service and may limit performance. Mediated access can also require extra effort to move data between the user and the Internet, since the on-line service may be an intermediate stopping point for the data. Most on-line services do not currently run Internet technology native to the service. This is especially true for e-mail and requires gateways that must translate between the Internet's e-mail codes and those of the on-line service. This is an opportunity for incompatibilities.

Messaging

Some users cannot obtain interactive access. They cannot send or receive information that works with the World Wide Web or other "real-time" services. For such users, e-mail is the only channel onto the Internet. What is astonishing is how useful this can be. While it does not permit the casual and extended information searching for which the Web is famous, it does permit participation in on-line dialogue and can also be used for retrieval of many files.

Styles of Use

Enthusiasm for the World Wide Web often results in expectations that it will fulfill all the communication needs for the Internet community. What is missed is that the Web is particularly good at one style of use and is not intended for the complementary use. The Web supports information "pull." Users decide when they want information, and then they go and pull it over. Control over such exchanges is fundamentally with the user. This is especially appropriate for browsing and interacting. Yet imagine that the only way to obtain information is to search for it. Imagine having no way of receiving information regularly, without having to go and get it yourself.

That's when information "push" is needed. The creator of the information can choose to send it to one or more recipients as soon as the information is available. The recipient does not need to check repeatedly. It will simply show up. This, of course, is the nature of e-mail, and its role is as essential to the conduct of business as are functions supporting information pull.[3]

Core versus Edges

As innovation continues on the Internet, a choice that must repeatedly be made is where to build in new features. The architectural issue is whether to add a feature to the infrastructure of the Internet itself or to tack it on at the edges. A little-appreciated aspect of Internet technology is that its better technical efforts have come from adding bits and pieces onto a simple core. The reason this is preferred is that it is easier to test and deploy.

To add a feature to an infrastructure, it must be widely deployed before it can be useful. Testing, too, often requires a complex sequence of system interactions. In contrast, adding a feature to the edge usually requires only that the "trading partners" cooperate before the feature is useful. As an example, imagine wanting to create a special application for group coordination or review among the branch offices of a company. Each branch office is likely to be attached to a different Internet provider. Then imagine being prevented from doing this unless and until the many different Internet providers all

---

[3] This terminology was suggested by Mark Smith, of Intel.

implement the service. In contrast, it is much simpler to deploy such a system if only the branch office computers need to add the application.

This distinction between "core" and "edges" is essential at each and every stage of system design. Unless there is a compelling need to the contrary, the golden rule is to take as much out of the core as possible.

Channel versus Object

When creating a service, such as security, the architectural choice of core versus edges is paramount. Placing a facility into the infrastructure can make it easier to use by virtue of hiding its details from the user of services. However, if its placement into the infrastructure is not done properly, then the burden can become higher!

In the case of security, the choice is whether to create security mechanisms that are established as part of the (interactive) communication channel between participants, or to wrap the security around the data object that is transmitted, independent of the specific type of channel that is used. Channel-based security can often be simpler and sometimes is the only available mechanism. On the other hand, it can—and does—lead to redundant mechanisms, one for each type of channel. Object security can—and should—result in one mechanism only, so that the choice of transmission channel does not matter. The same mechanism would apply for the same data, even when it was posted to a Web page and sent over e-mail.

ACCOUNT-CARD USE

Data communications services have been employed for financial transactions for many years. The recent popularity of automatic teller machines—rather different from data communication's version of ATM—is supported by a global infrastructure among banks and their associations. The same is true for the "back-end" processing of account-based credit- and debit-card transactions in the paper world. Formal exchange of purchase orders, invoices, waybills, and the like has been conducted for extended trading partner relationships in many industries for nearly twenty years, using standards developed under the rubric Electronic Data Interchange (EDI).

All of these can be done over the Internet, given sufficient bandwidth, reliability, and security by the infrastructure. Not surprisingly, the banking industry is likely to keep the "back-end" processing on a separate system, for extra safety. What is new, however, is having large-scale ability to conduct fully digital transactions among consumers and merchants and between new or occasional trading partners. Here much of the transaction requires no special security until the actual payment exchange. At this point data integrity, authenticity, and even privacy of the transaction often are required. When credit or debit cards (account cards) are used, the transaction needs to be tightly integrated into the card-processing organizations, such as Europay, MasterCard, Visa, and American Express. The size of the market that is likely to use such an on-line capability provides a compelling force for the technical and entrepreneurial communities. A variety of efforts by start-ups and established organizations are pursuing this opportunity with great vigor.

Payment Systems

Figure 1.1 shows a generic account-card service and the path traveled by the (16 + 4) digits of the account-card account number.[4] At its simplest, it entails the consumer, the merchant, and the processing system, which is here called the clearinghouse. In reality, the clearinghouse service usually entails multiple organizations, such as the bank that issues the card to the consumer and the bank that acquires the transaction from the merchant. It may also have one or more intermediaries, such as a bank-card processing association. In some cases all of these functions are performed by one organization, such as American Express.

The primary concern of the account-card organizations is reduction of risk. In particular, the organizations want to limit fraud through the unauthorized use of cards and account numbers. A distinguishing feature in the real world of card use is whether the merchant and client physically exchange the card. When they do, the risk is greatly reduced. Card organizations charge merchants for each transaction. That charge is much higher for "card not present" transactions. All transactions over the Internet are currently evaluated as card not present.

Bureaucratic requirements for account-card processing include proper identification of buyer and merchant, proper creation of an authorization instrument, and the ability to move the instrument into the card service and back out for charge-backs. Security requirements for this service are avoiding interception of sensitive data, such as account-card account number, by unauthorized third parties and preventing unauthorized use of the number. The term "unauthorized" is key. Fraudulent use of account numbers is an extremely serious problem for the card organizations, even without the advent of the Internet. The problem is growing explosively, and the account-card industry needs to find basic means of restricting the number of people

---

[4] The structure of this section derives from a presentation made by Marshall Rose in 1995. He is not, of course, responsible for any errors of translation or understanding here.

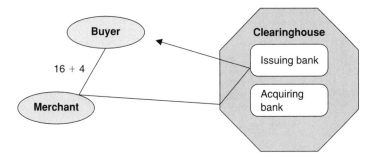

Figure 1.1 Account-card Participants

who know an account number. This means that there is pressure to keep even the merchant from seeing it.

This concern is exacerbated in the context of the Internet because it is possible to obtain many account numbers at the same time. A dishonest waiter at a restaurant gets numbers one at a time. A recent break-in to an Internet service provider netted the attacker 20,000 numbers! This is an interesting example of the core-versus-edges trade-off. Merchants compose a major portion of the consumer account-card infrastructure (core). One approach to solving the security concerns is to require all merchants to operate their services in an entirely secure manner. Unfortunately, this is not tractable since most merchants do not have the technical skills or the ability to provide the sustained operational focus required for high-quality network system security. A different approach is to place the bulk of the security mechanism into the hands of a trusted third-party service that specializes in these mechanisms.

Making the Internet Pay

Many new and established companies are developing and offering on-line purchase mechanisms over the Internet. Table 1.1 lists some of the early entrants, along with their World Wide Web home pages, for further reading.

In the remainder of this section, various schemes for permitting buyer/merchant transactions over the Internet are described; the schemes are given names, for convenient reference in this report. All of the schemes are in use today. Some will disappear, but the market is still evaluating appropriate roles for these alternatives, even as it develops additional ones.

The simplest distinction among the schemes is whether the Internet transaction involves only the buyer and merchant or whether a third-party service participates. In the first case the merchant interacts with the account-card organization(s) in the usual manner. In the second case the third-party

Table 1.1 Early Payment System Entrants

Commercenet	<http://www.commerce.net>
CyberCash	<http://www.cybercash.com>
DigiCash	<http://www.digicash.com>
First Virtual Holdings	<http://www.fv.com>
MasterCard	<http://www.mastercard.com>
Microsoft	<http://www.microsoft.com>
NetMarket	<http://www.netmarket.com>
Netscape	<http://www.netscape.com>
Open Market	<http://www.openmarket.com>
Visa	<http://www.visa.com>

service represents the account-card organization on-line, or is that organization itself. Since current paper- or plastic-based methods permit merchants access to account numbers, on-line schemes that do not use a trusted third party are subject to the same employee fraud and external attack concerns discussed earlier.

Clear

It is unlikely that a current account-card transaction will be monitored today by an attacker. While attackers can gain the ability to do monitoring, there is simply too little activity today to provide an interesting incentive. Consequently, there is some current transmission of account numbers in the "clear," with no authentication or privacy checks added. Since account numbers follow a representational, or format, pattern that can be detected even in free (unstructured) text, it is relatively easy for an attacker to identify such strings. When an attacker compromises this scheme—that is, when they are able to obtain account numbers—the user does not learn of the problem until receiving their next bill from the account-card organization. Hence transmission of account numbers in the clear is not advised.

ID

A small variation of the "clear" scheme is to register the account number with a merchant via non-Internet means (e.g., a telephone call) and use a special identifier (ID) instead. The ID, rather than the account number, is sent over the Net. This scheme is vulnerable to unauthorized use over the Internet but, of course, does not permit broader use of the account number.

Again, the owner of the account number does not learn of the theft until the monthly bill arrives.

ID Confirm

An interesting enhancement to the use of IDs is for its owner to be queried, separately, as part of each transaction. That is, the merchant or account-card processing service sends a query back to the "correct" user to see if the ID's use is valid for each purchase that is attempted. This simple addition to the ID scheme is remarkably powerful since it allows misuse to be detected quickly. It does not prevent "wiretapping" acquisition of the ID, but it greatly reduces the utility of its unauthorized use.

Secure Link

There are two sources of concern for unauthorized acquisition of account numbers: wiretapping during a transaction across the Net, and breaking into the on-line storage of those numbers by the buyer, merchant, or third party. It appears that this latter concern is remedied, first, by reducing the number of places that store the number and then "hardening" those places against attack. In the long run this will mean that buyers do not keep their numbers on-line but, instead, use smart cards, which provide a restricted access to the information while being highly tamper-resistant. It also means that merchants will never see the account number directly.

That leaves protection against wiretapping. A simple approach to this problem is adding privacy to the buyer-merchant communications channel. That is, rather than providing security that is wrapped around—and designed for—the details of an application such as account-card transactions, it is possible to simply put a generic privacy feature on the transport channel, creating a secure link between the buyer and the merchant. In simple cases this seems to work well, although it poses difficulties with large-scale use or when organizational firewall systems are in the path.

Mediated

The most elaborate approach has classic buyer-merchant and merchant-clearinghouse interactions, much like today, except that security technology is applied in an integrated fashion. It results in protection against both wiretapping and theft from the merchant's machine. Since this is an account-card transaction, the buyer and merchant each has a prior relationship with their point of contact into the account-card service. This relationship is modified to include acquisition of a private security code (encryption key). At the time of a purchase, the buyer encrypts information, such as the account number, with this security code so that the account-card service can decrypt it but the merchant cannot. The buyer then adds it to the rest of the transaction data, which is further encrypted using a key that the merchant *can* decrypt.

This protects the entire transaction against wiretapping. The merchant receives the data and decrypts the bulk of it—but not the account number—and then sends a similarly encrypted package to the card service for authorization. The account-card service receives the packet and decrypts the bulk of the data using the merchant's key and then decrypts the account number using the buyer's key. The service verifies the legitimacy of the transaction and then sends an encrypted response back to the merchant.

Getting There Openly

The Internet is based on openly developed technical specifications. This permits a broad base of input to their content and a level playing field among competitors. It also is the basis for satisfying the fundamental requirement of interoperability among the products from those competitors. For much of the payments-related work, however, things are proceeding down a proprietary path. And they are proceeding at a rapid pace.

IETF Standards Efforts

The Internet has developed its own method of creating standards, with procedures that are formal but organizational participation that is not. The organization that produces these standards, the Internet Engineering Task Force (IETF),[5] conducts a broad range of discussions and meetings to pursue enhancements to the Internet's technical base.

EDI

Electronic Data Interchange (EDI) comprises a large set of standards developed by various organizations, including the United States' ANSI and the United Nations' EDIFACT. These standards cover many different "structured" business transactions used between trading partners. EDI is already

---

[5] Information about the IETF and copies of its official documents (Request for Comments, RFC) and working papers (Internet drafts) can be accessed through the World Wide Web at <http://www.ietf.org>. IETF operations are described in [LYNRO93].

carried over a wide range of transport services, from specialized value added networks (VANs) to public X.25 networks and public X.400 e-mail networks to private links between the partners. EDI is designed for business-business transactions, whereas the current work in payments is primarily for consumer-merchant exchanges.

A recent IETF effort defined a means for carrying EDI via the Internet [CROC95a], through the use of a structuring and labeling mechanism called Multipurpose Internet Mail Extensions (MIME) [BOFR93, MOOR93, POST94]. MIME is used for e-mail and the Web.

Payments

Little open standards work is occurring for Internet-based payments. The major account-card associations and their partners dominate the work in this arena, since payment transactions ultimately must be processed by their services. They are responsible for assessing a transaction's risk and therefore for imposing requirements to reduce it. The tone of work in this arena is also making things interesting. It has shifted back and forth between private co-operation and vigorous public debate. As of this writing, it appears likely that MasterCard and Visa will produce a single, coherent specification. It is unclear whether alternative specifications, such as from Microsoft, will play a major or minor role.

However, account-card payment systems do not cover the full range of electronic commerce for which additional standards need to be developed. For example, account cards are only one form of payment and consumers need to be able to choose among the full range. Hence, there has been a recent effort to create some complementary work in the IETF. In particular, this work is likely to consider the carriage of account-card transactions over various transport services, such as the Web and e-mail, and the selection of payment method. There is also the possibility of trying to develop standards for exchanges earlier in the commercial relationship, such as for establishing the details of the purchase. That is, what is to be bought, and how much will it cost? A gleam in the eyes of researchers is the development of a standard for allowing automated *negotiation* (haggling) over the Internet.

(In)security

For formal commerce over the Internet to become accepted practice, the business world needs to be comfortable with the reliability of the Internet's performance and with its security against detection or modification of data. Currently the business community is skeptical; it needs to be convinced.

While most Internet performance really is quite good, security capabilities are largely nonexistent. In spite of the significant maturity of most of the underlying security technology, wide deployment in an open environment like the Internet is proving highly problematic. This is leading to multiple candidate solutions, some of which are proprietary.

Disturbing Trend

Proprietary development of technology is a key source of innovation. It gives a company an edge over its competition, a lead in the market. The counterpoint to these benefits is that proprietary technology can seriously increase customer costs and limit customer choice. In the world of open networking, it also limits or prevents interoperability among products from different vendors. The reality in the open-system market is that individual customers buy products from many vendors. Those products need to interoperate. When the products include proprietary enhancements, they usually cannot work together because they do not support the same features. This also makes customer networks considerably more complicated, since vendors often will provide similar features. Similar does not mean the same. Hence, each product will have a different way of solving the same problem.

How bad is the actual problem? Unfortunately, quite bad. In the last few years, the base of openly specified Internet protocols has increasingly been enhanced through the efforts of closed groups. A (small) sampling of these proprietary efforts follows; the citations are not intended to single out horrible offenders but, rather, to show an increasing industry tendency to ignore or bypass the open-standards process. The major concern should not be about particular vendors but instead the number and range of them and their impact on long-term competition and short-term interoperability.

More important is the matter of changing this trend. Vendors do not develop or provide open solutions out of a higher sense of good. They do it because the market demands it. For now the Internet mass market is too new to realize the basis of openness that was—and continues to be—essential for the operation and enhancement of the global service.

World Wide Web

Netscape Communications has developed very successful products for the Web. The Web technology that defines data to be displayed is called HyperText Markup Language (HTML). Netscape defined its own extensions and fielded them widely without coordinating with the rest of the community, in spite of general community agreement about the need for extensions of this type. This has led to Web pages that are designed specifically for Netscape user programs (browsers) and do not work well for users with other browsers. Worse, the Netscape extensions violate the underlying technical model on which HTML was based. An alternative approach would have been to coordinate with at least a subset of those doing development so that some degree of diversity was represented in the specification effort.

Netscape also developed its own "channel" security for private communications between the Web user and the Web server (i.e., customer and merchant). The company has stated that it intends to retain control over this specification, in spite of interest by the technical community in pursuing an open standard and fixing problems with the Netscape specification.

Security

The Internet standards community has pursued development of an open e-mail security standard for a number of years, resulting in a specification called Privacy Enhanced Mail (PEM) [LINN93, KENT93, BALE93, KALI93]. Various problems with that work led to a recently issued revised effort called MIME Object Security Services (MOSS) [GAMU95, CRFR95]. There is little installed base for this work, in either of its forms. The lack of timely success by this effort resulted in a private development, called Pretty Good Privacy (PGP) [GARF95]. Although saddled with a legally problematic history, which is now resolved, PGP has developed a real base of users. It is small but significant. Due to perceived problems with PGP and MOSS, a private vendor consortium has chosen to add yet another alternative into the pot, called Secure MIME (S/MIME) [RSA95]. Neither PGP nor S/MIME has been submitted into a standards process for open review and modification. Each participant in this shell game asserts the benefits of its own approach, of course.

Even the U.S. Postal Service is a player in the proprietary game. As noted earlier, public key technology makes it feasible to consider development of large-scale security services. Feasible is not the same as easy, however. A residual problem is the public certification of public keys; how does a recipient know that a given public key belongs to the purported author of a message? The PGP mechanism uses a highly informal method of certifying public keys. Another approach is to have a trusted third-party service offer public key certificates, much as is done in the paper world for notary publics.

The U.S. Postal Service has decided to pursue the market for such certificate "authorities." It is doing this through private contracts, developing a closed, proprietary approach. While it is making public presentations about this effort, the technical work is held close in spite of the need for multiple authorities. This makes it likely that the different authorities will follow different conventions and that users will need a special piece of software for each one.

Commerce

Other than work on EDI, all of the current attempts to develop specifications for Internet commerce are being conducted as proprietary efforts. The major payment efforts are through two small consortia led by Visa and Master-Card, respectively. Initially they collaborated, then developed separate specifications, and are again working collaboratively. Their previous specifications have been made publicly available, but the current work is not subject to general review or input.

Since EDI over the Internet often needs to obtain high degrees of security and reliability, the lack of established and accepted mechanisms for these services has prompted one company, Premenos, to offer a product that satisfies the requirement. The general perception is that it uses some technical components that follow standards and others that do not. Since the full details of the protocols that are followed are not published, customers are currently forced to use only the Premenos on both ends of the exchange. It may well be that only standards are followed, as Premenos asserts, but the fact that the set of protocols, and their style of use, are not published results in the same problem as if the technology were proprietary. For interoperability to be achieved, all potential vendors need access to *all* the technical details that describe "what bits go over the wire."

Basic Service

In a vein somewhat similar to the "proprietary" security and reliability service offered for EDI, there are some uses of "pure" Internet service that result in an environment that is not technically equal for all participants.[6] Microsoft's service offering, MSN, is generally characterized as a separate Internet. It is connected to the Internet but is not really part of it. This distinction is clearly true for the major on-line services, like America Online (AOL), Prodigy, and Compuserve. Their underlying technologies predate the commercial Internet and therefore are not native to it; interworking with the Internet requires gateways that (try to) translate between the environments. In

---

[6] Cautionary note: This is not an unrealistic call requiring all vendors to succeed or for all to succeed because one does. It is a concern about technical and operational choices by one, or a few, vendors that have the effect of locking out others.

the case of the established on-line services, most are moving to modify their underlying technologies to be Internet native.

Perhaps the strangest example of proprietary advantage comes from use of an Internet standard in an IETF-approved manner. The topic is addressing the information that specifies the destination or source of your packets of data. At the core of the Internet technology is the one, common piece that is used by all applications, called Internet Protocol (IP). It has a thirty-two-bit space for addresses, in which it needs to be able to have a unique value for every machine attached to the Internet. Thirty-two bits allow 2 billion such addresses, except that the address needs to be divided into substructures, which makes the real total much smaller. In reality, even today's relatively small Internet, with only some millions of hosts, is pressing the limits of that space; also, there is a serious technical requirement to structure the addresses in a fashion that facilitates the data relay machines' (routers') storage of addressing information. A new version of IP is being developed; in the interim we need to assign addresses more efficiently.

The current solution to this problem is called Classless Internet Domain Routing (CIDR), which defines additional hierarchy to the IP address [FULI93]. The proposed use of this scheme says that users of addresses get them from their providers. While such a requirement is logical and appears reasonable, the details of that specification give considerable leverage to larger providers at the expense of smaller ones. Smaller providers must get their block of addresses, to give to their own customers, from their "upstream" providers, whereas larger providers have permanent blocks. When customers change providers or when smaller providers change upstream attachments, they must change their addresses. Renumbering a large customer network or requiring a smaller provider to tell all its customers that they must renumber has a serious and negative impact on competitive position. It won't take customers long to realize that they are spared considerable pain by staying with a larger provider.

Lower Layers

The core of the Internet technology works well, but it does need enhancement. Along with others, Microsoft noticed deficiencies in the Internet technology, called DHCP, that allow hosts to be automatically configured when they attach to the Net and to the service that maps between host names and host addresses, called DNS. Unfortunately, Microsoft then wrote their own proprietary enhancements. An example of the effect is that the recent release of Microsoft's Windows 95® resulted in many Internet service providers getting a flood of customer support calls from new users who were getting unusual error messages. The messages were caused by incompatibilities between the Windows 95 use of DHCP and the standard service supported by the providers.

Groupware

When messaging and other on-line services are designed and used to support the operations of organized groups, then they are called "groupware." Internet e-mail and news services can be counted in this category, providing generic and limited capabilities. However, there is a special category of product which provides such capabilities in a coherent fashion. Lotus's Notes® and the recent Netscape CollabraShare® are proprietary examples. To be fair, groupware products have always been proprietary. The question is whether their technology will add to the repertoire of vendor-neutral open systems or will remain a set of closed shops.

GETTING THERE *WHEN*?

Where does all this leave eager or wary businesses? Can they use the Internet for commerce today? Should they? As with most things, the answer is that it depends.

Soon

Besides the philosophical and business question of open versus proprietary services, what other issues remain to be resolved before the Internet is comfortably competent for the full range of business uses?

Pervasive Security

In spite of technical maturity and the availability of multiple solutions, authentication and privacy technology are not widely deployed. This is the single most serious deficiency in the current Internet service. At the least it requires settling on one security technology and service.

Additionally, the requirement for independent, trusted agencies to certify keys so that their use can have legal substance is paramount. Without this ability, the basis for conducting formal on-line transactions is highly constrained. Authentication allows a recipient to verify that authors are who they purport to be. Privacy is protection against wiretapping by a third party. For contracts and other binding exchanges, it is also important to be able to prove to a third party that the transaction took place; this is called nonrepudiation. On-line services for nonrepudiation have historically been provided by the EDI value added network services through the use of simple logging. That is, all EDI traffic passes through the trusted, independent VAN. If the sender or the receiver of the traffic disputes whether it was received (or sent), the VAN logs can be checked.

There is technical work to provide automated nonrepudiation capabilities. Those developing it believe it will work, and they probably are right. However there is no operational history for such a mechanism; in particular, it has not been used within the control of a legal dispute. Such a service is essential for long-term use of the Internet when contract instruments are involved, but the slow change to case law is likely to make this take some time.

Other Commerce Protocols

Ideally, buyers and merchants should be able to conduct the entire buying and selling process through automated mechanisms, including the subtle interchange known as negotiation. In the extreme, it is primarily a psychological, not a technical, process, but simple forms of negotiating *can* be automated. This capability is not in the critical path of basic utility, but its appeal is enormous.

Role of Standardization

It is one thing to complain that vendors are not participating in open standards activities and another to try to find a balance. The community—and the industry—needs major specifications to be public so functions performed by products from different vendors can interoperate. Yet businesses need to be able to develop a competitive advantage. How can these two requirements be balanced?

Perhaps the real problem is confusing the agenda. There is a difference between innovating technology and holding on to it. Companies that innovate gain considerable advantage. This suggests that the best approach is for companies to continue to innovate and field new capabilities. When capabilities are proved in the field and/or the marketplace, the vendor should give the specification to the public, handing over control of changes to an open standards body. This gives companies a lead yet gives the community long-term control.

Now!

The Internet can give excellent service today, if an organization evaluates the choice of Internet service providers carefully and plans the other details of Internet use. The technology still requires some expertise to use fully. However, when that expertise is applied by all of the participants in a trading relationship, quality of service is excellent.

Activities that require high degrees of associated security can be achieved over the Internet today, but they require significant security technology and operations expertise. This is not an activity for the fainthearted, but neither is it on the leading edge or, worse, the "bleeding edge."

At a minimum, general communications, customer support, and marketing can be done, today, quite well and with minimal effort. Besides expanding the technology to make high-quality security practical, the majority of the work is merely(?) in improving ease of use.

REFERENCES

[BALE93]   Balenson, D. "Privacy Enhancement for Internet Electronic Mail, Part III: Algorithms, Modes, and Identifiers." RFC 1423. (1993)

[BOFR93]   Borenstein, N., Freed, N. "MIME (Multipurpose Internet Mail Extensions) Part One: Mechanisms for Specifying and Describing the Format of Internet Message Bodies." RFC 1521. (09/23/1993)

[CRFR95]   Crocker, S., Freed, N., Calvin, J., Murphy, S. "MIME Object Security Services." RFC 1848. (10/03/1995)

[CROC95a]   Crocker, D. "MIME Encapsulation of EDI Objects." RFC 1767. (03/02/1995)

[CROC95b]   Crocker, D. "To Be 'On' the Internet." RFC 1775. (03/17/1995)

[FULI93]   Fuller, V., Ti, T., Yu, J., Varadhan, K. "Classless Inter-Domain Routing (CIDR): An Address Assignment and Aggregation Strategy." RFC 1519. (09/24/1993)

[GAMU95]   Galvin, J., Murphy, S., Crocker, S., Freed, N. "Security Multiparts for MIME: Multipart/Signed and Multipart/Encrypted." RFC 1847. (10/03/1995)

[GARF95]   Garfinkel, S. *PGP: Pretty Good Privacy.* Sebastopol, CA: O'Reilly and Associates. (1995)

[KALI93]   Kaliski, B. "Privacy Enhancement for Internet Electronic Mail: Part IV: Key Certification and Related Services." RFC 1424. (02/10/1993)

[KENT93]   Kent, S. "Privacy Enhancement for Internet Electronic Mail: Part II: Certificate-Based Key Management." RFC 1422. (02/10/1993)

[LINN93]   Linn, J. "Privacy Enhancement for Internet Electronic Mail: Part I: Message Encryption and Authentication Procedures." RFC 1421. (02/10/1993)

[LYNRO93]   Lynch, D., Rose, M. *Internet System Handbook.* Reading, MA: Addison-Wesley. (1993)

[MOOR93]   Moore, D. "MIME (Multipurpose Internet Mail Extensions) Part Two: Message Header Extensions for Non-ASCII Text." RFC 1522. (09/23/1993)

[POST94]   Postel, J. "Media Type Registration Procedure." RFC 1590. (03/02/1994)

[RSA95]   RSA Data Security, Inc. <http://www.rsa.com/rsa/S-MIME>. (1995)

Chapter 2

Commercial Scenarios for the Web: Opportunities and Challenges

Donna L. Hoffman, Thomas P. Novak,
and Patrali Chatterjee

ABSTRACT

The potential of the World Wide Web on the Internet as a commercial medium and market has been widely documented in a variety of media. However, a critical examination of the Web's commercial development has received little attention. This paper proposes a structural framework for examining the explosion in commercial activity on the Web. First, we explore the role of the Web as a distribution channel and a medium for marketing communications. Second, we examine the factors that have led to the development of the Web as a commercial medium, evaluating the benefits it provides to both consumers and firms and its attractive size and demographic characteristics. Third, we discuss the barriers to commercial growth of the Web from both the supply- and demand-side perspectives. This analysis leads to a new classification of commercialization efforts that categorizes commercial Web sites into six distinct types: (1) on-line storefront, (2) Internet presence, (3) content, (4) mall, (5) incentive site, and (6) search agent. The first three constitute the "integrated destination site," and the latter three

A slightly different version of this paper originally appeared in the *Journal of Computer-Mediated Communication,* vol. 1, no. 3 (December, 1995). http://shum.huji.ac.il/jcmc/vol1/issue3/hoffman.html

represent forms of "Web traffic control." Our framework, argued in the context of integrated marketing, facilitates greater understanding of the Web as a commercial medium. It allows examination of commercial Web sites in terms of the opportunities and challenges firms face in the rush toward commercialization.

1. INTRODUCTION

The tremendous growth of the Internet, particularly the World Wide Web, has led to a critical mass of consumers and firms participating in a global on-line marketplace. The rapid adoption of the Internet as a commercial medium has caused firms to experiment with innovative ways of marketing to consumers in computer-mediated environments. These developments on the Internet are expanding beyond the utilization of the Internet as a communications medium to an important view of the Internet as a new market (Ricciuti 1995).

The Internet is a massive global network of interconnected packet-switched computer networks. Krol and Hoffman (1993) offer three (mutually consistent) definitions of the Internet: "(1) a network of networks based on the TCP/IP protocols; (2) a community of people who use and develop those networks; [and] (3) [a] collection of resources that can be reached from those networks." Note that there is no agreed upon definition because the Internet is at once a set of common protocols, a physical collection of routers and circuits, distributed resources, and even a culture of connectivity and communications.

The most exciting commercial developments are occurring on that portion of the Internet known as the World Wide Web (WWW). The WWW is a distributed hypermedia environment within the Internet that was originally developed by the European Particle Physics Laboratory (CERN). Global hypermedia allow multimedia information to be located on a network of interconnected servers around the world, allowing one to travel through the information by clicking on hyperlinks. Any hyperlink (text, icon, or image in a document) can point to any document anywhere on the Internet. The user-friendly, consumer-oriented home pages of the Web utilize the system of hyperlinks to simplify the task of navigating among the offerings on the Internet. The present popularity of the Web as a commercial medium (in contrast to other networks on the Internet) is a result of its ability to facilitate global sharing of information and resources and its potential to provide an efficient channel for advertising, marketing, and even direct distribution of certain goods and information services.

1.1. The World Wide Web as an Efficient Channel

Anecdotal evidence suggests that Web-based commercial efforts are more efficient and possibly even more effective than efforts mounted in traditional channels. Initial conjectures on efficiencies generated by on-line commercial efforts suggest that marketing on the Web results in "10 times as many units [sold] with 1/10 the advertising budget" (Potter 1994). It is about one-fourth less costly to perform direct marketing through the Net than through conventional channels (Verity, Hof, Baig and Carey, 1994). This fact becomes especially critical in the face of shortening technology and product life cycles and increasing technological complexity (IITA 1994). Consider the example of SunSolve Online, which in just a few months saved Sun Microsystems over $4 million in Frequently Asked Questions (FAQs) alone since Sun "reengineered information processes around the WWW" (Neece 1995).

1.2. The Web as an Active Model of Marketing Communications

Firms use various media to communicate with their current and potential customers. Marketing communications perform three functions: inform, remind, and persuade (Anderson and Rubin 1986). The traditional one-to-many marketing communications model for mass media is shown in Figure 2.1. In this passive model, firms (denoted by F) provide content through a medium to a mass market of consumers (denoted by C). The first two functions of marketing communications may be performed by traditional communication models. However, the persuasion function necessary for differentiating a product or brand is limited by the unidirectionality of traditional mass media.

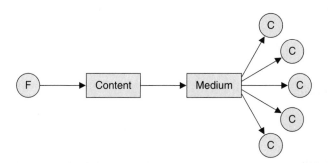

Figure 2.1 Traditional Mass Media Model of One-to-Many Marketing Communications

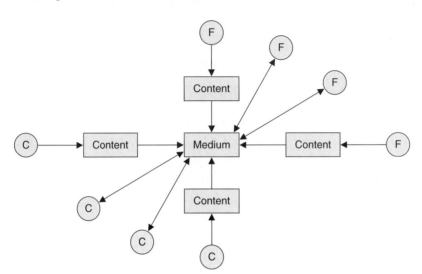

Figure 2.2 New Model of Marketing Communications for the Web

The Internet, a revolution in distributed computing and interactive multimedia many-to-many communication, is dramatically altering this traditional view of communications media. As Figure 2.2 indicates, the new many-to-many marketing communications model defining the Web offers a radical departure from traditional marketing environments (Hoffman and Novak 1994b, 1996c).

Figure 2.2 suggests that the Internet offers an alternative to mass media communication. Some applications on the Internet (e.g., personal home pages) represent "narrowcasting" to the extreme, with content created by and for consumers. As a marketing and advertising medium, the Web has the potential to radically change the way firms do business with their customers by blending together publishing, real-time communication broadcast, and narrowcast. As an operational model of distributed computing, the Net supports the following:

- Discussion groups (e.g., USENET news, moderated and unmoderated mailing lists)

- Multiplayer games and communications systems (e.g., MUDs, irc, chat, MUSEs)

- File transfer (ftp) and remote login (telnet)

- Electronic mail

- Global information access and retrieval systems (e.g., archie, veronica, gopher, and the World Wide Web)

From a business and marketing perspective, the most exciting developments are occurring on that portion of the Internet known as the World Wide Web. In this paper we present an initial attempt to organize the commercial activity on the Web thus far according to its business function. We identify two major categories of sites: "destination sites" and "Web traffic control sites." Under destination sites, we identify on-line storefronts, Internet presence sites, and content sites. These comprise the ultimate "destinations" housing a firm's virtual counterpart. The purpose of the Web traffic control sites is to direct consumers to these various destination sites. There are three major categories of Web traffic control: malls, incentive sites, and search agents. We argue for considering our framework in the context of "integrated marketing," in which various communications vehicles are coordinated to create a single, strategically appropriate marketing effort to maximize customer response (Schultz, Tannenbaum, and Lauterborn 1992; Tynan 1994).

2. THE WEB AS A COMMERCIAL MEDIUM

As a commercial medium, the Web offers a number of important benefits that can be examined at both the customer and the firm level. In this way, we can address both demand and supply issues. Buyer benefits, which arise primarily from the structural characteristics of the medium, include availability of information, provision of search mechanisms, and on-line product trial, all of which can lead to reduced uncertainty in the purchase decision. Firm benefits arise from the potential of the Web as a distribution channel, a medium for marketing communications, and a market in and of itself. These efficiencies are associated with Web technology and the interactive nature of the medium.

2.1. Consumer Benefits

One important consumer benefit associated with marketing on the Web is the access to greater amounts of dynamic information to support queries for consumer decision making. A recent Hermes survey of Web users found gathering purchase-related information was the most preferred Web activity (Gupta 1995). Further, the interactive nature of the Web and the hypertext environment allow for deep, nonlinear searches initiated and controlled by customers. Hence marketing communications on the Web are more consumer-driven than those provided by traditional media. In addition, recreational uses, manifested in the form of nondirected search behavior, can be an important benefit to consumers intrinsically motivated to use the medium (Hoffman and Novak 1996a).

The ability of the Web to amass, analyze, and control large quantities of specialized data can enable comparison shopping and speed the process of finding items (Wallace 1995). The Web facilitates trial and provides instant gratification; customers can test products on-line, which may stimulate purchase (e.g., Mathsoft browser, Dec Alpha AXP). There is also the potential of wider availability of hard-to-find products and wider selection of items due to the width and efficiency of the channel.

In addition, the advantages for industrial consumers are reduced costs to buyers from increased competition in procurement as more suppliers are able to compete in an electronically open marketplace. This increase in competition leads to better quality and variety of goods through expanded markets and the ability to produce customized goods (IITA 1994).

2.2. Benefits to the Firm

2.2.1. Distribution

Firm benefits arise partly from the use of the Web as a distribution channel. First, the Web potentially offers certain classes of providers participation in a market in which distribution costs or costs-of-sales shrink to zero. This is most likely for firms in publishing, information services, or digital product categories (Jones 1994). For example, digital products can be delivered immediately; hence, such businesses may encounter massive disintermediation or even the eventual elimination of middlemen (Michalski 1995). Moreover, buyers and sellers can access and contact each other directly, potentially eliminating some of the marketing cost and constraints imposed by such interactions in the terrestrial world. This may also have the effect of shrinking the channel and making distribution much more efficient (mainly due to reduced overhead costs through such outcomes as uniformity, automation, and large-scale integration of management processes). Time to complete business transactions may be reduced as well, translating into additional efficiencies for the firm. However, such potential efficiencies must be tempered with market realities (Kline 1995).

Second, business on the Web transfers more of the selling function to the customer, through on-line ordering and the use of fill-out forms (Michalski

1995), thus helping to bring transactions to a conclusion. This permits a third benefit in the form of capture-of-customer information. The technology offers the firm the opportunity to gather market intelligence and monitor consumer choices through customers' revealed preferences in navigational and purchasing behavior in the Web. Note, however, that many social, legal, and technological issues and drawbacks at the present level of technology prevent the full capitalization of this benefit (see, e.g., Caruso 1995).

2.2.2. Marketing Communications

At the present time, most firms use the Web primarily to deliver information about the firm and its offerings, and for both internal and external communication (Magid 1995; Sharples 1995) with other firms and consumers. The interactive nature of the medium (see Hoffman and Novak 1996a for discussion) offers another category of firm benefits since it is especially conducive to developing customer relationships. This potential for customer interaction, which is largely asynchronous under current implementations, facilitates relationship marketing and customer support (Cuneo 1995) to a greater degree than has been possible with traditional media.

Web sites are available on demand to consumers twenty-four hours a day. The interactive nature of the medium can be used by marketers to hold the attention of the consumer by engaging him or her in an asynchronous "dialogue" that occurs at both parties' convenience. This capability of the medium offers unprecedented opportunities to tailor communications precisely to individual customers, allowing them to request as much information as desired. Further, it allows the marketer to obtain relevant information from customers for the purposes of serving them more effectively in the future.

The simplest implementations involve engaging customers through the use of e-mail buttons located strategically on the site. More sophisticated implementations may involve fill-out forms and other incentives designed to engage customers in ongoing relationships with the firm. The objective of such continuous relationship building is dual-pronged: to give consumers information about the firm and its offering, and to receive information from consumers about their needs with respect to such offerings. Hence, effective customized advertising, promotion, and customer service (Berniker 1995) constitute the fifth benefit the commercial Web offers to the firm.

Most important, the Web offers an opportunity for competition on the "specialty" axis instead of the price axis. From a marketing perspective, it is rarely desirable to compete solely on the basis of price. Instead, marketers attempt to satisfy needs on the basis of benefits sought, which means pricing is dependent upon value to the consumer, not costs. Such opportunity arises when the offering is differentiated by elements of the marketing mix other than price. This results in the delivery of value-laden benefits, for example, convenience through direct electronic distribution of software, or enjoyment through a visually appealing and unusual Web site. As evidence that this is occurring, consumers indicated that price was the least important product attribute they considered when making on-line purchases (Gupta 1995). The ability to compete on dimensions other than price will become especially critical in categories where brands are perceived as substitutes, since it allows for more opportunities to differentiate along other dimensions.

2.2.3. Operational Benefits

Operational benefits of Web use for industrial sellers are reduced errors, time, and overhead costs in information processing; reduced costs to suppliers by electronically accessing on-line databases of bid opportunities, on-line abilities to submit bids, and on-line review of awards. In addition, creation of new markets and segments (Schrage 1995), increased generation of sales leads (Krumenaker 1995), easier entry into new markets (especially geographically remote markets), and faster time to market are facilitated (Wilder 1995). This is due to the ability to easily and cheaply reach potential customers and to the elimination of delays between the different steps of the business subprocesses (IITA 1994).

2.3. Size and Growth of the Internet and the World Wide Web

2.3.1. Internet Hosts

A main reason the Web is "hot" as a commercial medium is because of its current size, future growth prospects, and exceedingly attractive demographics. The most recent estimates put the worldwide number of host computers connected to the Internet at over 9.47 million, representing over 240,000 domains (Lottor 1996). This number has been approximately doubling annually since 1981. Over 2.4 million, or 26 percent, of these hosts are commercial domains (.com), while nearly 1.8 million, or 19 percent are educational (.edu) (Lottor 1996). The actual number of hosts connected to the Internet is probably much larger than 9.47 million, since there is an increasing trend for hosts to be installed behind firewalls. Hosts named "www" represent the largest and fastest-growing category of host computer connected to the Internet. In January 1996 over 76,000 host computers had this designation, up 2400 percent since January 1995 (Lottor 1996). It is reasonable to assume that such hosts represent Web servers (that is, the Web sites which individuals visit). Thus, 76,000 is a lower-bound estimate of the number of Web sites on the Internet.

The number of domains is also impressive. As of January 1996, there were over 170,000 commercial domains registered on the Internet with Inter-Nic, up from 29,000 at the beginning of 1995 (Walsh 1996). This represents a 586 percent increase in a single year. The number of registered .edu domains as of January 1996 was 2,261 (Walsh 1996). The dominance of commercial domains is a dramatic reversal from years past, when the Internet was dominated by educational hosts.

The Internet is a truly international communications medium; many dozens of countries are represented by over 128 international hosts, and international participation is increasing. Fifty-one country and global domains are experiencing annual growth rates in excess of 100 percent. The most rapidly growing country and global domains (among those above 10,000 hosts) are Singapore, .net, the Russian Federation, the U.S. domain (.us), Brazil, Finland, Japan, Israel, Italy, Poland, Taiwan, the United Kingdom, and Ireland (Rutkowski 1996). In absolute terms, the fastest-growing Internet domains (a six-month increase of at least 100,000 hosts) are .com, .net, .edu, the United Kingdom, the United States, Canada, Japan, Germany, and Australia (Rutkowski 1996). Since July 1995, twenty-eight countries or territories have connected to the Internet for the first time, including Albania, the Bahamas, Bahrain, Cuba, Ethiopia, Guatemala, Jordan, New Caledonia, Sri Lanka, Tonga, and Uganda (Rutkowski 1996).

Internet host distribution by country reveals that the top ten hosts (in July 1995) were the United States, with over 64 percent, followed by Germany with 5 percent, the United Kingdom and Canada with 4 percent, Australia with 3 percent, and Japan, the Netherlands, France, Finland, and Sweden each with 2 percent (Quarterman 1995). Current estimates put the U.S./non-U.S. host distribution at closer to 60 percent/40 percent, with roughly the same distribution across the top ten countries (Rutkowski 1996).

In January 1995 the number of U.S. networks connected to the Internet (a network is a communications medium that transports the information, or packets, to host computers connected to the Internet) was 26,681, and the number of international networks was 19,637 (Internet Society 1995). This number, now impossible to know, was forecasted to grow to roughly 100,000 networks connected to the Internet in 1996, with approximately half connected in the United States and half connected internationally (Rutkowski 1996).

2.3.2. World Wide Web Growth

Growth in Web sites is even more impressive than growth of the Internet; the Web grew a staggering 1758 percent in 1994 alone and doubles in size roughly every two to three months. More than 23,000 Web sites were found by the Web Wanderer in July 1995 (Gray 1995). Lottor (1996) estimates that there are at least 76,000 Web servers on the Internet, and this probably underestimates the total by as much as 20 percent. As of May 19, 1996, Digital's popular search engine Altavista (www.altavista.digital.com) indexed Uniform Record Locators (URLs) from over 225,000 Web sites.

In terms of content served up by these Web sites, Altavista indexed 30 million unique URLs and 11 billion words as of May 19, 1996. Inktomi (www.hotbot.com), launched May 20, 1996, currently indexes 50 million unique URLs, and Lycos (www.lycos.com) indexed 10.75 million unique URLs as of December 12, 1995 (at the end of 1994, Lycos indexed 1 million URLs).

Observers credit NSCA Mosaic (introduced in the spring of 1993) for jump-starting the growth of the Web. This stunning growth is a classic example of a rapid diffusion process (Rogers 1983) in which adoption is fueled by word-of-mouth communication, an internal influence (Bass 1969; Mahajan, Muller, and Bass 1990). Word-of-mouth centers around the uniquely interactive nature of the Web. Hoffman and Novak (1996a) discuss the unique characteristics of the Web medium as computer mediation, hypermedia, machine interactivity, network navigation, and telepresence.

2.3.3. Attractive Demographics

Computer-oriented consumers are "techno-savvy" (Ogilvy and Mather Direct 1994), and PC penetration in the United States is significant. The PC market is "young," since 58 percent of PC owners have had their computers for less than two years (Zeigler 1995). According to recent Odyssey Homefront Survey results (Vonder Haar 1995), one-third of U.S. households have a PC at home (up 27 percent from July 1994), 13 percent have CD-ROM drives, and 18 percent have modems. However, on-line service penetration remains low, with only 9 percent of American households subscribing to one or more on-line services.

The nonrepresentative Georgia Tech/Hermes survey of Web usage (Graphic, Visualization, and Usability Center 1996) reveals that the Web is starting to turn more mainstream. Females make up 29 percent of users globally (the percentage of females rises to 33 percent in the United States), 40 percent of Web users are thirty-six years old or over, almost a third of the respondents make less than $30,000 a year, and nearly half make less than $50,000 a year. As Hoffman (1996) notes, more middle class and working-class individuals are coming on-line everyday; occupationally, more students, more people in sales and service work, more retired people, and more people in a more diverse variety of occupations (e.g., day laborers, craftspeople, homemakers, and others), as well as people reporting smaller annual household incomes (especially under $30,000), are joining the ranks of the "wired."

SRI's (1995) psychographic analysis of the Web population gives further insight into the Web visitor and identifies two broad categories of the Web "audience." The first group, the "upstream" audience, represents 50 percent of the current Web population. This group is estimated to represent 10 percent of the U.S. population, is 77 percent male, educated (97 percent have at least some college education), and upscale. Members of this group are what SRI terms "actualizers": successful men and women with high self-esteem and active, "take-charge" lifestyles. Upstream Web visitors typically receive institutional subsidies for Web usage and represent the pioneer Internet users. Because most upstream users are already on-line, future Web growth must come from the "downstream" segment.

If the SRI analysis is valid, then the rate of adoption by the downstream segment, or "other half," will determine when and if the Web achieves critical mass as a commercial medium. The other half already on-line represents the lead users of the other 90 percent of U.S. society. This group is noticeably less gender-skewed than the upstream group (64 percent male and 36 percent female), younger (70 percent are under age thirty), and on its way to being just as educated (89 percent have at least some college education) since the group is comprised of students or recent college graduates. The other half are predominantly made up of what SRI refers to as "strivers" and "experiencers." According to SRI, strivers are unsure of themselves and seek approval from the world around them. In contrast, experiencers are enthusiastic and impulsive, seeking variety and excitement from life. An interesting finding that requires further study is that some of these other-half Web visitors appear not to find the Web valuable. Note, however, that the results of such surveys are not population-projectable, nor necessarily representative of the "typical" Web visitor. However, these early demographic surveys suggest that current Web consumers are leading-edge early adopters (Freeman 1995).

Motivated by Hoffman and Novak's (1994a) "call to arms" for a nonproprietary, industry-wide survey of Internet demographics, CommerceNet, a nonprofit consortium of firms dedicated to promoting electronic commerce, has funded the first-ever population-projectable, representative survey of who uses the Internet and why. Hoffman and Novak (1996b) estimate that

28.8 million people in the United States age sixteen and over have potential or actual access to the Internet, 16.4 million people use the Internet, 11.5 million people use the Web, and 1.51 million people have used the Web to purchase something. Hoffman and Novak also report that the demographics of Internet use depend on the particular usage segment and that strong relationships exist between usage segments and type of Internet access, computer ownership, and length of time of computer use.

3. BARRIERS TO COMMERCIALIZATION OF THE WEB

The barriers to consumer and firm adoption impact critical mass (Oliver, Marwell, and Teixeira 1985). Accumulated industry experience and anecdotal evidence strongly support the contention that the primary barrier to consumer adoption of the Web as a commercial medium is ease of access. Convenience of access is at the core of the adoption of any technological application and determines its ultimate success (Gupta 1995). In the context of the Web, ease of access is a multidimensional construct and includes high-speed access (the "bandwidth" problem), ease of finding a service provider, and the diffusion of the computer hardware/software/modem bundle into the home.

The secondary barriers are ease of use, price, and risk, including such factors as privacy and security. Ease of use includes issues such as the user-friendliness of the software, ease of software installation, and the like. The marketplace will weed out even technically feasible Web applications if they prove too complicated for the average consumer to use (Seaman 1995). Hence attempts to develop user-friendly technology are as important as the technology itself.

There is a great deal of concern regarding the security of financial information transmitted over the Internet and its impact on consumer willingness to buy or sell products (IITA 1994). This limitation is critical to mass adoption of the Web, especially since surveys of Web users indicate that vendor reliability and security of financial transactions are important to users (Gupta 1995). At this writing, such limitations impact consumer behavior on the Web; currently, the majority of consumers use the Web to browse or search much more than to actually make purchases (Booker 1995; Wintrob 1995).

The barriers to firm adoption arise from the Web measurement problem (Donaton 1995b). Firms are unsure of the number of people on the Net and how many people use the Web, and this uncertainty makes investment decisions difficult. In addition, there are no established criteria for judging the success of Web sites (Bellafante 1995). Hence, researchers need to develop concepts to shape standards. Such standards are critical to demonstrate the viability of the Web as a commercial medium, and to provide mechanisms for measuring investment opportunities and business success.

The commercial success of a firm's Web site depends in part on accurate information on market potential and consumer needs (Donaton 1995b). The Web provides multiple ways to reach a diverse and exciting set of markets. Determining the appropriate set of target market segments and evaluating the penetration of Web access technology in each market is the first step in developing an integrated marketing strategy.

Because critical mass for interactive technologies is "all-or-none" (Markus 1987), the Web will not be successful as a commercial medium until it achieves critical mass. An important first step in any marketing program, therefore, is determining how many people are on the Internet and what they are doing there (Hoffman and Novak 1994a). It is also necessary to define and estimate segments of Web behavior based on customer need. The economics of the Web can then be examined for each specific case to determine if the return on investment meets financial targets.

Some sites (e.g., Pathfinder, HotWired, and Internet Shopping Network) are attempting to capture data to address the preceding objectives by providing the option for visitor "authentication." In this process, visitors may register as subscribers in order to use the site fully (e.g., to search for specific content or to make a purchase). This enables the marketer to use demographic data and information on new and repeat visit patterns to strengthen its (and sponsors') marketing programs on the site. Ultimately, marketers may build detailed databases and tailor marketing programs specifically to individual visitors or groups of visitors.

4. MODELS OF WEB-BASED BUSINESS

Consider the following: As of April 11, 1996, a significant number of the 80,000-plus Web servers on the Internet represented commercial sites. Nearly 26,012 firms were listed in Open Market's (1996) "Commercial Services on the Net" directory, including 213 "malls" hosting at least fifteen commercial listings. In the Yahoo Companies directory (www.yahoo.com), there were 62,928 entries in categories as diverse as audio, automotive, funerals, home and garden, and shopping centers.

There is no doubt that a great deal of commercial activity exists on the Web and that this activity is increasing. However, the proliferation is confusing.

What sorts of business models are being implemented? Are some better than others? Two questions are especially relevant: Is anyone making any money? Where are the opportunities?

Profitability from commercial activity on the Web includes productivity savings, marketing and sales savings, and incremental or new revenue streams. Productivity savings arise from reduction in order and processing costs and more efficient inventory management. Increases in productivity on the "soft" side through more efficient personnel may also lead to productivity gains.

Savings may also be realized from efficiencies in the marketing and selling functions. The Web shifts more of these functions to the customer; savings result from reduced brochure printing and distribution costs and reductions in order taking as customers use fill-out forms to prepare their own orders. As control is also effectively transferred to the customer, we speculate that customer satisfaction might actually be increased.

Finally, incremental or new revenue streams are available for firms participating in digital commerce, through, for example, on-line sales, advertising revenues, or information brokering. Incremental revenues may be achieved for those firms that use the Web to expand into new channels of distribution and new market segments. Corporate training, electronic distribution, and maintenance provide additional revenue opportunities for appropriate firms. However, secure mechanisms for transactions are necessary to fully exploit the revenue-generating opportunities of the Web (Donaton 1995a).

Although we can address the potential for profitability, the question of whether anyone is making money on the Web remains largely premature. However, a careful examination of where the opportunities are can be undertaken. Despite the current frenzy of activity, there is little information on the types of business models in use and whether some have the potential to be more effective than others. Strategic insight is therefore needed into how sites are differentiated, how they may be designed more effectively, and how to attract customers to sites.

4.1. A New Classification of Commercial Web Sites

In integrated marketing programs, marketing managers combine elements of various media in order to maximize the effectiveness of a communications program (Belch and Belch 1995). Despite the intense interest in such coordinated efforts (see, e.g., Duncan and Everett 1993), there has yet to be widespread adoption and implementation of the concept (Cleland 1995e; Schultz 1995).

The concept of integrated marketing holds appeal and promise for business efforts on the World Wide Web because the Web offers enormous potential for developing customer relationships and customizing the offering to individual customers. In this section we define six functional categories of commercial Web pages. Each can be considered as an element in an integrated marketing program in the context of digital commerce. We discuss each category in detail and suggest how the elements may combine structurally to form the components of an integrated marketing program. The examples presented here were selected to reflect the range of practice regarding commercial activity on the Web, not necessarily best business practice. The reader should also be aware that as the Web is rapidly evolving, some links may have changed or disappeared altogether.

The six functional types are as follows:

- On-line storefront
- Internet presence (flat ad, image and information)
- Content (fee-based, sponsored, searchable database)
- Mall
- Incentive site
- Search agent, filters, and directories

These functional types provide the building blocks for a successful site. An integrated strategy should involve all of these, put to different use. Commercial Web site design includes on-line storefront sites, Internet presence sites, and content sites, as shown in Figure 2.3.

The main challenges for marketers are to attract visitors to the site and to generate significant repeat visits (Williamson and Johnson 1995). Awareness leads to trial or the initial site visit, so that the trial problem depends on "Web traffic control." However, sites will only be successful in the long run if they generate repeat traffic, which is far more difficult to achieve than trial. The repeat visit problem is partly a function of Web site design (Salomon 1995) and depends to a large extent on customer need.

4.1.1. On-line Storefront

These Web sites offer direct sales through an electronic channel via an electronic catalog or another, more innovative, format. The number of products presently being sold on a single site ranges from one to many. Consumers order goods via fill-out form, 800 number, registration, or snailmail. On-line

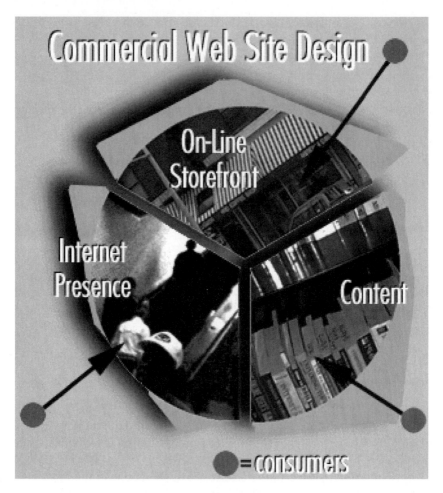

Figure 2.3 Commercial Web Site Design

storefronts cover a wide variety of offerings; examples include Absolutely Fresh Flowers, Adventurous Travelers Bookstore, Alaska River Adventures, Ann Hemyng Candy, CDNow, 800-Flowers, Freeway Enterprises Person-to-Person Web Sites and Greeting Cards, HeadFirst, Internet Shopping Network, Samsonite Luggage Express, San Francisco Music Box Company, Shrink-Link, Think Big, Tower Records, and Virtual Vineyards. A recent innovator in this category is Security First Network Bank (FSB), the world's first Internet bank, which offers on-line consumers the ability to open accounts, pay bills, and manage their finances via the World Wide Web.

Opportunities abound for the on-line storefront model. It combines elements of direct marketing with in-store shopping and has the potential to be vastly more efficient than either. In this approach there are tremendous opportunities for customization and relationship marketing. A much broader definition of product and service categories becomes possible in this environment. The ultimate developments are those products that can exist or be consumed only on the Web (see, e.g., Freeway Enterprises' offering of electronic greeting cards for person-to-person Web sites).

However, the on-line storefront model poses a number of challenges. Current access speeds can make on-line shopping frustrating and tedious. Additionally, the terrestrial approach to shopping necessarily sets the standards for on-line offerings. In many cases the on-line versions pale in comparison to real-world experiences of flipping through glossy catalogs or shopping in department stores. Because the technologies for secure transactions (e.g., on-line payment) are not mature yet, security and privacy are major issues that have yet to be addressed satisfactorily in this medium. Finally, the consumer behavior issues are completely unknown. For example, we have little idea how to stimulate "trial" and "repeat," do not yet know what the most effective segmentation bases will be for on-line shopping, and understand little about the impact of marketing tools such as custom-designed incentives.

4.1.2. Internet Presence Sites: Flat Ads, Image, and Information

Internet presence sites provide a virtual "presence" for a firm and its offerings. They may also serve to signal to current and prospective customers and competitors that the firm is on the cutting edge, possibly driven by "mimetic isomorphism" (DiMaggio and Powell 1983). We identify three types of Internet presence sites: flat ad, image, and information.

Flat ads are single-page electronic flyers with no hypermedia links. They could just as easily appear in a newspaper or magazine, though a flat ad is decidedly less sophisticated than its print counterparts. We expect the evolution in this category to include hypermedia, particularly as Web browsers like Netscape integrate real-time audio and video (e.g., Sun Microsystem's Java multimedia language) (Johnson 1995). Michael's bespoke tailors, Weightlifting 101, and Xopix represent current examples of flat ads.

In Internet presence image sites, the consumer appeal is emotional rather than rational. Information about the product, if any, is provided in the context in which the product is consumed or has meaning to the consumer. Such sites appear to be especially suited to products that have low hard-information content. Examples include Evian, Late Show with David Letterman on Eye on the Net @ CBS, L. L. Bean, Miller Genuine Draft, P&G's Sunny Delight, Paramount Pictures Online Studio, Planet Reebok, and Zima.com.

Information sites provide detailed, rational information about the firm and/or its offering. Internet presence information sites can take on innovative and sophisticated forms and can be used to facilitate navigation. One objective of such sites is to build a relationship with the consumer even before the need to purchase the product or service arises (Rechtin 1995). Examples include American Airlines, Andersen Consulting, Apple Computer, Club Med, FedEx, Forrester Research, Goldman, Sachs & Co., HeadsTogether/Bookworm, L. L. Bean, Lotus, MathSoft, Sun Microsystems, Sun-Maid Raisins, and Volvo.

Opportunities for Internet presence sites include the ability to reach motivated customers with an information- or image-rich communications message. Because the entry barriers are so low, smaller firms can set up Internet presence sites as well as (or in some cases even better than) larger firms. We believe that Internet presence sites represent the future of advertising and marketing communications on the Web.

Challenges include the actual execution, that is, what is the best way to implement such a concept? Executional challenges are greater for image sites, but the rewards may be greater as well, since image sites may be more likely to generate flow, the "glue" holding the user in a site (Hoffman and Novak 1996a). A final challenge is how managers can evaluate the effectiveness of such sites.

4.1.3. *Content: Fee-Based, Sponsored, and Searchable Database*

In fee-based content sites, the provider supplies and/or pays for content, which the consumer pays to access. Fee-based content sites are expected to proliferate as secure payment mechanisms are implemented. To date, however, the model has met with only limited success, perhaps because consumers may be unwilling to pay for content delivered in this manner. A recent trend is toward information brokering and usage-based pricing, as with NewsPage, where visitors are able to access news summaries at no charge but incur a small fee for the full text of a story. Other examples include QuoteCom and Washington Weekly.

Sponsored content sites sell advertising space to reduce or eliminate the necessity of charging fees to visitors (Donaton 1995b). Thus, as with magazines in the terrestrial world, advertising appears from a variety of sources and underwrites the editorial content. A recent trend is toward sponsored "entertainment" content and sponsored search agents (see later text). Typical current examples of sponsored content sites include HotWired, Triangle Online, and Washingtonian Online. Some sponsored content sites combine elements of the Internet presence model and the mall. Examples of such hybrids include GNN, iWORLD, and Pathfinder.

In the third type of content model, merchants or advertisers pay a provider for information placement in an organized listing in a searchable database. The unit of analysis is a person, service, or information source, all of the same type. This is the inverse of the fee-based content model. Selected examples include Catalog Mart Home Page, Comspace.com: Orange County, E-Zines Database, Medical Illustrators, NYNEX BigYellow, Single-Search, and the Virtual Headbook.

Opportunities abound for content sites, as they closely parallel traditional media models. At the present there is generally no (sponsored content) or at most a small (fee-based) charge to consumers to consume the content. Some firms (e.g., Wired and Time/Warner) offer a new channel for expansion. Firms adopting this model have the opportunity to reach an advertiser-coveted audience. In addition, such sites may provide meaningful exposure that would otherwise be lost in the unstructured clutter that currently typifies the Web (Cleland 1995d). Additionally, content sites can demonstrate innovation, are more efficient than their terrestrial counterparts, and are, in theory, easy to implement. However, the challenges for content sites arise because of this perceived ease of implementation. The close parallels to traditional media represent significant execution hurdles for content sites. How best to measure and optimize consumer response to advertising in sponsored content sites is completely unknown.

4.1.4. Mall

The mall site typically constitutes a collection of on-line storefronts, each of which may contain many different categories of goods for sale. The provider charges rent in exchange for the virtual real estate and may offer a variety of services to the storefront (Gaffin 1994). Some malls also accept advertising, as with, for example, the Internet Mall. Other examples include the Branch Mall, CyberMart, eMall, and Shopping 2000.

4.1.5. Incentive Site

The incentive site represents a unique form of advertising that attracts a potential customer to a site. The objective is to pull the user to the commercial site behind it, thus helping marketers generate traffic to their Web sites (Cleland 1995a). The content may be transitory in nature and may appear to serve as a "public service announcement" or offer incentives. From the context of Web traffic control, incentive sites serve the same function as malls.

Some efforts may be especially sophisticated, as in directory services such as Open Market. Other examples include Cupid's Cove, Digital's Altavista, and Lucky Leprechaun's Lane.

4.1.6 Search Agents, Filters, and Directories

The purpose of these sites is to identify information, other Web sites, or offerings on those or other Web sites through keyword search of a database that either is based on software agents that filter information based on user preferences, extends throughout the Web, or is based on provider selection criteria. These can represent innovative and sophisticated use of intelligent agent technology. A recent trend in such sites is the emergence of fee-based (e.g., InfoSeek) or advertiser-sponsored (e.g., Yahoo) search agents. Other examples are Firefly, Lycos, Magellan, Open Text, Rex: Adaptive Newspaper Service, and Web Crawler, with additional contenders entering the market regularly. Newer search agents such as BargainFinder incorporate increased assistance to the user in the search process.

In terms of opportunities, there are many novel ways to generate traffic to a destination Web site. There is also the potential to model the diffusion of site visitors as a function of where the consumer entered the site from. Recently, search agent sites have shown potential as high-traffic vehicles for advertising sponsorship.

Web traffic control sites face a number of challenges. The proliferation of commercial Web sites means that it is increasingly difficult to find anything on the Web, especially if one is not looking for it! Therefore, identifying pivotal cross-linking opportunities will be critical.

5. SUMMARY AND CONCLUSIONS

We have proposed a framework for evaluating the commercial development of the World Wide Web on the Internet. Our categorization scheme organizes the explosion of commercial activity and identifies two major categories of sites: destination sites and Web traffic control sites. Destination sites include on-line storefronts, Internet presence sites, and content sites. These comprise the ultimate "destinations" competing for consumers' share of visits on the Web. Web traffic control sites, including malls, incentive sites, and search agents, function to direct consumers to these various destination sites. We have argued that the marketing objective is to integrate these sites into a coordinated plan designed to generate initial visits and secure repeat visits.

Our systematic categorization also serves to focus strategic attention on the following:

- Understanding evolution of sites and structural characteristics over time: Examining the attributes underlying Web site structure can lead to insight into what makes a successful site.

- Gaining insight into categories that do not yet exist: Since site characteristics will change over time, tracking changes will suggest where the development is headed.

- Keeping an eye on the leading edge to gain a differential advantage: From a developmental point of view, managers need to identify the extent to which firms are following existing models or developing new models. One path to a differential advantage will be to create innovative sites in less crowded categories, particularly as sites proliferate.

The models identified here reinforce the idea that the firm's relationship with the customer must take advantage of a key feature of the medium, namely, interactivity, and that such relationships must be updated continuously. The interactive nature of the Web is especially conducive to relationship building and offers marketers new opportunities to create stronger brand identities that have the potential to translate to brand loyalty (Upshaw 1995).

Future work should focus on empirically estimating the relative distributions of firms across these different categories and the types of firms within each category. Research efforts should especially concentrate on developing integrated marketing approaches that specify the ways in which these different elements can be combined for maximum advantage.

The Internet, especially that portion known as the World Wide Web, has the potential to radically change the way businesses interact with their customers. The Web frees customers from their traditionally passive role as receivers of marketing communications, gives them much greater control over the information search and acquisition process, and allows them to become active participants in the marketing process.

However, significant adoption barriers to commercialization preclude predictable and smooth development of commercial opportunities in this emerging medium. Commercial development of the Web must follow the demand ("demand pull"), instead of being driven by "gold fever." Firms will reap the benefits of innovation in interactivity by being closer to the customer than ever before.

REFERENCES

Anderson, Patricia M., and Leonard G. Rubin (1986). *Marketing Communications.* Englewood Cliffs, NJ: Prentice-Hall.

Bass, Frank M. (1969). "A New Product Growth Model for Consumer Durables." *Management Science* 15 (January): 215–227.

Belch, George E., and Michael A. Belch (1995). *Introduction to Advertising and Promotion: An Integrated Marketing Communications Perspective.* Homewood, IL: Irwin.

Bellafante, Ginia (1995). "Strange Sounds and Sights." *Time,* 145-12 (Spring), 14–16.

Berniker, Mark (1995). "Sony Online Debuts Internet Site." *Broadcasting and Cable,* February 20, 51.

Booker, Ellis (1995). "Web Users Cruising for Info, Not Purchases." *Computerworld,* February 20, 6.

Caruso, Denise (1995). *New York Times,* Monday, June 24.

——— (1995a). "Online Offers Truly Receptive Promotion Target." *Advertising Age,* March 20, 18.

——— (1995b). "Online Soon to Snare 100-Plus Newspapers." *Advertising Age,* April 2, S-6, S-13.

——— (1995c). "A Gaggle of Web Guides Vies for Ads." *Advertising Age,* April 17, 16.

——— (1995d). "Internet Surfing with a Purpose." *Advertising Age,* May 15, 18.

——— (1995e). "Few Wed Marketing, Communications." *Advertising Age,* 66(9), February 27, 10.

Cortese, Amy (1995). "Cyberspace." *Business Week,* February 27, 78–86.

Cuneo, Alice Z. (1995). "Internet World Show Spurs Online Commerce Debate." *Advertising Age,* April 17, 16.

DiMaggio, Paul, and Walter W. Powell (1983). "The Iron Cage Revisited: Institutional Isomorphism and Collective Rationality in Organizational Fields." *American Sociological Review* 48: 147–160.

Donaton, Scott (1995a). "Web News with a Personal Touch." *Advertising Age,* April 3, 25.

——— (1995b). "Pathfinder Blazes a Trail to Ads," *Advertising Age,* April 10, 19.

Donlin, Dennis (1995). "Scaling New-Media Mountains." *Advertising Age,* March 27, 22.

Duncan, Thomas R., and Stephen E. Everett (1993). "Client Perceptions of Integrated Marketing Communications." *Journal of Advertising Research* 33 (May/June): 30–39.

Fawcett, Adrienne Ward (1995). "Trading Scissors for Modems." *Advertising Age,* June 5, 14.

Filo, Jerry, and David Yang (1995). "Yahoo—A Guide to the WWW." [URL: http://www.yahoo.com/]

Freeman, Laurie (1995). "From Salesman's Web to Online Web." *Advertising Age*, April 3, S-30, S-31.

Gaffin, Adam (1994). "Mall-Hopping on the Internet." *Network World*, October 10, 4.

Graphic, Visualization, and Usability Center (1996). "GVU Fourth WWW Users' Survey." [URL:http://www.cc.gatech.edu/gvu/user_surveys/User_survey_Home.html]

Gray, Matthew (1995). Comprehensive List of Sites. [URL: http://www.netgen.com/cgi/comprehensive]

Gupta, Sunil (1995). "HERMES: A research Project on the Commercial Uses of the World Wide Web." [URL: http://www.umich.edu/~sgupta/hermes/]

Hoffman, Donna L. (1996). "Cyberspace to Congress: The Net is Mainstream—and it Votes!" Microtimes, no. 148, March 4. [www.microtimes.com/prof.html]

Hoffman, Donna L., and Thomas P. Novak (1994a). "Wanted: Net.Census." *Wired*, 2.11, November.

——— (1994b). "Building New Paradigms for Electronic Commerce." *Hot-Wired* (Intelligent Agent Section), December 29. [URL:http://www2000.ogsm.-vanderbilt.edu/intelligent.agent/index.html]

——— (1996a). "Marketing In Hypermedia Computer-Mediated Environments: Conceptual Foundations." *Journal of Marketing* 60(3):50–68.

——— (1996b). "Internet and Web Use in the United States: 1995 Baselines for Commercial Development." *Communications of the ACM*, December, forthcoming.

——— (1996c). "A New Marketing Paradigm for Electronic Commerce." *The Information Society*, forthcoming.

IITA (1994). "Electronic Commerce and the NII." Information Infrastructure Technology and Applications Task Group, National Coordination Office for High Performance Computing and Communications, February.

Internet Society (1995). [ftp://ftp.isoc.org/isoc/charts/]

Johnson, Bradley (1995). "A Cure for the Common Web Site?" *Advertising Age*, June 5, 18.

Jones, Russ (1994). "Digital's World-Wide Web Server: A Case Study." *Computer Networks & ISDN Systems*, 27-2 (November): 297–306.

Kelly, Keith J. (1995). "Top Newspapers Link for Online Network." *Advertising Age*, April 24, 14.

Kline, David (1995). "'Friction-Free' Foolishness." *HotWired*, September 11. [URL:http://www.hotwired.com/market/95/37/index1a.html]

Kroll, Ed, and Ellen Hoffman (1993). "FYI on `What Is the Internet?'" Network Working Group Request for Comments: 1462; FYI:20. [URL: gopher://ds1.internic.net/00/fyi/fyi20.txt]

Krumenaker, Larry (1995). "Setting Up Shop on the World Wide Web." *Information World Review*, 102 (April): 13–14.

Lotter, Mark K. (1996). "Internet Domain Survey January 1996." *Network Wizards.* [URL: http://www.nw.com/zone/www/report.html]

Magid, Lawrence (1995). "Populism Thrives Online." *Informationweek,* 514, February 13, 74.

Mahajan, Vijay, Eitan Muller, and Frank M. Bass (1990). "New Product Diffusion Models in Marketing: A Review and Directions for Research." *Journal of Marketing* 54 (January): 1–26.

Markus, M. Lynne (1987). "Toward a 'Critical Mass' Theory of Interactive Media: Universal Access, Interdependence, and Diffusion." *Communication Research* 14, (October): 491–511.

Michalski, Jerry (1995). "People Are the Killer App." *Forbes ASAP,* June 5, 120–122.

Mullich, Joe (1995). "Web Sales Opportunities, Dangers Abound." *Advertising Age's Business Marketing* 80-4 (April): T-4.

Neece, Jerry (1995). "Caught in a Net of Support." *New York Times,* Sunday, June 11.

Ogilvy and Mather Direct (1994). "The Techno-Savvy Consumer." [URL: http://www.img.om.com/img/hp012000.html]

Oliver, Pamela, Gerald Marwell, and Ruy Teixeira (1985). "A Theory of Critical Mass. I. Interdependence, Group Heterogeneity, and the Production of Collective Action." *American Journal of Sociology* 91: 522–556.

Open Market (1996). "Commercial Sites Index." [URL: http://www.directory.net/]

Potter, Edward (1994). WELL Topic "Commercialization of the World Wide Web" in the Internet conference on the WELL. November 16.

Quarterman, John (1995). Matrix Maps Quarterly, vol. 2 (4), 42–43, Matrix Information and Directory Services, Inc. (MIDS), Austin.

Rechtin, Mark (1995). "Selling Autos Online." *Advertising Age,* April 3, 32.

Ricciuti, Mike (1995). "Database Vendors Hawk Wares on Internet." *InfoWorld,* January 9, 10.

Rogers, E. M. (1983). *Diffusion of Innovations.* New York: Free Press.

Rutkowski, Anthony (1996). "Strategic Note —Latest Internet Statistics." General Magic Strategic Note, February 21. [www.genmagic.com/internet/]

Salomon, Allan (1995). "Making the Post Office Interactive." *Advertising Age,* March 20, 20.

Schrage, Michael (1995). "Web Spinners." *Adweek,* February 20, 20.

Schultz, Don E. (1995). "IMC Is a Great Idea, But Does It Have 'Legs'?" *Marketing News,* May 8, 12.

Schultz, Don E., Stanley I. Tannenbaum, and Robert F. Lauterborn (1992). *Integrated Marketing Communcations.* Lincolnwood, IL: NTC Business Books.

Seaman, Barrett (1995). "The Future Is Already Here." *Time,* 145-12 (Spring), 30–33.

Sharples, Hadley (1995). "Vendors Explore On-line Services." *Graphic Arts Monthly* 67 (March): 75–79.

SRI (1995). "Exploring the World Wide Web Population's Other Half." SRI International. [future.sri.com/vals/vals-survey.results.html]

Tynan, Kevin B. (1994). *Multi-Challen Marketing: Maximizing Market Share with an Integrated Marketing Strategy.* Chicago: Probus Publishing Company.

Upshaw, Lynn (1995). "The Keys to Building Cyberbrands." *Advertising Age,* May 29, 18.

Verity, John W., Robert D. Hof, Edward C. Baig, and John Carey (1994). "The Internet: How It Will Change the Way You Do Business?" *Business Week,* November 14, 80–88.

Vonder Haar, Steven (1995). "Not So Fast: Study on PC Market." *Inter@ctive Week,* September 25, 16.

Wallace, David J. (1995). "Shopping Online: A Sticky Business." *Advertising Age,* April 10, 20.

Walsh, Mike (1996). "The 01/05/96 Snapshot." *Internet Info.* [www.webcom.com/~walsh/stats.html]

Wilder, Clinton (1995). "An Electronic Bridge to Customers." *Informationweek,* January 16, 38–39.

Williamson, Debra Aho, and Bradley Johnson (1995). "Web Ushers in Next Generation." *Advertising Age,* May 29, 13.

Wintrob, Suzanne (1995). "Cyberspace Consumers Still Just Looking, Not Buying." *Computing Canada,* April 12, 34.

Ziegler, Bart (1995). "Shares of Homes with PCs Rises to 31% in Poll." *Wall Street Journal,* February 6, sect. B, p. 5, col. 1.

Ziethaml, Valarie A. (1981). "How Consumer Evaluation Processes Differ between Goods and Services." In *Marketing of Services,* ed. James H. Donnelly and William R. George. Chicago: American Marketing Association.

Chapter 3

An Evaluation of the World Wide Web as a Platform for Electronic Commerce

Daniel W. Connolly

ABSTRACT

The architecture and implementation of the World Wide Web are evaluated with respect to Douglas Englebart's requirements for an open hyperdocument system. Englebart's requirements are derived from experience in using computer-supported collaborative work (CSCW) to support large-scale electronic commerce.

INTRODUCTION

The study of *electronic commerce* often focuses on security, cryptography, and electronic currency and payments. But commerce is more than just the exchange of money. It includes research, development, marketing, advertising, negotiation, sales, and support, if not more. It follows that a successful platform for electronic commerce will enhance all these activities. A strategy of integrating cryptographic security techniques into existing disconnected systems is not as likely to succeed as an attempt to automate collaborative work in general.

The World Wide Web is targeted at collaborative work in this way. It borrows many design principles from the research in computer-supported collaborative work (CSCW), which showed how effective hypermedia systems can be for knowledge capture, knowledge exchange, and collaboration in general. In comparison to even the early hypertext research systems, the Web is fairly simple and somewhat limited, yet it is extremely widely deployed and exploited. Is the Web technology ultimately limited? Is it a passing phenomenon, or is it a viable long-term platform for collaborative work—and in particular, for electronic commerce?

The first uses of the Web for electronic commerce were probably motivated by the same factors that motivated its use in other disciplines: the novelty of the system and the investment value of experimenting with information technology. But the value of a network increases as the square of the number of connected resources. Before long, the low cost of entry, low administrative overhead, and the volume of accessible data made using the Web cost-effective regardless of its novelty in such disciplines as research and education.

By now, the demographics of the user base make the business case for advertising and marketing on the Web quite simple. It is no longer clear whether the user base increases in response to reduced prices and increased service (e.g., major on-line service providers have added Internet and Web access, lowered prices, and funded directory services) or the other way around. But it is clear that the user base is increasing and the services are increasing—exponentially.

The Web currently provides a sufficient platform for many business ventures. And each day, the critical mass of users, services, experience, and infrastructure for another venture is achieved. But will it become a platform for widespread electronic commerce? Or are there fundamental requirements that will never be met?

This question looms large, as many businesses invest heavily in this technology and even more consider the possibility of doing so. This report considers the requirements established not by the business community but by the researchers in the field of CSCW who first considered the application of hypermedia systems to electronic commerce. In *Knowledge-Domain Interoperability and an Open Hyperdocument System*, Douglas Englebart condensed the results of much of the research into twelve requirements [ENG90]. Here the Web is evaluated with respect to each of the requirements: Has it been met? If not, can it? What are the obstacles, and what are the most promising developments in each area?

ESSENTIAL ELEMENTS OF AN OPEN HYPERDOCUMENT SYSTEM

Englebart's research was directed at large-scale knowledge work, for example, the interactions between a major manufacturer in the aircraft industry and its contractors, subcontractors, and so on. Research and experimentation led to the following requirements:

1. Mixed object documents

2. Explicitly structured documents

3. View control of object's form, sequence, and content

4. The basic "hyperdocument"

5. Hyperdocument "back-link" capability

6. The hyperdocument "library system"

7. Hyperdocument mail

8. Personal signature encryption

9. Access control

10. Link addresses that are readable and interpretable by humans

11. Every object addressable

12. Hard-copy print options to show address of objects and address specification of links

OVERVIEW OF WEB ARCHITECTURE

In order to evaluate the Web with respect to Englebart's requirements, some background on the architecture is essential. The Web is a hypermedia distributed information system. A distributed information system allows users to access (read, search, navigate) documents from a wide variety of computers connected via a network. A hypertext system is one where the documents have links in and between each other, so that readers are not constrained to a sequential reading order. Finally, a hypermedia system integrates images, sounds, video, and other media with text in documents.

The Web incorporates a wide variety of information sources on the Internet into a coherent information system. The user experience on the Web is as follows:

1. An initial document is presented to the user, consisting of text, graphics, sounds, animation, and so on.

2. The user can choose one of the links in the document and request to
   visit the document on the other end of the link. The link specifies the
   address of another document.

3. The system retrieves the document at that address and presents it to
   the user, and the process repeats.

PROTOCOLS AND ADDRESSING SCHEMES

A Uniform Resource Identifier (URI), is a name or address for an object in
the Web [URI]. For example:

http://www.w3.org/
ftp://ds.internic.net/rfc/rfc822.txt

Each URI begins with *scheme:*, where *scheme* refers to an addressing or naming scheme. For example, URIs beginning with "http:" refer to objects accessible via the HTTP protocol; "ftp:" refers to FTP objects, and so on. New
schemes can be added over time.

There are a number of information retrieval protocols on the Internet:
FTP, gopher, WAIS, and so on. In the Web user experience, they behave similarly: a server makes a collection of documents available. A client contacts a
server and makes a request to access one or more of the documents by giving
a command telling what sort of access (read, write, etc.) and some parameters that indicate the relevant document(s). Finally, the server fulfills the request, for example, by transmitting the relevant document to the client.

The HTTP protocol is designed specifically for the Web [HTTP]. It is ex-
tensible, with support for the widely used features of existing protocols,
such as file transfer and index searching, plus support for some novel features, such as redirection and format negotiation.

DATA FORMATS

There is no one data format for all Web documents—each document may
have its own format. In fact, it may be available in many formats. Each data
format has a name, or an Internet Media Type. Internet Media Types, aka
content types, are part of Multipurpose Internet Mail Extensions [MIME], a

collection of enhancements to Internet mail to accommodate rich media. Most Internet Media Types are just standardized names for existing data formats; for example, text/plain for normal ASCII text; image/gif for images in GIF format, and so on.

The MIME standard also introduces some new data formats. The multipart/mixed is a *compound* data format—it allows several pieces of media to be combined into one, for transmission via e-mail, storage in a file, and so on.

Hypertext Markup Language (HTML) is a data format designed specifically for the Web. It combines the features of a typical structured markup language (paragraphs, titles, lists) with hypertext linking features.

HTML is an application of the Standard Generalized Markup Language (SGML) [SMGL], a technology for specifying structured document types. HTML is one such document type, but there are many others—as many as anyone cares to dream up. TEI, DocBook, and Pinnacles are just a few of the types of SGML documents used in the Web [NCSASGML].

EVALUATING THE WORLD WIDE WEB

This evaluation measures the World Wide Web against each of Englebart's requirements, discussing strengths, weaknesses, and promising developments.[1]

Mixed Object Documents

> . . . to provide for an arbitrary mix of text, diagrams, equations, tables, raster-scan images (single frames, or even live video), spreadsheets, recorded sound, etc.—all bundled within a common "envelope" to be stored, transmitted, read (played), and printed as a coherent entity called a "document."

The first Web documents contained only text, but support for icons and images was added to NCSA Mosaic in 1993. Since then, Web pages with mixed text and graphics have been the rule, and sound and video are not uncommon. As a recent development, tables are widely deployed. Support for equations is still essentially in development, and diagrams are generally limited to rasterized snapshots.

---

[1] Portions of this article were excerpted, with permission, from *Knowledge-Domain Interoperability and an Open Hyperdocument System* by Douglas C. Englebart. Proceedings of the Conference on Computer-Supported Cooperative Work (CSCW '90), Copyright © 1990 Association for Computing Machinery, Inc.

Exchange of spreadsheets and other rich data sets associated with proprietary software packages is supported to some extent, but its use is generally limited to small communities of interest that agree to use the packages.

This demonstrates that, at least to some extent, the requirement for mixed object documents is met. But it is not met completely: the tools for composing mixed object documents are primitive, and many features of a comprehensive compound document architecture are lacking.

Authoring Tools

The intent of the original design of the Web was that documents would be composed in direct-manipulation fashion from a rich set of media objects. The initial prototype was done on the NeXTStep platform, which allows drag-and-drop editing of rich text documents, including raster images, encapsulated postscript images, sounds, and diagrams. The NeXTStep platform includes an architecture and a set of development tools for adding new object types to the mix available on the desktop.

Research systems such as Hyper-G provide many of these features, and recently products such as NaviPress and FrontPage have begun to provide these features to the Web user base at large.

Compound Document Architecture

The two technologies used to create compound documents on the Web are URIs and MIME. Objects can be linked together by using their addresses. For example, the HTML A, IMG, FORM, and LINK elements specify URIs of linked objects. Links are typed to indicate various relationships between objects such as parent/child, precedes/succeeds, supports/refutes, and so on. The MIME multipart facility allows several pieces of content to be combined into one entity. Support for typed links and multipart data is deployed only to a limited extent.

The combination of URIs and MIME supports the entire existing Web information space. Still, compared with compound document architectures such as OpenDoc, OLE, Fresco, LINCKS [LINCKS], or HyTime, many facilities are lacking.

Facilities for diagrams, equations, screen real estate arbitration, event management, versioning, transactions, link indirection, and aggregation have been developed for various Web applications, but there are no standard facilities. Standards for such facilities might result in a critical mass of shared technology that would make feasible classes of applications that were previously too costly.

Explicitly Structured Documents

> . . . where the objects comprising a document are arranged in an explicit hierarchical structure, and compound-object substructures may be explicitly addressed for access or manipulation of the structural relationships.

The HTML used to represent most Web documents is a structured document format. Elements of HTML documents are explicitly tagged, and structure can be inferred from the tags. Not all substructures may be explicitly addressed—only anchor elements and embedded objects. Fragment identifiers in URIs allow compound-object substructures to be explicitly addressed.

Other hierarchical structures are possible but not yet supported. One facility that is notably lacking from Web implementations is transclusion—the ability to include one text object inside another by reference, for example, including an excerpt of one document inside another or building a document out of section and subsection objects.

Even if transclusion were supported, compound text documents would probably be prohibitively expensive: the overhead for a transaction in the current version of the HTTP protocol is very high; hence the protocol is inefficient for retrieving a number of small objects in succession. This inefficiency is being addressed in efforts to revise the protocol.

Because HTML is essential to interoperability, it is restricted to document structures that are universally applicable. In many situations, a custom document type would support more expressive collaboration. Widespread support for custom SGML document types would enable such collaboration.

SGML is not the only structured document technology available. The multipart media types support explicit hierarchical structure, and support for them is being deployed.

The Web architecture clearly supports the requirement for structured documents. But the deployed software provides limited support. The Web is predominantly used in a "publish and browse" fashion; data transmitted across the Web are largely throwaway data that look good but have little structure. In order to use the Web as a rich collaborative platform, much more support for structured documents will be needed.

View Control of Object's Form, Sequence, and Content

> . . . where a structured, mixed-object document may be displayed in a window according to a flexible choice of viewing options—especially by selective level clipping (outline for viewing), but also by filtering on

content, by truncation or some algorithmic view that provides a more useful view of structure and/or object content (including new sequences or groupings of objects that actually reside in other documents). Editing on structure or object content from such special views would be allowed whenever appropriate.

View control can be achieved on the Web by custom processing by the information provider. A number of views can be provided, and consumers can express their choice via links or HTML forms. For example, gateways to database query systems and fulltext search systems are commonplace. Another technique is to provide multiple views of an SGML document repository.

Another approach to view control is client-side processing. After the document is transmitted, the reader's software could filter, sort, or truncate the data. About the only such control in wide deployment is the ability to turn off embedded images. Outline views with folding have been proposed [FOLD], but the cost of transmitting text that isn't displayed has presented a barrier.

Stylesheets are a mechanism for presenting the same data in different forms, using fonts, colors, and space to give visual structure. Support for stylesheets is an important ongoing development. In some systems [LINCKS], stylesheets are much more than that: they control form, sequence, and content, as Engelbart described. For example, in LINCKS, the same document can be presented and edited in abstract form, outline form, or full form depending on which stylesheet (generic presentation descriptor, in their jargon) is in effect.

At the extreme end of the spectrum, stylesheets give way to arbitrary programs that display data and interact with the reader. In a distributed system, running arbitrary programs can have dangerous consequences. But advances such as Safe-Tcl and Java make this technique of "active objects" feasible.

It is clear that the Web architecture supports custom view control. It remains to be seen whether some view control mechanisms are sufficiently valuable to be standardized.

The Basic "Hyperdocument"

. . . where embedded objects called "links" can point to any arbitrary object within the document, or within another document in a specified domain of documents—and the link can be actuated by a user or an automatic process to "go see what is at the other end," or "bring the other-end object to this location," or "execute the process identified at the other end." (These executable processes may control peripheral devices such as CD-ROM, and videodisk players.)

This requirement is clearly met. The hyperdocument as described previously is the epitome of the Web page. The only exception is that Englebart refers to links as "special objects," whereas in the Web links are not addressable "first-class" objects—not in implementations, and not in the architecture.

Hyperdocument "Back-Link" Capability

> . . . when reading a hyperdocument on-line, a worker can utilize information about links from other objects within this or other hyperdocuments that point to this hyperdocument—or to designated objects or passages of interest in this hyperdocument.

The design of the Web trades link consistency guarantees for global scalability. Links are one way, and the reverse link is not guaranteed to exist. Aside from the intractability of maintaining global link consistency, another barrier to a distributed back-link service is privacy. Some links are sensitive, and their owners do not want them easily discovered.

These barriers do not, however, prevent Web users from utilizing back-link information. Some Web server tools (FrontPage) maintain back-link information for the local site. And the HTTP protocol includes a mechanism— the Referer: field—that allows information providers to gather back-link information for their site.

Finally, there are search services that traverse the Web building full-text search indexes. Some (Altavista) take advantage of the links they encounter to offer back-link services.

The Hyperdocument "Library System"

> . . . where hyperdocuments can be submitted to a library-like service that catalogs them and guarantees access when referenced by its catalog number, or "jumped to" with an appropriate link. Links within newly submitted hyperdocuments can cite any passages within any of the prior documents, and the back-link service lets the on-line reader of a document detect and "go examine" any passage of a subsequent document that has a link citing that passage.

There are no guarantees of access on the Web today. A few commercial web service providers guarantee server availability on a 24×7 basis, but this does not guarantee access to the entire global user base—any network interruption between the reader and the provider can prevent access.

In a distributed system, absolute guarantees are impossible. But reliability can be made arbitrarily good by investing in redundancy. A number of strategies for caching and replication (including Harvest) are being explored, standardized, and deployed.

Catalog numbering systems have not matured either; this is known as "the URN problem." A number of promising proposals have been made [PATH], [STANF], but none is widely deployed.

Digital libraries are an active field of research. ARPA is funding research, and the Online Computer Library Center (OCLC) is conducting experiments.

Hyperdocument Mail

. . . where an integrated, general-purpose mail service enables a hyperdocument of any size to be mailed. Any embedded links are also faithfully transmitted—and any recipient can then follow those links to their designated targets in other mail items, in common-access files, or in "library" items.

Internet mail is possibly the world's most widely deployed information system. MIME standardizes facilities for attachments and compound documents, among other things. Though nearly every new mail system supports MIME, the installed base of pre-MIME mail systems is still significant—a majority by many estimates. User interfaces that integrate e-mail (and USENET news) into the Web user experience are anticipated, but have not been deployed.

Personal Signature Encryption

. . . where a user can affix his or her personal signature to a document, or a specified segment within the document, using the private signature key. Users can verify that the signature is authentic and that no bit of the signed document or document segment has been altered since it was signed.

There are a number of digital signature standards, but none has been globally adopted and deployed on the Web. One barrier is patent licensing. A critical feature of Web technology that led to its rapid deployment was its royalty-free copyright status. Patents on public-key cryptography prevent digital signature technology from being deployed without license negotiations. Another barrier is export control legislation. Implementations of cryptographic techniques such as encryption are considered munitions by many governments, and there are strict controls on the export of such technologies. The largest barrier is social and educational. Digital signature techniques will have to be tested in production use, and users will have to be educated about the related issues before commerce can depend on this technology.

Access Control

... Hyperdocuments in personal, group, and library files can have access restrictions down to the object level.

The distributed nature of the Web allows information providers to implement any access control policy they choose, down to the object level.

Minimal support for user name/password authentication is widely deployed. This allows information providers to implement access control based on users and groups of users, but this basic facility is not robust in the face of concerted attack.

A number of mechanisms for strong authentication and confidentiality, as well as billing and payment, are being standardized. A complete discussion of these mechanisms is beyond the scope of this document.

Link Addresses That Are Readable and Interpretable by Humans

... one of the "viewing options" for displaying/printing a link object should provide a human-readable description of the "address path" leading to the cited object; AND, that the human must be able to read the path description, interpret it, and follow it (find the destination "by hand" so to speak).

Document addresses in the Web are designed so that they can be transcribed—written on envelopes, recited over the phone, and so on. Each URI scheme has an associated public specification of how to interpret and follow its path description. By and large, URIs are sensible to those familiar with the conventions—http://www.ford.com is the address of Ford Motor Company, for example. But portions of URIs are allowed to be opaque by design—they may be pointers into an index, checksums, dates, and so on.

Every Object Addressable

... in principal, every object that someone might validly want/need to cite should have an unambiguous address (capable of being portrayed

Table 3.1 Coverage of Requirements

Requirement	Architecture Support	Standard Facilities	Ubiquitous Facilities	Local/Proprietary Facilities
1. Mixed object documents	YES: format negotiation, typed links	PART: URI, HTML, IMG, INSERT, MIME link types*	PART: GIF in HTML	YES: JPEG in HTML, Java/Safe-Tcl in HTML, OLE, OpenDoc, Fresco
2. Explicitly structured documents	YES: fragment identifiers	YES: HTML, SGML, MIME	PART: HTML	YES: Panorama, OLE, LINCKS
3. View control of object's form, sequence, and content	PASS	PART: HTTP, CGI	NO	YES: DynaWeb, Java/Safe-Tcl, style-sheets
4. The basic "hyperdocument"	YES	YES: URI, HTML	YES: URI, HTML	
5. Hyperdocument "back-link" capability	PASS	PART: referer	NO	YES: local link map, back-link service
6. The hyperdocument "library system"	PASS	NO	NO	NO

7. Hyperdocument mail	PASS	YES: MIME	YES: MIME	
8. Personal signature encryption	PASS	NO	NO	YES: S-HTTP, PEM, S/MIME, PGP, PKCS-7
9. Access control	YES	PART: basic auth	ART: basic auth	YES: MD5, SSL, S-HTTP, PGP, smart cards, etc.
10. Link addresses that are readable and interpretable by humans	PART: URI	PART: URI	PART: URI	
11. Every object addressable	Objects: YES substructures: PASS	PART: URI	PART: URI	
12. Hard-copy print options to show address of objects and address specification of links	PASS	NO	NO	YES: HTML2LaTeX

in a manner as to be human readable and interpretable). (E.g., not acceptable to be unable to link to an object within a "frame" or "card.")

Every object on the Web is addressable, but not every substructure within objects that someone might need to cite has a standard addressing mechanism, for example, individual pages in a postscript document, lines in a text file, or pixels in an image. These structures are, in principle, addressable. Only a standard syntax for URI fragment identifiers to address them is lacking.

In HTML documents, elements can be named and addressed, but there is no mechanism to address unnamed elements. For parties that do not have write access to a document, this presents a problem. One solution would be to allow elements to be addressed by their structural position. There are a number of standard technologies for addressing elements of SGML documents (and hence HTML documents): TEI pointers, HyTime location ladders, and DSSSL queries. Any of these could be incorporated into Web software. Another possibility is to address strings within a document by pattern matching. One annotation system [BRIO] uses patricia trees for stable pointers into documents.

Hard-Copy Print Options to Show Address of Objects and Address Specification of Links

> . . . so that, besides online workers being able to follow a link-citation path (manually, or via an automatic link jump), people working with associated hard copy can read and interpret the link-citation, and follow the indicated path to the cited object in the designated hard-copy document. Also, suppose that a hard-copy worker wants to have a link to a given object established in the online file. By visual inspection of the hard copy, he should be able to determine a valid address path to that object and for instance hand-write an appropriate link specification for later online entry, or dictate it over a phone to a colleague.

Most of the installed base of Web client software allows users to view link address; but ironically, that option is not available for printing in many cases. It would be a straightforward enhancement, well within the bounds of the existing architecture.

WEB ARCHITECTURE AND FACILITIES

In Table 3.1, each each horizontal row represents one of Englebart's requirements. The vertical columns are as follows:

Architecture support: Is the requirement explicitly addressed in the Web architecture? Does the architecture passively allow the requirement to be met by applications? Or does the architecture conflict with the requirement?

Standard facilities: Are there standardized facilities that meet the requirement? Partially meet the requirement?

Ubiquitous facilities: Some facilities are standardized, but not required of all systems, or not supported by all installations. What facilities are assumed to be supported by all participants in the Web?

Local/proprietary facilities: Has the requirement been met within the architecture by local applications or with the use of proprietary facilities?

Each cell contains an evaluation of whether the requirement is met (YES, NO, PASSive, or PARTial), followed by a list of relevant facilities. Missing facilities are marked with an asterisk.

CONCLUSIONS

Support for Englebart's requirements is far from ubiquitous. But the architecture in no way prevents these requirements from being realized, and the quantity of resources integrated into the system provides ample motivation for research and development. In each area where facilities to meet the requirement are not ubiquitous, a demonstration of sufficient facilities has taken place. This gives confidence that the requirements will eventually be met and become infrastructure. If in fact Englebart's requirements are an effective way to measure the viability of a platform for electronic commerce, the Web is very likely to be a viable platform for some time to come.

REFERENCES

[BRIO] M. Röscheisen, C. Mogensen, and T. Winograd. "Beyond Browsing: Shared Comments, SOAPs, Trails and On-line Communities." *Proceedings of the Third International World-Wide Web Conference, Darmstadt, Germany.*

[ENG90] Douglas C. Englebart. *Knowledge-Domain Interoperability and an Open Hyperdocument System.* Proceedings of the Conference on Computer-Supported Cooperative Work (CSCW '90), copyright © 1990 Association for Computing Machinery, Inc., pp. 143–56. (AUGMENT, 132082.)

[FOLD] Mark Torrance. *Proposal—Foldable Anchor Inclusion.* (torrance@ai.mit.edu) message to www-talk@w3.org, Tue, 26 Jul 94 13:40:42 EDT.

[HTML] T. Berners-Lee and D. Connolly. *HyperText Markup Language Specification*—2.0. IETF RFC 1866, November 1995.

[HTTP] T. Berners-Lee, R. T. Fielding, and H. Frystyk Nielsen. *Hypertext Transfer Protocol—HTTP/1.0.* Work in progress, MIT, UC Irvine, CERN, March 1995.

[LINCKS] P. Lambrix, M. Sjölin, and L. Pagdham. "LINCKS—A Platform for Cooperative Information Systems." Unpublished manuscript, Department of Computer and Information Science, LiTH, Sweden, 1993.

[MIME] N. Borenstein and N. Freed. *MIME (Multipurpose Internet Mail Extensions) Part One: Mechanisms for Specifying and Describing the Format of Internet Message Bodies.* September 1993.

[NCSASGML] Lucy Ventresca, Welcome to SGML on the Web. NCSA and SoftQuad. Work in progress.

[PATH] D. LaLiberte and M. Shapiro. "The Path URN Specification." Internet draft 07/26/1995.

[STANF] Terry Winograd. "Stable Network File URLs as a Mechanism for Uniform Naming." Early draft version 12/2/93.

[SGML] International Standards Organization 8879. "Information Processing—Text and Office Systems—Standard Generalized Markup Language (SGML)." 1986.

[URI] T. Berners-Lee. rfc1630.txt "Universal Resource Identifiers in WWW: A Unifying Syntax for the Expression of Names and Addresses of Objects on the Network as Used in the World-Wide Web." (Format: TXT=57601 bytes), June 1994.

This document is available on the World Wide Web at: http://www.w3.org/pub/WWW/Collaboration/ECommerceEval

PART 2

General Business and Policy

Part Two deals with political and legal issues that need to be resolved before electronic commerce can become a reality. The Internet and electronic commerce have become so important in our society that it is natural to expect them to attract governmental attention. In Chapter 4 James B. Rapp lists the issues that are currently at the center of attention in Washington. They include intellectual property rights, privacy, financial crimes, specifically tax evasion, regulations of electronic banking, consumer protection including pornography, and federal versus state legal jurisdictional questions. As Rapp points out, the current administration is very much involved in the development of the Internet and electronic commerce. Rapp's article outlines these issues and indicates the various industry groups that are involved in influencing the outcomes.

In Chapter 5 Dorothy E. Denning describes the technical, legal, and political issues in key escrow management. While security and privacy protection for communications are critical for the growth of electronic commerce, in some circumstances access to information by governmental agencies is needed to protect society from illegal activities. Creating an acceptable legal process to access communications and developing the associated technically sound key escrow policy are challenges that need to be resolved. Denning's paper outlines the past approaches and presents her views for the establishment of a global key management system.

In Chapter 6 A. Michael Froomkin discusses the public key concept as one of the foundations for secure electronic commerce. It is widely recognized that there must be a trusted third party to maintain the public keys or else the security system can be compromised. Froomkin's article delves into the legal and institutional issues of third-party certification, how it can be done, and the legal obligations of the parties involved. Since most of the literature on security is concerned with the possibility of breaking the encryption algorithm, consideration of third-party certification and the associated problems raises an entire collection of new challenges.

Chapter 4

Electronic Commerce: A Washington Perspective

James B. Rapp

ABSTRACT

Electronic commerce issues and conduits such as the Internet have arrived in Washington not in an application sense but in a policy sense. A U.S. Treasury financial crime unit head expresses concern about money laundering and tax evasion via the Internet; a group of 160 telephone service resellers petition the Federal Communications Commission (FCC) to place restrictions on Internet telephony; and certain U.S. federal agencies desire the ability to access encrypted private electronic transmissions.

The current crop of futurists tell us that old-order industrial-society governments will react to the shift toward a new-order information/electronic commerce society, but they have not really told us how they will react or what is happening at this time. This chapter will take the next step and offer a "snapshot" of the current Washington environment as it relates to issues impacting electronic commerce.

For two reasons, much of this chapter will focus upon Internet-related issues: (1) At present, the Internet is one of the primary communication tools that will be used in the conduct of electronic commerce; and (2) most of the policy debate in Washington has centered around the Internet, probably as a result of the significant media attention it has received. However, the issues raised could apply to almost all electronic commerce delivery vehicles and application systems.

Finally, the purpose of this chapter is to make electronic commerce interests aware that public policy issues need to be on their "radar screens" when making business decisions, as they will impact pricing, service and product offerings, and marketing approaches. The chapter also explores what to expect in the future, and why and how to take a proactive approach.

INTRODUCTION

Electronic commerce issues and conduits such as the Internet are now on the "radar screens" of Washington's federal policy and law enforcement officials. "The players," which in Washington parlance means relevant participants, include the executive branch, Congress, and "other players," such as the media.

In late 1993 the Clinton administration launched the National Information Infrastructure (NII) initiative in order to ensure that a nation of information "haves" and "have-nots" would not emerge, and that seamlessness of technologies take place. The NII initiative is based upon the premise that while the private sector will construct the "information superhighway," government must play a major role. The National Telecommunications Information Administration (NTIA) and the Information Infrastructure Task Force (IITF) have been leading advisory bodies and implementers of the NII initiative; however, in many instances this role has been overtaken by other departments and agencies.

The Congress, in both a technical implementation and a policy sense, has been much slower to adapt to electronic information media than the executive branch. However, since late 1995 this has changed dramatically. Congressional electronic mail and World Wide Web sites have been established, hearings are taking place on issues impacting electronic commerce, and the establishment of an Internet Task Force and a Congressional Technology Working Group has occurred.

A number of issues relevant to electronic commerce have been reviewed within the Clinton administration and are now being looked at by Congress. Important issues include copyright/intellectual property, privacy, financial crime, tax, electronic banking/currency, content, international, universal service, labor, consumer protection, cryptography, and federal versus state legal/regulatory authority.

Politics plays a role in Washington's involvement in the advent of the information age and electronic commerce. The Clinton administration has been a big proponent of public-private "dual-use" Internet/electronic commerce programs. However, the Republican-controlled Congress has attempted to scale back monies for these efforts, arguing that winners and losers should not be selected by government and that the private sector will quite ably take the United States into the emerging information age. Many in the Republican congressional majority look upon "dual-use" programs as executive branch patronage.

Factors driving Washington's interest in cyberspace and electronic commerce include media attention and trendiness. The media have focused on the Internet, which along with electronic commerce is a trendy topic today. Politicians look for "political mileage," and federal bureaucrats like to implement programs related to hot-button issues.

Another factor driving governmental interest in cyberspace and electronic commerce is fear. The technology opens up the possibility of a diffusion of power from centralized bureaucracies to many communities spread throughout the globe. Old-order industrial-society Washington interests will go to great lengths to maintain power during the transition to the new-order information age. Monetary authorities are fearful that electronic currency transactions may enable massive tax avoidance and cause a lack of monetary stability and control.

What should electronic commerce interests do? (1) Keep abreast of government and law enforcement initiatives, and adjust electronic commerce business models accordingly. (2) Contact elected officials in a proper manner in order to ensure that the private sector plays a major role in the development of the electronic commerce regulatory environment and does not wholly leave it up to government. (3) Look for new business opportunities that government regulations and laws will spawn. (4) Be a good Netizen and educate electronic commerce "newbies," particularly the media.

Education of business, government, and the public at large over the next three years is crucial to the development of electronic commerce. Working groups consisting of business, government, and academic interests must be formed to explore electronic commerce issues in respect to how they will impact the international business sector, international economies, and society in general.

I. THE PLAYERS

The Executive Branch

The Clinton administration has taken a very active role in attempting to foster Cyberspace development.[1] In September 1993, Vice President Albert Gore launched the NII initiative, intended to enable all Americans to better communicate through the utilization of a multitude of electronic delivery systems (i.e., Internet, cable, wireless, telephone). The administration looks on

---

[1] See Addendum I: Other Players.

the NII as crucial to the future economic competitiveness and well-being of the United States. Although the administration states that the private sector will be the major architects of the NII, it believes that government must play a major role in order to ensure that leveraged developmental resources are available and that all citizens have access.

In keeping with this agenda, the Clinton administration has proposed nine fundamental principles to guide the initiative: (1) promoting private sector investment; (2) extending the "universal service" concept to ensure that information resources are available to all at affordable prices; (3) acting as a catalyst to promote technological innovation and new applications; (4) promoting seamless, interactive, user-driven operation of the NII; (5) ensuring information security and network reliability; (6) improving management of the radio frequency spectrum; (7) protecting intellectual property rights; (8) coordinating with other levels of government and with other nations; and (9) providing access to government information and improving government procurement [NII93].

The NTIA, a part of the U.S. Department of Commerce, initially took a lead role in carrying out NII initiatives as outlined in the 1993 Agenda for Action. However, as is typical in government, numerous other agencies and departments are now involved in cyberspace and electronic commerce developmental issues; thus, the NTIA is now one of many players.

The White House formed the IITF, a policy advisory panel composed of senior federal officials assisted by the public/private sector, Advisory Council NII, to articulate and implement the administration's vision for the NII [IITF95]. In reality, both the NTIA and the IITF have what could be characterized as a "hot and cold" history, in that they have accomplished significant research and policy recommendations; however, implementation and continuity have been less apparent.

The Federal Secure Infrastructure Program (FSIP) has been established and is supported by the General Services Administration (GSA), the National Security Agency (NSA), the U.S. Postal Service, the Department of Defense, and the Department of the Treasury. One of the first initiatives of the FSIP, the Paperless Federal Transaction for the Public, will seek to create an infrastructure that will enable any government agency to securely interface and accomplish transactions with outside businesses and the general public. The effort will make heavy use of the Internet through the use of secure World Wide Web servers, browsers, and client encryption tokens. An open platform will be created to ensure ubiquity for all agencies, as well as outside users.

Envisioned uses include access to IRS records and tax information, the ability to digitally sign and receive payment for federal contracts, the provision of access to Veteran's and Social Security benefits, and the secure transmission and receipt of electronic mail [MM96].

Congress

Until late 1995, Congress was considerably behind the executive branch in addressing Internet-related policy issues and making use of Internet technology. This was likely a function of the 1994 turnover in power, the allocation of resources elsewhere, and reluctance of older members and staff to enter the information age.

Further, some members of Congress with a significant private sector bent did not believe the government should be involved in information infrastructure development and issues to the extent that the Clinton administration has deemed necessary [PUHL95].

Much of this has changed since late 1995. A majority of House and Senate members have electronic mail capability, and many have established World Wide Web home pages on the Internet. Cyber-savvy members, such as Representative Vernon Ehlers (MI), now envision a state-of-the-art Intranet system that will enable members and staff to communicate and work more efficiently.

Hearings have been held on a variety of issues, including content, copyright/intellectual property protection for digital products, and electronic currencies. Bipartisan working groups such as the Congressional Internet Caucus and the Congressional Information Technology Working Group have been established as educational forums in the hope of minimizing government obstacles to information technology development.

Special Interest Groups

The Media

Often looked upon as the fourth branch of government, the media must be included in any discussion of governmental matters. Over the past year, sensationalist stories about Internet content and other "hot-button" issues have received much international media attention. For example, a story on the CBS television program *48 Hours* detailed how pipe bombs constructed by two teenagers accidentally detonated, resulting in the death of one of the teens. The CBS correspondent readily encouraged the surviving child to mention that bomb-making information is available on the Internet [CBS95].

For better or worse, the media seem to have Internet mania these days, and as long as it continues, it will drive political interests in Washington. This could potentially impact federal policies and certain developmental aspects of a primary electronic commerce conduit—the Internet.

Other Special Interest Groups

Through the mobilization of votes, campaign contributions, and media influence, other special interests will play a major role in shaping policies that impact electronic commerce:

Civil liberty. Civil liberty groups keep abreast of topics such as content, privacy, government encryption policy, international government Internet actions, and any issues that affect the civil liberties of cyberspace participants. Active civil liberty groups with a Washington presence include the Center for Democracy and Technology (CDT), the Electronic Frontier Foundation (EFF), now headquartered on the West Coast, the American Civil Liberties Union (ACLU), and the Electronic Privacy Information Center (EPIC).

Industry groups. Industry groups represent member interests through congressional legislation, lobbying, and educational programs. Examples include the Software Publishers Association (SPA), which is active in cryptography and intellectual property issues; the Business Software Alliance (BSA), which has an agenda similar to that of the SPA; the Electronic Messaging Association (EMA); the Interactive Services Association (ISA), a group with significant support from major on-line service providers, such as America Online™, and the Information Technology Association of America (ITAA).

Individual companies. Large companies will often directly seek to influence matters in Washington by working through their own representatives or by hiring high-powered public relations and/or law firms.

Public policy organizations. A number of public policy organizations are addressing Internet and electronic commerce issues. Several examples are the Progress and Freedom Foundation (PFF), the Manhattan Institute for Public Policy, and the Discovery Institute.

II. THE ISSUES

Copyright/Intellectual Property

A big issue related to the advent of electronic commerce is compensation for producers of written content, software, and other digitally transmitted items of value. Washington is attempting to address this issue. A Commerce Department and U.S. Patent and Trademark Office White Paper recommends amending the copyright law to cover the digitally networked environment. The paper addresses the fair use issue, whereby copywritten material may be used in some instances by libraries, academic institutions, and other parties for educational purposes. However, firm recommendations have not been made, and the issue is under further review [IP95].

Congressional legislation has been introduced (S. 1284), intended to "amend title 17 to adapt the copyright law to the digital networked environment of the National Information Infrastructure" [SEN95]. While there is little controversy over formally extending traditional copyright protection to electronic transmissions, the discussion of copyright liability has become heated. Specifically, content producers wish liability to be placed not only on individual violators but also on on-line and Internet service providers. The service providers believe it is impossible to be responsible for copyright violations; however, at a minimum, content producers want providers to be held liable when the infringement is brought to their attention and no action is taken [COPY96].

Content producers and service providers have reached tentative agreement on four main points: (1) the copyright owner has the major responsibility for discovering copyright violations; (2) some sort of notice and legal framework should be put in place; (3) on-line service providers should be held liable if found to be direct infringers; and (4) limited liability should be in place for carriers acting as simple conduits [HATC96].

Increasingly, the model for digital product distribution will be through alternative channels such as internetworked systems instead of traditional retail outlets. For example, through resellers, Microsoft Corporation has commenced a pilot program to distribute twenty of its top-selling computer software programs over the Internet [DIST95]. This distribution method has the potential to further exacerbate the already burdensome problem of software piracy.

Industry groups such as the SPA and BSA attempt to bring legal action against software thieves, and are reviewing various legislative and legal remedies in this area [COPS96].

Other private sector models are being reviewed. For example, "virtual magistrates" might be formed to resolve on-line copyright/intellectual property disputes. Teams of private arbitrators would be established in the expectation of dealing with disputes in a more timely network-oriented fashion than is possible through traditional legal channels [PMNY96].

Privacy

Privacy is an extremely important issue that electronic commerce interests must be sensitive to. According to a Times Mirror Survey, interconnected databases holding information and the potential loss of privacy worried 20 percent of respondents "a lot" and 30 percent "some" [SURV95]. Medical and credit histories, buying habits, and other sensitive consumer information is easily obtained.

In addition, questions are being raised about employee on-line use. New software products enable companies to monitor the amount of employee time spent on the Internet and the sites visited, and may even block certain sites. Companies claim this practice is reasonable since their equipment is being used and the employee is on their time. However, questions have been raised as to the degree of allowable monitoring, and disclosure practices, before individual privacy rights are violated [MONI96].

To this end, the Department of Commerce NTIA asserts that there is a lack of uniformity among existing privacy laws and regulations for telephone and video services and warns that other services such as "those available over the Internet are almost entirely unprotected." The NTIA believes it will become increasingly difficult to apply existing privacy laws and regulations to communications service providers as services and sectors converge and new technologies evolve.

To address this perceived problem, the NTIA proposes a framework geared toward the general public and encompassing two fundamental elements, notification and consent. Within this framework, telecommunications and information service providers would notify individuals about their information practices, abide by those practices, and keep customers informed of subsequent changes to such practices. Service providers would be free to use information collected for stated purposes once they obtained consent from the relevant customer. Affirmative consent would be required with respect to sensitive personal information. Tacit customer consent would be sufficient to authorize the use of all other information.

It is claimed that this approach, if embraced by industry, would allow service providers and their customers to establish the specific level of privacy protection offered in a marketplace transaction, free from excessive government regulation, so long as the minimum requirements of notice and consent are satisfied. The NTIA is of the opinion that because considerable flexibility is allowed in giving notice and securing consent, implementation should not be overly burdensome. In fact, it is felt that electronic commerce purveyors will actually benefit through greater use if consumers perceive that their privacy rights would be respected when using the NII.

The NTIA urges the private sector to adopt privacy protection, or the government may see fit to take action [PRIV96].

The U.S. Federal Trade Commission (FTC) is also taking an active role in respecting the preservation of consumer privacy by business interests. Issues being explored include:

The Use of Consumer Information

How is personal information currently used by on-line businesses? What do consumers know about the use of consumer information in on-line marketing and commercial transactions? What kinds of disclosure and notice might be provided to consumers? What choices can or should consumers have in exercising control over uses of personal information? How can the security and accuracy of personal information used on-line be assured? Are voluntary standards useful in this area?

Electronic Regimes for Protecting Consumer Privacy On-line

Can technological standards such as the Platform for Internet Content Selection (PICS) be used as models to facilitate automatic disclosure of privacy policies and the availability of consumer choice regarding the use of personal information?

Consumer and Business Education in On-line Privacy Issues

What are the various means of educating consumers and industry about the use of personal information in on-line transactions? What kinds of heightened protections might be afforded medical and financial information? What role, if any, should such information play in on-line transactions?

The Impact of the European Commission's Council Directive on the Protection of Personal Data

What does the directive require of government and industry with respect to the free flow of personal information? Can industry satisfy the directive's "adequacy" requirement through the use of interactive privacy regimes?

The Collection and Use of Information about Children

What information is currently collected about children, and how is it being used? Is it appropriate to place limits on the on-line collection and/or use of information from and about children? What limits could be recommended? Who may consent and exercise choice in this context [FTC96]?

Financial Crime, Tax, and Electronic Banking

The ability to conduct anonymous or nondecipherable (encrypted) electronic monetary transactions has monetary, tax, and central bank authorities taking a hard look at electronic payment mechanisms. The Financial Crimes Enforcement Network (FinCEN) is exploring how electronic monetary payments could play a role in money-laundering and tax-evasion schemes. The physical bulk of ordinary currency is often a hindrance for money launderers and others. In contrast, electronic currency has no bulk, and a nearly infinite amount can be stored on silicon chips, that might be embedded in smart cards.

Tax evasion is another concern. At present, individuals and businesses that attempt to illegally evade taxes through cash payments are faced with the need to deposit this currency in an account. Electronic currency holds the potential to be electronically sent anywhere in the world through the global electronic networks, which could make certain forms of financial crime significantly easier. With the development of electronic currency, it is believed that some new methods to declare and search for illegal currency being shipped may need to be developed.

The United States has laws that prohibit financial transactions with specifically designated nations, such as Iran. Electronic currency makes it far more difficult to police these types of transactions effectively [FINC95].

In addition to federal concern about nonreported financial transactions and revenue loss, states are beginning to explore how they will be able to collect retail sales taxes on electronic commerce transactions.

Questions currently being explored include the following:

1. What actions can be taken to promote cooperative development of suitable tax concepts by both states and industry?

2. What premises or principles need to be adopted to guide the development of consumption-based transactional taxation of on-line services?

3. Should any tax be separately codified or made an integral part of the existing sales and use tax?

4. Is there a potential for unreasonable tax avoidance that counsels the need for a compensatory use tax?

5. To what extent can local taxes be accommodated?

6. Are on-line services best conceptualized as the sale of a service, the sale of an intangible, or neither?

7. How should the risk of multiple taxation be managed?

If a fair and rational system of state transactional taxation is to be achieved, development of reasonable "Nexus"[2] standards is paramount.

Determining the geographic situs of the underlying sale that is the subject of the tax is another important issue in appropriately apportioning transactional taxation of inherently interstate activity [MTC95]. A report released by the Center for Community Economic Research (CCER) asserts that at some point on-line commerce will boom and could pose a devastating loss in state and local government revenue due to uncollected sales taxes. The report recommends reducing or eliminating sales taxes and centralizing revenue collection at the state and national level [NN95].

U.S. Federal Reserve authorities are tracking electronic payment mechanisms, as well as the possible advent of electronic nonbank financial institutions. Paul Bauer, an economic adviser with the Federal Reserve Bank of Cleveland, states:

> In the United States roughly 85% of the "value" exchanged in trade already flows electronically over Fedwire, Chips, and Automated Clearing House (ACH). Most electronic money schemes target cash or the Internet. Cash probably accounts for about 85% of the transactions in the U.S., but less than 1/2% of the "value."
>
> A more common view is that "consumer" electronic payments pose no new challenges, just the same concerns in a different guise. All payment instruments must be concerned with the possibility of fraud, counterfeiting, settlement risk, consumer protection, etc. The means to address these risks may be different, but the underlying sources are the same as in the physical world.
>
> After resolving whether electronic money is secure or not, the Federal Reserve, along with the Treasury and state governments are probably most concerned about Seigniorage, Reg E, deposit insurance, Reserve Requirements, and escheatment laws. [PB96].

The federal government currently earns substantial revenue from what is sometimes referred to as "Seigniorage" on its currency issue. In effect, holders of the roughly $400 billion of U.S. currency are lending interest-free to the government. In 1994, for example, the Federal Reserve turned over $20 billion of its earnings to the Treasury, most of which was derived from

---

[2] See Addendum II: Nexus.

Seigniorage on Federal Reserve notes. Should some U.S. currency get replaced by stored-value products (which are private monies), this source of government revenue would decline.

One possible solution under review is some manner of government-issued electronic currency. It is felt that this would probably stem Seigniorage losses, provide a riskless electronic payment product to consumers, and prevent private sector monopolization.

The question of whether and how to apply the Electronic Fund Transfer Act (EFTA) and the Federal Reserve's Regulation E to these products has received considerable attention from industry participants, at the Federal Reserve, and in Congress. Among other things, Regulation E limits consumers' liability for unauthorized electronic withdrawals from their accounts, provides procedures for resolving errors, and requires institutions to provide disclosures, terminal receipts, and account statements. Federal Reserve interests argue that uncertainty surrounding the application of Regulation E may be holding back the development of the industry; resolving this question would help clarify some of the major risks that consumers may bear.

To this end, the Federal Reserve opposes congressional legislation, such as H.R. 1858, which would exempt all stored-value cards and a potentially wide range of other products, including transactions through the Internet, from the EFTA and Regulation E. Under current regulations, stored-value balances issued by depository institutions would be treated as transaction accounts and hence subjected to reserve requirements. However, the Federal Reserve does not currently have the authority to impose reserve requirements on nondepository institutions. Further, nonbank issuers may be free from reporting obligations, regulation, and supervision by federal banking agencies. Thus there is a potential issue of disparate treatment of bank and nonbank issuers [AB95].

While publicly the Federal Reserve and other central bank authorities may not wish to raise the alarm about electronic payment mechanisms, one would imagine that internally there must be concern about an increase in the use of nontraditional payment channels.

Content

Content issues have been among the first aspects of the Internet that have caught the eye of both the general public and government and law enforcement interests. A survey of 427 Internet users found significant worry about children's access to pornography on the Internet and on-line services (80 percent of respondents), with just over half favoring steps to control cyberporn. However, one-third favored a private sector self-regulating approach rather than governmental intervention [INTE95].

In 1996 Congress passed the Communications Decency Act (CDA), which imposes severe monetary and imprisonment penalties on parties that create, transmit, or make available "indecent" material to anyone under age eighteen. Upon its passage, civil liberty and commercial interests challenged the constitutionality of the legislation, claiming the CDA is in violation of U.S. First Amendment free speech rights. This action has temporarily restrained enforcement of the CDA, pending court ruling. The U.S. Supreme Court is expected to ultimately decide the outcome of this legislation.

The software and communications industry is busy taking proactive measures to develop private sector solutions to content issues. For example, the PICS, a cross-industry working group, is busily developing technologies to afford interactive media users control over content they and their children may access. Content providers will be able to voluntarily label the content they create and distribute, enabling end users to screen and control access via software tools such as preconfigured World Wide Web browsers [W3C96].

No matter what occurs in respect to CDA, as well as private sector efforts to promote nongovernmental solutions, given the emotional (and political) aspects of content issues, it is expected that international government and law enforcement interests will continue to monitor and involve themselves in a significant manner.

International

Electronic commerce is "going international." For example, the International Business Exchange (IBEX), backed by major multinational companies including AT&T, General Electric Information Services, SHL Systemhouse, and Dun & Bradstreet, in conjunction with the U.S. Chamber of Commerce, is providing businesses, via on-line networks, the ability to line up suppliers, negotiate contracts, make and receive bids, and arrange the delivery of goods and services around the world [IBEX96].

While ventures such as IBEX are at the vanguard of international electronic commerce, practitioners must be cognizant of the fact that international government interests now recognize that electronic networks transcend international boundaries and open up whole new avenues of ideas and freedom of expression that may be at odds with traditional informational/expression controls. Many countries are taking steps to deal with this phenomenon. For example, the European Commission, which represents many European countries, is actively seeking to draft a global convention on ethics, legislation, and the Internet. It wishes to come up with methods for official agencies to "protect the interests of children, and outlaw criminal activity on the Internet" [EC96].

In Asia, new Internet regulations are being imposed on a regular basis. Vietnam has only a single government-controlled Internet service provider (ISP). Singapore requires that political and religious sites be "registered." Malaysia has set up a regulatory body to monitor the Internet, including "politically incorrect" Usenet Newsgroups. In China, every ISP and user must register with the police, proffering up a written statement that material deemed harmful to the country will not be accessed or downloaded [VW96].

The question must be raised as to whether government authorities will be able to impose desired regulations, and, if so, the impact on electronic commerce purveyors if they must adhere to an international maze of regulations or a stifling set of unitary international standards.

In Washington, the Departments of State, Treasury, Defense, and Commerce, the NSA, and other U.S. government bodies are readily exploring avenues to establish international treaties, standards, or snooping capabilities in the electronic age.

Universal Service

A cornerstone of the Clinton administration's argument for government involvement in the evolution of information communication media like the Internet is the assurance that all Americans will enjoy full and open access. The administration is committed to working with the private sector to connect every classroom, library, hospital, and clinic in the United States to the NII by the year 2000. Concerned that the United States faces the risk of a widening gap between information "haves" and "have-nots," the administration seeks to ensure that public institutions can serve as public access sites to prevent this from occurring, at least during the interim period before households generally become hooked up to the NII [GOAL94].

The Commerce Department is reviewing the whole concept of universal service, as pertains to new information services. Historically, the long-standing government commitment to the achievement of universal service has meant the widespread availability of "basic" plain old telephone service (POTS), at affordable rates. Questions being explored include the following:

1. Is competition alone enough to ensure that advanced network services will become readily accessible on a reasonably equal basis across the country, reducing the need for universal service regulation?

2. In a purely market-driven scenario free of regulation, would "electronic redlining" take place, in which low-income and minority neighborhoods would be "systematically underrepresented" in the deployment of advanced services? A policy that the administration supports is to have libraries, schools, and "other access centers" provide electronic access for

those who would otherwise have to do without. Proponents claim that this would be a good transition mechanism, making desirable services more widely available without incurring the risks and cost of mandating universal provision of uneconomical or unwanted services.

3. What sort of services should be included in a redefinition of universal service? Pursuant to the new Telecommunications Act of 1996, one consideration is to track what services seem most in demand in the marketplace. Services that meet a certain threshold would be selected for inclusion in the redefinition of universal service. A potential way for government to get around the difficult task of identifying particular services would be to define universal service in terms of a network connection that would enable customers to access any service available via such a network. The problem here is that government officials would have to make difficult decisions about the type of network connection to be provided.

4. To what extent should universal service address customer premises equipment (CPE)? The government recognizes that without appropriate equipment, such as a computer, a connection and access to services is meaningless. The government is also aware of the potential expense for CPE and of the difficulty in deciding upon what constitutes necessary CPE.

5. What sort of sources of monetary contributions might potentially be tapped? One proposal is to require all service providers delivering services over the public switched network to contribute proportionally to universal support mechanisms. Various tax schemes have also been proposed by special interests, such as a general tax on revenues, a telecommunications sales tax, a tax on telecommunications equipment, or a property tax on carriers. It has also been suggested that commercial advertising on the information highway could be used to fund universal service objectives.

6. Distribution of subsidies. The current universal service scheme distributes subsidies to select areas regardless of individual need. Under expanded universal service methods, new models, such as vouchers, are being reviewed as a means to target subsidies to the needy and truly underserved [UNIV94] [JM96].

In a "hands-on" effort to foster universal Internet access, the NTIA oversees the Telecommunications Information Infrastructure Assistance Program (TIIAP). TIIAP, a matching fund program (50 percent federal, 50 percent nonfederal), is aimed at the establishment of public access Internet sites and Internet-oriented education programs, particularly in rural and underserved areas. Grantees have primarily consisted of universities, libraries, city government interests, and nonprofit community organizations [DG95].

The Federal Communications Commission (FCC) is involved in the universal service debate. Comments by FCC Chairman Reed Hundt indicate that the commission is taking a hard look at a future scheme for Internet access fees. There seems to be concern, both within and outside the commission, about the use and advent of emerging voice and visual technologies, in that they might short-circuit the traditional access fee collection scheme, whereby telephone long distance and business services are priced at a higher rate in order to help pay for residential, rural, and disadvantaged areas—thus ensuring universal service.

In one of the first instances of a business sector "running to Washington" for protection from the perceived threat of the Internet and the new cyber environment, the America's Carriers Telecommunication Association (ACTA), a trade association supported by 160 small and medium-sized telephone carriers, has petitioned the FCC to regulate Internet telephony. ACTA argues that Internet phone software vendors are effectively enabling the same service as their member firms, just using a different network. They believe that Internet telephony should be regulated and incur access charges, or that regulation/access charges on ACTA carriers should be lifted.

Opponents of Internet phone regulation argue that the quality of Internet phone communications is not anywhere close to what ACTA members provide. Further, at present, most Internet phones cannot interoperate, due to a lack of standards. All of this has evoked strong criticism from the Internet community and has even been opposed by large telecommunication carriers such as AT&T [MK96].

The FCC may begin deliberations on whether to regulate Internet telephony. However, as FCC Internet policy analyst Mark Corbitt states: "An alternate view is that Internet voice will introduce a new quality of voice communications with a different cost basis that will co-exist but not substitute for guaranteed bandwidth communications. It is premature to predict a set of variables (i.e., improvements in technology, network congestion, rate of adoption, usage model or the economic impact)" [MC96].

Universal Service and Infrastructure

A longer-term universal service goal is the introduction of broadband (networks capable of large-scale data handling) capability into the residential setting. Consumer-oriented electronic product sales would benefit, as well as afford workers and entrepreneurs the opportunity to conduct business in multiple settings. Unfortunately, the implementation of broadband is not occurring as quickly as had been projected. Possible factors accounting for this may be "high cost and no established demand." Further, it is thought that initially broadband may find its way into urban multifamily units prior to single family units [BBND95].

In many emerging countries, such as China, Chile, Argentina, and Malaysia, state-of-the-art fiber networks are being laid. In Great Britain, U.S. cable companies have been busily wiring homes with hybrid coaxial/fiber systems that enable video and telephone services. Groundbreaking wireless communication systems have also been implemented in Great Britain. Prior to this telecommunications "renaissance," Britain's phone system was marginal; however, government deregulation has seemingly reversed the tide [IW95].

Several questions arise in relation to the United States:

1. Is the slow progression of residential, and to some extent business, broadband solely due to lack of economic demand and consumer acceptance, or is it possible that past government telecommunications policies bear some responsibility?

2. If the United States is slow to implement broadband, in what manner might this impact U.S.-based electronic commerce?

3. How will the Telecommunications Act of 1996, legislation touted as fostering competition, impact the proliferation of business/residential broadband?

Internet Gridlock

Is one of the primary electronic commerce conduits, the Internet, facing a congested future? The "free" nature of the Internet has pretty much enabled most individuals with access the ability to send and receive unlimited amounts of data. However, with the growing number of users and the increasing trend toward byte-hungry video, audio, and high-grade graphics, there is concern that the Internet may become overloaded, impeding electronic commerce.

Trunk line operators such as Sprint are upgrading Internet links to enhance capacity, and the National Science Foundation, in cooperation with MCI, is experimenting with a high-speed Internet backbone system. Still, should bandwidth become problematic, some in the Internet/electronic commerce industry, such as Internet visionary Vinton Cerf, foresee the possible implementation of some sort of payment system as a method of moderating overload [CERF95].

The FCC is looking into the issue of network congestion as a potential justification for access fees, which raises questions about how charges might impact electronic commerce purveyors and Internet users in general.

Labor Issues and Electronic Commerce

While the advent of electronic commerce will spur productivity gains, and create whole new businesses (and jobs), ultimately creating significant wealth and economic development, transitional labor issues may evolve. For example, airlines such as American, Southwest, United, and Delta are now selling tickets on the World Wide Web directly to passengers. While this is a boon to the airlines and to consumers, it spells trouble for travel agents, who earn a 10 percent commission on each ticket and account for 80 to 85 percent of all bookings on the ten largest U.S. airlines [JLNY96].

World Wide Web sites are being created to sell securities directly from companies to investors; eventually they could eliminate the need for many costly brokerage services, or even physical stock exchanges [MS96]. Electronic banking may significantly lessen the need for branch banking (and staff), as well as labor-intensive check processing. Other disciplines ripe for structural change include real estate brokerage and automobile shopping, as well as many other business segments that rely on middlemen [EBB96].

Some proponents of electronic commerce envision the day that virtual corporations will be the norm, meaning work will be less dependent on formal work sites, instead being diffused to wherever employees with access to communications devices are located. What this all means is that workers who are able to adapt to the new information age will easily assimilate into new jobs and work styles; however, a large percentage of the population may encounter trouble coping with rapid change and a whole new work structure. In some instances this "left-out segment" may seek to bring about laws that will slow the move to an electronic work environment.

It is important that both industry and academia be aware of the social consequences of this transition, and work to make the shift as inclusive and painless as possible in order to head off government impediments and societal discord.

Consumer Protection

The FTC has released a consumer alert entitled "Online Scams: Road Hazards on the Information Superhighway." The document warns that internetworked systems could become the next medium of choice for electronic commerce scam artists [SCAM95].

A collective FTC and state "scam-fraud" database is now maintained. One could imagine that at some point this might be available on-line to aid consumers in spotting "red-flagged" electronic scam artists. However, liability issues would need to be addressed in respect to the listing process [BBUR96].

Cryptography

Many present and soon-to-be electronic commerce purveyors are of the opinion that relevant encryption systems are crucial to secure financial and business transactions. Current U.S. law permits the use of strong encryption technology for domestic applications, although the exportation of strong encryption products is restricted.[3]

In 1995 the Clinton administration proposed that export encryption key strength be increased, with the proviso that a private key escrow system be implemented. This would afford government and law enforcement authorities court-order accessibility to encrypted data. The proposal was not well received by computer software/hardware, business, and civil liberty interests, which cited the following as problematic:

- Interoperability and other provisions viewed by many as vague and a backdoor method to impose a key escrow or other limited system domestically.

- Proposed key length increases on exportable key escrow products have been thought by some to be inadequate given the continuing increase in computing power.

- Limitations on key strength might afford government (and other parties) a secondary method of decryption beyond the key escrow system.

- The provisions would force users in other countries to utilize U.S.-based escrow of all keys until bilateral access agreements were in place. U.S. commercial interests believe this is unacceptable to international commercial interests, citing lengthy treaty negotiations and administrative burdens, among other factors [DW95].

Congress has introduced S. 1726, the Promotion of Commerce On-Line in the Digital Era (Pro-CODE) Act of 1996. The stated purpose of the act "is to promote electronic commerce through the use of strong encryption." Primary provisions include the following:

---

[3] See Addendum III: Current Encryption Export Policies.

1. Restricting the Department of Commerce with respect to the promulgation or enforcement of regulations, or the application of policies, that impose government-designed encryption standards.

2. Promoting the ability of U.S. businesses to sell computer hardware and software internationally that incorporate strong encryption by restricting federal or state regulation of the sale of such products and programs in interstate commerce; prohibiting mandatory key escrow encryption systems; and establishing conditions for the sale of encryption products and programs in foreign commerce [PROC96].

U.S. House of Representatives members have introduced H.R. 3011, the Security and Freedom Through Encryption (SAFE) Act, which, among other measures, suggests that key escrow does not adequately address security concerns and hampers U.S. business interests.

Twenty-seven members of Congress sent a letter to President Clinton, urging him to either publish a final rule on the implementation of a key escrow encryption proposal or relax export controls on encryption programs and products that do not have a key escrow feature [SAFE96].

Both Pro-CODE and SAFE have enjoyed widespread bipartisan congressional support, as well as support from privacy and industry interests. The primary provisions allowing stronger exportable encryption products and the abolition of a key escrow system seemingly backed the administration into a tight corner in a political sense. In response, the White House has offered another plan that it is hoped will meet with approval and acceptance. Provisions include the following:

- The establishment of Key Management Infrastructure (KMI). An international infrastructure for key escrow encryption, including a key sharing plan, would be accomplished.

- Large companies would be allowed to "self-escrow" keys, but the utilization of government Certificate Authorities (CAs) to hold keys for other concerns would be required. CAs would be independent but would be under the authorization and scrutiny of the federal government.

- Where keys are escrowed in the United States, or a government-to-government escrow agreement is in effect, current export controls would in certain instances be eased [EPIC96].

On the surface, while the latest administration proposal seems to meet criticisms such as easing export restrictions to some extent and allowing large companies to "self-escrow" keys, in many instances it is not very different from previous proposals. Key escrow, which has come under major criticism, is still at the center of the proposal. This factor, combined with numerous bureaucratic nuances such as the establishment of international agreements (which could back a key escrow system into the U.S. domestic market), as well as the costs and time required for adherence to a key escrow system, may elicit continued resistance.

Leading cryptography authority Pat Farrell also shares the view that the proposal is not substantively different from prior ones. However, he does feel that one positive aspect is an easing up on export products incorporating the Data Encryption Standard (DES), a standard that offers stronger protection against computerized attacks than allowable under present export controls, as in his estimation DES is already pervasive [PF96].

It will be interesting to see if key escrow survives, or whether other alternatives will be arrived at to meet the needs of national security and law enforcement concerns, while at the same time generating greater acceptance outside of government.

Federal versus State

If these government regulations are going to be promulgated for the Internet and electronic commerce, some interests, such as America Online's director of public policy Bill Burrington, would actually prefer preemptive federal laws and regulations rather than the perceived nightmare of having to deal with a "crazy quilt" of various state regulations. Privacy and content are examples of such issues that could be subject to vagaries of state laws [BBAOL96].

III. ELECTRONIC COMMERCE AND WASHINGTON POLITICS

As a result of the Republican takeover of Congress, a continuation of the Clinton administration's NII effort has to some degree been sidelined. The Congress, primarily Republican congressmen elected in 1994, proposed elimination of the NTIA, and elimination or reduction in funding of dual-use programs. However, much of the fervor for these reductions has lessened, and it seems that many members now recognize that government does have at least some constructive role to play.

Electronic commerce conduits such as the Internet are now squarely in the purview of politicians and bureaucrats for several reasons. Politicians are media-driven and focus on issues that are in the spotlight. Politicians score points by introducing legislation that enshrines them as protectors of the meek from pornography, bomb makers, and anarchists.

Federal bureaucrats desire involvement in hot-button issues. The result can sometimes be agency overlap and the buildup of fiefdoms. Should media attention wane, so too may political interest.

Politicians and bureaucrats are beginning to realize that international electronic communication networks could diffuse power from a central location, which has them concerned. Government and law enforcement authorities like control and stability, and they will go to great lengths to maintain the status quo. Revenue authorities fear a potential loss of tax revenue through hidden electronic currency financial transactions.

IV. WHAT TO DO

By being involved in the unfolding policy debate, electronic commerce practitioners can both mold the debate and benefit from it. Specifically, it is important to:

1. Keep abreast of what government authorities are doing (including state and local), inputting relevant factors into electronic commerce business operating models.
   - If imposed, taxes, access fees, and regulations will impact pricing of services and operating strategies.
2. Work through or form interest coalitions.
   - Politicians take notice of large numerical voter counts and campaign contributions. The old axiom that there is strength in numbers applies to the new world of electronic commerce.
3. Contact individual senators/congressmen, and executive branch interests using a "correct" method.
   - Write intelligent letters that make sense.
   - Call the offices of elected officials (including district offices) to register an opinion.
   - Use reasoned and constructive comments.
   - Contact state and local political interests as well.
   - Be persistent and consistent. Another old axiom, "The squeaky wheel gets greased," applies in politics.
4. Look for new opportunities that may arise from legislation or public policy.

- Congressional content legislation literally created the content-filtering industry. Forthcoming legislative initiatives may present similar opportunities.

- Washington is digitizing untold amounts of information that could potentially be repackaged and sold.

5. Be a good Netizen, and encourage media interests and others to be such.

- There are many new cyberspace and electronic commerce entrants, as well as coverage by the media. As appropriate, more experienced practitioners should educate newcomers in a friendly, constructive manner.

CONCLUSION

A goal of this chapter has been to convince electronic commerce interests of the crucial need to keep abreast of government and law enforcement initiatives. This is particularly important over the next few years, as at present electronic commerce rules and regulations are only beginning to be formulated.

The private sector should take an active role in developing an electronic commerce regulatory/law enforcement framework that is reasonable to both business and consumer interests; otherwise government will step in.

Much education of consumers, government, media, and law enforcement is needed. Academic, business, and government interests must put together well-thought-out research initiatives to explore the many facets of electronic commerce, imparting key findings on an appropriate basis.

ADDENDUM I: OTHER PLAYERS

1. National Institute of Standards and Technology (NIST): NIST, an appendage of the Commerce Department, is responsible for formulating technical standards on encryption export policy.

2. U.S. Patent and Trademark Office: This office is actively reviewing copyright/intellectual property issues as they relate to electronic commerce.

3. Department of the Treasury: The Financial Crimes Enforcement Network (FinCEN), an agency of the U.S. Department of the Treasury, serves as the U.S. government's primary source of expertise regarding money laundering. In addition, the FinCEN is a major source of

expertise regarding international and domestic financial crimes, and the effect on the financial services community and the financial markets in which criminals operate. As such, FinCEN is charged with remaining abreast of all significant new developments affecting finance, banking, and capital markets, and examining the potential and existing impact of these innovations on the financial community [FINC95].

The Internal Revenue Service (IRS), the revenue collection arm of the U.S. Treasury Department, is exploring how electronic financial transactions may impact upon its mission. Specifically, the IRS is concerned about unreported financial transactions. It is also looking into on-line taxation filing, and the ability to disperse refunds and receive payments electronically.

4. Federal Trade Commission (FTC): The FTC is responsible for educating consumers about fraudulent selling schemes. The FTC may also bring actions against offending parties.

5. Department of Justice/FBI: The Justice Department and FBI investigative unit are America's law enforcement branch. They are now seeking to expand their watch to Internet/on-line service computer crime.

6. Department of Defense: The Clinton administration is a big proponent of defense conversion and "dual-use" public/private sector programs. The Technology Reinvestment Project (TRP), funded by both defense and nondefense federal agencies, is such a program that has included electronic commerce initiatives. CommerceNet is an example of a TRP-funded project [COMN96].

7. Department of State: The State Department is involved in the debate over encryption export standards; it is a likely candidate to be involved in international electronic network issue squabbles or treaties.

8. Federal Communications Commission (FCC): The FCC regulates common carrier telephone service, as well as broadcast television and radio. Comments by Chairman Reed Hundt in respect to Internet access fees suggest the FCC is also taking a hard look at this area [CW95].

The Telecommunications Act of 1996 potentially gives the FCC some authority to regulate the Internet, although, to what extent, and how this might be accomplished is not yet clear.

9. Postal Service: Electronic mail (e-mail) is among the most regularly used on-line activities [SURV95].

The U.S. Postal Service is developing a new suite of services to enter the electronic commerce arena. Pilot projects have been established with the Federal Aviation Administration (FAA), the Internal Revenue Service (IRS), the Social Security Administration (SSA), the

Government Services Administration (GSA), and additional private sector companies.

The Postal Service acknowledges that e-mail could provide a competitive option to traditional mail; however, it believes that traditional mail will continue to be a viable service and a complement to e-mail.

The Postal Service believes it will be a major participant in electronic commerce for the following reasons:

- Consumers view the Postal Service as a trusted third-party provider.

- The Postal Service has the resources and existing infrastructure to offer universal services to all, bridging the gap between information "haves" and "have-nots."

- The Postal Inspection Service has the unique ability to investigate any attempts at fraud.

- The Postal Electronic Commerce Services' Electronic Postmark will provide at least four assurances regarding a given transaction: that a document existed at a specific point in time; that the document was no longer in the originator's control; that the document will be afforded Postal Service protections under existing laws and regulations; and that the resultant digital signature will make the document nonmodifiable so that, if it is changed in any way between processing by the Postal Service and receipt by the receiving party, it will not authenticate.

- The Postal Service wants to help federal and state agencies assure customer privacy and assumed integrity of correspondence. The Social Security Administration has asked the Postal Service to assist it in the establishment of an electronic distribution system. Private sector companies may also be allowed to distribute government benefits electronically, if they meet strict guidelines [JG96].

ADDENDUM II: NEXUS

The application of a taxing state's sales or use tax is defined by the laws of that state. (For purposes of this guideline, application of a taxing state's sales or use tax includes a duty to collect a sales tax or a use tax from the customer of the out-of-state business.) Application of a state's sales and use tax is nonetheless subject to the existence of requisite nexus under the due process clause and the commerce clause of the U.S. Constitution. This guideline informs business of the signatory states' practice with respect to determining whether an out-of-state business has sufficient contacts with a taxing state under the due process clause and commerce clause of the U.S.

Constitution to support application of a taxing state's sales or use tax, including a duty to collect a sales tax or a use tax from the out-of-state business customer. The guideline reflects the signatory states' best understanding of applicable law and represents an effort to minimize post-transactional assessments reflecting constitutional understandings for which no advance notice has been given. In determining the possible application of a taxing state's sales or use tax under the Constitution of the United States, the statement makes no distinction between the vendor and vendee form of a sales and use tax. The signatory states understand that if a set of circumstances will support the constitutional application of one form of tax, the same set of circumstances will support application of the other form of tax [AICPA94].

APPENDIX III: CURRENT ENCRYPTION EXPORT POLICIES

Authorities

The export of cryptographic products is regulated by the Department of State pursuant to the Arms Export Control Act (AECA) and its implementing International Traffic in Arms Regulations (ITAR), and by the Department of Commerce pursuant to the Export Administration Act (EAA) and its implementing Export Administration Regulations (EAR). No license is required for the import of cryptographic hardware or software. There are no federal laws regulating the use of cryptographic products within the United States. A license is required for the export of cryptographic products to all destinations except Canada. Applications are reviewed by the Department of Defense (NSA) for national security implications and by the Department of State for foreign policy concerns. The export licensing policy is consistent with U.S. national security and foreign policy. The Department of Commerce controls the export of rudimentary cryptographic products containing cryptographic functions generally limited to purposes such as data authentication, password protection, and access control. Products that are determined to be covered by the Commerce Control List (CCL), with certain foreign policy exceptions, may be exported under a general license.

Procedures

- Autolist: For products reviewed and approved by the NSA for export to approved classes of end users and end uses. Permits Department of State to process license applications for such products without further review by the NSA.

- Distribution arrangements: Single license vehicle for export of approved products to classes of end users in countries or regions. Avoids need for licenses on an export-by-export basis.

- Distribution agreements: Permits single license for export of approved products to identified distributors. Again, avoids export-by-export licensing.

- Personal use exemption: Products exported for the personal use of the exporter are excepted from pre-export license requirements.

Policies

- Products designed to use cryptography for access control/authentication purposes are export controlled as dual use commodities pursuant to the Export Administration Act.

- Product manufacturers determine if their products are access control/authentication devices.

- Generally, access control/authentication products are exportable under general license procedures.

- Mass-market software products verified as implementing RC2/RC4 encryption algorithms, with 40-bit key space limitations, are designated dual-use items, to be controlled under the Export Administration Act, after a onetime review completed within seven working days of submission.

- Mass-market software implementing other encryption algorithms and key space lengths for confidentiality are reviewed on a case-by-case basis for designation as dual-use items and control under the Export Administration Act. By regulation, reviews must be completed within fifteen days of submission.

- Generally, licenses are approved for export of products to be used in protecting U.S. proprietary information (i.e., intellectual property).

- U.S. companies and their subsidiaries are allowed to export products with strong encryption for their internal use.

- Confidentiality encryption products that incorporate the Data Encryption Standard (DES) are routinely approved for export to:
  - Financial institutions and financial applications

- Protecting financial information in electronic commerce applications

- Confidentiality encryption products that incorporate the Data Encryption Standard (DES) are favorably considered for export to:

  - Applications involving protection of personal medical data

  - Parking and toll systems; debit applications; other transaction-based systems in which encryption is configured to perform identified specific transactions [CRYP96].

REFERENCES

[AB95] Alan S. Blinder, vice chairman, Board of Governors of the Federal Reserve System. Testimony before the Subcommittee on Domestic and International Monetary Policy of the Committee on Banking and Financial Services, U.S. House of Representatives, Washington, DC, October 11, 1995.

[AICPA94] American Institute of Certified Public Accountants (AICPA). "Nexus Guideline for Application of a Taxing State's Sales and Use Tax to a Remote Seller." October 24, 1994.

[BBAOL96] Bill Burrington, director of policy, America Online. Vienna, VA, personal electronic mail and voice communication, May 14, 1996.

[BBND95] Northern Business Information (A Datapro/McGraw Hill unit). "Will Residential Broadband Ever Happen?" *Newsbytes,* September 7, 1995.

[BBUR96] Becky Burr, attorney, U.S. Federal Trade Commission. Washington, DC, personal communication, May 16, 1996.

[CBS95] *48 Hours,* CBS Television, October 12, 1995.

[CERF95] Vinton Cerf, senior vice president, MCI Data Network Systems. Reston, VA, personal electronic mail communication, July 14, 1995.

[COMN96] CommerceNet (http://www.commerce.net/information/background.html), 1996.

[COPS96] "Cops on the Net." *PC Magazine Online* (http://www.pcmag.com), April 18, 1996.

[COPY96] "Bill Attacks Copyright Minefield." *Washington Post,* April 15, 1996.

[CRYP96] "Enabling Privacy, Commerce, Security and Public Safety in the Global Information Infrastructure." Draft paper, Interagency Working Group on Cryptography Policy, Executive Office of the President, Washington, DC, May 20, 1996.

[CW95] Networked Economy Conference. *Communications Weekly,* Washington, DC, September 12, 1995.

[DG95] David Gardner, legislative affairs specialist, U.S. Department of Commerce NTIA. Washington, DC, personal communication, September 1995.

[DIST95] *PC Week Online* (http://www.pcweek.com), October 16, 1995.

[DW95] Daniel Weitzner. Privacy and Security Policy Issues Raised by Commercial Key Escrow Systems. Center for Democracy and Technology, Washington, DC, September 7, 1995.

[EBB96] E. B. Baatz. "Will the Web Eat Your Job?" Webmaster, International Data Group, Framingham, MA, May/June 1996.

[EC96] "European Commission Working on Internet Regulation." Newsbytes News Network via Individual, Inc., May 3, 1996.

[EPIC96] EPIC Analysis of Administration Crypto Policy Paper (http://www.epic.org). Electronic Privacy Information Center (EPIC), May 1996.

[FINC95] Financial Crimes Enforcement Network (FinCEN), "Electronic Currency: An Overview." Distributed with FinCEN personal written communication, Vienna, VA, September 20, 1995.

[FTC96] Announcement of Public Workshop on Consumer Privacy on the Global Information Infrastructure (http://www.ftc.gov). U.S. Federal Trade Commission, Washington, DC, May 1996.

[GOAL94] *Goals 2000.* Executive Office of the President, Washington, DC, January 1994.

[HATC96] "Hatch Intends to Move Forward with NII Copyright Bill." Washington Telecom News, Phillips Publishing. Potomac, MD, May 13, 1996.

[IBEX96] International Business Exchange, U.S. Chamber of Commerce. Washington, DC, brochure/personal communication, May 1996.

[IITF95] Information Infrastructure Task Force (IITF) Fact Sheet. Washington, DC, September 24, 1995.

[INTE95] "Internet Users Favor Limits on Cyberporn." Survey by Intelliquest, Austin, TX, September 9, 1995.

[IP95] U.S. Department of Commerce NTIA. "Report on Intellectual Property and the National Information Infrastructure" (http://www.ntia.doc.gov). Washington, DC, September 1995.

[IW95] "Global Markets Heating Up." *Interactive Week* (http://interactive-week.ziff.com/~intweek/), September 25, 1995.

[JG96] Janice Gould, program analyst, U.S. Postal Service, New Electronic Businesses. Washington, DC, personal electronic mail communication, May 23, 1996.

[JLNY96] Jane Levre. "On-Line Airlines Bode Ill for Travel Agents." *New York Times* (http://www.nytimes.com), May 2, 1996.

[JM96) James W. McConnaughey, senior economist, Office of Policy Analysis and Development, U.S. Department of Commerce NTIA. Washington, DC, personal written communication, May 9, 1996.

[KP95] Karen Pearce, legislative assistant, Science Committee, U.S. House of Representatives. Washington, DC, personal communication, October 18, 1995.

[MC96] Mark Corbitt, Internet policy analyst, U.S. Federal Communications Commission (FCC). Washington, DC, personal electronic mail communication, May 8, 1996.

[MK96] Margaret Kane. "Internet Telephony Awaits FCC Call." *PC Week Online* (http://www.pcweek.com), May 6, 1996.

[MM96] Michael Moeller. "Government Agencies Build Secure Transaction Platform." *PC Week Online* (http://www.pcweek.com), May 20, 1996.

[MONI96] "Does Your Company Monitor Your Web Use?" *PC Magazine Online* (http://www.pcmag.com), April 19, 1996.

[MS96] Michael Selz. "Small Stock Issuers Find New Market on Internet." *Wall Street Journal Interactive Edition* (http://interactive.wsj.com), May 14, 1996.

[MTC95] Multistate Tax Commission. Sixth Annual Business/ Government Dialogue on State Tax Uniformity, Pre-event announcement, Topic II: State Transactional Taxation of On-line Services. Washington, DC, September 8, 1995.

[NII93] National Information Infrastructure—Agenda for Action (http://ntia.doc.gov). Washington, DC, September 15, 1993.

[NN95] Nathan Newman. "Proposition 13 Meets the Internet: How State and Local Government Finances Are Becoming Road Kill on the Information Superhighway." Center for Community Economic Research, University of California at Berkeley, August 16, 1995.

[PB96] Paul Bauer, economic adviser, Federal Reserve Bank of Cleveland. Cleveland, OH, personal electronic mail communication, May 20, 1996.

[PF96] Pat Farrell, senior technology consultant, American Management Systems. Arlington, VA, personal communication, May 28, 1996.

[PMNY96] Pamela Mendels. "Got an Online Beef? Tell It to the Virtual Judge." *New York Times Company* (http://www.nytimes.com), April 21, 1996.

[PRIV96] U.S. Department of Commerce NTIA. Privacy and the NII: Safeguarding Telecommunications-Related Personal Information (http://www.ntia.doc.gov). Washington, DC, October 23, 1995.

[PROC96] U.S. Senate. S. 1726 Pro-CODE. Washington, DC, May 6, 1996.

[PUHL95] Peter Uhlmann, legislative director, Rep. Christopher Cox (CA), U.S. House of Representatives. Washington, DC, personal communication, September 28, 1995.

[SAFE96] U.S. House of Representatives. Letter to President Clinton, released by Rep. Robert Goodlatte, Washington, DC, May 15, 1996.

[SCAM95] U.S. Federal Trade Commission. Online Scams: Road Hazards on the Information Superhighway (http://www.ftc.com), Washington, DC, 1995.

[SEN95] U.S. Congress, Senate. National Information Infrastructure Copyright Protection Act of 1995, S. 1284, 104th Cong. 2nd sess., 1995.

[SURV95] Survey about Americans "Going Online." Times Mirror Center for the People and the Press, October 16, 1995.

[UNIV94] U.S. Department of Commerce NTIA. Inquiry on Universal Service and Op Access Issues, *Federal Register*, v. 59, no. 180. Washington, DC, September 19, 1994.

[VW96] Vivienne Walt. "The Internet Meets the Thought Police." *Wall Street Journal Interactive Edition* (http://interactive.wsj.com), May 4, 1996.

[W3C96] World Wide Web Consortium (http://www.w3.org/...228/ Microsoft.html), February 28, 1996.

Chapter 5

International Encryption Policy

Dorothy E. Denning

ABSTRACT

Cryptography policy must promote the use of strong encryption on the global information infrastructure, but without unnecessarily hindering the ability of governments to get access to communications and stored information in criminal and terrorist investigations. One approach that has received considerable attention from both governments and the international business community involves archiving keys with trusted third parties within a key management infrastructure. The archived keys would enable recovery of encrypted data by the owners of the data in case of lost or damaged keys, and by governments under due process of law and strict accountability. This chapter describes international initiatives to develop a key management infrastructure with key archive and recovery, how such an approach might work, and potential obstacles to approaches that would ensure government access.

INTRODUCTION

Information. Global connectivity. Electronic commerce. Competition. Economic espionage. Global organized crime. Chemical, biological, and nuclear weapons. Terrorism. Conflict. Economic and social instability. Violations of privacy and human rights. Erosion of trust. These are some of the global realities we live with today. They explain why cryptography must be an integral part of the global information infrastructure (GII) to protect privacy,

This article also appeared in *Computer Fraud and Security,* July, 1996.

intellectual property, and financial assets, and to provide a foundation of trust for electronic commerce. They also explain why we ought to proceed thoughtfully in the deployment of this technology.

An encrypted GII is completely without precedent in world history. It is not the same as a private conversation on the beach. It allows individuals and groups, anywhere and anytime, to communicate securely across time and space. Nor is it the same as a locked door or filing cabinet. Locks can be picked and doors broken down. Unbreakable codes empower the individual to communicate and store records in total secrecy, beyond the reach of crooks and court orders alike. The concern is that while preventing many crimes, encryption will facilitate others, leading to large-scale economic and human losses. Encryption can be hazardous even to users. If keys are lost, valuable data can become inaccessible. In developing an encryption strategy for the GII, therefore, it is worthwhile to seek one that will meet the security and data recovery needs of users of the GII without unnecessarily undermining the ability of governments to enforce the law and protect public safety and national security.

Most major countries, including the United States and other New Forum (formerly Coordinating Committee for Multilateral Export Controls, or COCOM) countries, regulate exports of encryption technology.[1] A few, including France, China, Israel, and Russia, regulate its import and use. These controls have limited, though not prevented, the spread of strong encryption to adversaries throughout the world. While this has helped protect vital national security interests, it has also hampered the widespread deployment of robust encryption technology to protect the legitimate interests of organizations and individuals, and it has threatened the economic competitiveness of companies in export-controlled countries. Business and government alike recognize that changes are needed to meet the security requirements for the GII, ensure a level playing field in the information technology global market, and still protect law enforcement and national security interests.

One approach that has received considerable attention from both governments and the international business community involves archiving (or escrowing) keys with trusted third parties within a key management infrastructure. The archived keys would enable recovery of encrypted data by the owners of the data and by governments under due process of law and strict accountability. When combined with key escrow, strong encryption would be freely exportable and importable in conformance with international standards and government-to-government agreements. The standards, which would apply to encryption products and key management services, would be developed through standards bodies with representation from industry and government. They would be open and nondiscriminatory. Key agreements between governments would allow governments to access keys in foreign countries where necessary pursuant to criminal investigations, while preserving privacy rights and protecting against foreign espionage.

Encryption cannot be used effectively across the GII (or any network) without a key management infrastructure. Indeed, lack of a global infrastructure is one reason the use of encryption is not more widespread. A key management infrastructure provides signed certificates for public keys, certificate distribution, authentication of users, revocation and expiration of keys, time-stamping and notarization of electronic documents, dispute resolution, and key archiving. These services are performed by trusted entities, sometimes called trusted third parties, which ensure confidentiality, integrity, authenticity, nonrepudiation, and availability of information and services. Public-key certificates are issued by a trusted certificate authority (CA), which first establishes proof of identity of the person owning the corresponding private key and then signs a certificate containing the user's identity, public key, and period of validity. Separate keys can be used for encryption (confidentiality protection) and digital signatures (authentication and nonrepudiation), with separate certificates issued for each. With an escrowed infrastructure, a certificate for a public encryption key would not be issued unless the corresponding private decryption key is archived. The key holder could be the CA itself or a separate key escrow authority. Private signature keys need not be archived as they are not needed for data recovery.

Use of an escrowed infrastructure and compatible products would be voluntary. The incentive would be access to strong, globally interoperable encryption systems and key management services that meet high standards of assurance for confidentiality, integrity, and data recovery. Users would get extremely strong security and privacy for stored data and for international as well as domestic communications, backup protection for keys, assurance that their information will not be disclosed to governments or anyone else except under due process, and liability protection in case keys are compromised or misused. The information technology industry would get to export strong cryptography into a global market with a level playing field.

This chapter describes various initiatives to develop a key management infrastructure with key archive and recovery, how such an approach might work, and potential obstacles to approaches that would ensure government access.

INITIATIVES

Beginning with the Clipper initiative in 1993, the Clinton administration has embraced an encryption policy based on key escrow with trusted third parties. This policy includes development of federal standards for key escrow encryption, adoption of key escrow within the federal government, and liberalization of export controls for key escrow encryption products. The objective has been to promote encryption in a way that does not unnecessarily undermine law enforcement and national security objectives, and to do so through export controls and government use of key escrow rather than mandatory controls on the use of encryption.

In the Clipper system, the escrow mechanism was independent of any key management infrastructure.[2] The administration is now proposing an approach in which data recovery services would be integrated into the key management infrastructure and tied to the issuance of public-key certificates.[3] The goal is to allow ready export of any encryption product that uses an escrowed infrastructure regardless of algorithm, key length, or hardware or software implementation. Existing export controls place severe restrictions on key length (40 bits for a general export license), so this represents a significant advance. Keys could be held within the United States or in any country that has a government-to-government key agreement with the United States. Such agreements would recognize that authorized government access must be preserved consistent with the legally recognized privacy interests of the citizens of each country.

In the interim, until an escrowed key infrastructure is developed and agreements are in place, the administration will continue its initiative to allow ready export of 64-bit software or 80-bit hardware products with key escrow.[4] It will permit, prior to formal government-to-government agreements, exports of products that use an escrowed infrastructure to approved markets, consistent with policies of the destination country. Further, prior to establishment of a multinational infrastructure with key recovery, it will permit export of products that require the use of an escrowed infrastructure, on a case-by-case basis, to any destination with which the United States has government-to-government agreements.

In addition to allowing overseas escrow of keys, the policy would allow organizations to escrow their own keys if they can meet the performance requirements. The government proposes to seek legislation that would shield escrow authorities within an organization from internal pressures during an investigation. Legislation would also be sought to criminalize the unauthorized disclosure or use of keys, authorize civil actions against those responsible, specify the circumstances in which keys could be requested and released, and establish liability protections for key holders who exercise due prudence in fulfillment of their obligations.

Outside the United States, Canada is building its public-key infrastructure using the Nortel Entrust product line for its underlying security architecture. Entrust supports optional key escrow through the certificate authorities.

The certificate authority for an organization, which may be internal to the organization, holds the private keys of users when recovery is desired.

In Europe, the British government is proposing to license trusted third parties providing encryption services to the general public.[5] The TTPs, which in some cases might be within a company, would hold and release the encryption keys of their clients under appropriate safeguards. The licensing regime would seek to ensure that TTPs meet criteria for liability coverage, quality assurance, and data recovery. It would allow for relaxed export controls on encryption products that work with licensed TTPs. The private use of encryption would not be regulated. A system design for a key management infrastructure from Royal Holloway will be tested in product demonstrations.

France has waived its licensing requirement on the use of encryption when keys are escrowed with government-approved key holders, effectively trading licenses on the use of encryption for licenses governing the operation of trusted TTPs. To get a license, an organization providing TTP services would have to operate in France.

The European Commission is proposing a project to establish a European-wide network of TTPs that would be accredited to offer services that support digital signatures, notarization, confidentiality, and data integrity. The trust centers, which would operate under the control of member nations, would hold keys that would enable them to assist the owners of data with emergency decryption or supply keys to their national authorities on production of a legal warrant. Australia is also considering the development of a key infrastructure with TTPs.

In recognition of the need for international coordination of encryption policy, the Organization for Economic Cooperation Development (OECD), which includes the United States, Australia, Canada, Europe, Japan, and New Zealand, is drafting guidelines for cryptography policy that would promote encryption on the GII while balancing the needs of consumers, industry, public safety, and national security. The OECD has been working closely with several industry associations, including the Business-Industry Advisory Council (BIAC) to the OECD, the International Chamber of Commerce (ICC), the INFOSEC Business Advisory Group (IBAG), and a quadripartite group consisting of the European Association of Manufacturers of Business Machines and Information Technology Industry (EUROBIT), the Information Technology Industry Association of Canada (ITAC), the Information Technology Industry Council (ITI) in the United States, and the Japan Electronic Industry Development Association (JEIDA).[6]

The guidelines, which are being prepared by a Group of Experts on Cryptography Policy under a parent Group of Experts on Security, Privacy, and Intellectual Property Protection in the GII, are due to be completed by early 1997. While the guidelines will not require any particular approach, they are likely to provide a framework wherein encryption with key escrow could work internationally through international standards and government-to-government agreements.

The Open Group (formerly X/Open and OSF) is pursuing standards for a public-key infrastructure. It is working with law enforcement and other government agencies, as well as with the international business community, to build an infrastructure that would support key archive and recovery.

In all of these initiatives, certain basic principles are emerging as a foundation for making encryption widely available on the GII. These include (1) robust and trusted security; (2) choice of encryption method, key length, and key holder; (3) open, market-driven standards developed through international standards bodies with industry and government representation; (4) recognition of national responsibilities and regulations to protect privacy, promote commerce and economic well-being, maintain social order, and protect national security; (5) government access to the plaintext of encrypted communications and stored data under due process and strict accountability; (6) liability protection for the owners of encrypted data who escrow their keys and for key holders responding to legitimate government requests; and (7) international cooperation and harmonization of policies to the extent possible, with bilateral agreements so that a government can conduct an investigation within its jurisdiction even when the keys needed for decryption are held outside its borders. Each of these principles is to be interpreted in the context of the whole, where the needs of consumers, industry, and government are all valued and balanced with each other. Thus, free choice and market-driven standards are relative to government regulations, but any regulations that are adopted must be such that users find the products and services meeting those regulations to be technically and legally acceptable.

Many of the difficulties in bringing forth the widespread use of encryption have less to do with encryption policy than with the lack of technology to facilitate its integration into applications and networks. This is being remedied with the development, internationally, of cryptographic application programming interfaces (CAPIs), which allow the cryptographic functions to be isolated in modules separate from the rest of the software. CAPIs are playing a major role in experiments conducted under the International Cryptography Experiment (ICE), an informal international alliance of individuals and organizations working together to promote the international use of encryption that meets the needs of users and business as well as those of law enforcement and national security.[7] ICE calls for a series of experiments that demonstrate the international use of encryption in common applications.

HOW KEY ESCROW MIGHT WORK

With an escrowed infrastructure, a user's private encryption key would be archived with a trusted key holder prior to issuance of the corresponding public-key certificate.[8] If the user's certificate authority is the key escrow agent, then these operations can be done together. Otherwise, the certificate authority would need proof that the key has been escrowed, say, through an escrow certificate digitally signed by the key holder.

Actual escrowing of keys could be performed off-line, with the user physically present at the key archive site. Either the user can generate a random public-private key pair and give a copy to the escrow agent, or else the escrow agent can generate the key pair and give a copy to the user. All this can be done electronically so that the keys need never be in human-readable form. For example, a user's keys could be generated on a smart card or PC card belonging to the user and then read into an escrow agent workstation, or they could be generated on the workstation and downloaded onto the card.

Standards for key holders would be developed to establish performance criteria for key integrity, confidentiality, accessibility, auditability, and recovery and use. They would help ensure that requests from government agencies are handled legally, expeditiously, and with confidentiality. If a law enforcement agency is conducting a wiretap, for example, it is important that the subject not be informed of the investigation, at least prior to completion. Entities meeting these standards would be certified or accredited in some way. Escrow agents would generally be in the private sector.

Users could choose any key holder that is certified as meeting the standards. They would not be forced to escrow their keys with their government. Nor would their government or any other government be able to get their keys at will. Government access to plaintext or keys would be strictly limited and subject to due process and international agreements. All such accesses would be audited. Through contracts and criminal law, key holders would be accountable for their actions and liable for abuses of keys. They would not, however, be liable for responding to lawful requests by owners or government officials operating under due process. Governments would be held accountable for their use of keys and data recovery services.

Qualifying organizations would be able to hold their own keys as long as their internal key escrow services meet the standards. This would provide assurance that the escrow unit would respond to court orders and maintain confidentiality of investigations of employees. The key holders would be protected from company internal pressures through appropriate legal safeguards. Self-escrow, however, is a difficult issue, as it could potentially lead to a situation where government agencies could not conduct a surreptitious wiretap against a criminal or terrorist organization. Some mechanism is needed to minimize the chances of such a group qualifying as an escrow agent.

Key escrow agents must provide a high level of assurance that keys are not compromised or misused. This can be achieved through a variety of safeguards, including auditing, separation of duties, access controls, physical security, encryption, and trusted operating systems. One control that is particularly effective is to split the keys into components, with each component controlled by a different group of people so that trust is not concentrated in a single entity. Then a key cannot be misused without collusion. Some technological approaches to key escrow would allow the user to split a key and escrow it with separate entities in such a manner that the entities can, without combining their parts, verify that their components would together form the user's private key. In some cases, data recovery is possible without ever reassembling the private key; instead, the key holders share in the decryption of the message key (or plaintext).

With key escrow, data recovery is possible through services provided by the key holders and information transmitted or stored with the encrypted data. An encrypted message, for example, could contain a header with the message key encrypted under the public encryption key of each recipient.[9] Access is then possible using the private encryption key of any recipient (by default, the sender can also be a recipient so that access is possible through the sender's key). The key holders could either release the private encryption key or use it to decrypt and release the message key. The data are then decrypted with the message key.

The data recovery services provided by key escrow agents would be available to the owners of the keys and to government officials with the legal authority to access the encrypted data. Owners would have to prove their identity and rights to the keys. In the case of a corporation or other type of organization, designated officers of the organization would have permission to obtain the keys of employees on behalf of the organization. This is essential to protect against the death, termination, or loss of an employee and to enable criminal investigations of an employee. Government agencies would similarly have to establish their legal authority, normally through a court order, to a key and the information that will be decrypted with it. If the escrow agent is in a foreign country, the government of the country seeking access would additionally need an agreement with the foreign government that would allow access, possibly subject to approval by the foreign government.

In the case of stored data, there are obvious benefits to owners for archiving keys: if the keys are lost, the data are lost. For certain types of communications, for example, real-time network connections, key escrow has no obvious benefits to the owners: if the keys are lost, new keys can be generated and the data retransmitted. Indeed, with some protocols, keys are generated on the fly and discarded when the connection is closed. However, retransmission is not possible with all forms of communication. In the case of electronic mail, for example, there would be no guarantee of the sender retaining the original message. Phone calls would be similar when the receiver is a voice mailbox and the message is recorded for later playback. Thus, key escrow is also useful to the owners of certain types of encrypted communications, but there may be some applications where it would not be selected by choice, particularly if it added to the cost.

In order to accommodate import and export of strong encryption and user choice of key holders, mutual assistance agreements would be established between countries. These agreements would give governments access to foreign data recovery services, though not necessarily direct access to keys or key holders. In that way, a government can get access to data encrypted with products that are exported from or imported into its borders in the case of a major criminal or terrorist investigation falling within its jurisdiction. Under such agreements, a multinational company or any company with foreign offices would be able to escrow its keys in its home country if so desired. Access to keys by foreign governments would be very tightly controlled to protect users from foreign espionage.

Encryption products that operated only with an escrowed key infrastructure would be generally exportable and importable. Unlike the situation under current regulations, key length would not be a factor for exportability. Thus, users would have access to strong encryption systems both for domestic and for international use. Standards for algorithms and implementations would be set by standards groups.

The preceding outlines one possible approach to a global key management infrastructure with key escrow. There are, of course, many issues and details to be worked out, including international agreements, standards, liability protection, certification of escrow agents, self-escrow, legislation, and how or whether escrow fits into specific applications. These are being addressed by the OECD and individual governments in collaboration with industry and other interested parties. The American Bar Association is addressing the nature of contractual arrangements for key escrow.

POTENTIAL OBSTACLES TO KEY ESCROW WITH GOVERNMENT ACCESS

Although the international business community has been generally supportive of efforts to find a balanced, international approach that would accommodate government access, much of that support has been motivated by export controls. Under such controls, an approach based on key escrow offers a possible way forward toward widespread availability of strong encryption, global interoperability, and a level playing field in the encryption and information technology markets. However, if export controls were dropped, then industry support for accommodating government access could diminish substantially. There would still be interest in key escrow, but only insofar as it serves the data recovery needs of users and is totally optional (i.e., not required for export or for use of the key management infrastructure).

Within the United States, there has been considerable pressure from the information technology industry to lift export controls on encryption on the grounds that they harm the competitiveness of U.S. industry in the global market. As a result of this pressure, bills have been introduced in the Senate and the House to lift export controls (S. 1587, S. 1726, and H.R. 3011).[10] Thirty-seven members of the House sent a letter to President Clinton on May 15, 1996, asking him to abandon his administration's key escrow encryption policy proposal and immediately liberalize export controls on non–key escrow encryption programs and products. The bills offer no alternative mechanism for protecting public safety and law enforcement interests. If passed, they would likely undermine efforts at finding a balanced approach, accelerate the spread of unbreakable encryption, and aggravate the problems for law enforcement here and in other countries. While attempting to satisfy the economic objectives of U.S. industry, they could ultimately subvert those same objectives by facilitating economic crimes. On June 7, 1996, Senators Specter and Kerrey sent a letter to Senator Leahy, sponsor of both Senate bills, recommending that Congress proceed cautiously with the legislative initiative so that its full implications could be discerned. They noted that industry representatives are meeting with the administration to address the issues and that both Congress and the administration are reviewing the congressionally mandated study conducted by the National Research Council.[11]

U.S. business is understandably concerned about export controls. Many countries have more liberal controls than in the United States, giving their companies a competitive advantage. For example, several New Forum countries allow ready export of mass market and public domain encryption software (e.g., DES and RSA, which are tightly controlled in the United States), as permitted by the old COCOM agreements. It is also unclear to what extent the agreements are binding. There have been reports that Japan is allowing the export of RSA with 1024-bit keys in hardware; however, Japanese officials have said they are still controlling exports.[12]

As a result, the global market for products that use encryption is not a level playing field. Although import controls, trust in supplier, and overall product desirability dampen the effect of export restrictions, exportability is nevertheless a factor in industry competitiveness. If accepted by all major countries, the key escrow approach outlined here, with international standards for strong, exportable encryption products and services, could even out the playing field so that export controls are not a major factor in sales. However, if countries that have a substantial information technology industry do not agree to the approach, then those that do could be at a competitive disadvantage.

Another potential obstacle to widespread use of key escrow is acceptability. Large-scale deployment of key escrow introduces some risk into the infrastructure. Key escrow is not likely to be accepted unless users are convinced that these risks have been made negligible through technical, legal, and procedural safeguards, and that they will be able to recover losses in case of abuse. Users will want to be able to pick key holders they trust. They will want assurances that key escrow will not be exploited by corrupt governments to violate human rights and that government-to-government agreements will not make them vulnerable to foreign espionage. Even with these safeguards and assurances, some people may see any form of mandatory key escrow as an affront to human dignity or right to privacy. The approach outlined here would not require that users escrow their keys; however, persons not doing so would be unable to take advantage of the escrowed security infrastructure for global interoperability.

Key escrow also adds to the cost and complexity of the security infrastructure. Although the infrastructure must support some form of escrow anyway to support consumer and business needs for data recovery, requirements for government access will increase the cost by some factor, particularly if the requirements lead to regulation of escrow agents or use of escrow in situations where consumers and businesses do not need it. If criminals and terrorists do not use escrow, at least for their internal communications (they may use it to interoperate with the rest of the world), then the extra costs to provide for government access may not be justified.

Even if an escrowed infrastructure is developed and accepted by many users, an unescrowed key infrastructure could emerge as an alternative. Such an infrastructure could support global interoperability for an encryption system such as PGP (Pretty Good Privacy), which is available worldwide over the Internet despite export controls, or for strong encryption products developed in a country without export controls. Indeed, PGP already has an informal public-key infrastructure based on a web-of-trust model under the control of users. Given the cost and complexity introduced by key escrow and the need to develop international standards and agreements to make it work, an alternative, unescrowed infrastructure could emerge anyway to fill an immediate need for a public-key infrastructure. It is also possible that there will be no single key infrastructure but rather several, some escrowed and some not. These could arise in the context of specific applications such as electronic mail, electronic payments, and Internet Protocol (IP) level encryption.

The National Research Council study recommended against an aggressive approach to key escrow, arguing in part that it is untested, at least on a large scale. However, an intensive effort will help resolve the policy issues, establish an appropriate legal framework, promote development of key escrow products and services, encourage establishment of TTPs, and test various approaches. Moreover, internationally business and government are rapidly acquiring operational experience with key escrow as organizations install a data recovery capability to protect their own assets. An escrowed infrastructure is integral to several encryption products and application environments, including the Defense Messaging System, which eventually will support about 2 million users, Nortel Entrust, and PC Security Stoplock KE, which is being used by Shell Group enterprises worldwide to meet their confidentiality, integrity, and data recovery needs.

CONCLUSIONS

Cryptography policy must promote the use of strong encryption on the GII, but without unnecessarily hindering criminal and terrorist investigations. Thus, it is important that we continue efforts to develop an escrowed key infrastructure based on voluntary use and international standards and agreements. Doing so will help establish a basis for confidence in key escrow. It will also demonstrate the value of key escrow to users for data recovery and to governments for investigating cases of crime and terrorism. If key escrow can be shown to be safe, valuable to users and society, and cost-effective, then it likely will be accepted and adopted widely. If not, then it will be properly rejected on the basis of evidence, not emotion. But until an alternative mechanism is found that adequately balances commercial needs with law enforcement requirements, key escrow remains, above all other considerations, the only show in town. The law enforcement and national security interests are too important to dismiss key escrow at this time, and key escrow offers a potential way forward toward a safe and secure GII.

NOTES

1. For a description of cryptography regulations and their effect on the market, see "A Study of the International Market for Computer Software with Encryption" (Washington, DC: U.S. Department of Commerce and the

National Security Agency, 1996); see also James P. Chandler, "Identification and Analysis of Foreign Laws and Regulations Pertaining to the Use of Commercial Encryption Products for Voice and Data Communications" (Proceedings of the International Cryptography Institute 1995: Global Challenges, National Intellectual Property Law Institute, September 21–22, 1995).

2. For a description of Clipper and its key escrow system, see Dorothy E. Denning and Miles Smid, "Key Escrowing Today," *IEEE Communications* 32, no. 9 (September 1994): 58–68. Available through Dorothy Denning's Cryptography Project page on the World Wide Web: http://www.cosc.georgetown.edu/~denning/crypto.

3. "Enabling Privacy, Commerce, Security and Public Safety in the Global Information Infrastructure" (draft paper issued by the Office of Management and Budget, May 17, 1996). Available through the Cryptography Project (see note 2).

4. For a discussion of the administration's 64-bit software key escrow initiative, see Dorothy E. Denning and William E. Baugh Jr., "Decoding Encryption Policy," *Security Management*, February 1996, 59–63. Available through the Cryptography Project (see note 2). Or see Dorothy E. Denning and William E. Baugh Jr., "Key Escrow Encryption Policies and Technologies," *Information Systems Security* 5, no. 2 (Summer 1996): 44–51.

5. "Regulatory Intent Concerning Use of Encryption on Public Networks" (London: Department of Trade and Industry, June 10, 1996). Available through the Cryptography Project (see note 2).

6. At a business-government forum sponsored by the OECD-BIAC-ICC in December 1995, IBAG issued a statement of seventeen principles supporting a key escrow approach and calling for industry-led voluntary, consensus, international standards. The quadripartite group issued a similar statement calling for harmonization of national cryptography policies and industry-led international standards. Both statements are available through the Cryptography Project (see note 2).

7. Information about ICE is available through the Cryptography Project (see note 2) or http://www.tis.com.

8. This section sketches one possible approach to key escrow. For a taxonomy of key escrow features and options, see Dorothy E. Denning and Dennis K. Branstad, "A Taxonomy of Key Escrow Encryption," *Communications of the ACM* 39, no. 3 (March 1996): 34–40. Available through the Cryptography Project (see note 2).

9. Normally, a message is encrypted using a symmetrical (single-key) algorithm such as the Data Encryption Standard. Asymmetrical (public-key) encryption is used to transfer the session key from the sender to the receiver or to establish the session key through an interactive protocol between the two parties.

10. Full text of the Senate and House bills is available through the Cryptography Project (see note 2).

11. Kenneth Dam and Herbert Lin, eds., *Cryptography's Role in Securing the Information Society* (Washington, DC: National Research Council, National Academy Press, 1996). Available through the Cryptography Project (see note 2).

12. A subsidiary of Nippon Telephone and Telegraph has begun the manufacture and shipment of encryption chips with 1024-bit RSA. See statements by Jim Bidzos, president of RSA Data Security Inc., and James Barksdale, president and CEO of Netscape Communications Corp., before the Senate Committee on Commerce, Science and Transportation, Subcommittee on Science, Space and Technology, June 12, 1996.

Chapter 6

The Essential Role of Trusted Third Parties in Electronic Commerce

A. Michael Froomkin

By now it is well known that the Internet is a global, but insecure, network.[1] It is also increasingly well understood that cryptography[2] can contribute greatly to the transactional security that Internet commerce so obviously lacks.[3] What is less well understood is that cryptography is only part of the security story. Many cryptographic protocols for secure electronic transactions require at least one trusted third party to the transaction, such as a bank or a "certification authority" (CA). These partly cryptographic, partly social, protocols require new entities, or new relationships with existing entities, but the duties and liabilities of those entities are uncertain. Until these uncertainties are resolved, they risk inhibiting the spread of the most interesting forms of electronic commerce and causing unnecessary litigation.

This chapter aims to describe what CAs do, explain why they are important to electronic commerce, and suggest that they are likely to provoke some interesting legal problems. It does not attempt to describe a complete

---

[1] The FBI estimates that 80 percent of the computer crime it investigates involves the Internet. DAVID ICOVE ET AL., COMPUTER CRIME: A CRIMEFIGHTER'S HANDBOOK 129 (1995).

[2] For an explanation of cryptographic techniques, see *infra* Part I.A–C.

[3] *See generally* A. Michael Froomkin, *The Metaphor Is the Key: Cryptography, The Clipper Chip, and the Constitution*, 143 U. PA. L. REV. 709 (1995).

legal regime for the regulation of CAs in electronic commerce.[4] The coming wave of faceless electronic commerce presents a number of challenges; opportunities for fraud and error and for the prevention of fraud and error are interwoven with the solutions to these difficulties. Although accounts of fraud in commercial electronic transactions (as opposed to simple theft of data or services by a stranger) on the Internet remain very rare, this may reflect the low level of Internet commerce today more than any virtues of the medium.[5]

Utah was the first state to attempt to provide a regulatory framework for CAs. The Utah Digital Signature Act provides for a safe harbor against most liability for those who qualify.[6] No one has qualified to date,[7] and the act does not define the duties and liabilities of those who do not qualify for the safe harbor.[8] Clarification of the duties and liabilities of CAs in the absence of legislation should thus serve the interests of all parties to an electronic transaction in which a certificate plays a role. Other states, and perhaps someday the U.S. Congress, will eventually have to decide whether to enact digital signature laws of their own, and they may find it helpful to have a better understanding of the legal background against which a comprehensive legislative program may be drawn.

Before embarking on a discussion of the role of trusted third parties in electronic commerce, it is useful to review basic cryptographic techniques such as public-key cryptography and digital signatures. Cryptographically sophisticated readers should skip to Part I.D., which begins a description of CAs and discusses the various types of digital certificates they may issue, or

---

[4] Attempts to do this are in progress. The state of Utah passed a Digital Signature Act in 1995, UTAH CODE ANN. tit. 46, ch. 3 (1995), and amended it in 1996. Digital Signature Act Amendments, 52nd Leg., Gen. Sess., 1996 Utah Laws 188 (LEXIS, Code library, UTCODE file) (to be codified at UTAH CODE ANN. tit. 46, ch. 3) (hereinafter all cites to the UTAH CODE ANN. incorporate the 1996 amendments). As of November 1995, no certification authorities had qualified under the Utah Act. *See* Introductory Commentary, History and Current Status of the Utah Act *1, *available online* URL http://www.state.ut.us/ccjj/digsig/dsut-int.htm. The Information Security Committee of the Section on Science and Technology of the American Bar Association issued the Craft Digital Signature Guidelines for public comment which ended in January 1996. Draft Digital Signature Guidelines, *available online* URL http://www.state.ut.us/ccjj/digsig/dsut-gl.htm [hereinafter ABA Draft Guidelines]. The guidelines are currently being revised. The state of California has passed a statute delegating to the secretary of state powers to make rules regulating the use and verification of digital signatures. *See* 1995 Cal. Legis. Serv. Ch. 594 (A.B. 1577) (West). On March 29, 1996, Washington State approved a digital signatures statute with an effective date of January 1, 1998. *See* Washington Electronic Authentication Act, 1996 Wash. Legis. Serv. Ch. 250 (S.B. 6423) (WL, WA LEGIS Library).

[5] "The Net currently is a universe of browsers rather than shoppers." Larry Marion, *Who's Guarding the Till at the CyberMall?*, DATAMATION, Feb. 15, 1995, at 38, 41.

[6] UTAH CODE ANN. § 46-3-309 (1996).

[7] Introductory Commentary, History and Current Status of the Utah Act, *supra* note 4, at *1.

[8] UTAH CODE ANN. § 46-3-201(5).

to Part II, where the discussion of the application of these techniques to Internet commerce begins. In order to show just how hard it can be to determine what legal rules apply to this new world of electronic commerce, Part III offers an introductory discussion of the liability of a CA that issues an erroneous certificate.

I. CRYPTOGRAPHIC KEYS, DIGITAL SIGNATURES, DIGITAL CERTIFICATES, AND THE PEOPLE WHO ISSUE THEM

A. Public-Key Cryptography

A *public-key cryptosystem* is one in which messages encrypted with one key can only be decrypted with a second key, and vice versa. A strong public-key system is one in which possession of both the algorithm and one key gives no useful information about the other key and thus no clues as to how to decrypt the message.[9] The system gets its name from the idea that the user will publish one key but keep the other one secret. The world can use the public key to send messages that only the private key owner can read; the private key can be used to send messages that could only have been sent by the key owner.

With the aid of public-key cryptography it is possible to establish a secure line of communication with anyone who is using a compatible decryption program or other device. Sender and receiver no longer need a secure way to agree on a shared key. If Alice wishes to communicate with Bob, a stranger with whom she has never communicated before, Alice and Bob can exchange the plaintext of their public keys. Then, Alice and Bob can each encrypt their outgoing messages with the other's public key and decrypt their received messages with their own secret, private key. The security of the system evaporates if either party's private key is compromised, that is, transmitted to anyone else.

Thus, if Alice wants to send a secure e-mail message to Bob, and they both use compatible public-key cryptographic software, Alice and Bob can exchange public keys on an insecure line. If Alice has Bob's public key *and knows that it is really Bob's*, then Alice can use it to ensure that only Bob, and no one pretending to be Bob, can decode the message.

---

[9] See BRUCE SCHNEIER, APPLIED CRYPTOGRAPHY: PROTOCOLS, ALGORITHMS AND SOURCE CODE IN C 470–74, 501–2 (1996) (stating that security of public-key systems depends on inability of factoring large numbers rapidly or on the continuing inability of mathematicians to solve the long-standing problem of calculating discrete logarithms).

The problem facing Alice in this scenario, however, is that there is no more reason to trust an e-mail message purporting to be from Bob that says "Here is my public key" than there is to trust any other e-mail message purporting to be from Bob. Lacking independent confirmation, Alice has no way of knowing whether the message is really from Bob or from an imposter. (Bob has the same problem regarding Alice.) One bit looks exactly like another, making it possible for Mallet to forge messages purporting to come from either Alice, Bob, or both.[10] And, if Mallet is able to masquerade as Bob in an e-mail message, Mallet can just as easily send Alice his own public key, claiming that it belongs to Bob. Without help from a source external to the Internet communication, either a trusted third party or some "out-of-band" (non-Internet) communication that is reliable, Alice has no way of assuring herself of the authenticity of any e-mailed communication from a stranger, regardless of what it says. Alice needs some assurance to feel confident that she is not sending the details of a tender or her financial details to a malicious stranger who might seek to profit from it at her expense. Of course, if the message is from someone Alice already knows, the message itself may provide internal clues of its authenticity—for example, the clichéd scenario in war movies in which soldiers radio from behind enemy lines and identify themselves by telling their buddies about a well-remembered poker hand.

A third-party registry of public keys does not really solve Alice's and Bob's problem unless the registry also certifies the accuracy of the information it contains. Suppose that Carol runs an Internet directory service that contains names, e-mail addresses, and public keys. Being a generous person, Carol invites anyone to sign up for free and makes no effort to check the data submitted to her. Alice has no way of knowing whether the entry for Bob was sent in by Bob, or whether it was sent in by Mallet claiming to be Bob. If Mallet sent it in, he will have an entry with Bob's name, Mallet's e-mail address, and Mallet's public key. A directory service alone is thus of little value in providing the assurance as to Bob's identity that Alice wants.[11]

The World Wide Web (Web) introduces some complications into this picture but does not alter the basic substance. Although at this writing it is very difficult for Alice to completely mask the identity of the account accessing a Web page, prototype anonymous Web browsers are currently being developed.[12] Even if Alice does not have access to an anonymous browser, there is no way for Bob to know whether Alice is using an account that can be traced to her, or an account procured under a pseudonym, or a hacked account belonging to someone else entirely. Similarly, in the ordinary course, Bob's Web

---

[10] This is the classic "man-in-the-middle" attack. *Id.* at 48–49.

[11] One method of addressing this problem is the "web-of-trust" approach. *See infra* note 26.

[12] Prototype anonymous Web proxies are in development. *See, e.g.,* Anonymizer FAQ, *available online* URL http://anonymizer.cs.cmu.edu:8080/faq.html.

address identifies his Web page as residing on a particular machine whose physical location can be deduced from information readily available on the Internet,[13] although the address itself is less informative than a telephone number.[14] However, some services sell anonymous Web pages,[15] and Web addresses can be hacked; furthermore, messages to and from a Web server also are at least theoretically subject to a "man-in-the-middle" attack by which message packets are intercepted and replaced with the attacker's messages.[16]

B. Digital Signatures

Public-key systems also allow users to append a *digital signature* to an unencrypted message. A digital signature encrypted with a private key uniquely identifies the sender and connects the sender to the exact message. When combined with a digital time stamp,[17] the message can also be proved to have been sent at a certain time. Anyone who has the user's public key can then *verify*[18] the integrity of the signature. Because the signature uses the original text as an input to the encryption algorithm, if the message is altered in even the slightest way the signature will not decrypt properly, showing that the message was altered in transit or that the signature was forged by copying it from a different message.[19] A digital signature copied from one message has an infinitesimal chance of successfully authenticating any other message.[20]

---

[13] For a more detailed description of these mechanisms, see BRENDAN P. KEHOE, ZEN AND THE ART OF INTERNET (1992), *available online* URL http://www.cs.indiana.edu/docproject/zen/zen-1.0_3.html.

[14] For example, the organization that created www.trilateral.com is (almost certainly) not the real Trilateral Commission. *See* The Trilateral Commission, *available online* URL http://www.trilateral.com (including humorous cites and links to "other conspiracies").

[15] *See, e.g.,* Community ConneXion, The Internet Privacy Provider, *available online* URL http://www.c2.org/web.phtml.

[16] *See* SCHNEIER, *supra* note 9, at 48–49.

[17] *See infra* Part I.D.4.

[18] The Utah Digital Signature Law states that: "Verify a digital signature" means, in relation to a given digital signature, message, and public key, to determine accurately that: (a) the digital signature was created by the private key corresponding to the public key; and (b) the message has not been altered since its digital signature was created.
    UTAH CODE ANN. § 46-3-103(40).

[19] Digital signatures achieve this by computing a *hash value* of the message and then encrypting the hash value with the user's private key. *See infra* text following note 59 (describing hash functions). The recipient checks the digital signature by decrypting the hash value with the sender's public key, then comparing the hash value with the hash value of the file received. If the two numbers are the same, the file is authentic and unchanged. *See* Paul Fahn, RSA Laboratories, Answers to Frequently Asked Questions about Today's Cryptography § 2.13 (1993), *available online* URL http://www.rsa.com/pub/faq/faq.asc.

[20] *See* SCHNEIER, *supra* note 9, at 38 (noting that a digital signature using a 160-bit hash has only a one in 2^{160} chance of misidentification).

Again, however, the utility of a digital signature as an authenticating tool is limited by the ability of the recipient to ensure the authenticity of the key used to verify the signature. If Alice uses her private key to sign an otherwise unencrypted message, Bob can verify that Alice really sent it only if Bob knows Alice's public key.[21] In order to rely on the authenticity of that public key, however, Bob needs to get it from some source other than the "Alice" sending the message, because if Mallet is forging a message from Alice he will send his own public key as well, claiming that it actually belongs to Alice. Since Mallet has the private key corresponding to the public key he sends Bob, Bob's attempt to verify the signature of the forged message will result in a confirmation of the message's authenticity—even though it is not really from Alice at all. In contrast, if Bob has access to Alice's real public key from some outside source, and uses it to verify the message signed with Mallet's private key, the verification will fail, revealing the forgery.

In short, if Alice and Bob are strangers with no alternate means of communication, then no digital signatures, indeed no amount of cryptography standing alone, will reliably authenticate or identify them to each other without the assistance of some outside source to provide a link between their identities and their public keys. Any outside source that reasonably inspires trust will suffice: for example, the telephone company might include its public key in the monthly phone bill, or corporations might publish their public keys in the newspaper. Or the outside source could be a trusted third party such as a mutual friend, a government agency, or a business that offers online verification services.

C. Certification Authorities

A *certification authority* (CA) is a body, either public or private, that seeks to fill the need for trusted third party services in electronic commerce by issuing digital *certificates* that attest to some fact about the subject of the certificate.[22]

---

[21] Even if Bob does not know that the public key belongs to Alice, the key may have value in identifying a series of messages as emanating from a single source calling itself "Alice." This property is particularly valuable in establishing the continuity of a pseudonym in public forums, in preventing "nym collision" (in which two or more parties accidentally use the same pseudonym), or "nym hijacking" (in which Mallet sends messages signed "Alice" in order to free ride on the good reputation "Alice" has accumulated among those familiar with her messages). *See* A. Michael Froomkin, *Flood Control on the Information Ocean: Living with Anonymity, Digital Cash, and Distributed Databases*, 15 PITT. J.L. & COMMERCE (forthcoming 1996).

[22] *See generally* WARWICK FORD, COMPUTER COMMUNICATIONS, SECURITY: PRINCIPLES, STANDARD PROTOCOLS AND TECHNIQUES 93–101 (1994). The International Telecommunications Union defines a CA as a body "trusted by one or more users to create and assign certificates." MICHAEL S. BAUM, U.S. DEPARTMENT OF COMMERCE NATIONAL INSTITUTE OF STANDARDS AND TECHNOLOGY, FEDERAL CERTIFICATION AUTHORITY LIABILITY AND POLICY: LAW AND POLICY OF CERTIFICATE-BASED PUBLIC KEY AND DIGITAL SIGNATURES 5 (1994) (quoting ITU-T, X.509 § 3.3 (1993)).

In order for either Bob or Alice to be willing to accept certificates issued by Carol, a CA, Bob and Alice must have confidence that Carol's public key is really Carol's and not another manifestation of the wily Mallet. One way to achieve this confidence is to have an identifying certificate from Trent, another CA, certifying Carol's key. CAs that certify other CAs are said to participate in a *certificate chain*, with a *root certificate* at the bottom of the tree.[23] Unfortunately, this just shifts the problem to the validity of Trent's CA's public key.

One solution to this problem contemplates a governmental role in certifying the keys of CAs. The root key would belong to a state or federal agency, and the few CAs that met state licensing requirements would be rewarded with government certification of their root key.[24] These CAs would then certify the root keys of organizations that wished to manage their own certificates. A CA might certify the root key of ABC Corp., which would in turn be used to certify the keys of, for example, the key manager in each corporate division, which in turn would certify the keys of salespeople, purchasing agents and press secretaries.

The more levels there are in a certification tree, the more certificates Alice needs to check to ensure that Bob's certificate remains valid. Suppose that Bob's digital signature is supported by a certificate issued by CA1, which has a public key certified by CA2, in turn certified by CA3, which in turn is certified by a state government. If the state government issues a notice of revocation for the certificate of CA3 because, for example, someone has broken its private key, all certificates descending from CA3 are now suspect. If CA3 could say with certainty that its key remained safe until a particular date, then certificates bearing a secure time stamp showing that they were issued before that time would still be reliable.[25] Alice can work all this out, but it takes some computing time, and it may require accessing as many different databases as there are CAs, which also could be costly or time-consuming.[26]

---

[23] Warwick Ford, *Advances in Public-Key Certificate Standards*, SIG SECURITY, AUDIT & CONTROL REV., July 1995, at 9, 10.

[24] *See, e.g.,* UTAH CODE ANN. §§ 46-3-104, 46-3-201.

[25] The time stamp from an outside source is essential. Alice cannot trust a certificate from CA3 that *claims* to have been issued during the safe period because the party forging the certificate could be lying about the time as well. A certificate with an outside time stamp proving that it was issued before CA3's key was compromised can be revalidated by a new, trustworthy certificate from CA3 or any other CA, thereby extending its life span considerably. *See* Dave Bayer et al., *Improving the Efficiency and Reliability of Digital Time-Stamping, in* SEQUENCES II: METHODS IN COMMUNICATION, SECURITY, AND COMPUTER SCIENCE 329, 332–33 (Renato Capocelli et al. eds., 1993).

[26] Certification authorities are not the only means by which strangers can be persuaded to trust each other. An alternate system, called the web-of-trust, blurs the distinction between CAs and users. Every participant in a web-of-trust system is able to issue notices about whom they know and trust, and there is no central authority. In this system, Carol may provide a directory of

The few CAs currently in operation have dealt with the absence of an agreed root certification authority by simply signing their own keys and posting the self-certified key on their Web sites.[27] The self-certified key is then mirrored on other computers.[28] This self-certification, in which the CA relies on its reputation gleaned from other business dealings, fits a model of relatively flat certification hierarchies, in which users turn to CAs, be they suppliers or the U.S. Postal Service, that they already know in other contexts. One expert predicts that the wave of the future will be relatively flat hierarchies, in which organizations have a root certificate for internal purposes that is certified by at most one other CA.[29] It is simply too early to know which certification model will predominate, but it is interesting to consider that today the major indicator of the authenticity of most accountant's and lawyer's opinions provided to third parties is the letterhead (easily forged) and the representation of authenticity by the party proffering the opinion.

---

e-mail addresses and public keys (the *key server*), but if so, she makes no representations at all as to their ownership or authenticity. Users then provide authenticating statements for each other. Typically this is done by meeting face-to-face and showing identification, and then by exchanging public keys signed with their private keys. Alternately, users can exchange "key fingerprints"—a short form of the key that points to the key's location on the key server. If Alice wishes to make it easy for people she has not met to contact her securely, Alice must upload these authentications to the key server. If Alice has her key signed by David, whom Bob knows or trusts, Bob can safely assume that the signature purporting to be from "Alice" is not in fact an impostor's. Suppose, however, that Alice and Bob do not have any friends in common, but that Bob's friend David has signed Ted's key, and Ted has signed Alice's key. From Bob's point of view this is not as good as if David, whom he knows, had signed Alice's key, but it is considerably better than nothing. Bob needs to decide how many intermediaries he is willing to accept before he considers a public key to be unreliable. The increase in the length of the chain of authentication can be offset by finding multiple routes to Alice. For example, Bob may still feel reasonably secure if he can establish three relatively long but independent chains of authentication. *See* Philip Zimmermann, PGP™ User's Guide Volume I: Essential Topics (Oct. 11, 1994), *available online* URL ftp://net-dist.mit.edu/pub/PGP. This web-of-trust approach is the foundation of the PGP encryption system.

The web-of-trust model has the advantage of being independent of any central authority. It has the disadvantage that it requires Alice either to trust strangers when she has no friends in common with Bob or to accept that there are large numbers of people with whom she cannot securely communicate. In contrast, the CA model is designed to make it possible for all strangers to communicate regardless of whether they have any friends in common, and to define with some precision the degree of trust that they can put in the CA's representations about strangers. This chapter discusses CA-based systems, but this is not intended to denigrate the utility of a web-of-trust system. If it is true that all people are within six degrees of separation from each other, the web-of-trust may be a valuable system.

[27] *See, e.g.*, The Sun CA's Certificate, *available online* URL http://www.incog.com/self.html; Internet PCA Registration Authority Root Key Information, *available online* URL http://bs.mit.edu:8001/ipra.html; Netscape Test Certification Authority, *available online* URL http://home.netscape.com/newsref/ref/netscape-test-ca.html.

[28] Mirroring makes Mallet's job more difficult; however, if Mallet is able to filter all messages from Alice's computer to the rest of the world, no amount of mirroring will defeat him.

[29] Warwick Ford, Looking into the Crystal Ball: Certificates Revisited, Presentation at the Worldwide Electronic Commerce Conference (Oct. 20, 1995).

D. Certificates

A *certificate* is a digitally signed statement by a CA that provides independent confirmation of an attribute claimed by a person proffering a digital signature. More formally, a certificate is a computer-based record that (1) identifies the CA issuing it, (2) names, identifies, or describes an attribute of the subscriber, (3) contains the subscriber's public key, and (4) is digitally signed by the CA issuing it.[30]

As a formal matter, a certificate binding a fact to a public key does not need to have a description of the level of inquiry used to confirm the fact. Bob would be foolish, however, to trust a certificate that made no representation, if only through incorporation by reference, as to the nature of the inquiry used. While a zero-inquiry certificate issued by "Certificates-R-Us" is, in some sense, a real certificate, its attestational value is low.

In practice, CAs will probably offer a range of certificates, graded according to the level of inquiry used to confirm the identity of the subject of the certificate. For example, VeriSign, a company that has recently begun advertising its willingness to provide identifying certificates[31] under the unfortunate name of "Internet driver licenses" for the Information Superhighway,[32] proposes four different classes of certificates that will be compatible with Netscape World Wide Web browsers. Class 1 certificates, designed for "casual Web browsing and secure e-mail use," certify only "the uniqueness of a name or e-mail address."[33] VeriSign will issue Class 1 certificates in response to an e-mailed request by the subject.[34] In contrast, VeriSign will only issue a Class 2 certificate, which is more expensive, only after receiving "third party proofing of name, address and other personal information provided in the on-line registration process."[35] To obtain a Class 3 certificate, the subject must pay still more money and appear in person or present "registered

---

[30] *See* Ford, *supra* note 23, at 9. The Utah Act defines a "certificate" as a document that "names or identifies its subscriber." Utah Code Ann. § 46-3-103(3)(B). Arguably, this could be read to limit the reach of the act to identifying certificates. Alternately, one could read the act to say that any certificate that binds an attribute of the subscriber to the subscriber's public key "identifies" the subscriber in some manner. This seems the better reading since the act clearly contemplates certificates other than identifying certificates, and even defines a "transactional certificate" as "a valid certificate incorporating by reference one or more digital signatures," Utah Code Ann. § 46-3-103(37), albeit stating a "transactional certificate is a valid certificate only in relation to the digital signature incorporated in it by reference." Utah Code Ann. § 46-3-103(39)(B).

[31] Identifying certificates are described *infra* Part I.D.1.

[32] VeriSign, Class 1 Digital IDs, *available online* URL http://www.verisign.com/netscape/class1.html. The name is unfortunate because it implies that an identifying certificate is, or should be, a prerequisite to Internet access.

[33] *Id.*

[34] *Id.*

[35] VeriSign, Class 2 Digital IDs, *available online* URL http://www.verisign.com/netscape/class2.html.

credentials."[36] VeriSign also contemplates a bespoke certificate, Class 4, that would be issued after the subject is "thoroughly investigated."[37]

CAs are likely to issue several types of certificates, notably *identifying certificates, authorizing certificates, transactional certificates,* and *time stamps.*

1. Identifying Certificates

An identifying certificate, such as the ones being offered by VeriSign,[38] connects (the technical term is "binds") a name to a public key. The act of the CA in checking that the name corresponds to something in the nondigital world binds the name to an identity. Careful and accurate identification is not a trivial task: the cost of verifying the identities of all holders of U.S. Social Security cards and reissuing the cards would exceed $1.5 billion.[39] Of course, for digital communications, the "name" need not necessarily be either a unique name or even a real name. The "name" could be "Darth Vader X" or "John Smith" or "John Smith, 1000 Main Street, Eugene, Oregon, Social Security Number 123-45-6789." In addition to being stored on computers connected to the Internet, certificates could be stored on smart cards and could be used for issuing driver's licenses and public benefits, or conducting banking and other transactions.

In order to issue a certificate stating that a particular public key belongs to Alice, the CA generates an electronic message containing Alice's name, a statement as to the type of inquiry used to ascertain that the person purporting to be Alice is really Alice, and her public key. The CA signs this message with its private key. What happens next depends on the type of service the CA offers. The CA might publish the resulting certificate on a World Wide Web site available to anyone with Internet access, or give the certificate to Alice, or contract with Alice to honor e-mailed requests for the certificate from all comers. In some cases these choices might affect the legal regime that applies to the CA.[40]

Armed with an identifying certificate from a reputable CA, Alice is in a much better position to persuade Bob that the digital signature she proffers

---

[36] VeriSign, Class 3 Digital IDs, *available online* URL http://www.verisign.com/netscape/class3.html.

[37] VeriSign, Class 4 Digital IDs, *available online* URL http://www.verisign.com/netscape/class4.html.

[38] *See supra* text accompanying notes 32–37.

[39] Lawrence O. Gostin, *Health Information Privacy,* 80 Cornell L. Rev. 451, 459 (1995) (citing *Hearing on the Use of the Social Security Number as a National Identifier before the Subcomm. on Social Security of the House Comm. on Ways and Means,* 102d Cong., 1st sess. 24–25 (1991) (statement of Gwendolyn S. King, commissioner of Social Security, estimating the cost of reissuing the cards from $1.5 to $2.5 billion).

[40] *See infra* Part III.A.1.

really belongs to her and not to Mallet. If the CA is a reputable entity, and if its digital signature on the certificate can be verified,[41] Bob no longer has to trust Alice's electronic word because he now has confirmation from an independent source. Bob's attempt to verify the CA's digital signature requires that he have access to some independent means of ensuring that what purports to be the CA's public key is authentic, and not yet another scam by the cunning Mallet. Since the CA is in the business of providing such assurances, perhaps for a small fee, it may make economic sense for the CA to provide customers such as Alice and Bob with the means to confirm the authenticity of its public key, such as routine publication in a newspaper. The CA might also establish the accuracy of its public key by reference to a special "root" certificate established either by trade usage or by a government agency.

Even a certificate that can be verified is not ironclad proof of an identity. For example, Bob might foolishly have shared the passphrase to his private key with a family member, who then takes advantage of this disclosure to make transactions under Bob's name. Bob's passphrase might have been carelessly chosen and cracked by Mallet. "Bob" might even *be* Mallet if the CA were negligent, or if Mallet is so good at fooling CAs that even the CA's reasonable care was insufficient to penetrate Mallet's deception.

The risks that the reality represented by the certificate is out-of-date can be controlled, but not eliminated, by ensuring that certificates are dated when issued, stated to have limited periods of validity, or be subject to periodic reconfirmation by the CA, and by having Alice check the *certificate revocation list* (CRL)[42] maintained by the CA to warn recipients of certificates known to be no longer reliable. The absence of either rules or usages of trade determining who has a continuing duty to monitor the accuracy of data in certificate means that Alice has to make some difficult decisions. In addition to routinely checking the right CRL, Alice might decide that she will accept only certificates that state that their date of issue was within thirty days. If Alice is extremely cautious, she can decide to accept only certificates that are very recent, maybe less than a day old, or even limit herself to certificates issued within minutes or microseconds. She still bears some risk, but it is reduced.

As for the risk of receiving an erroneous certificate, Alice will have to make a judgment as to which certificates from which CAs she will accept. This decision is likely to be based on the CA's reputation and on the representations that the CA makes about the level of inquiry undertaken to issue a

---

[41] Recall that "to verify" a digital signature is to confirm that the public key associated with the party whose name appears on the message properly produces a numerical result that uses the plaintext as an input to the algorithm. *See supra* notes 19–20 and accompanying text.

[42] *See* Ford, *supra* note 23, at 10. For more on CRLs, see *infra* notes 107–8 and accompanying text.

certificate. To return to the VeriSign example,[43] Alice might decide not to accept "Class 1" certificates but to require at least "Class 2." Or she might decide that there was something about the limitations on liability asserted by VeriSign that displeases her and so choose to refuse all its certificates because she prefers a competitor's promises. Whatever the level of inquiry promised by a CA, however, it is always possible that the CA was negligent or that Mallet simply outsmarted it. For Alice, these are the risks of the trade, much as merchants bear some risk of forged signatures and counterfeit money in more mundane commerce.

2. Authorizing Certificates

Although identifying certificates are likely to be the most popular type of certificate in the short run, in the medium term CAs are likely to begin certifying attributes other than identity. An authorizing certificate might state where the subject resides, the subject's age, that the subject is a member in good standing of an organization, that the subject is a registered user of a product, or that the subject possesses a license such as bar membership. These authorizing certificates have many potential applications. For example, law professors exchanging exam questions on the Internet could require that correspondents demonstrate their membership in the Association of American Law Schools (AALS) before being allowed to have a copy of the questions.

It is illegal to export high-grade cryptography from the United States without advance permission from the federal government,[44] but there are no legal restrictions on the distribution of strong cryptography to resident aliens or U.S. citizens in the United States. The lack of a reliable means to identify the geographic location of a person from an Internet address creates a risk of prosecution for anyone making cryptographic software available over the Internet.[45] For example, if Alice is making high-grade cryptography available for distribution over the Internet, she might protect herself from

---

[43] *See supra* notes 32–38 and accompanying text.

[44] *See generally* International Traffic in Arms Regulations, Pub. L. No. 90-629, 90 Stat. 744 (codified at 22 C.F.R. §§ 120–130 (1995)) (ITAR). The ITAR are administered by the Office of Defense Trade Controls in the State Department. If the State Department chooses, it can transfer jurisdiction of an export application to the Commerce Department. The statutory authority for the ITAR is the Arms Export Control Act (codified as amended at 22 U.S.C. § 2778 (1994)).

[45] Whether such a prosecution could succeed is a question beyond the scope of this chapter. Since the instruction to download software is issued by the recipient's computer, an argument can be made that the "export" is committed by the recipient, not the owner of the software. In any case, the risks incident to being a test case are substantial: up to a $1 million fine and ten years in jail. 22 U.S.C. § 2778(c) (1994).

considerable risk by requiring that Bob produce a valid[46] certificate from a reputable CA, stating that he is a U.S. citizen or green card holder residing in the United States, before allowing him to download the cryptographic software.

Alice substantially reduces her risk under the ITAR by requiring Bob to produce an authorizing certificate demonstrating his citizenship, but even this does not eliminate her risk. Alice's major remaining risks are that: (1) the CA's statement was erroneous; (2) Bob has lost control of his digital signature and it has fallen into the hands of Mallet, who is not a U.S. citizen or permanent resident, or is abroad; and (3) something about Bob has changed since he procured the certificate, for example, he has moved abroad, has lost his citizenship or green card, or has died and his private key is held by his executor or heir.[47]

A certificate binding the geographic location, age, or other attribute to a public key can contain the name of the subject of the certificate, but the public key suffices if it was generated in a secure manner and is sufficiently long to be unique. Nameless, anonymous certificates create the possibility for sophisticated anonymous Internet commerce. For example, persons wishing to purchase materials that can be sold only to adults might obtain "over 18" certificates that bind this attribute to a public key but do not mention their name.[48] Similarly, a financial institution might issue a certificate linking a public key to a numbered deposit account.

3. Transactional Certificates

A third type of certificate, the transactional certificate,[49] attests to some fact about a transaction.[50] Unlike an identifying certificate or an authorizing certificate, a transactional certificate is not designed to be reused or to bind a fact to a key. Instead, the certificate attests that some fact or formality was witnessed by the observer. For example, if Alice is a lawyer officiating at a

---

[46] For a discussion of what "valid" means in this context, see *supra* text following note 42.

[47] Succession creates special problems for any system based on public-key cryptography. Any means Bob uses to create a backup copy of the passphrase to his private key introduces a new risk to his security. On the other hand, robust social protocols akin to those currently used in banking are needed to permit an executor or heir to enter into transactions that have been designed to require Bob's digital authorization.

[48] For an example of an anonymous age credentialing service targeting persons seeking access to "over 18" Web services, see Validate, *available online* URL http://www.zynet.com/~validate/services.html.

[49] Transactional certificates are sometimes referred to as *attesting certificates* or *notarial certificates*.

[50] The Draft ABA Digital Signature Guidelines define a "transactional certificate" as a "certificate for a specific transaction incorporating by reference one or more digital signatures." ABA Draft Guidelines, *supra* note 4, § 1.30.

digital closing, and Bob is her client, Bob can digitally sign a document. Alice then issues a certificate attesting that Bob digitally signed it in her presence. The certificate might contain the text of the document,[51] Bob's digital signature of the document, and Bob's public key, all of which would be signed with Alice's private key. The resulting certificate would be evidence that Bob affixed his signature in Alice's presence.[52] A transactional certificate of this type might suffice to transmit a deed to a public official for recordation.[53]

The differences between Alice's transactional certificate and Alice's digitally signed confirmation that she received Bob's document are primarily legal rather than technical. Indeed, from a cryptographic perspective, a transactional certificate is little more than an ordinary electronic document digitally signed with the CA's private key.

The potential legal differences are many and varied. First, the act of affixing the signature likely will carry with it the type of formality associated with a closing, or perhaps even with a notarial act in a civil law country. Indeed, the American Bar Association and the U.S. arm of the International Chamber of Commerce are exploring the creation of an American legal specialization to be known as a CyberNotary®.[54] A CyberNotary would be a lawyer able to demonstrate that she has the ability to issue certificates from a trusted computing environment. The hope is that civil law jurisdictions will come to accept a CyberNotary's certification as legally sufficient authentication and recordation of legal acts executed in the United States. If so, a power of attorney or the transfer of corporate shares certified by a CyberNotary in the United States would be recognized and enforced in those jurisdictions, even when an ordinary U.S. lawyer's or U.S. notary's certification would not suffice.[55]

Second, a certificate will typically contain representations by the CA as to the level of inquiry conducted by the CA, or will at least incorporate a general policy statement by reference. In contrast, an ordinary digital signature adds no content to the message being signed.

Third, the CA may add link information to the document being signed, such as a secure time stamp from a trusted time-stamping service.[56]

---

[51] Or, in some cases, a hash value, *see infra* text following note 59, and a pointer to the actual document.

[52] This example is drawn from the ABA Draft Guidelines, *supra* note 4, § 1.30.3.

[53] *See id.*

[54] In 1994 the Council of the ABA Section of Science and Technology resolved that its Information Security Committee should work with the ABA Standing Committee on Specializations to draft a proposal for ABA accreditation of the CyberNotary as recognized legal specialization. ABA Section of Science and Technology Section Minutes (Aug. 8, 1994) (copy on file with author). For updated information on the CyberNotary project, see Theodore Sedgwick Barassi, *The CyberNotary: Public Key Registration and Certification and Authentication of International Legal Transactions, available online* URL http://www.intermarket.com/ecl/cybrnote.html.

[55] *See* Barassi, *supra* note 54.

[56] *See infra* Part I.D.4.

Fourth, by issuing a transactional certificate, a CA subjects herself to a completely different, and arguably far more benign, liability regime than does a CA who issues an identifying certificate. A transactional certificate is by nature a single-purpose certificate. While an unlimited and unknowable number of third parties may rely on it, the nature of their reasonable reliance is largely, perhaps completely, within the control of the CA. A lawyer who officiates at a closing, for example, might certify that she examined corporate documents and that the corporate officers were duly authorized to enter into the transaction; this is no different from what lawyers engaging in due diligence do today. It is, however, different from issuing an identity or creditworthiness credential to a person who might then use it to run up an unlimited amount of debt or other obligations.

4. Digital Time-Stamping Services

A *time stamp* is a cryptographically unforgeable digital attestation that a document was in existence at a particular time. It is not difficult to show that a document existed after another event: one need only include a reference to something that happened earlier, which could not have been predicted before it happened.[57] For example, before it became easy to doctor images, kidnappers could demonstrate that their victim was still alive by photographing him holding the front page of a newspaper. Sometimes, it is enough to prove that a document was signed or an event occurred after a given date, as in statute-of-limitations questions. Often, however, it is equally (if not more) important to show exactly when it happened, or to prove that it happened before another date. If Alice quotes the headlines in last Tuesday's newspaper, it proves that she wrote the document no earlier than last Tuesday, but it gives Bob no way of telling whether she wrote it on any of the days since then. The "creation date" or "modification date" appended to documents by many word processing systems is also of little or no evidentiary value since it is a trivial matter to alter these dates, or to change the time on a computer's internal clock.[58] Alice's digital signature on the document tends to show that Alice wrote it and that no one else has altered it, but the signature adds nothing to the credibility of Alice's claim as to when she wrote it.

The only way to prove beyond doubt that a document was created before a certain time is to "cause an event based on the document, which can be

---

[57] Bayer et al., *supra* note 25, at 329. *See generally* Charles R. Merrill, The Digital Notary™ Record Authentication System—A Practical Guide for Legal Counsel on Mitigation of Risk from Electronic Records (June 22, 1995) (footnote omitted from title) (unpublished manuscript, on file with author).

[58] *See, e.g.*, Rudolph J. Peritz, *Computer Data and Reliability: A Call for Authentication of Business Records under the Federal Rules of Evidence*, 80 Nw. U. L. Rev. 956, 960 (1986).

observed by others."[59] If Alice publishes the text of her document in the newspaper, she can prove that it had to exist at the time it was published. This is expensive, uses a lot of newsprint, and destroys Alice's privacy. A better method is for Alice to publish a *hash value* of her document. A hash value is a large number produced by a *hash function* that takes the entire document as its input. The hash functions used in this manner have three properties that allow them to serve as a kind of fingerprint for a document. First, hash functions are public—anyone can repeat the calculation if he or she has the original document. Second, the hash function is a *one-way function*: if Alice sends Bob a file purporting to be the document that produced a hash value she published in the newspaper five years ago, Bob can easily confirm that the document's hash is the same, but possession of the hash value alone does not allow anyone to re-create the document. Third, although it is not impossible for two different documents to produce the same hash value, the odds against it are so high as to make this probability infinitesimal.[60] Therefore, even a slight alteration to a document will change its hash value, making it essentially impossible for Alice to create a document with the same hash value as the one whose hash value she published in the past. Even if Alice were to put supercomputers to work to find another set of bits that produced the same hash value as the original digital document, there is no chance at all that this document would have letters and numbers in an order that produced intelligible text.

Of course, for most transactions it is impractical to rely on publication in a newspaper for authentication. This creates a business opportunity for CAs. Carol, a CA, can provide a simple time-stamping service by providing an attesting certificate that Alice sent Carol a hash value of a document at a certain time.[61] Carol might automate the process by having an Internet service that returned a dated and digitally signed certificate every time a subscriber sent her a hash value. Alice does not have to trust Carol with her data, because all Carol ever sees is the hash value. Now Bob no longer has to take Alice's word for when she wrote the document; he only need believe that Carol is telling the truth about Alice. If Carol is a reputable CA, her certificate may inspire this trust. If Bob is very mistrustful, however, he may be concerned that the system would fall apart if Alice can persuade Carol to backdate a time stamp.

A more secure method of time-stamping documents exists. In this system Bob does not have to trust Carol because there is no way for her to backdate a time stamp. Rather than simply signing the hash value of Alice's document,

---

[60] *See* Schneier, *supra* note 9, at 30–31.
[61] *See id.* at 76.

Carol sends Alice a digitally signed document reciting the hash values of Alice's document, the hash values of the last few documents submitted for time-stamping and the e-mail addresses of their owners. Now the only way to forge a time stamp is to suborn both Carol and many other users of the system. A weekly summary hash of the "tree" of the many documents submitted is published in the Sunday *New York Times* and is therefore unchangeable.[62] It is currently being marketed by its inventors as the "Digital Notary™."[63]

II. INTERNET COMMERCE: FRAUD'S PLAYGROUND?

Judging by the low amount of civil fraud (as opposed to crime) to date, the Internet's reputation as fraud's playground is undeserved. Yet this may be the rare case in which expectations accurately predict a possible future. While there may be a great deal of Internet advertising and information exchange, there are still relatively few transactions for value over the Internet. As the amount of Internet commerce grows, the opportunities for fraud may grow unless security and authentication measures also grow.

The CA's role in identification and authentication is particularly important for transactions that have effects which extend over time. In basic consumer transactions, where something is exchanged for money, there may be no need for certificates—a credit card suffices, with the issuer fulfilling the role of the third party. If the goods are not forthcoming or if they are other than they were represented to be, the customer can simply stop payment. If the goods are satisfactory, ordinarily the customer does not care whether the seller was who he or she claimed to be.

The picture changes dramatically, however, as soon as the transaction has lasting effects. If the communications are part of an ongoing relationship such as instructions to a broker, or if the terms of sale allow payments to be delayed, or if there is any question of a warranty or service contract, the parties have a much greater interest in identifying and authenticating each other.

A. Simple Sales

Although estimates vary, it is widely agreed that electronic commerce over distributed networks, such as the Internet, is set for explosive growth. One

---

[62] *See* Bayer et al., *supra* note 25, at 331–32.

[63] *See* Surety Technologies Homepage, *available online* URL http://www.surety.com; SCHNEIER, *supra* note 9, at 78–79; Merrill, *supra* note 57.

guesstimate suggests that approximately 16 percent of consumer purchases may be electronic transactions by the turn of the century,[64] a date now less than five years in the future. Definitions of electronic commerce differ; this chapter concentrates on commercial activities such as sales and negotiations carried out over insecure distributed networks such as the Internet.

Internet commerce presents challenges that are not present, or are present in nearly harmless form, in traditional transactions carried out face-to-face. These problems include the following:

<u>Basic Transactional Issues</u>

• How to move value.

• How to ensure that communications are secure from eavesdroppers.

<u>Merchant's Desires</u>

• Authentication: Knowing the buyer's identity before making the sale may assist in proof of order and guarantee of payment. The merchant also may wish to build up a database of customers and their buying profiles.

• Certification: The merchant may need proof that the buyer possesses an attribute required to authorize the sale. For example, some goods may be sold only to those licensed to use them; other goods require that the purchaser be over eighteen. Some products cannot be sold in some parts of the country, and others cannot be exported.

• Confirmation: The merchant needs to be able to prove to any third party involved in the transaction (such as a credit card company) that the customer did indeed authorize the payment.

• Nonrepudiation: The merchant wants protection against the customer's unjustified denial that he or she placed the order, or that the goods were not delivered.

• Payment: The merchant needs assurance that payment will be made. This can be achieved by having payment before sale, at the time of sale, or by provision of a payment guarantee. A credit reference by a trusted third party provides a lesser form of assurance, but it at least demonstrates that the buyer is capable of making the payment.

---

[64] Kelley Holland & Amy Cortese, *E-Cash Could Transform the World's Financial Life: Where E-Cash Will Take Off*, Bus. Wk., June 12, 1995, at 66, 70.

- Anonymity: In some cases the merchant may want to control the amount of transactional information disclosed to the customer.

Buyer's Desires

- Authentication: Confirming the seller's identity prior to purchase helps ensure that goods will be genuine and that service or warranties will be provided as advertised.

- Integrity: Protection against unauthorized payments.

- Recourse: Comfort that there is recourse if the seller fails to perform or deliver.

- Confirmation: A receipt.

- Privacy: Control over the amount of buyer/transactional information disclosed to third parties.

- Anonymity: Control over the amount of transactional information disclosed to the merchant.[65]

Cryptographers would have us believe that most of the problems on this list that arise from Internet commerce and are not present in physical commerce can be solved, and the good news is that this is largely correct. The bad news, unless you happen to be a lawyer, is that the cryptographic solutions currently available are not simply mathematical. They frequently rely on the intervention of a trusted third party who is a certificate-issuing CA. Issuing certificates entails the creation of new entities, new businesses, and new relationships for which the duties and liabilities are currently uncertain.

The law of sales is complex, as the many sections of the Uniform Commercial Code (UCC) testify. Shifting any sale to an electronic medium can add further complexity. To better understand the nature of the new problems posed by electronic commerce, and the ways in which they are reduced by the introduction of a trusted third party, it helps to begin by considering this list of issues in the context of an extremely simple sale, one that includes no documents of title and in which both goods and payment (or a promise to pay that functions as a close substitute, for example, a check or credit card transaction) are exchanged by face-to-face parties contemporaneously with the moment of contract formation.

---

[65] This list is an adaptation and simplification of the more formal and extensive list in Mihir Bellare et al., *ikp—A Family of Secure Electronic Payment Protocols* (July 12, 1995), *available online* URL http://www.zurich.ibm.ch/Technology/Security/publications/1995/ikp.ps.

1. Face-to-Face Sales

When Alice, a buyer, purchases food at the local grocery store from Bob, the merchant, in a face-to-face sale, there is no problem with moving value: Alice tenders paper money and coin,[66] food stamps, or, if Bob permits it, Alice may choose to write a check, pay with an ATM card, a debit card, a credit card, or even in some cases buy "on account." Ordinarily, there is no particular need to ensure that the transaction is secure from Mallet, an eavesdropper, since there is little that Mallet could do with the information and even less that Mallet could do to hurt either Alice or Bob.[67] However, on the occasions when Alice and/or Bob would desire privacy or anonymity, they might find these difficult to obtain.

The documentation of the transaction differs slightly depending on whether it is a cash sale, or if there is a third party involved such as a bank or credit card company.[68] If there are just two parties, Alice and Bob typically keep copies of a receipt. If there is a third party, additional documents are generated, such as a check, an electronic ledger entry and a paper receipt in the case of an ATM card, or a credit card slip.[69] These pieces of paper also serve as proof of order in the unlikely event that it is questioned. Similarly, each of these payment mechanisms has well-developed ways of ensuring that consumers are protected from unauthorized payments.[70] On the other hand, buyer repudiation and nonpayment are issues in face-to-face commerce. A cash payment cannot easily be repudiated, but it may be counterfeit. A check can be dishonored by the bank, and under U.S. law, embodied in Regulation E, Alice has the right to contest a credit card payment up to two months later.[71]

---

[66] Payment in paper money or coin may create a demand for change. Problems may ensue if Bob lacks the correct change.

[67] If Alice is careless, Mallet might be able to obtain Alice's credit card receipt, obtain her credit card number, and use it to run up charges on her credit card.

[68] The discussion in the text greatly simplifies reality to underline the differences between face-to-face commerce and electronic commerce. In the ordinary check sale, there may well be multiple banks, since at a minimum, the check is likely to be drawn on one bank, deposited to a second, and cleared by a third. Similarly, some credit card transactions involve multiple parties.

[69] There is a significant difference between "on-line" clearance, in which Bob checks that the credit/debit card has sufficient credit/funds before authorizing the purchase, and "off-line" clearance, in which the purchase is not recorded with the credit card company until after the fact. In either case, transaction recording and customer profiling are possible if an electronic payment mechanism is used.

[70] For example, Alice's cash cannot be paid out unless it is stolen; checks cannot be drawn unless Alice's signature is forged, and even then the bank may have a duty to refuse payment. The holder of a credit card or debit card is only liable for the first fifty dollars fraudulently charged to the card. 15 U.S.C. § 1643(a)(1)(B) (1994); 12 C.F.R. § 205.6(b) (1995) (limiting consumer liability to $50 for most unauthorized electronic funds transfers).

[71] *See* 12 C.F.R. § 205.6(b)(2)(ii).

Because physical goods are exchanged in a physical place, Alice has a number of indicators that suggest, although they do not prove, that she will have recourse in the event that the purchase is not satisfactory. First, Alice knows where the store is: its physical presence suggests that Bob may have assets that can be attached, even if only a lease and the contents of the shop.[72] The accessibility of the store's physical location also makes it easier for an irate customer to create bad publicity, either in the store itself or in the store's community, creating a further incentive for Bob to resolve any difficulty.[73] Furthermore, knowing the location of the store gives Alice an indication of the legal system that is likely to have jurisdiction over any conflict.

The physicality of the transaction also protects Bob. If authorization is required, Bob can demand that appropriate documents be displayed (for example, proof of age, unless Alice's appearance seems sufficient proof), and he can examine the credentials for authenticity. Bob also has some protection in the event that the transaction goes badly. Seeing Alice offers some chance of providing a description (or a store camera video) in the event of nonpayment or fraud. The face-to-face aspect of the relationship means that in many cases,[74] Alice will have to return the goods to claim reimbursement. Thus, typically Alice will be unable to continue to enjoy the products after claiming a refund.

2. Telephone Sales

Telephone sales lack the face-to-face aspect of a sale in a store. As a result, the parties are likely to have less knowledge about each other. In addition, telephone sales, like catalog sales, introduce a time lag between the order and its fulfillment, during which many things can go wrong: the goods may be discovered to be different from what the buyer had imagined they would be, the goods may spoil or be damaged in transit, either party may change its mind or become insolvent, and so on.[75]

The party who placed the call obviously knows the number she dialed, although if Alice calls Bob via an 800 number, that telephone number alone reveals little or nothing about Bob's location.[76] The recipient of the call may also

---

[72] The shop suggests, but does not prove, that Bob has attachable assets, since these assets may be encumbered by liens and mortgages with priority.

[73] Other than bad publicity, most jurisdictions limit Alice's self-help remedies in the event of a dispute.

[74] Consumables, perishables, and easily copied materials excepted.

[75] The UCC supplies a large variety of techniques that address each of these problems, and more. *See generally* RICHARD E. SPEIDEL ET AL., SALES AND SECURED TRANSACTIONS 452–60 (1993).

[76] Indeed, some firms, notably airlines, commonly switch calls from 800 numbers to operators located abroad. Catherine Cleary, *Telemarketing Harnesses Technology and Blarney*, IRISH TIMES, Dec. 29, 1995, at sec. 3, supp. 7 (LEXIS, News Library, Curnws file).

know the calling party's number if caller ID is available. Indeed, calls to an 800 number automatically disclose the number of the calling party.[77] If Bob uses a database indexing telephone numbers to addresses, credit histories, or buying patterns, he may have considerable information about Alice regardless of who places the call. On the other hand, if Alice is an ordinary consumer, her information about Bob will depend largely on sources extrinsic to the call (for example, catalogs, advertising, prior dealings) and the firm's reputation, if any. In addition, returning goods or getting redress may be more difficult with a faraway party. Not only may the relevant legal system be inaccessible or expensive to access, but Alice's inability to bring her complaint to the attention of other shoppers reduces her bargaining power with Bob.

Although impersonation is certainly possible at the grocery store,[78] it is easier over the telephone. Lacking the ability to verify signatures or identify the physical characteristics of the buyer, Bob runs an increased risk of making sales to persons using stolen credit card numbers (although this risk is attenuated by using on-line clearing). Similarly, because it is difficult to verify identity over the telephone, Alice runs an increased risk that the person claiming to be Bob is actually Mallet.

Although value cannot be exchanged by cash or check at the time of sale, mailed payment can be a prerequisite to shipment. As a practical matter, consumer telephone sales tend to be made by debit or credit card because this medium of payment gives the merchant considerable assurance of Alice's ability to pay, but not necessarily a guarantee that payment will actually be made. The credit card company's inability to ensure nonrepudiation[79] becomes a positive advantage because Alice can transact knowing that payment can be suspended if Bob, or the person claiming to be Bob, fails to perform in some material way. Similarly, the ability to repudiate transactions means that while the call may be subject to eavesdropping or diversion, these acts are of limited value to a third party so long as Alice checks her credit card bill carefully for unauthorized purchases.[80]

3. Internet Sales

Internet sales are likely to take two general forms: ordinary commerce in tangible things and information commerce. Ordinary commerce in tangible

---

[77] *See* Edmund L. Andrews, *New Rules Are Approved for Nationwide Caller ID*, N.Y. TIMES, May 5, 1995, at D5.

[78] As the volume of trademark infringement suits demonstrates, goods as well as people can be inauthentic.

[79] *See supra* note 71.

[80] Typically, merchants do not receive payment from a credit card sale until the repudiation period has passed.

things will greatly resemble common transactions today: purchases that are currently carried out by telephone, ordinary mail (for example, catalog sales), and even in person. Ordinary rules of commercial law presumably will continue to apply to these transactions, subject to one vital difference: without taking some special measures to identify each other, the parties will be saddled with a risk that their counterpart will not be who she professes to be. Transactions that use a telephone require that someone dial a telephone number. The use of that telephone number implicates a record that ultimately could identify the party called. In some cases the number alone will provide the identification; in other cases it may be necessary to invoke the aid of the legal process, or of the telephone company. Nevertheless, the telephone number provides some kind of link to a physical presence, for at least one of the two parties to the communication.[81] An Internet e-mail address, by contrast, gives the recipient no reliable information about the person sending the message.

Information commerce is more of a departure from traditional sales. It has the immediacy of a face-to-face transaction, but little mutual identifying information need necessarily be exchanged. In information commerce, unlike ordinary commerce in tangible things, there may be no package to help identify the sender after the goods are delivered. Instead, both parties will conduct the exchange electronically: the buyer will send digital cash, and the seller will send information.[82] Some of these transactions may be sizable, such as the sale of access to proprietary databases or the purchase of computer software, but others are likely to be very small. For example, providers of information on the World Wide Web might choose to charge a fraction of a penny to each person accessing their pages.[83] Browsers may be configured to pay these charges, up to a predefined limit, without ever troubling the user. Existing credit card systems are too expensive for such microcharges.[84] Microcommerce in information will require a digital payment system that does not rely on the (expensive) participation of a third party such as a credit bureau or credit card issuer.[85] If such a payment system could be widely

---

[81] The call record may also identify the caller, but this is less certain. The caller could place the call from a pay phone.

[82] Whether the exchange is performed simultaneously or in series is up to the parties.

[83] *See* Arnold Kling, *Banking on the Internet, available online* URL http://www.e1c.gnn.com/gnn/meta/finance/feat/archives.focus/bank.body.html.

[84] *See, e.g.,* Electronic Cash, Tokens and Payments in the National Information Infrastructure § 1.1, *available online* URL http://www.cnri.reston.va.us:3000/XIWT/documents/dig_cash_doc/ElecCash.html. The average U.S. credit card purchase today is $60. *Id.*

[85] Steve Glassman et al., *The Millicent Protocol for Inexpensive Electronic Commerce, available online* URL http://www.research.digital.com/SRC/millicent/papers/millicentw3c4/millicent.html, argues that even digital coins are too expensive for microtransactions, and that a new form of "scrip" needs to be deployed for microtransactions. Proposals for two schemes that may meet the exacting requirements of efficient microtransactions can be found in Ronald L. Rivest & Adi Shamir, *Payword and MicroMint: Two Simple Micropayment Schemes* (Apr. 3, 1996), *available online* URL http://theory.lcs.mit.edu/~rivest/RivestShamir-mpay.ps.

deployed, the potential for growth of Internet information commerce is enormous.

Identifying or authenticating certificates can provide all the information that a party might reasonably want for both information commerce and ordinary commerce in tangible things. Whether it makes sense to require a certificate at all depends on the amount of the transaction, the mode of payment, and the cost and delay associated with use of a certificate. Of course, even when it makes sense to use a certificate to verify identifying information about a transactional counterpart, this serves only to restore the parties to an informational position akin to what is commonplace in other more familiar transactions. It does not in any way reduce the need for the existing, and complex, rules about consideration, delivery, breach, title, security interests, fraud, or any of the myriad other issues addressed by the UCC and other commercial and criminal law.

a. Transactional Issues: Moving Value and Authentication   If Alice has no hardware available to her other than her computer,[86] she can choose to move value to Bob across the Internet with a debit card, a credit card, or electronic cash.[87]

(1) Debit Cards and Credit Cards   Today, the simplest way for Alice to pay Bob across the Internet is to use a debit card or credit card. This payment mechanism has the great virtue of familiarity. It uses established mechanisms to apportion risk of nonpayment and repudiation. Although it is vulnerable to eavesdropping, the risk may be smaller than commonly believed.

If Alice sends out unencrypted credit card information on the Internet, she takes a chance that a third party will intercept the information. To date, however, there are no reported cases of credit card information acquired by eavesdropping on an Internet transaction being used to make a purchase.[88]

---

[86] Smart cards, sometimes called electronic wallets, also can be configured to be stores of value. Rather than digital cash embodied in "coins" that are a series of numbers in a cryptographic envelope, an electronic wallet contains a counter that records the amount of money held on the card. Movement of value on and off that counter can be hedged with a number of cryptographic safeguards. For example, cards can be programmed to only accept value from cards that properly identify themselves. Smart cards can be used to transfer value across the Internet if both parties to the transaction have smart cards or the equivalent, and both have computers outfitted with appropriate card readers. For a taxonomy of smart card types, see David Chaum, *Prepaid Smart Card Techniques: A Brief Introduction and Comparison*, *available online* URL http:// ganges.cs.tcd.ie:80/mepeirce/Project/Chaum/cardcom.html.

[87] One can also imagine other, less practical, systems, including barter transactions, by which Alice and Bob exchange services or digitizable products (software, poems).

[88] In contrast, in one incident, credit card information belonging to more than 20,000 customers that had been stored in an insecure database was compromised. *See* JONATHAN LITTMAN, THE FUGITIVE GAME 325, 348 (1996) (reporting apparent copying of credit card records by Kevin Mitnick).

When one considers that the same credit card information is easily available to every employee of every merchant who accepts credit and debit cards, and can be acquired by examining paper credit card slips retained by any restaurant or dumped in the trash at any mall, it is easy to see why few people go to the considerably greater trouble of attempting to obtain credit card numbers by monitoring large volumes of Internet traffic.

If Alice wants greater security, she can encrypt her credit card data before sending it. Similarly, Bob may want assurances that Alice is who she purports to be. Bob may want Alice to send her order encrypted with her private key, thus uniquely identifying the order as emanating from her. For a greater level of security, Alice and Bob may require that identifying certificates from a reputable CA accompany the exchange of public keys.[89] On the other hand, since the debit/credit card issuer/administrator fulfills some of the functions of a trusted third party already, and charges the same commission regardless of whether Alice and Bob exchange certificates, they may decide to take the risk.[90]

Although debit and credit cards are the easiest means of transferring value over the Internet, and require little if any legal innovation, they have some disadvantages as well. Neither debit nor credit cards are suited to small transactions because verification and clearing impose significant fixed costs on every transaction.[91] Because one of the most likely applications of Internet sales is microcharges—pennies or fractions of a penny—for the right to view information such as a World Wide Web page, this inability to handle tiny transactions strongly suggests the need for an alternate payment mechanism. Furthermore, the utility of credit and debit cards is critically dependent on the continuing applicability of the consumer's liability being capped at fifty dollars in the event that a credit card number is copied in transit or misused by the recipient. Without the fifty-dollar limit, Alice would face an enormous danger of her credit card information going awry, either because Mallet managed to penetrate Bob's security and copy all messages as they were sent to Bob's store, or because Mallet fooled Alice into sending him the credit card information by pretending to be Bob, or because Bob was careless and Mallet hacked his database. Any change in this regulatory regime would

---

[89] Alternately, Alice and Bob may find each other's public keys on a keyserver that is part of the National Information Infrastructure; the keyserver may itself demand a valid certificate as a condition of the listing, or it may contain (optional?) pointers to the databases where the certificates reside.

[90] The risk is not negligible; the consumer risks a fifty-dollar charge, 12 C.F.R. § 205.6(b), and considerable hassle, plus potential damage to a credit rating. The merchant takes the risk of nonpayment since the credit card company will not pay the merchant if the customer fails to pay.

[91] *See, e.g.,* Stefan Brands, Centrum voor Wiskunde en Informatica (CWI), *Offline Electronic Cash Based on Secret-Key Certificates* 1–2 (Report CS-R9506 1995), *available online* URL ftp:// ftp.cwi.nl/pub/brands/CS-R9506.ps.Z.

cause Alice, and indeed all consumers contemplating electronic transactions, to need both encryption and authentication.[92]

(2) Electronic Cash   Electronic cash implementations vary.[93] While generalizations are hazardous, most true digital cash systems that are entirely software-based (for example, do not rely on a smart card or other physical token to provide authentication or to store value) use some variation of the "digital coin." A digital coin is a sequence of bits, perhaps signed with an issuing financial institution's private key, that represents a claim of value.[94]

Software-based digital coins are potentially suitable for small transactions, such as charging a penny or less to view a Web page, where credit cards would be prohibitively expensive.[95] Unfortunately, since bits are easy to copy, digital coin schemes require fairly elaborate mechanisms to prevent a coin from being spent more than once. One method of preventing double spending is to require that coins be cleared in real time. If Alice offers a coin to Bob, Bob immediately accesses the issuing bank to make sure that the coin is valid and has not previously been spent.[96] A necessary consequence of this protocol is that if Alice uses a digital coin to pay Bob, Bob cannot spend it directly. Instead, Bob must either deposit the coin in an account at the issuer or turn it in for another digital coin or conventional money.[97] An on-line clearing system can be configured to ensure that the bank does not know who gave Bob the coin (payor anonymity), but the bank will know that Bob received the coin (no payee anonymity).

While Bob might clear large payments from a single source on-line by making a real-time connection to the bank to ensure that the coins have not

---

[92] Whether Regulation E should apply to electronic money has been a matter of some debate in Congress. *See, e.g., Bill's EFTA and Reg E Exemptions Need Reworking, Blinder Tells Panel,* BNA BANKING DAILY, Oct. 12, 1995, at *2 (Lexis, News library, Curnws file). ("Blinder said that he could support an extensive, and perhaps blanket exemption from Reg E for stored-value cards of $20, but that there are questions about whether such an exemption is appropriate for large amounts transferred over computer networks.")

[93] *See, e.g.,* PETER WAYNER, DIGITAL CASH: COMMERCE ON THE NET (1996) (surveying a large number of existing and proposed systems); Froomkin, *supra* note 21, at Part III.B.2 (surveying fewer systems in more detail).

[94] *See generally* Froomkin, *supra* note 21, at Part III.B.

[95] Charging and payment might be built into the browser. Alice might program her browser to pay any fee up to a set amount, say two cents, without asking for confirmation. Glassman argues that even digital coins are too expensive for microtransactions, and that a new form of "scrip" needs to be deployed for microtransactions. *See* Glassman et al., *supra* note 85.

[96] One U.S. financial institution currently offers a "DigiCash" implementation with real money. *See* Mark Twain Banks, Providing Global Investment Solution, *available online* URL http://www.marktwain.com.

[97] *See* David Chaum, *Achieving Electronic Privacy,* Sci. Am., Aug. 1992, at *1–2, *available online* URL http://ganges.cs.tcd.ie/mepeirce/Project/Chaum/sciem.html (discussing electronic cash); Ecash Homepage, *available online* URL http://www.digicash.com/ecash/ecash-home.html.

previously been spent, this may be impractical and uneconomical for transactions measured in pennies or less. Instead, Bob will accumulate a hoard of small digital coins and send them to the bank to clear in batch lots. This off-line clearing opens a window of opportunity for unscrupulous parties to engage in multiple spending. In order to forestall this, a bank issuing coins that will be redeemed off-line is likely to require that Alice encode some identifying information about herself onto the coin. The system can be set up so that no one, not even the bank, can read this information so long as Alice spends the coin only once. A second attempt to spend the coin will disclose Alice's identity and allow the issuer to sue her for fraud and perhaps report her to the authorities for criminal charges of fraud or theft.[98] Barring a complex money-laundering protocol,[99] Bob cannot respend this type of coin either, and must turn it into the bank just as if it had been cleared on-line.[100]

This feature reduces the need for Alice and Bob to exchange certificates; in essence, the digital coin carries its own certification. If Bob is particularly concerned about the possibility of double spending, or if the percentage of respent coins being tendered to Bob reaches unacceptable levels, Bob may choose to restrict even his microsales to parties that can provide an identifying certificate. Bob's decision will turn in part on the cost and delay associated with a certificate as opposed to the cost and delay of having the bank help him trace double spenders.

b. Confirmation Issues: Proof of Order, Nonrepudiation, Receipt, and Recourse

All that Alice needs in order to prove that Bob made a promise to buy or to pay is a message including the promise signed with Bob's digital signature.[101] The issue of proving the promise is separate from whether a digital signature is a "signature" for legal rules that require that a writing bear a signature.[102] Alice will find it less cumbersome to prove Bob's promise if she has access to a certificate, valid at the time of Bob's promise, that links Bob to the signature appearing on the message. However, a certificate may

---

[98] If the coins are cleared off-line, and the double-spender has received value from the payee, then there is clearly theft from the payee. Whether the double spender can be charged with attempted theft from the bank may depend on whether the relevant jurisdiction allows prosection for attempted "impossible" crimes. Since in most protocols the bank checks the validity of every coin before exchanging it for value, there was no possibility that it would actually suffer a loss; the offense against the bank is thus "impossible," and in some jurisdictions arguably noncriminal.

[99] *See infra* text accompanying notes 102–4.

[100] *See* Froomkin, *supra* note 21, at part III.B.3.

[101] Electronic writings ordinarily satisfy the Statute of Frauds. *See* John R. Thomas, Note, *Legal Responses to Commercial Transactions Employing Novel Communications Media*, 90 MICH. L. REV. 1145 (1992); Merrill, *supra* note 57, at 3. A digital time stamp may add evidentiary value. *Id.* at 1.

[102] Whether a digital signature is a "signature" is beyond the scope of this chapter. *See generally* BENJAMIN WRIGHT, THE LAW OF ELECTRONIC COMMERCE § 16 (2d ed. 1995).

not be strictly necessary, depending on the payment mechanism and the nature of the transaction.

Debit and credit cards leave an information trail that can assist Alice in finding Bob, and vice versa. Because a payor might have an anonymous or pseudonymous debit/credit card,[103] or because a payee might have disappeared in the time since the transaction was recorded, the trail is not perfect. However, the trail of information is significant, and not much different from what would likely be in a certificate, so it is likely to make the certificate somewhat redundant.

Digital cash can be designed to protect the anonymity of the payor who does not double spend. A prudent payee who is tendered digital cash with this anonymizing feature may seek an identifying certificate from the payor if the transaction makes it important to know her. As most digital cash schemes do not protect the anonymity of the payee, the payor will request an identifying certificate only if the cost of the certificate is less than the expected value of the cost of persuading the bank to release the payee's identity on an occasion where this might be needed, adjusted for the danger that the payee will get away before being identified. The cheaper and quicker it is to use a certificate, the more likely it will be used.

The introduction of a coin laundry service that offered payees an opportunity to exchange coins anonymously would greatly increase the payor's need for a certificate from the payee. A coin laundry would break the guaranteed link between the identity of the payee and the coin, whether or not Bob actually avails himself of the service. If Alice knows that Carol's coin exchange is in business, Alice will have to be more wary about sending coins to Bob, a stranger. Now, if Bob takes the coin and defaults on the transaction, it is no longer obvious that the bank will be able to identify Bob when Alice asks it to reveal who redeemed her coin. If the bank tells her that the coin was redeemed by Carol's money-changing service, and Carol's service is located in a foreign jurisdiction, perhaps one with strong bank secrecy laws,[104] Alice may find it very difficult to find out who Bob really is and where he lives. In these circumstances, Alice may find that she wants an identifying certificate from Bob after all.[105]

---

[103] For a description of how to obtain an anonymous credit card, *see, e.g.,* Vaxbuster, *Safe and Easy Charging,* 4 PHRACK Issue 44, File 20, *available online* URL http://-www.fc.net:80/phrack/files/p44/p44-20.html.

[104] Banks are increasingly unwilling to provide truly anonymous bank accounts. *See, e.g.,* William W. Park, *Anonymous Bank Accounts: Narco-Dollars, Fiscal Fraud, and Lawyers,* 15 FORDHAM INT'L L.J. 652, 668–69 (1991–92). Governments are increasingly unwilling to allow banks based within their regulatory reach to offer this service, in part because of the Council of Europe Money Laundering Convention whose reach extends beyond Europe. *See* EuroWatch, *Banking Secrecy: Liechtenstein Signs European Money Laundering Convention* (July 28, 1995) (LEXIS News library, Curnws file).

[105] I am greatly indebted to Hal Finney for alerting me to this scenario.

Consumers will have an increasing need for anonymous commerce as merchants become more adept at assembling computerized databases on their customers, and as these databases themselves become valuable commodities.[106] Anonymous certificates are likely to play an essential role in anonymous commerce since they will help induce parties to trade with one another when they are unable to identify each other.

B. Ongoing Transactions

As we have seen, there is a somewhat reduced need for a CA's services when payment and goods are exchanged simultaneously, although the need for a trusted third party is not eliminated. In part this is because the payment schemes already incorporate a trusted third party—the credit card company or the digital cash issuer—who is likely to be capable, if pushed, of providing some identification of the defaulting party in the event the transaction goes badly.

In contrast, any communication in which the exchange of funds and goods is not immediate, or which looks either backward or forward in time, creates a strong and continuing need for authentication and/or identification. For example, if Alice has an account with a broker, Bob, both Bob and Alice have a strong interest in ensuring that any buy or sell order regarding Alice's account be from Alice and no one else, and that this fact be easily provable should it ever be called into question. Similarly, parties negotiating on the Internet will want to ensure that they know who they are communicating with in order to keep secrets from their rivals. No supplier will wish to accept orders for goods that are sold on terms that allow payment at a future date, even from a regular customer, without assurances that the key used to sign the order is one belonging to a person authorized to place the order.

It is important to recall that, much like in the nonelectronic world, the authentication/identification problem in these circumstances has two parts. Bob wants a certificate showing that Alice is who she says she is and/or that Alice is authorized to do what she wants to do. In addition, Bob needs an assurance that the certificate issued to Alice remains valid. Alice could have left her job as purchasing agent, or she could have discovered that someone has learned her passwords. In the nonelectronic world, customers frequently take these things on faith; in the electronic world, such faith is less reasonable and thus likely to be less frequent.

In order, therefore, to be willing to rely on a certificate issued to Alice for transactions of any value, Bob needs easy access to a CRL[107] that will allow

---

[106] *See* Froomkin, *supra* note 21, at part IV.

[107] *See supra* text accompanying note 42 (describing the Certificate Revocation List).

him to establish that Alice's certificate has not been revoked or suspended. When Alice shows Bob her certificate (or when Bob contacts Carol to get a copy of Alice's certificate) Bob—or Bob's software—will check to see whether the certificate has been revoked,[108] much like credit cards are checked against lists of suspended cards today. Bob thus needs an easy way to identify and get access to the CRL that would list Alice's certificate if there were something wrong with it. And every CA needs an efficient and reliable means of communicating its CRL to potential users of certificates.

Fortunately, the means for achieving these ends are now at hand. The recognized standard for certificates is the X.509 standard maintained by the International Telecommunications Union (ITU).[109] Previous editions of this standard defined a relatively rigid and inflexible form for a certificate, one that was not well suited to the legal requirements of digital commerce. In particular, neither the original X.509 standard nor the revision known as X.509 (ver 2) made provisions for a certificate to carry information about the CRL. Instead, the original X.509 standard provided information about how to contact the CA, and the user was expected to be able to use this information either to identify the CRL or to contact the CA for more information.[110] A recent change in the X.509 standard, now known as X.509 (ver 3), solves these problems. The new standard defines a data location where a CA can put information that will allow Bob to find the CRL quickly, such as the Internet address (URL) of the applicable CRL.[111] The new standard, which is being mirrored in standards developed by ANSI X9 (which adopts standards for banks) and ISO/IEC, also includes a data field in which a CA can insert information about how to find the policies that apply to the certificate, such as the level of inquiry undertaken before issuance.[112]

III. THE DIFFICULTY OF IDENTIFYING THE RIGHTS AND DUTIES OF PRIVATE CERTIFICATION AUTHORITIES

As electronic commerce grows, it will become increasingly important to define the rights and duties of CAs. This will not be an easy task, particularly

---

[108] A certificate also might be suspended for a brief period, pending inquiries as to whether it should be revoked. A prudent CA that received an emergency telephone call asking that a certificate be revoked might suspend it while waiting for proof that the person making the request had the authority to do so. *Cf.* Utah Code Ann. §§ 46-3-306, 307 (providing for suspension of a certificate).

[109] Ford, *supra* note 23, at 9. The ITU was formerly known as the Consultative Committee on International Telephony and Telegraphy (CCITT).

[110] *Id.* at 10, 11.

[111] *Id.* at 12–14.

[112] *Id.* at 13.

once electronic commerce becomes more international. International transactions intensify the problems caused by the divergences between legal systems and tend to raise the stakes in choice of law.[113] "The consumer cannot and indeed *will* not participate effectively in the . . . market where economic and legal conditions are obscure."[114] Although international issues are beyond the scope of this chapter,[115] identifying and applying the relevant substantive law can be a moderately complex problem even when the focus is restricted to one state in the United States.[116]

The duties and potential liabilities imposed on private[117] CAs by U.S. law are unclear, as might be expected from the dearth of applicable legislation,[118] the complete absence of case law, and the very small number of currently functioning CAs. Legislation attempts to provide clarity: the Utah Digital Signature Act provides for a safe harbor against most liability for those CAs who qualify. No CAs have qualified to date, and the act in any event does not define the duties and liabilities of CAs who do not qualify for the safe harbor.[119] Clarification of the duties and liabilities of these CAs in the absence of legislation should thus serve the interests of all parties to an electronic transaction in which a certificate plays a role. As other legislatures debate whether to enact digital signature laws of their own, they may find it helpful to have a better understanding of the legal background against which they are working. This section seeks to begin a discussion of that background by addressing a sample problem: Who, under existing law, is liable for an erroneous certificate?

The importance of clarifying a CA's liabilities will grow further if one aspect of the recently passed Utah Digital Signature Act becomes a national model. If Alice wants to persuade a jury that the pen-and-ink ("holographic") signature on a contract or note is in fact Bob's, but Bob claims that it is a forgery, Alice must bear the burden of proving that Bob's signature is genuine. Digital signatures are nearly impossible to forge, and the Utah Digital Signature Act thus reverses the presumption of authenticity for digital

---

[113] Peter Sutherland, *The Internal Market after 1992: Meeting the Challenge, Report to the EEC Commission by the High Level Group on the Operation of Internal Market* (1992), identified consumer uncertainty as a major impediment to the realization of a single European market.

[114] Stephen Weatherill, *The Role of the Informed Consumer in European Community Law and Policy*, 2 CONSUMER L.J. 49, 59 (1994).

[115] For a discussion of the likely reception of digital signatures in Canadian law, see Serge Parisien, *Aspects Juridiques et Technologiques des Mécanismes de Signature Électronique: Une Analyse Comparative*, available online URL http://www.droit.umontreal.ca/Palais/Invites/AQDIJ/Colloque_10_11_95/Parisien/parisien_udm.html.

[116] Because this chapter already exceeds the length limits suggested by the editors of this symposium volume, it does not include any discussion of choice of law issues.

[117] For a discussion of the liabilities of a public CA, see BAUM, *supra* note 22.

[118] *See supra* note 4.

[119] *See supra* notes 6–8. As this chapter went to press, Utah was joined by the State of Washington. *See supra* note 4.

signatures. Under the Utah Act, a digital signature that can be verified by a valid certificate is presumed to belong to the subscriber listed in the certificate.[120]

Utah's presumption means that Alice can have greatly increased confidence in the enforceability of Bob's digital signature so long as Alice can verify Bob's digital signature with a valid certificate issued by a registered CA. This increased confidence could be of great value in everything from automated microtransactions to large international transactions where the parties are strangers.

On the other hand, the presumption creates a danger for a consumer who loses control of his or her digital signature. Although implementational details will vary, most digital signatures are likely to be protected with at least a passphrase, a more complex version of the PIN number that protects most bank cards today. Some digital signatures may require both a passphrase and a hardware token (for example, a smart card), or even the passphrase, the hardware token, and a biometric authentication (for example, a thumbprint scan). In the absence of the most heroic biometric security measures, however, the consumer is at risk that someone will acquire the hardware token and either guess the passphrase or obtain it by eavesdropping or some other means. If this happens, the Utah legislation creates a spectre of unlimited liability that can only be capped once the consumer reports that the digital signature has been compromised. Since there is likely to be a lag between loss of control of the signature and discovery of that fact, a reasonable consumer might well choose to avoid this risk by not creating a digital signature at all.[121] Utah's presumption seems considerably less unreasonable when applied to large, sophisticated organizations using the signatures for substantial transactions.

A. Liability for Erroneous Certificates

Inevitably, certificates will issue with false statements, and third parties will rely on them to their detriment. In the absence of much state[122] or federal regulation, it will fall to the courts to determine who should bear the liability when this happens. They will have a difficult task.

1. Is a CA Selling a Good or a Service?

The difficulties in determining a CA's duties and liabilities begin with how one characterizes the CA's provision of a certificate. Is the CA providing an

---

[120] Utah Code Ann. § 46-3-406 (1996).

[121] *See* Benjamin Wright, Eggs in Baskets: Distributing the Risks of Electronic Signatures, *available online* URL http://www.sig.net/~jbc/signatur.html.

[122] *See supra* note 4 for a summary of state legislation to date.

investigative "service" of which the certificate is an embodiment or memorial—much like a lawyer's opinion letter or a valuer's opinion—or is the certificate that the CA is selling a "good," or is the transaction a mixture of a good and a service? The characterization determines whether Article 2 of the Uniform Commercial Code (UCC) applies to the CA's provision of a certificate.

If the CA is selling a "good," then Article 2 of the UCC applies.[123] If Article 2 applies, it brings with it a menu of default rules, as well as provisions for statutes of limitation and express and implied warranties including, in particular, the implied warranty of merchantability[124] and the warranty of fitness for a particular purpose.[125] Article 2 of the UCC also imposes limits on the disclaimers of those warranties.[126] Article 2 of the UCC is not, however, uniform in ways that would matter greatly to CAs, their customers, and relying third parties. For example, section 2-318 of the UCC offers states a choice of three different rules governing the seller's warranty liability to third parties. One version of section 2-318 limits the run of the CA's warranties to persons in the family or household of the buyer[127] but leaves the common law unchanged as to the effect of the warranty on "other persons in the distributive chain."[128] A CA in such a state will have whatever liability to third parties the common law of the state imposes: for example, the liability for negligent misrepresentation discussed later. The UCC's second version of section 2-318 extends the run of the CA's warranties to all natural persons "who may reasonably be expected to use . . . or be affected by the goods."[129] CAs subject to this provision will find that they are subject to warranty claims for "defective" (that is, erroneous) certificates to all natural third parties, since the reliance of such third parties could reasonably be expected. The UCC's third version of section 2-318 includes artificial as well as natural persons among the third parties who can make warranty claims.[130] CAs in such states will provide the certificates that should, all other things being equal, command the most trust; they also will face the largest potential liability. The problem from the point of view of a person trying to decide whether a certificate is reliable is that they

---

[123] U.C.C. § 2-102 (1994); *see also* note 132.

[124] U.C.C. § 2-314.

[125] U.C.C. § 2-315. An example of a claim under section 2-315 might be against a CA that had provided a certificate signed with an insecure key or a key known to be compromised.

[126] *See* JAMES J. WHITE & ROBERT S. SUMMERS, UNIFORM COMMERCIAL CODE ch. 12 (4th ed. 1995).

[127] U.C.C. § 2-318, alternative A. This alternative is the most commonly used of the three. WHITE & SUMMERS, *supra* note 126, at 392 n.3.

[128] U.C.C. § 2-318, cmt. 3.

[129] U.C.C. § 2-318, alternative B. This alternative is the least frequently used of the three, but it has been adopted in six states. WHITE & SUMMERS, *supra* note 126, at 393 n.6.

[130] U.C.C. § 2-318, alternative C. This alternative, or some form of it, is used in at least eight states. WHITE & SUMMERS, *supra* note 126, at 393 n.7.

will not necessarily know which of these provisions happen to apply unless the certificate tells them. In addition to the three official versions of section 2-318, a number of states use formulations of their own, further complicating matters.[131] If the UCC applies to the sale of a certificate, this lack of uniformity could impose a large burden on Bob when Alice asks him to accept Carol's certificate. Unless Bob and Alice happen to live in the same state as Carol, they will need to know which state's law applies, and whether that state's law allows Bob to take comfort from Carol's express and implied warranties about the reliability of her certificate.

If, on the other hand, the CA is selling a "service," then the UCC Article 2 is by its own terms inapplicable.[132] It is not obvious that Article 2 should apply to the provision of a certificate. UCC section 2-105(1) defines "goods" as "all things . . . which are moveable at the time of identification to the contract for sale other than the money in which the price is to be paid, investment securities . . . and things in action."[133] Since a certificate is highly movable, it might seem to be a "good" under this definition. This temptation should be resisted: a certificate is only a little closer to the classic definition of a "movable good" than is a surveyor's or valuer's report. A certificate resembles a professional's opinion in that a certificate ordinarily is the tangible memorial of a process of analysis in which the subject's credentials were checked in some manner. On the other hand, a certificate differs from a professional's opinion in some ways that may be relevant. Any trustworthy CA will be managed by a professional—someone who knows how to run a trustworthy computer system—but it is not inevitable that the actual checking of credentials in all cases will be the sort of activity traditionally undertaken by professionals. If Carol's certificates are founded on checking the subject's passport, it may well be that the person who actually examines Alice's passport and issues her certificate is a clerk who has been trained in passport authentication, not an expert like a surveyor or valuer. There is no policy reason, however, why the classification of a certificate as a good or service should turn on whether the person making the report happens to be a professional. Furthermore, the certificate is not the only thing that the CA sells. In addition to the certificate and the investigatory services that it embodies, the CA also maintains (or contributes to) a CRL, without which a certificate is untrustworthy and thus of little or no value.[134]

---

[131] WHITE & SUMMERS, *supra* note 126, at 393 n.8.

[132] *See* U.C.C. § 2-102 ("Unless the context otherwise requires, this Article applies to transactions in goods. . . ."). Proposed revisions to Article 2 may extend its coverage to include "service contracts." *See* Raymond T. Nimmer, *Intangible Contracts: Thoughts of Hubs, Spokes, and Reinvigorating Article 2*, 35 WM. & MARY L. REV. 1337, 1374, 1389 (1994). This change would greatly increase the likelihood that Article 2 applies to the provision of a certificate.

[133] U.C.C. § 2-105(1).

[134] *See supra* text accompanying notes 107–8.

Courts may, however, with some justice, view the CA's role as combining elements of provision of a service and the sale of a good. In such "mixed" cases, courts consider the applicability of Article 2 of the UCC to be a question of fact concerning the nature of the transaction. If the seller is providing a hybrid of a good and a service, the majority of states use a "predominant factor" test to determine whether Article 2 of the UCC should apply.[135] Under this test, the court attempts to determine the parties' intentions as to what was important. If the transaction is predominantly for the sale of goods, Article 2 of the UCC applies; otherwise it does not.[136] Other states either use a "final product" test, which looks at what is left when a contract is completed,[137] or attempt to determine which classification best serves public policy.[138] As the courts have failed to achieve anything approaching uniformity in how they characterize the facts about mundane transactions,[139] it is entirely possible that courts in different jurisdictions will disagree about how best to characterize a CA's provision of certificates in the absence of legislation. Furthermore, some courts divide hybrid sales into the provision of a "good" and a "service" and then apply Article 2 of the UCC to the "goods" portion of the transaction.[140] CAs may be able to manipulate this characterization in some jurisdictions. For example, a CA that gives a client a certificate may be more likely considered to be selling a "good" than a CA that enters into a "service contract" by which the CA agrees to make the certificate available on a Web page to all who wish to see it.

The view that a CA is providing a service (or a hybrid in which the service element predominates) appears more convincing than the alternative under either the "predominant factor" test or the "final product" test.[141] Although it is true that a CA provides a "movable" thing to the client, that thing is digitized information[142] that is essentially useless without other

---

[135] WHITE & SUMMERS, *supra* note 126, at 3–4.

[136] *Id.; see also* Crystal L. Miller, Note, *The Goods/Services Dichotomy and the U.C.C.: Unweaving the Tangled Web*, 59 NOTRE DAME L. 717 (1984).

[137] Miller, *supra* note 136, at 726.

[138] *Id.* at 728–29.

[139] *See* 1 RONALD A. ANDERSON, ANDERSON ON THE UNIFORM COMMERCIAL CODE § 2-105:51 (3d ed. 1981); Miller, *supra* note 136, at 717–20.

[140] *See* WHITE & SUMMERS, *supra* note 126, at 3–4.

[141] Whether this result best serves public policy is a difficult question, one that may become easier to answer once certificate-based electronic commerce becomes more commonplace and CAs have more of a track record.

[142] One issue in this context is whether that information is an "intangible" since it is generally but not universally agreed that Article 2 of the UCC does not apply to intangibles. Several writers have argued that the UCC should apply to software, even though it has properties that make it appear to be an "intangible." *See, e.g.,* Andrew Rodau, *Computer Software: Does Article 2 of the Uniform Commercial Code Apply?*, 35 EMORY L.J. 853 (1986); Bonna L. Horovitz, Note, *Computer Software as a Good under the Uniform Commercial Code: Taking a Byte Out of the Intangibility Myth*, 65 B.U. L. REV. 129 (1985). Indeed, the courts that have spoken on this issue appear to be in

supporting information provided by the CA on a continuing basis. To issue a certificate worthy of trust, the CA must: (1) have a valid and verifiable certificate of its own; (2) conduct the inquiry on which the certificate will be based; (3) accurately state facts in the certificate, including both the facts about the subject and the facts about the CA's investigation; and (4) maintain a CRL.[143] The CA's continuing duty to maintain the CRL in a form that can be rapidly and efficiently used by persons wishing to rely on a certificate is in itself significant evidence that the service element predominates in what the CA is selling. On the other hand, a CA that does no investigation at all and/or a CA that does not maintain a CRL may not be providing a "service." In that case, there is a real question whether the "good" being offered is fit and proper for its purpose.

Article 2 is being revised to extend its reach to "intangibles" such as computer software and data.[144] Thus, even if a certificate is outside the scope of Article 2 today, it does not necessarily follow that it will be outside the scope of Article 2 as ultimately revised. Nevertheless, so long as the revisions do not extend Article 2 to services, the argument that the service aspect of maintaining the CRL predominates over the sale of data as a "good" should remain valid.

A decision that a CA provides a service does not resolve all the ambiguities about a CA's liabilities in the absence of legislation, but it does provide a framework in which questions can be asked and answered. The next section briefly examines one of the ways in which a CA might face liability in the absence of a statute or other norms defining the rights and duties of a CA in order to demonstrate the legal complexities created by the introduction of a CA into a transaction. Of course, some scenarios are easy: if a CA is willfully or grossly negligent, or a CA conspires with the subject of the certificate, the CA should obviously be liable for its acts and omissions. Other scenarios, beyond the scope of this preliminary exploration, are not as straightforward. These include the following:

- The certificate is accurate, but the transaction goes wrong for some other reason.[145]

---

general agreement that the UCC should apply to software. *See* Mark A. Lemley, *Intellectual Property and Shrinkwrap Licenses*, 68 S. CAL. L. REV. 1239, 1249 n.38 (1995) (noting that "most courts and commentators have concluded that distribution of mass-market software constitutes a sale of goods, thus invoking the UCC"). It could be argued that a certificate on a disk is more "tangible" than a certificate on a Web site, but this privileges form over substance.

[143] ABA Draft Guidelines, *supra* note 4, § 3.11 cmt. 4.

[144] *See* Nimmer, *supra* note 132.

[145] A CA should not be liable for the ways in which accurate certificates may be used by others. Both the Utah Digital Signature Act and the draft ABA Guidelines create a safe harbor from liability for a CA that has made accurate representations and complied with certain other requirements. *See, e.g.,* UTAH CODE ANN. § 46-3-304(4)(a) (providing for subscriber's indemnification of CA against claims due to subscriber's misrepresentation); *id.* § 46-3-309(2) (creating safe harbor against liability in excess of reliance limit stated in certificate for licensed CAs and limiting

- The security of Alice's key is compromised and Mallet uses it, along with Alice's publicly available certificate, to impersonate Alice.[146]

- Alice revokes her key because she learns of Mallet's actions, but Mallet manages to transact during the period between Alice's revocation notice to Carol and Carol's posting of a certificate revocation.[147]

- The security of Carol's key is compromised, and Mallet begins issuing bogus certificates or bogus certificate revocations.[148]

- Carol erroneously lists Alice's key as revoked, and Bob refuses to transact with Alice.[149]

- The "meltdown scenario": there is a major discovery in number theory or computation, and the algorithms on which Alice's and Carol's keys are based are no longer secure.

2. Misrepresentation, Whether Willful or Negligent, of CA's Client, Not Detected by CA

Assume that Alice makes a negligent or willful misrepresentation when procuring a certificate from Carol, a CA. The misrepresentation might be about Alice's identity, or her credit rating, or her employment. Carol fails to detect the misrepresentation. Alice then uses the certificate to transact with Bob, but either fails to pay or defrauds Bob in some manner. Assume further, for simplicity, that Bob can show that his reliance was reasonable,[150] that he

---

recovery in tort to compensatory damages). As a general matter, this makes sense: there is no reason why a CA should be involved in Alice's securities claim against Bob if the CA's only involvement was to provide accurate identifying certificates for the people involved. Of course, a different result would be appropriate if the CA provided an attesting certificate that was materially misleading. Different rules might arguably be appropriate for certain consumer transactions.

[146] Unless Alice and Carol have made a special arrangement, a CA should have no duty to monitor the use of a certificate that they have agreed will be publicly available. Once notified of a key compromise, a CA should have a duty to publish this in the CRL "quickly." ABA Draft Guidelines, *supra* note 4, § 3.11 cmt. 4.

[147] Presumably the critical issue in this scenario will be whether Carol acted quickly enough. The common-law approach to this problem would rely on usages of trade, but it is difficult to do this when (1) there is as yet no "trade" to speak of, and (2) technology is changing very rapidly.

[148] Liability here may in part depend on how the key was compromised. There are differences between an inside job, penetration of Carol's systems by a hacker (perhaps due to bad security), an extraordinarily lucky brute force attack on Carol's key, advances in key-cracking technology (which raise the question whether these advances should have been anticipated), or Carol's failure to update her keys.

[149] This scenario resembles a bank dishonoring a check when there are sufficient funds in an account or a credit card clearer erroneously reporting that a credit limit has been exceeded or the card stolen.

[150] The degree to which Bob's reliance actually was reasonable may turn on a number of factors. One of the most important is the content of the certificate itself. If the certificate states that it should not be relied on for transactions over $5, Bob's reliance on the certificate for a $1 million transaction is unreasonable.

would not have transacted with Alice but for her presentation of a verifiable certificate, and that the misrepresentation was material to the transaction.

If Carol made representations in the certificate as to the level of the inquiry used to verify Alice's claims about herself, the first issue is whether Carol should have detected Alice's misrepresentation given the promised level of inquiry. If Carol's practice statement proudly advertises that certificates are handed out to all comers, without any checking whatsoever, it is difficult to see how Carol could justly be accused of any form of negligence, assuming she accurately parroted Alice's claims, as long as it remains unreasonable to assume that all CAs conduct a minimum level of verification of their customers' assertions.[151] At this early stage in the development of certificate-backed electronic commerce, there are no usages of trade that might help define the standard of care that one might expect of a CA. There are, at present, no licensing or professional bodies whose standards could serve as the basis for a legal norm.[152] Perhaps someday CAs, like doctors and lawyers, will not be allowed to disclaim a minimum degree of investigation, or will only be allowed to disclaim after getting the client to acknowledge informed consent based on reading harrowing disclosures of the risks, but in the short term the representations contained in the certificate itself are likely to be the starting—and ending—point for defining the CA's duty to investigate.[153]

If, however, Carol claims that her certificates only go to people she has "thoroughly investigated,"[154] it may be reasonable to find that she was negligent in issuing the certificate containing the false information submitted by Alice. By asserting that she conducted an independent investigation, Carol negates any defense she may have as a mere republisher of Alice's statement.[155] And if Bob has reasonably relied on Carol's certificate to his detriment, Carol may be liable to Bob under either contract or tort principles.[156]

a. Liability in Contract for Negligent Misstatements

Carol's potential contractual liability depends in part on with whom she has a contract.

---

[151] *But see supra* notes 141–43 and accompanying text (suggesting that a CA who makes no representations as to service may be selling a "good" subject to UCC because no service is provided).

[152] A document such as the proposed ABA Digital Signature Guidelines, *see* ABA Draft Guidelines, *supra* note 4, may in time come to play this role.

[153] For a discussion of the similar problem of defining negligence in the absence of established usages of trade for Internet security professionals, see Michael Rustad & Lori E. Eisenschmidt, *The Commercial Law of Internet Security*, 10 HIGH TECH L.J. 213, 243–52 (1995).

[154] *See supra* text accompanying note 37.

[155] Unless they have reason to know of the errors, publishers and book distributors are not liable for errors in works they publish and sell. *See, e.g.*, ALM v. Van Nostrand Reinhold Co., 480 N.E.2d 1263 (Ill. App. 1985) (dismissing negligence claim against publisher of allegedly unsafe "how-to" book); Cardozo v. True, 342 So. 2d 1053 (Fla. Dist. Ct. App.) (holding UCC did not make book dealer liable to purchaser of cookbook for lack of adequate warnings as to poisonous ingredients used in recipe), *cert. denied*, 353 So. 2d 674 (Fla. 1977).

[156] Other remedies are available if Article 2 of the UCC applies. *See supra* part III.A.1.

Carol's contract may be with Alice, the subject of the certificate, or it may be with another party, such as Alice's employer. But Carol does not have a contract with Bob, Alice's victim, who is the person most likely to sue. Nor does she have a contract with David, who was impersonated by Alice.

(1) **Liability to Alice** If Alice benefited from Carol's error, she is unlikely to sue. If the error hurt Alice in some way, Alice's claim turns on Carol's failure to detect Alice's own error. In such cases, Alice's recovery is likely to be limited by her breach of contract in misinforming Carol. Even if Alice were able to persuade a court to grant her compensation, the measure of damages is likely to be restitution (that is, whatever Alice paid for the certificate) since she appears to have neither a reliance interest nor an expectation interest.[157]

(2) **Liability to Alice's Employer** Carol may have issued Alice's certificate at the request of Alice's employer, TED Corp. By failing to detect the falsity of Alice's claim that she was TED's vice president in charge of purchasing when in fact she was a file clerk, Carol may have breached her contract with TED Corp. If Alice used the certificate in a way that harmed TED Corp., perhaps by buying tickets to Rio, TED Corp. has a contract claim against Carol, although Carol again may have a partial defense of contributory negligence on the part of TED Corp.'s apparent agent, Alice, and possibly against anyone else at the company who may have corroborated her claims. Again, the measure of damages is likely to be restitution, since there is neither a reliance interest nor an expectation interest, although this time the amount of the contract may be somewhat larger.

(3) **Liability to Bob, Whom Alice Defrauded** Bob's hope of recovering under the contract between Carol and Alice (or Alice's employer) turns on his ability to characterize that contract as a third-party beneficiary contract of which he was an intended beneficiary.[158] Bob's ability to so characterize himself may also affect his right to recover in tort in states that adhere to a strong privity rule.[159]

Traditionally, Bob's hopes would have been slim. The first Restatement of Contracts divided third-party beneficiaries into three classes: "donee beneficiaries," "creditor beneficiaries," and "incidental beneficiaries."[160] Incidental beneficiaries have no contractual right against either party to the contract.[161]

---

[157] *See* L. L. Fuller & William R. Perdue, Jr., *The Reliance Interest in Contract Damages*, 46 YALE L.J. 52 (1936) (defining three types of contractual interests).

[158] *See* RESTATEMENT (SECOND) OF CONTRACTS § 302 (1979); David M. Summers, Note, *Third Party Beneficiaries and the Restatement (Second) of Contracts*, 67 CORNELL L. REV. 880 (1982).

[159] *See* Gary Lawson & Tamara Mattison, *A Tale of Two Professions: The Third-Party Liability of Accountants and Attorneys for Negligent Misrepresentation*, 52 OHIO ST. L.J. 1309, 1319 (1991).

[160] *See* Restatement of Contracts § 133 (1932).

[161] *Id.* § 147.

Bob is not a creditor beneficiary because the purpose of the contract between Alice and Carol is not to confer a gift on him. According to the first Restatement, Bob is a donee beneficiary when "it appears from the terms of the promise in view of the accompanying circumstances that the purpose of [Alice] in obtaining the promise . . . is . . . to confer upon [Bob] a right against [Carol]" that Bob would not otherwise have.[162] While it is certainly correct that Alice procured the certificate from Carol in order to show it to people like Bob and that this type of use was foreseeable, ordinarily there would be little reason to believe that Carol knew or should have known that Alice intended to show the certificate to Bob. In the era when privity reigned, Bob would not have been able to claim to be an intended beneficiary of the agreement without being specified as such when Alice procured the certificate.[163]

Today, the picture is murkier.[164] "The *Restatement First* test, the intent-to-benefit test and its variations, and the *Restatement Second* tests are all inadequate and indeed largely meaningless."[165] Courts have relaxed the privity requirement in contract, as in tort,[166] replacing it with tests such as

> the balancing of various factors, among which are extent to which the transaction was intended to affect the [beneficiary], the foreseeability of harm to him, the degree of certainty that the [beneficiary] suffered injury, the closeness of the connection between the defendant's conduct and the injury, and the policy of preventing future harm.[167]

Nevertheless, courts remain reluctant to allow everyone to be a potential third-party plaintiff in contract actions.[168]

---

[162] *Id.* § 133(1)(a).

[163] *See, e.g.*, Ultramares Corp. v. Touche, 174 N.E. 441, 445 (N.Y. 1931) (Cardozo, J.). Cardozo wrote:

In the field of the law of contract . . . the remedy is narrower where the beneficiaries of the promise are indeterminate or general. Something more must then appear than an intention that the promise shall redound to the benefit of the public or to that of a class of indefinite extension.

Id.; Moch Co. v. Rensselaer Water Co., 159 N.E. 896, 897 (N.Y. 1928) (Cardozo, J); Restatement of Contracts § 145 (1932); *see also* Restatement of Contracts § 147 ("An incidental beneficiary acquires by virtue of the promise no right against the promisor or the promisee.")

[164] *See* Harry G. Prince, *Perfecting the Third Party Beneficiary Standing Rule under Section 302 of the Restatement (Second) of Contracts*, 25 B.C. L. Rev. 919 (1984) (summarizing wide variety of judicial responses to third-party benefit claims).

[165] Melvin A. Eisenberg, *Third-Party Beneficiaries*, 92 Colum. L. Rev. 1358, 1385 (1992).

[166] *See* William L. Prosser, *The Fall of the Citadel (Strict Liability to the Consumer)*, 50 Minn. L. Rev. 791 (1966) [hereinafter *Fall of the Citadel*]; William L. Prosser, *The Assault upon the Citadel (Strict Liability to the Consumer)*, 69 Yale L.J. 1099 (1960).

[167] Lucas v. Hamm, 364 P.2d 685, 687 (Cal. 1961) (citing Biakanja v. Irving, 320 P.2d 16, 19 (Cal. 1958)), *cert. denied*, 368 U.S. 987 (1962).

[168] *See, e.g.*, Eisenberg, *supra* note 165, at 1374; Summers, *supra* note 158, at 893. Note that the breach by Alice of her contractual promise to tell the truth may not inevitably prevent recovery from Carol by a third party. *See* Lewis v. Benedict Coal Corp, 361 U.S. 459 (1960). *But see* Restatement of (Second) of Contracts § 309(1)–(2); Eisenberg, *supra* note 165, at 1413 n.188.

Bob's position is not much clarified by the Restatement (Second) of Contracts, which provides that a third party may enforce a contract if he is an "intended beneficiary," that is, "if recognition of a right to performance in the beneficiary [Bob] is appropriate to effectuate the intention of the parties and . . . the circumstances indicate that the promisee [Alice] intends to give the beneficiary the benefit of the promised performance."[169] Whether the contract between Alice and Carol was for Bob's benefit or for Alice's depends entirely on how one chooses to look at it. Alice procures the certificate in order to induce Bob to transact with her. Alice wants Bob to rely on the certificate; perhaps Carol does also since this enhances the market for her product.[170] But Alice wants Bob to rely because it benefits her, not because it benefits him. The glass is either too empty or too full. Either the holder of the certificate, Alice, is the intended beneficiary because the certificate gives her something to show to Bob, or Bob is the intended beneficiary because without the benefit he will not transact with Alice.[171] Either no third party is intended or they all are.

(4) Liability to David, Whom Alice Impersonated   Suppose that Alice persuades Carol to issue a certificate stating that Alice is David, an innocent third party. Alice then uses this certificate to defraud Bob, or just runs up a large number of debts she fails to pay. David may be justly aggrieved when a parade of unhappy Bobs comes to his door demanding payment. At the very least he will waste time straightening out the mess; his credit rating may be damaged; he may have to pay a lawyer. Like Bob, however, David's remedies, if any, are in tort. Indeed, David's contractual case is nonexistent since there is not even an argument that David was an intended beneficiary of the agreement.

b. Liability in Tort for Negligent Misrepresentation   Recovery in tort is generally premised either on the breach of a duty of care, or on strict liability.[172]

---

[169] RESTATEMENT (SECOND) OF CONTRACTS, § 302(1). For a dissection of this section and its associated comments, see Eisenberg, *supra* note 165, at 1382–84.

[170] Furthermore, the courts are not in agreement as to whether Alice's intent, Carol's intent, or their joint intent should control. *See* Jean F. Powers, *Expanded Liability and the Intent Requirement in Third Party Beneficiary Contracts*, 1993 UTAH L. REV. 67, 73–74.

[171] There is great merit to Professor Eisenberg's complaint that:

> the entire enterprise of finding an intent to benefit the third party as an end is misguided. Except in some cases involving true donee beneficiaries, the intent of the contracting parties is typically to further their own interests, not the interests of a third party. Accordingly, the question whether there is an intent to benefit the third party as an end normally cannot generate a meaningful answer.

Eisenberg, *supra* note 165, at 1381.

[172] *See infra* Part III.A.2.b(4) (discussing imposition of strict liability on CAs).

Unlike their contract claims, the various parties' tort claims will in no way be undermined by any breach of contract Alice may have committed in misrepresenting facts to Carol, except of course for Alice, who may suffer from estoppel, unclean hands, or comparative fault. If Carol has a tort duty to issue accurate statements, it exists outside the contract. Nevertheless, the contours of Carol's duty of care will, to a great extent, be defined by the representations she makes about the level of inquiry she promises to make before issuing a certificate. In a sense, therefore, the contract does define the tort;[173] anyone who relies on the certificate can reasonably be expected to take the trouble to read the terms incorporated into the certificate. For example, if Carol says in her certification practice statement, incorporated by reference in the certificate, that she requires applicants to show their passports but she in fact failed to ask Alice to show hers, she is guilty of negligence. Or, if Carol says that she checks passports, and did so, but failed to notice that Alice presented a crude forgery that could have been detected with ordinary care,[174] she is guilty of negligence. Conversely, if Carol did everything she said she would do, but Alice proffered a superbly faked passport, then Carol is not guilty of negligence. Bob and David may still be able to recover in this last case, however, if Carol is strictly liable for the accuracy of her certificates.[175] Even if Carol is not strictly liable, David may be such an attractive plaintiff that he stands to recover if his lawyer can find a way to get him to the jury.[176]

If Carol, the CA, breaches her duty of care in checking the facts about Alice recited in the certificate, she potentially is liable for making a negligent misrepresentation.[177] This liability may run to Bob (Alice's victim), to David (if Alice impersonated him), to Alice's employer (if the certificate was pursuant to a

---

[173] *Cf.* RESTATEMENT (SECOND) OF TORTS § 299A cmt. c (1965) ("In the ordinary case, the undertaking of one who renders services in the practice of a profession or trade is a matter of contract between the parties. . . .")

[174] The definition of "ordinary care" is itself an issue. If there is an industry, trade usages may supply a guide, *see supra* note 147. Otherwise, judges and juries will have to resort to general principles of ordinary care by reasonable people in like circumstances, whatever those may be.

[175] *See infra* Part III.A.2.b(4) (discussing applicability of strict liability to CAs).

[176] Perhaps David's lawyer might accuse Carol of a privacy tort, or of casting David in a false light by identifying him with the evil Alice.

[177] The misrepresentation is clearly of a matter of fact, not opinion, as those terms are used in the RESTATEMENT (SECOND) OF TORTS, §§ 538A, 548A.

> In some cases one could also hypothesize other claims against Carol, including false representation under 15 U.S.C. § 1125(a)(2) (1994) (trademark), which requires neither privity nor negligence, or a privacy tort. If Alice manages to acquire a certificate saying she is David, David may have a tort claim for appropriation of name or likeness, *see* RESTATEMENT (SECOND) OF TORTS § 652C ("One who appropriates to his own use or benefit the name or likeness of another is subject to liability to the other for invasion of his privacy"), or a false light claim against Carol, *id.* § 652E (publicity placing another in false light that is offensive, based on reasonable person standard, subjects publisher to liability if published with knowledge of or reckless disregard as to falsity), or perhaps even a new tort of impersonation.

contract with the employer), and perhaps even to Alice, subject to her contributory or comparative negligence or unclean hands if she committed a fraud.[178]

A threshold issue, however, is to whom the negligent misrepresentation in the certificate is addressed. If Bob got his copy of the certificate from Carol's Web site where she publishes certificates, Bob has a tort claim for a negligent misrepresentation that Carol made directly to him, although contract privity is absent.[179] David cannot make this claim—he is a third party, and his ability to recover depends on how the applicable state's law treats third parties claiming injury from negligent misrepresentation to another. On the other hand, if Carol gives the certificate to Alice and Alice sends a copy of it to Bob, the negligent misrepresentation was made to Alice, and Bob is reduced to a third party.

States differ greatly on when a third party can obtain redress for negligent misrepresentations.[180] Some require only that the third party's reliance be foreseeable; most follow the Restatement (Second) of Torts rule which is an uneasy, and sometimes unclear, compromise between the two views; a few require contract privity.

(1) Foreseeability States   A small, but perhaps growing,[181] number of states determine who may bring a third-party negligent misrepresentation claim by applying traditional tort analysis focusing on foreseeability. Carol clearly would be liable to Bob in these states, regardless of how he obtained the certificate, since it is completely foreseeable that persons such as Bob would rely on the certificate. Carol should be liable to David as well, since it is foreseeable that a person whose good name is misappropriated in a certificate will be harmed. Both the equities and an economic analysis favor David since he is completely innocent, he had no notice, and there is nothing he could have done to protect himself from Alice.

(2) Restatement States   Most states follow the rule set out in section 552 of the Restatement (Second) of Torts[182] and allow a third party to sue if he or she

---

[178] *See* 9 Stuart M. Speiser, et al., The American Law of Torts §32:74, at 367 (1992).

[179] There may be interesting choice of law problems if Carol and Bob live in different jurisdictions.

[180] *See generally* Jordan H. Leibman & Anne S. Kelly, *Accountants' Liability to Third Parties for Negligent Misrepresentation: The Search for a New Limiting Principle*, 30 Am. Bus. L.J. 347 (1992).

[181] James R. Adams, *No Privity Required for Negligent Misrepresentation Action*, 60 Def. Couns. J. 601 (1993).

[182] *See, e.g.*, Bily v. Arthur Young & Co., 834 P.2d 745, 773 (Cal. 1992) (adopting Restatement (Second) of Torts § 552 approach). The relevant part of section 552 states:

1. One who, in the course of his business, profession or employment, or in any other transaction in which he has a pecuniary interest, supplies false information for the guidance of others in their business transactions, is subject to liability for pecuniary loss caused to them by their justifiable reliance upon the information, if he fails to exercise reasonable care or competence in obtaining or communicating the information.

is within the group of actually foreseen (not all foreseeable) users, the "limited group of persons for whose benefit and guidance" to whom the author knows the "recipient intends to supply" the statement.[183] Unfortunately, the Restatement rule is difficult to apply to a CA. The potential class of persons who will be shown a certificate and asked to rely on it is large, much like an appraiser's or accountant's report. Indeed, the potential class is as large as or larger than those who might rely on a report regarding a publicly traded security; the possible transactions are more diverse, and the reliance by the third party is more likely to be a "but for" element of the transaction. Furthermore, any CA must be aware of these facts. Because the whole point of having a certificate is to enable the holder to show it to someone who will rely on it, there is no question that the recipient of a valid and verifiable certificate should be within the zone of foreseeable users, that is, among those entitled to "justifiable reliance."[184]

The problem with this line of reasoning, however, is that it seems to prove too much. While section 552 of the Restatement (Second) is not a model of clarity, it is a compromise that was not intended to expand the class of potential third-party plaintiffs to the entire world.[185] The class of potential users of a certificate is all users of electronic commerce, indeed all users of e-mail or the World Wide Web, which may equal a good fraction of the world someday; allowing a right of action to this entire group threatens to collapse into the foreseeability test, and thus to exceed the boundaries that section 552 was designed to create. There has been a trend toward allowing third parties to assert negligent misrepresentation claims against professionals, but this trend has not been uniform across states, nor even across professions within individual states.[186] Some have argued that professional opinions such as audits are intended primarily for the benefit of third parties and that accountants should therefore be liable to these essentially foreseeable parties,[187] but many others strongly oppose this idea.[188] Part of this debate concerns the extent to

---

2. Except as stated in Subsection (3), the liability stated in Subsection (1) is limited to loss suffered (a) by the person or one of a limited group of persons for whose benefit and guidance he intends to supply the information or knows that the recipient intends to supply it; and (b) through reliance upon it in a transaction that he intends the information to influence or knows that the recipient so intends or in a substantially similar transaction.

[183] RESTATEMENT (SECOND) OF TORTS § 552(2)(a); *see, e.g.,* Rosenblum Inc. v. Adler, 461 A.2d 138, 145 (N.J. 1983).

[184] *Arthur Young & Co.,* 834 P.2d at 772.

[185] *See* RESTATEMENT (SECOND) OF TORTS § 552 cmt. a (noting that liability for negligent misstatement is more restricted than for fraudulent misrepresentation).

[186] *See* Lawson & Mattison, *supra* note 159, at 1310.

[187] *See, e.g.,* Howard B. Wiener, *Common Law Liability of the Certified Public Accountant for Negligent Misrepresentation,* 20 SAN DIEGO L. REV. 233, 250 (1983); Richard D. Holahan Jr., Note, Security Pacific Business Credit, Inc. v. Peat Marwick Main & Co.: *Just in Case You Had Any Doubts—There Is No Tort of Negligent Misrepresentation in New York,* 13 Pace L. Rev. 763, 771–76 (1993).

[188] *See, e.g.,* Victor P. Goldberg, *Accountable Accountants: Is Third-Party Liability Necessary?,* 17 J. LEGAL STUD. 295 (1988); Thomas L. Gossman, *The Fallacy of Expanding Accountants' Liability,*

which accountants can foresee the uses to which their clients will put their work product, but commentators have also argued that unfettered liability is disproportionate to the wrong, might discourage socially useful behavior (such as audits of litigation-prone industries), might be expensive to administer, or might otherwise impose greater social costs than benefits.[189]

The CAs' circumstances are materially different from the accountants' in one important respect. If Bob acquires a certificate from Alice, that certificate has almost no value to Bob except as a means of facilitating transactions with other parties.[190] *Every* recipient of a certificate who suffers because of the CA's negligence thus falls squarely within the Restatement (Second) section 552 class of persons who suffer loss "through reliance upon [the negligent misrepresentation] in a transaction that [the CA] intends the information to influence or knows that the recipient so intends or in a substantially similar transaction."[191] It may be that the CA's resulting liability is unfairly large or socially detrimental, but it is hardly incidental or unexpected.

(3) Privity States   A few states, notably New York, still follow the older rule that if Bob is a third party he can only recover for Carol's negligent misrepresentation to Alice (that Alice then furnished to him) if he is in a relation of privity with Carol, although some of these states slightly relax the qualifications for privity.[192] The policy reason for attempting to limit the class of potential plaintiffs claiming negligent misrepresentation is in deference to what are considered to be legitimate fears of indeterminate liability to third persons. In the infamous words of Justice Cardozo in *Ultramares Corporation v. Touche,* "If liability for negligence exists, a thoughtless slip or blunder, the failure to detect a theft or forgery beneath the cover of deceptive entries, may expose accountants to a liability in an indeterminate amount for an indeterminate time to an indeterminate class."[193]

The classic cases about negligent misrepresentation, such as *Ultramares,* involve a common fact pattern in which Bob receives Carol's negligent misrepresentation (regarding, for example, an accountant's report) from Alice. If Bob got the certificate from Alice, his third-party negligent misrepresentation

---

1988 COLUM. BUS. L. REV. 213; John A. Siliciano, *Negligent Accounting and the Limits of Instrumental Tort Reform,* 86 MICH. L. REV. 1929 (1988).

[189] *See, e.g.,* Siliciano, *supra* note 188, at 1944.

[190] The picture is somewhat more complicated if Alice's employer obtains the certificate for Alice, since the certificate may have uses within the organization.

[191] RESTATEMENT (SECOND) OF TORTS §552(2)(b). Arguably these third parties are thus within the "limited group of persons for whose benefit and guidance [Alice] intends to supply the information or knows that the recipient intends to supply it," *id.* § 552(2)(a), even if this "limited group" is in fact limited only to those with computers.

[192] *See* 9 Speiser, *supra* note 178, § 32:75, at 370.

[193] Ultramares Corp. v. Touche, 174 N.E. 441, 444 (N.Y. 1931).

claim hews closely to the *Ultramares* facts, giving Bob little hope of recovery against Carol in a privity state.

Bob's position in a privity state such as New York is more complicated if he got Alice's certificate directly from Carol's Web site. It is as if the accountants in *Ultramares* had published the accounts to the world with their client's consent. Yet Bob still has no contract privity with Carol. As a formal matter, staying squarely within the language of *Ultramares*, Bob's claim is unchanged. Nor does the direct provision of the certificate have any formal effect on Bob's status as a potential third-party beneficiary of the contract—a status that would substitute for privity[194]—since Carol's and Alice's intentions are a necessary element of Bob's third-party beneficiary contract claim,[195] and their intentions are not affected by the mode of delivery.

Carol's claim that she did not foresee Bob's reliance rings particularly hollow if she placed Alice's certificate on the World Wide Web herself rather than giving it to Alice; Bob's claim of justifiable reliance on a certificate published by Carol in this manner seems strong. Nevertheless, since a certificate issued by Carol is used, foreseeably, by the same people in the same way for the same purposes regardless of whether it happens to pass through Alice's hands on the way to Bob, it seems overly formalistic to make a distinction between the legal consequences of the two distribution models. Indeed, with the exception of the case where Alice notifies Carol that she intends to give Bob the certificate, Bob is just as much—or as little—an intended third-party beneficiary whether Alice publishes the certificate or Carol does. Because in practice the two distribution methods are barely distinguishable, especially when one considers that Carol continues to manage the CRL regardless of who distributes the certificate, there is a danger that Bob's tort claim would fail in a strong privity state such as New York even if he got Alice's certificate directly from Carol.[196]

Whatever this result may say about general tort principles applicable in New York, it is not a sensible result in the special context of a CA who issues a certificate at the request of a client, particularly if the CA publishes the certificate. The rule in *Ultramares* was crafted to protect accountants and other professionals from being subjected to unforeseen, arguably unforeseeable, liability by the actions of a client in cases where the person issuing a report could reasonably believe that the report was for the client's own, private, use.[197] A CA issuing a certificate, especially an identifying certificate, knows full well

---

[194] *See* Lawson & Mattison, *supra* note 159, at 1319.

[195] *See supra* note 169 and accompanying text.

[196] *Cf.* Holahan, *supra* note 187. A CA that wanted to take on liability in such a state in order to signal that its certificates were reliable would either have to draft a contract that made its intentions very clear, or it might have to adopt a business model in which Carol does not put Alice's certificate on a Web page, and does not make it available to all, but instead provides an automated e-mail credential response service in which Carol meters Alice's usage of the certificate, and perhaps charges accordingly.

[197] *See supra* note 193 and accompanying text.

that the client's entire purpose in acquiring the certificate is to show it to third parties who will rely on it. By publishing the certificate itself, the CA removes itself from the *Ultramares* facts. Even if the client publishes the certificate, the CA must logically know that the client intends to do so. The CA cannot, therefore, credibly claim surprise when an unknown third party relies on the certificate in a manner consistent with the CA's representations in that certificate because the certificate exists solely to be relied upon by strangers. The common law should reflect this reality, particularly in the case where the CA itself is the publisher, even in a strong privity state.

(4) Strict Liability for CAs? Strict liability is most commonly applied in cases involving goods, such as defective products, and ultrahazardous activities. Furthermore, strict liability traditionally allows recovery for personal injury but not for "economic loss." Traditionally, strict liability would thus seem to have had little to do with the issuance of certificates: they are not ultrahazardous in the usual sense of the term,[198] and they are probably not "products."[199] However, one commentator suggests that a certificate which used a faulty algorithm to produce the CA's digital signature might be found to have a design defect.[200] Given that some jurisdictions separate "hybrid" good-service transactions into the part that is a good and the part that is a service,[201] it may be useful to consider briefly the economic principles that might underlie the imposition of strict liability as they apply to certificates as "goods." Indeed, there is a policy argument that a regulatory approach to the law of certification authorities might want to take these factors into account in assigning liability, particularly in the absence of the consensus as to what constitutes due care for a CA needed to give teeth to the CA's duty of care.

Imposition of a strict liability regime eliminates the need to find privity: liability follows the good.[202] There is no requirement that the plaintiff show fault by defendant; instead, the sole issue is whether the product performed adequately. The Restatement (Second) of Torts section 402A imposes strict liability on products with an unreasonably dangerous defect.[203] Prosser defined this class of products as those that are "not safe for such a use that can be expected to be made of [them], and no warning is given."[204]

---

[198] *But see supra* text at notes 120–21 (discussing proposals to make consumers presumptively liable for all transactions with their digital signature supported by valid certificate).

[199] *See supra* text accompanying notes 133–34 (making the argument that certificate is not a "good" for UCC purposes).

[200] Baum, *supra* note 22, at 130–31.

[201] *See supra* note 140 and accompanying text.

[202] *See* MacPherson v. Buick Motor Co., 111 N.E. 1050 (N.Y. 1916).

[203] RESTATEMENT (SECOND) OF TORTS § 402A, cmt. i (1977) (discussing definition of "unreasonably dangerous").

[204] Prosser, *Fall of the Citadel, supra* note 166, at 826.

The Learned Hand test, as reformulated by Dean Calabresi, suggests that courts should impose strict liability on the least-cost avoider.[205] As between Carol and anyone but Alice, Carol will in most cases be the least-cost avoider of the loss caused by an inaccurate certificate. If Alice and Bob are strangers, Bob has no means of testing the validity of the representations in the certificate: his inability to confirm Alice's claims about herself is the precise reason he wants the certificate in the first place.[206] As between Carol and Alice, however, Alice is ordinarily the least-cost avoider of Alice's errors.

The net effect of a policy that makes Alice strictly liable to everyone for her own errors in a certificate, and makes the CA strictly liable to everyone but Alice for the CA's failure to detect Alice's misstatements, would be to turn the CA into an insurer for Alice's veracity in every case where Alice disappears or lacks the assets to satisfy a judgment.[207] There is also a danger that imposing strict liability on Carol removes the incentive for Alice to take care that her statements to Carol are accurate. For Carol to agree to be a CA under these terms would require that Alice provide either extraordinarily strong assurances as to her claims, or that Carol charge prices large enough to pay for a generous insurance cover.

B. Contractual Attempts to Limit Private CA Liability

Even absent strict liability, the current uncertainty as to the state of the law gives a CA an incentive to be overcautious. A lawyer retained by a CA is likely to respond by attempting to have the CA disclaim any responsibility for anything it says. Thus, for example, the disclaimer offered by an early entrant to this market, in its standard contract with purchasers of certificates entitling them to run a Netscape-compliant "secure server," states:

> VERISIGN DISCLAIMS ANY WARRANTIES WITH RESPECT TO THE SERVICES PROVIDED BY VERISIGN HEREUNDER INCLUDING WITHOUT LIMITATION ANY AND ALL IMPLIED WARRANTIES OF MERCHANTABILITY OR FITNESS FOR A PARTICULAR PURPOSE. VERISIGN MAKES NO REPRESENTATION OR WARRANTY THAT ANY CA OR USER TO WHICH IT HAS ISSUED A DIGITAL ID IN THE VERISIGN SECURE SERVER HIERARCHY IS IN FACT THE PERSON OR ORGANIZATION IT CLAIMS TO BE WITH

---

[205] *See* GUIDO CALABRESI, THE COST OF ACCIDENTS: A LEGAL AND ECONOMIC ANALYSIS (1970); Guido Calabresi & Jon T. Hirschoff, *Toward a Test for Strict Liability in Torts*, 81 YALE L.J. 1055, 1077 (1972).

[206] *See generally* Section I *supra*.

[207] There is also some danger that under a strict liability regime, the fact that Carol was willing to become an insurer for Alice might itself be a signal that Carol was not trustworthy.

RESPECT TO THE INFORMATION SUPPLIED TO VERISIGN. VERISIGN MAKES NO ASSURANCES OF THE ACCURACY, AU- THENTICITY, INTEGRITY, OR RELIABILITY OF INFORMATION CONTAINED IN DIGITAL IDs OR IN CRLs COMPILED, PUBLISHED OR DISSEMINATED BY VERISIGN, OR OF THE RESULTS OF CRYP- TOGRAPHIC METHODS IMPLEMENTED. NO ORAL OR WRITTEN INFORMATION OR ADVICE GIVEN BY VERISIGN OR ITS EM- PLOYEES OR REPRESENTATIVES SHALL CREATE A WARRANTY OR IN ANY WAY INCREASE THE SCOPE OF VERISIGN'S OBLIGA- TIONS. SOME JURISDICTIONS DO NOT ALLOW THE EXCLUSION OF IMPLIED WARRANTIES, SO THE ABOVE EXCLUSION MAY NOT APPLY TO YOU.[208]

Leaving aside the issue of the enforceability of this language, especially as applied to third parties,[209] if Carol in fact "makes no representation or warranty" that the holder of one of her identifying certificates "is in fact the person or organization it claims to be with respect to the information sup- plied to" Carol, and if she also disclaims "the accuracy, authenticity, in- tegrity, or reliability of information" the certificate provides, one is entitled to ask how much point there is to having one of Carol's certificates.[210] The answer depends primarily on what Alice and Bob decide they need in order to feel comfortable transacting with each other. If a certificate provides trans- actional confidence, at least in the absence of alternatives, then it suffices. Carol's desire to protect her service's reputation may, in any case, provide Alice and Bob with some comfort that Carol has been verifying the accuracy of Alice's assertions.

---

[208] VeriSign Corp., Secure Server Legal Agreement 3, *available online* URL http://www. verisign.com/netscape/legal.html. VeriSign's policies continue to evolve. Later versions of its Certification Practice Statement should be available online http://www.verisign.com/reposi- tory/CPS/.

[209] In California, where VeriSign is located, the disclaimer will not work if a certificate is a good because an "as is" disclaimer or one which disclaims "all implied warranties that would other- wise attach to the sale of consumer goods under the provisions of this chapter," CAL. CIV. CODE § 1791.3 (West 1985), must be "a conspicuous writing . . . attached to the goods." *Id.* § 1792.4(a). It is unclear how one achieves this for a certificate. For a survey of limits on disclaimers in the United States see Donald F. Clifford Jr, Non-UCC STATUTORY PROVISIONS AFFECTING WARRANTY DISCLAIMERS AND REMEDIES IN SALES OF GOODS, 71 N.C. L. REV. 1011 (1993).

[210] Indeed, one can imagine a court throwing out the disclaimers as unconscionable. *See* U.C.C. § 2-302; *see also id.* at cmt. 1 (suggesting courts should strike as unconscionable clauses "contrary to public policy or to the dominant purpose of the contract"). This section has been applied to many kinds of contracts other than those for goods "either by analogy or as an expression of a general doctrine." E. ALLAN FARNSWORTH, CONTRACTS § 4.28, at 325 (2d ed. 1990); *see also* RE- STATEMENT (SECOND) OF CONTRACTS § 208 (1979); CAL. CIV. CODE § 1670.5 (West 1985). *Compare* Wile v. Southwestern Bell Tel. Co., 549 P.2d 903 (Kan. 1976) (finding disclaimers of liability for error in telephone book not unconscionable) *with* Allen v. Michigan Bell Tel. Co., 232 N.W.2d 302 (Mich. Ct. App. 1975) (finding disclaimers for errors in telephone book to be unconscionable).

Similarly, because the law today offers a CA no obvious means of pegging its liability according to the degree of investigation that went into a certificate, a CA in operation today may seek to reduce its liability to the minimum. Again, VeriSign provides an example in its standard contract:

> NEITHER PARTY WILL BE LIABLE TO THE OTHER FOR ANY CONSEQUENTIAL, INDIRECT, SPECIAL OR INCIDENTAL DAMAGES, WHETHER FORESEEABLE OR UNFORESEEABLE, ARISING OUT OF BREACH OF ANY EXPRESS OR IMPLIED WARRANTY, BREACH OF CONTRACT, MISREPRESENTATION, NEGLIGENCE, STRICT LIABILITY IN TORT OR OTHERWISE, EXCEPT ONLY IN THE CASE OF WILLFUL MISCONDUCT, DEATH OR PERSONAL INJURY WHERE AND TO THE EXTENT THAT APPLICABLE LAW REQUIRES SUCH LIABILITY. THE PARTIES AGREE THAT VERISIGN'S TOTAL LIABILITY HEREUNDER SHALL NOT EXCEED THE AMOUNTS PAID BY CUSTOMER TO VERISIGN UNDER THIS AGREEMENT EXCEPT TO THE EXTENT THAT SUCH LIABILITY AROSE FROM VERISIGN'S WILLFUL MISCONDUCT. SOME JURISDICTIONS DO NOT ALLOW THE LIMITATION OR EXCLUSION OF LIABILITY FOR INCIDENTAL OR CONSEQUENTIAL DAMAGES, SO THE ABOVE LIMITATION OR EXCLUSION MAY NOT APPLY TO YOU.[211]

With this disclaimer, the CA seeks to limit its liability to its client for anything other than its own "willful misconduct" to the amount the subscriber paid for the certificate, which is likely to be a very small sum in most cases. The desire to limit liability in this manner is a response to the largely unpredictable and potentially capacious liability that a CA might encounter in the absence of a statute or other norms defining its rights and duties. Unfortunately, this response threatens to undermine the certificate itself. A certificate that contains a warning that it is not to be trusted seems ill suited to fill a trust-building role in electronic commerce. A world in which such warnings are routinely given and routinely ignored suggests that at least one party's expectations will be disappointed.

C. Is CA Legislation Needed to Resolve Liability for an Erroneous Certificate?

A CA's fundamental duty, whether in contract or tort, should be to make accurate representations in a certificate. In a certificate worthy of reliance, these representations will concern not only facts about the subject of the

---

[211] VeriSign Corp., *supra* note 208, at 3.

certificate but also facts about the CA itself. To inspire confidence, a certificate should state (or incorporate by reference) the identity of the CA, the facts upon which the identification of the subject of the certificate is based, the degree of investigation performed by the CA to confirm the facts stated by the subject of the certificate, the start and end dates of the certificate's validity, and the location of the relevant CRL. CAs might choose to include additional information, such as a recommended reliance limit for transactions based on the certificate.

One can imagine that as the number of CAs grows, certificates will eventually begin to be issued that bear all the indicia of reliability through the operation of market mechanisms. This is an uncertain process, however, and it is not instantaneous. Furthermore, the existing uncertainty about the substantive law applicable to CAs increases the risk involved in running one. All other things being equal, this will raise the cost of certificates, as risk-averse parties may be unwilling to enter the market, reducing the number of competitors.

1. The Case for Legislation

The case for legislation begins with the observation that the legal climate for CAs is uncertain. Uncertainty increases costs and discourages transactions.[212] In the case of CAs it threatens to produce overpowerful incentives for CAs to underproduce certificates and/or disclaim all liability for certificates, which threatens to limit their utility.[213] It is also likely to lead to considerable litigation until all the relevant rules are identified.

As we have seen, absent legislation, a CA's liability is potentially high. Much of the social benefit of having a certificate-based system of electronic commerce is forgone if Carol's exposure to liability is so high that the cost of insurance is enormous. In that case Carol will self-insure, and will declare bankruptcy if a large claim is decided against her, which does not help the injured parties and creates a risk that CAs will not last. Alternately, Carol will have to charge high prices and issue few certificates, which also defeats the purpose of the system.

A CA's liability can be fixed by legislation, but this requires a policy choice as to what the appropriate level of liability should be. The Utah Act

---

[212] *See generally* Karl N. Llewellyn, *Why We Need the Uniform Commercial Code*, 10 U. FLA. L. REV. 367 (1957).

[213] However, the existence of standards such as X.509 impose significant constraints on CA behavior. For example, to comply with X.509 a CA must uniquely identify itself in a certificate. *See* Ford, *supra* note 23, at 12. Failure to produce a certificate that complies with the standard designed into systems that use certificates will result in users rejecting the certificate.

provides one model. Under that act, a CA that complies with relatively oner-ous requirements[214] is granted a safe harbor from consequential damages, and indeed from most liability in excess of a reliance limit stated in the cer-tificate, even if the CA itself is guilty of a negligent misstatement.[215] It is cer-tainly possible to imagine other levels at which the CA's liability might be fixed in the event that it is negligent, levels that create an additional incen-tive to be careful but fall short of open-ended liability.[216]

Another reason legislation might be needed is to make provisions for certificates issued by a CA that later goes out of business. A CA cannot re-call all of its certificates; a bankrupt CA might have no incentive to even notify its former clients that it was ceasing operations. Some certificates, particularly transactional certificates, may be on documents with a long life span. The need to check the validity of the digital signatures on a deed may not arise until many years after it is affixed, but the need is no less real. If the CA is to go out of business in a manner that does not undermine the utility of such certificates, someone must be found to store the certifi-cates that validate the CA's key and to take over the management of the CA's CRL, without which all of its certificates must be considered un-reliable.[217]

Legislation may also serve the goal of consumer protection (depending on its content), since a statute can require that CAs carry insurance or re-serves to meet any claims for their errors. CAs resemble notaries public in that both verify the authenticity of signatures, and it may follow that, like

---

[214] These requirements include: having a secure system, trusted personnel, clear certification policies, insurance, a CRL, a certificate from the root CA operated by the state, regular financial audits of its balance sheet, and regular security audits of its computer systems. UTAH CODE ANN. § 46-3-201, -202, -203, -301, -307.

[215] The Utah Act states that a CA which complies with its terms is:

> B. Not liable in excess of the amount specified in the certificate as its recommended reliance limit for either:
> (I) a loss caused by reliance on a misrepresentation in the certificate of any fact that the licensed certification authority is required to confirm; or
> (II) failure to comply with [rules relating to the proper issuance of a certificate] in is-suing the certificate;
> C. Liable only for direct, compensatory damages in any action to recover a loss due to re-liance on the certificate, which damages do not include:
> (I) punitive or exemplary damages;
> (II) damages for lost profits, savings, or opportunity; or
> (III) damages for pain or suffering.

Id. § 46-3-309(2).

[216] On the other hand, once the decision to have comprehensive legislation has been made, the case seems overwhelming for reemphasizing that a CA should never be liable for anyone's use of an accurate certificate that the CA had no reason to suspect was no longer accurate—even if this is certain to be the common-law result absent legislation.

[217] Utah addresses these issues in its administrative rules issued pursuant to Section 104 of the Utah Digital Signature Act. *See id.* § 46-3-104(3).

notaries, CAs "require some level of licensing by governmental entities" to ensure public confidence.[218]

A single standard should also prevent the duplicative litigation that would otherwise be required to identify the relevant rules in many jurisdictions. Furthermore, the likelihood that different jurisdictions will have different liability rules reduces the utility and ease of use of certificates. Without new laws, uniformity among states, much less among nations, is unlikely. The American Bar Association is working on Guidelines for Digital Signatures,[219] and the Commissioners on Uniform Laws are studying the issue.

While the liability and uncertainty arguments have power, the strongest argument for legislation is that it would create an opportunity to standardize the rights and duties of CAs, their customers, and those who rely on certificates, regardless of the jurisdiction in which they happen to reside. It is possible to imagine a system in which users grade certificates according to the liability regime that applies, but it seems unwieldy and inefficient to force users (or their software) to take account of factors such as the effect of the geographic location of the CA and the trading parties on the choice of law. This is especially true when information about geographic location may not necessarily be accessible to participants in Internet commerce.[220] Users cannot reasonably be expected to keep abreast of changes in the law of multiple jurisdictions, and the challenge of programming a certificate system to do more than classify certificates by their reliance limits seems daunting. One can imagine the introduction of yet another intermediary that would perform this rating function, but requiring the introduction of a trusted fourth party to rate trusted third parties seems to be too much of a good thing. A uniform national or even international rule would be much easier to understand and to administer.

2. The Case against Legislation

The case against new legislation is that it would be too much too soon, and perhaps too unfair. First, although the idea of a CA is not new, commercial CAs are so new that the industry barely deserves to be called a fledgling. At this stage, with few providers, few clients, and few certificates, it is difficult to foresee how certificates will actually be used with sufficient precision to draft rules that will last. Any statute written today, including the Utah Act, is

---

[218] Henry H. Perritt Jr., *Access to the National Information Infrastructure*, 30 WAKE FOREST L. REV. 51, 100 (1995). On the other hand, equal public confidence might be achieved by clear legal rules that either impose liability on CAs for their errors or at least make it possible for CAs to signal their confidence in their certificates by undertaking a measured amount of liability.

[219] *See* ABA Draft Guidelines, *supra* note 4.

[220] *See generally* Froomkin, *supra* note 21.

a first draft. Second, it is at least conceivable that the marketplace will provide an adequate solution without regulation. If a competitive market in certificates arises, it is possible that a struggle to the top[221] (or market stratification) may ensue, and that CAs may find that a willingness to back their certificates with at least some kind of guarantee may make their certificates more attractive to clients and third parties.[222]

The clients' interests depend in large part on how they plan to use the certificate. If Alice plans to use the certificate to transact with Bob, Alice wants the least expensive certificate that Bob will find acceptable.[223] Bob, on the other hand, may want a certificate that gives him recourse against the CA if Alice succeeds in defrauding him and turns out to be an imposter. Similarly, Alice's demands regarding the assurances she wants to receive about Bob will play a large role in the level of assurance Bob will want to be able to display. In other words, neither Alice's nor Bob's interests are necessarily well served by a world in which CAs have no liability to either of them under any circumstances. The CA itself may benefit from a regime in which it at least has the option of taking on liability to demonstrate its confidence in the certificates. Although the Utah Act allows CAs to take on additional liability if they want, market pressures arguably may produce optimal outcomes without regulation.

Even if Carol says that her Class A certificates are not suitable to transactions of more than five cents, Alice may be able to use the certificate millions of times in an hour. It might, however, be possible for Carol to say that Class A certificates are only suitable for transactions of five cents or less *and* that each individual third party may rely on a certificate only once per day. This would impose an additional, but perhaps not unreasonable, record-keeping obligation on Bob since now he has to make sure that Alice has not used the certificate with him that day. Bob is of course free to dispense with this record keeping, but if he does so he bears the risk that the certificate is erroneous because his reliance on the certificate in excess of its terms is not justified. Even if such a scheme were feasible, it would only protect Bob against overreliance on a once-a-day certificate. It would not protect Alice against Mallet's misuse of her signature if he gained control of it. Because a digital signature supported by a valid certificate can be used to transact with a very large number of people in a short period of time, only usage monitoring by

---

[221] *See generally* Ralph K. Winter Jr., *State Law, Shareholder Protection, and the Theory of the Corporation*, 6 J. LEGAL STUD. 251 (1977).

[222] The Utah Act allows CAs to take on additional obligations to clients or others if they so desire. UTAH CODE ANN. § 46-3-302(3).

[223] If Alice plans to transact with many people, she will have to trade the expense of the certificate against the likelihood that it will be accepted by those with whom she wishes to transact.

the CA itself, or by the CA's agent managing a unique CRL, could turn the reliance limit into an effective protection against multiple use. Unfortunately, there is reason to doubt whether it is technically and economically feasible for a CA to do this;[224] there has been no suggestion that any potential CA is interested in shouldering this substantial burden.

Utah's approach to the CA liability question creates two categories of CAs. Those that comply with the relatively strict requirements of the Utah Act by proving their technical and financial security can benefit from a very safe harbor from liability for erroneous certificates.[225] Noncomplying CAs are left to the tender mercies of the background law. The commentary to the Utah law notes that CA liability limits are justified because "one of the principal impediments to the emergence of certification authorities has been the uncertainty of the legal risks such a business would undertake."[226] Indeed, when the Utah Act was enacted in early 1995, there were no commercial CAs offering certificates to the public in the United States, nor were there any as of February 1, 1996.

By early 1996, however, Netscape 2.x browsers came equipped to recognize certificates issued by CommerceNet, MCI Mall, ATT, RSA, and Netscape.[227] Although at this writing these entities have yet to begin issuing certificates on a large scale, it seems plausible that they will do so even in the absence of legislation. If they do begin issuing certificates on a large scale in the absence of legislation, the argument that they require substantial protection from liability in order to enter the market will be at least weakened, and perhaps even proved wrong. "Perhaps" is, however, the strongest word appropriate at this time. The willingness of large organizations to enter the market in advance of legislation that they may reasonably expect will provide liability shields does not necessarily prove that they would remain willing to issue certificates if it became clear that the legislation was not going to materialize. Some CAs may choose to take a calculated short-term risk to expose themselves to high liability in order to grab market share and create brand-name recognition. These same CAs might be unwilling to shoulder the risk in the long term. Nevertheless, to an opponent of legislation, "perhaps" is good enough since the crux of the argument is that one should wait and see.

---

[224] One of several obstacles to any system that seeks to count the number of uses of a certificate is that both certificate lists and CRLs are easily copied. If Bob runs a high-volume, low-margin business, in many cases it will be far more efficient for him to copy an entire CRL at random intervals, and take the risk of honoring a revoked certificate from time to time, than to continually contact the CA to check individual certificates.

[225] *See* UTAH CODE ANN. § 46-3-309.

[226] *Id.*, cmt. a, *available online* URL www.state.ut.us/ccjj/digsig/dsnt-act.htm.

[227] Netscape 2.01, Options menu, Security Preferences menu, Site Certificates menu; *see generally* Netscape Handbook: Application Features, *available online* URL http://home.netscape.com/eng/mozilla/2.01/handbook/docs/appans.html#C37.

Similarly, the opponent of legislation is unlikely to be fazed by the preliminary evidence that fear of liability has forced one CA to include scatter-shot disclaimers in its certificates.[228] Even if one agrees that if this practice persisted it would risk undermining the utility of certificates, there is arguably little to be gained by legislating before the market for certificate policies has had an opportunity to reach equilibrium.[229]

Finally, if the market requires standardized rules, the competition between states may provide them without federal assistance, as demonstrated by the predominant role of Delaware's corporate law.[230] Perhaps Utah, or some other state, or even a foreign country, will become the address of choice for CAs that wish to signal their trustworthiness.

3. The ABA Digital Signature Guidelines

One of the difficulties in determining the duties and liabilities of CAs in the absence of legislation is the paucity of trade practices or best practices.[231] A further difficulty is that lawyers and judges are generally unfamiliar with the purpose and functions of digital signatures and CAs. The ABA Section on Science and Technology's Information Security Committee is attempting to address these problems with its Digital Signature Guidelines. At this writing, the first, still unofficial, exposure draft is being revised.[232] This chapter has avoided discussing the draft guidelines because of their preliminary nature and the likelihood that they might change significantly by the time this chapter is published. Whatever their final form, however, it is already clear that the guidelines stand a chance of influencing both the practice and regulation of CAs and that they warrant careful reading.[233]

CONCLUSION

Persons who are not previously acquainted, but wish to transact with one another via computer networks such as the Internet, will need a means of

---

[228] *See supra* note 211 and accompanying text.

[229] A supporter of legislation would be likely to counter that the process of finding this equilibrium would require enormous amounts of wasteful litigation.

[230] *Cf.* Roberta Romano, *Competition for Corporate Charters and the Lesson of Takeover Statutes*, 61 FORDHAM L. REV. 843 (1993) (discussing competition among states for the business of corporate charters).

[231] *See supra* note 153 and accompanying text.

[232] ABA Draft Guidelines, *supra* note 4. The comment period ended January 15, 1996.

[233] In the spirit of full disclosure, I should confess that I am a quondam member of the ABA's Information Security Committee and was involved in drafting parts of the draft guidelines.

identifying or authenticating each other. One means of achieving this is to introduce a trusted third party into the bilateral relationship. This third party, a Certification Authority, can vouch for a party by issuing a certificate identifying her, or attesting that she possesses a necessary qualification or attribute. CAs may become essential to much, but not all, electronic commerce. Although at this writing there are few CAs in operation, and what electronic commerce takes place rarely relies on certificates, the dollar value of electronic commerce is forecast to grow quickly. If it does, the demand for CA's services should grow rapidly as well.

Outside the states of Utah and Washington, which have passed comprehensive digital signature acts but currently have no CAs qualified to take advantage of their terms, state rules likely to be applicable to CAs are unclear. Basic concepts, such as whether a CA's sale of a certificate is the sale of a "good," a "service," or the mixture of the two for UCC Article 2 purposes, remain to be determined. State common-law rules concerning the liability of a CA for negligent misrepresentations in a certificate are anything but uniform, and in some cases likely to be unclear also.

The more general lack of regulatory and legal standardization that these examples evince may prove to be a large impediment to the development of reliable electronic commerce. A national—or even possibly international—standard for accurately signaling what a certificate promises, and the extent to which a certificate can reasonably engender reliance, may be needed. Such a standard is unlikely to emerge until the relevant legal rules that already exist are identified; the development of standards is also likely to be retarded by the great diversity of legal regimes in different jurisdictions that may be involved in a single transaction. Whether it would be best to produce the needed legal standardization through legislation, the judicial process, or market mechanisms such as the bargaining process and the usages of trade, is debatable. However, until some standardization is achieved, users of digital signatures will find it difficult to determine what degree of commercial reliance to place on a representation in a certificate.

Standards aside, the current uncertainty about the law creates a climate in which CAs have an enormous incentive to understate the reliability of their certificates in order to avoid exposure to liability whose contours are difficult to predict. This understandable behavior undermines the justified reliance that CAs should be designed to achieve; if it persists, legislation to balance CA incentives and liability is likely to become necessary. State legislation holds out the promise of clearer rules and the avoidance of much litigation, but today this clarity comes at the price of having to determine the distributional consequences of mistakes by CAs and the people who use certificates before there is any significant evidence of the nature and patterns of certificate use and abuse.

After a reasonable period of experimentation in which market-driven certificates that do not purport to be worthless have a chance to surface, it will be appropriate to consider whether the national interest in a functioning national information infrastructure might be better served by uniform national rules. The CA equivalent of Delaware's corporate law might emerge from a competition among state regulatory authorities. If not, uniformity could be achieved via the traditional channels for state law harmonization, such as model laws and uniform acts, or by federal legislation. In addition to these national standards, at least minimal international norms for certificate recognition and CA regulation will become increasingly necessary as electronic commerce becomes more global.

ACKNOWLEDGMENTS

Tom Baker, Caroline Bradley, Patrick Gudridge, Trotter Hardy, Richard Hausler, Francis Hill, Mark Lemley, Jessica Litman, Charles Merrill, Daniel Murray, and Katie Sowle provided helpful comments on earlier drafts of this paper. I am also grateful to Alan Asay, Bob Jueneman, Chuck Miller, and many other past and present members of the ABA Information Security Committee for helpful discussions of many technical questions; Richard Field, Hal Finney, and Lucky Green for sharing their expertise regarding electronic cash and related matters; Ann Klienfelter, Claire Donnelly, Sue-Ann Campbell, and Nora de la Garza for reference and information retrieval help; Rosalia Lliraldi for secretarial assistance; and Erica Wright for research assistance. I am particularly grateful to Keith Aoki, Richard Painter, and the University of Oregon School of Law for inviting me to participate in this Conference on Innovation and the Information Environment. Unless otherwise noted, this article attempts to reflect legal and technical developments up to February 1, 1996.

This article was originally published in 75 Oregon Law Review 49 (1996).

PART 3

Pricing and Electronic Transactions

Part Three deals with issues in electronic payments. Two of the papers in this part are concerned with the payment process, while the third deals with the management of network bandwidth.

In Chapter 7, Nathaniel S. Borenstein and coauthors describe the experiences of First Virtual Holdings' first year as a financial intermediary that provides payment services. The paper is divided into two parts. The first part describes the experiences of the people in First Virtual as they operate their company while situated in different geographic locations. The second describes the approach First Virtual has developed to support buyer-seller payments. In its current implementation, no cryptography is used to achieve security and authentication. One emphasis of First Virtual is to provide technical support so that the Internet problems that impact a transaction can be resolved. Of course, the discussion implicitly assumes that the commodities are digital, possibly informational or entertainment products. The emphasis is on the practical issues of operating a cost-effective financial intermediary. For example, the company's view is that the introduction of cryptographic features has to be weighed against the cost of using those features and the expected benefits of defeating attacks in the payment system. Another practical problem that First Virtual is very much concerned with is the language issue. The company wants to provide a Japanese-language version to support transactions in Japan, or to support a Japanese customer buying a product in Germany. Related to this are customer support problems that range from network-computer failure to an inability of a user to understand the instructions to carry out the transaction.

Alok Gupta, Dale O. Stahl, and Andrew B. Whinston apply economic principles to electronic commerce in Chapter 8. The authors focus on the challenge of allocating network bandwidth in an economically efficient manner. They suggest using prices so that urgent needs are recognized and provided for in the allocation process. To support this contention, they argue that the value of a product or service is a function of the electronic delivery time which could easily vary depending on the network load. For example, if someone is sending a recipe to their grandmother, the delivery time is probably not critical. If the same person, however, needs certain financial information to decide on a stock market trade, then response time is critical. The authors note that prices play a role in obtaining accurate measures of time dependent end user values. Without prices, there is a natural tendency for every user to insist on high quality response time. While economic theory deals with the role of prices, it does not specify mechanisms to deal with the real time formation of prices. The authors have specified and tested a price formation mechanism that in simulation tests dramatically improves network performance.

In Chapter 9, B. Clifford Neuman sets forth requirements for an electronic payment system and briefly describes the different types of payment models. He discusses how some payment systems are based on the secure transfer of credit card information while others depend on the use of an electronic currency. These payment systems offered by different financial intermediaries will differ on the degree of security provided, the reliability, scalability and the possibility of providing anonymity to buyer and seller. Neuman emphasizes that there will be many different kinds of payment servers competing on the basis of charges and the characteristics of the payment system. In addition, he also discusses the importance of compatibility between financial intermediaries. This issues gains particular importance depending on the nature of the transaction.

Chapter 7

Perils and Pitfalls of Practical Internet Commerce: The Lessons of First Virtual's First Year

Nathaniel S. Borenstein, John Ferguson, Gerald Hall,
Carlyn Lowery, Richard Mintz, Darren New,
Beverly Parenti, Marshall T. Rose, Einar Stefferud,
Lee Stein, Carey Storm, Ed Vielmetti,
Marc Weiser, and Pierre-R. Wolff

ABSTRACT

Unlike many would-be players in the field of Internet commerce, First Virtual[TM1] chose to announce its payment system only after it was fully operational and to operate it initially with relatively little publicity hype, while learning from the experience of its use. In the company's first year of operation, it has experienced exponential growth and gained substantial experience with and insight into the nature of Internet commerce. In this chapter, the First Virtual team discusses both the lessons we have learned from a year's experience with the actual operation of an Internet commerce system and the prospects for the future.

This chapter begins with a short description of First Virtual and its Internet Payment System, which may be skipped by those already familiar with the company's system at the conceptual level. Next we consider the lessons learned, focusing on five key areas: the organizational aspects of an Internet

---

[1] First Virtual, VirtualPIN, and InfoHaus are registered trademarks of First Virtual Holdings Incorporated.

service company, the need for an Internet-based intermediary in the payment process, the security and administrative issues involved in operating an Internet commerce server, the customer service issues in dealing with a user community as diverse as the Internet, and, finally, the myths and realities surrounding the use of cryptographic technology for Internet commerce. Finally, we look to the future, with projections about the possible evolution of First Virtual's system in particular and Internet commerce in general.

I. WHAT IS FIRST VIRTUAL?

First Virtual Holdings is a company that was formed in early 1994 to facilitate Internet commerce. The first product offering from First Virtual was an Internet payment system, which was developed quietly and publicly announced as a fully operational open Internet service on October 15, 1994.

First Virtual's system differs in many ways from all other proposed approaches to Internet commerce, most notably in the fact that it does not rely on encryption or any other form of cryptography to ensure the safety of its commercial transactions. Instead, safety is ensured by enforcing a dichotomy between nonsensitive information (which may travel over the Internet) and sensitive information (which never does), and by a buyer feedback mechanism built atop existing protocols.

In a nutshell, First Virtual's payment system is built on top of preexisting Internet protocols, notably the SMTP/RFC822/MIME (e-mail), telnet, finger, FTP (file transfer), and HTTP (Web) protocols. Because these protocols are "insecure" in the sense that they carry no strong proofs of identity, it is necessary to design a payment system in such a way as to provide much stronger guarantees. While others have focused on achieving this goal using cryptography, First Virtual designed a higher-level protocol based on e-mail callbacks.

In the First Virtual system, a buyer and seller may use any procedure or protocol to meet and decide to transact business. While this often occurs when a buyer browses a seller's Web page, it also frequently happens by e-mail, FTP, Internet Relay Chat, or even off-Net entirely, and it could easily happen in the future via protocols that do not exist today. Once the buyer and the seller have an intent to do business, they submit a transaction to First Virtual. That transaction can be submitted via standard e-mail or via a new protocol, SMXP, designed by First Virtual for real-time exchange of MIME (e-mail) objects.

When First Virtual is asked to process a financial transaction, it looks up the buyer's VirtualPIN™ (account identifier) in its database and finds the buyer's e-mail address of record. An e-mail message is dispatched to the buyer, asking the buyer to confirm the validity of the transaction and his or her commitment to pay, which the buyer can respond to with a simple answer of "yes," "no," or "fraud." Only when the buyer says "yes" is a real-world financial transaction actually initiated. Simple attacks based on Internet "sniffing" are rendered unappealing because their value is sharply limited by the fact that a VirtualPIN, or First Virtual ID, is not useful off the Net, and require e-mail confirmation for use on the Net. More sophisticated attacks require criminals to break into the victim's computer account and monitor the victim's incoming mail, a crime that is much more easily traced. It is also worth noting that such a break-in would also probably yield access to the victim's encryption keys in any commerce schemes that make use of public key cryptography for encryption.

In First Virtual's system, the valuable financial tokens that underlie commerce—notably credit card numbers and bank account information—never appear on the Internet at all. Instead, they are linked to the buyer's VirtualPIN by First Virtual when the customer applies for a First Virtual account, a procedure that involves an off-Internet step for the most sensitive information. Currently, the sensitive information is provided by either an automated telephone call (for buyers to provide their credit card number) or by postal mail (for sellers to provide their bank account information). However, it would also be possible to provide the VirtualPINs automatically en masse to buyers, for example, by direct mailing from the credit card issuers as is done with traditional ATM PINs.

The exclusion of the most valuable (to criminals) information from the Internet data stream eliminates any need for encryption, which in turn eliminates the need for any nonstandard software on the buyer's end. Ordinary e-mail—which effectively represents the lowest common denominator of Internet connectivity—is all that anyone needs in order to participate. The simplicity of this approach gained First Virtual more than a year's head start in the marketplace over the encryption-based approaches, and greatly lowered the entry barrier to anyone wishing to become a First Virtual user.

Another unusual feature of the First Virtual system is that it is explicitly designed for entrepreneurs. There is no screening process for sellers, allowing anyone on the Internet to open a new business. The system even includes an automated information server, the InfoHaus,™ that will (for an additional fee) make information continuously available for sale by Web, FTP, and e-mail, even for sellers who do not have their own Internet servers.

Full details about the First Virtual system are available elsewhere, as documented in the references. In this chapter, we will concentrate on the lessons we have learned from a full year of operating that system, processing transactions for real money. However, the system is sufficiently different from most other proposed approaches to Internet commerce that we have prepared a rather lengthy list of commonly raised concerns about First Virtual, and our responses, as Appendix A to an extended version of this paper, available on our Web pages at http://www.fv.com/pubdocs/fv-austin.txt.

II. WHAT HAVE WE LEARNED?

A. Organizational Issues

First Virtual has attracted some notice as an extreme example of a "virtual company." The company was certainly unusual in its initial organization: The four founders lived in San Diego, Orange County, Silicon Valley, and northern New Jersey. We promptly hired additional team members in distant parts of the same and other states. There were no physical offices until fifteen months after the company was founded (eight months after the system became operational). The servers were set up in a high-security machine room of Electronic Data Systems (EDS) in a suburb of Cleveland; the data 800 number was answered in Atlanta, Georgia; the voice 800 numbers started out in Portland, Oregon, but were then changed to move around from city to city. Marketing was handled from Washington, D.C., and public relations from San Diego. The company hired lawyers in San Diego, Los Angeles, Chicago, New York, Washington, and Cheyenne. Legally, First Virtual was a Wyoming corporation.

Some aspects of this decentralization worked well and were quite fun. Certainly it was always fun to tell the story of our "virtual office," as in the previous paragraph! But there were serious problems as well. While three of the four founders were longtime Internet veterans, one was not, and approximately half of the early employees (all the nontechnical ones) were Internet "newbies" who had to learn the ropes of working with others completely via the Internet. This is a nontrivial endeavor. The larger the company grew, the more seriously its productivity was impeded by communications difficulties, which ultimately led to the decision to consolidate the bulk of operations—and particularly new hires—in a small number of offices.

The biggest problems in running a distributed company were the more mundane aspects of any corporation—administrative tasks, scheduling meetings, making presentations to customers, and so on. There were a frightening number of near misses in which people were told of important meetings or discussions at the last minute, and an appalling number of emergency red-eye flights. It was much harder to gather people together for informal brainstorming sessions and other creative gatherings. The distributed nature of the company made it difficult to ensure that the company would speak with a unified voice in its public statements and difficult to avoid wasteful duplication of efforts. It is also far harder to integrate new hires into a virtual environment, particularly if they are not by temperament the kind of independent workers who function best in such an environment.

More specifically, the actual supervision of remotely located employees was a constant management challenge. The more distant these employees were from the initial founding and vision of the company, and the less clearly they understood the "big picture" of the company's strategy, the less likely they were to be able to execute their jobs productively without close supervision. This, in turn, was reflected directly in the degree to which their remote location was perceived as an impediment to their productivity.

Given these problems, it is tempting to say that virtual companies don't work. This is an oversimplification, and an irrelevant one in any event. First Virtual, in particular, could not have been created any other way. Its four founders were successful people who lived in four different parts of the country, and it was never a serious possibility that three of them would relocate in order to start a highly speculative new venture. (Later, as the company grew, some such moves did in fact take place.)

More generally, almost any Internet service company will by nature be somewhat "virtual," if only because of the need to support fully international operations. If you're going to be able to communicate with Internet-based customers around the world, in many languages, it is almost inevitable that you will end up with operations spread out to many countries, connected to each other primarily via the Internet. Thus the right question to ask is not "Should an Internet company be virtual?" but rather "How virtual should an Internet company be?" or perhaps "How can the advantages of a distributed company be maximized and the disadvantages minimized?"

What worked best were creative projects executed by small, strongly motivated, highly skilled teams. The basic technologies in First Virtual were all created by such teams, whose members never shared an office. However, the need for communication and clear task delegation among the team members argued for regular in-person meetings. Two-day monthly staff meetings, scheduled on a totally regular basis for the same days each month, have proven sufficient for such tasks.

Another ultimate strength of our operation, despite occasional problems, was the customer support system. Because all of First Virtual's customers have e-mail, the company is able to do nearly all of its customer support over the Internet. Our customer support operators are distributed across the United States, but this has not proven to be a problem. In general, the operators have worked well, and customer service has functioned well without paying rent for any office space.

One human and social benefit of a company with distributed customer support is that it creates a set of jobs that require a high level of mental skills but can be performed by people with severe physical disabilities. For example, First Virtual's senior customer support representative, one of the authors of this paper, is severely disabled in a manner that might inhibit his employment in many traditional work environments. By computer, from his home, he communicates using voice dictation software and has interacted with thousands of First Virtual customers who never had any inkling that he was disabled at all. We believe that, just for this benefit alone, it is well worth tolerating some of the more challenging aspects of a distributed corporation.

As the customer support staff grew, however, it became clear that while skilled customer service operators work well remotely, training is made more difficult by distance. Accordingly, a major current focus of the customer service department is the production of improved training materials for new operators.

An intangible factor that requires special attention in a virtual environment is employee morale. It is relatively easy for an employee working remotely to come to feel "out of touch" with the company as a whole. Regular meetings are helpful in this regard, as are frequent phone conversations. (All senior management employees were required to get three-way calling service, and they often chained together several three-way calls as an inexpensive mechanism to establish larger conference calls.) The customer service department is also contemplating morale-boosting incentives (e.g., a "silly question of the week" contest) that will facilitate friendly competition and communication among the customer service operators, whose entire job consists of dealing with the system's "rough spots."

In short, having everybody together at a single site is absolutely not a prerequisite for doing business on the Internet, which should be a relief to anyone contemplating serious international operations. However, a distributed operation carries some very specific pitfalls in terms of communication, efficiency, and motivation, which need to be understood and addressed by management early on. It also seems very compelling to try to centralize those operations that can be centralized, such as marketing, operations, and corporate administration.

B. The Need for an Internet Intermediary

One complaint that has been voiced about both First Virtual's system and several other proposed approaches to Internet commerce is that they create a new intermediary between the customer, the merchant, and the financial institutions. Our experience to date strongly suggests that this is not a bug but a feature, and that all parties involved will increasingly see the necessity of such an intermediary as the nature of Internet commerce becomes clearer.

The simple fact is that the Internet is a complex set of technologies and services that simultaneously make commerce possible and also form a barrier to the conduct of that commerce. The distributed, anarchic nature of the Internet makes certain classes of service oddities inevitable, including temporary partial network outages, total or partial communication failures either unidirectionally or bidirectionally, subtle incompatibilities between software on the buyer's and seller's ends, and much more.

What is often overlooked is that, from the buyer's perspective, the following two situations are indistinguishable: (1) a technical failure, possibly even one caused by an invisible intermediate third party, that prevents a reputable merchant from either delivering paid-for merchandise or notifying the buyer of its nondelivery and the refund procedures; (2) an unscrupulous merchant who defrauds customers for a quick profit. In our experience, the first case is far more common, but buyers are remarkably quick to assume the second case. This is in part human nature and in part the result of the strangeness of cyberspace business relationships, in which one sends money to some unseen person on the other side of the planet.[2]

Customers naturally expect and demand that the provider of payment services will mediate such situations and help to resolve them. Whoever performs that service is, ipso facto, a new intermediary in the payment process, to facilitate the resolution of problems in the Internet-specific aspects of the transaction. It seems unlikely that Internet commerce can flourish without such an intermediary. While it is certainly conceptually possible that such services could be provided by existing financial institutions, it must be remembered that the resolution of these problems can be quite complicated technically. Debugging obscure problems with incompatible implementations of Internet protocols is not a core competence of most financial institutions.

By analogy, people rarely object to the role played, in modern commerce, by parcel delivery services and telephone companies. If the Internet were somehow centrally administered, then the Internet-specific aspects of financial

---

[2] Over time, established brand-name identities may help reassure customers in such situations, but this is itself problematic. Brand identity in cyberspace may be too easily damaged by technical circumstances beyond the control of the identified corporation. Moreover, the establishment of brand identities will be in opposition with the egalitarian tendencies of the Internet, which will tend to promote small entrepreneurs or "micromerchants." Finally, anyone with an established brand identity needs to worry a good deal, on the Internet, about impostors speaking in their name.

transactions would be handled by that central administration in a manner that parallels the worlds of telephone and parcel services. However, the anarchic nature of the Internet leaves it without any central authority to resolve technical issues that pit buyers against sellers, and these are of paramount importance to the conduct of commerce. Therefore, some kind of Internet service bureau seems essential for investigation and resolution of these problems.

To make all of this more concrete, a few examples are given here. The First Virtual team has encountered dozens, perhaps hundreds, of these situations, many of them caused by "sophisticated" multinational corporations, and sees no likelihood that they will stop arising in the foreseeable future. Each new Internet software package or site seems to introduce new bugs arising from incompatible protocol implementation and the like, and *all* of these have an inevitable effect on the conduct of commerce. The following are a few selected examples:

FTP bugs: Some browser software puts an arbitrarily low maximum size on ftp file transfers. The net result is that the buyer gets a truncated file, which is often useless (e.g., for software). However, the seller, who believes that the buyer has successfully downloaded the software, sends a bill through First Virtual. (Sometimes the seller should have been able to tell that the download was aborted, but sometimes this is impossible.) This problem was first introduced when a Fortune 500 computer company began selling products using First Virtual, which demonstrates that technical sophistication is no protection.

Connectivity glitches: Sometimes a partial Internet outage occurs after a buyer has paid for access to a site but before he or she has been able to reap the benefit of it. From the buyer's perspective, this looks like an attempt to "take the money and run."

Catastrophic failures on the seller end: If a site sells subscriptions, and then has a catastrophic hardware failure, they are often unable even to tell their customers about the problem. Naturally, the paying customers feel the need to complain to someone and perhaps seek a refund.

Protocol violations: There are many well-known software vendors that provide broken implementations of core Internet protocols. Merchants that seek to make use of some of the higher-end features of the Internet are quite likely to encounter customers whose software doesn't work right. From the customer's perspective, it's difficult not to blame a merchant who promised a daily picture delivery by e-mail if the customer sees only a daily message that appears to be garbage (because of a broken MIME, or Multipurpose Internet Mail Extensions, implementation, for example). Such bugs are far from rare—they are found in widely used software from some of the most well-known software vendors.

Unanticipated e-mail limitations: Any services that sell information by e-mail, or particularly that provide e-mail–activated robots, are likely to encounter problems with software that imposes arbitrary limitations. For example, the Prodigy system currently truncates e-mail subject headers to an extremely short length, which messes up many robots that key off the subject headers, leaving Prodigy customers feeling cheated when they don't get a proper response.

Unidirectional communication: Many merchants attract customers to their Web pages, where they ask the customer for an e-mail address. Unfortunately, nearly half of all Internet users make a mistake when asked to type in their e-mail address, and thus provide an address that does not work.

Software configuration bugs: The widely used Netscape browser, for example, can be used to send mail but in its configuration-setting mechanism makes no attempt to verify that the user-supplied e-mail address is correct (or even syntactically legal!). Thus a surprising number of Netscape users never receive any replies to their e-mail, and never know why.

The preceding examples are used for illustration only; the actual number of such problems appears to be, for all practical purposes, without limit. Each major new service that comes on-line seems to exhibit at least one of these bugs, at least for a while. (The recently released Microsoft Network exhibits almost all of them, and more!) As long as the Internet is full of such glitches, there must inevitably be some kind of Internet-based intermediary for commercial transactions conducted via the Net. In order to resolve these situations, the intermediary must have a deep understanding of the way the Internet protocols actually work. In the last year, First Virtual's team has come to supplement that deep understanding with hundreds of detailed examples, most of which are reflected in patches to the system that work around other peoples' bugs.

In the long term, it is important for the Internet community to achieve a much greater degree of interworking between applications at the highest levels. Internet commerce will increase the demands of Internet users for service providers to provide software that works with everyone else's software, instead of application software that includes so-called features that do not interwork with other software. First Virtual believes that market demand for interworking applications will in due course persuade all Internet software vendors to more closely adhere to the open Internet Engineering Task Force

(IETF) standards. For now, however, there are substantial problems of interoperability and confusion caused by vendors trying to unilaterally define or extend the standards for Internet applications. First Virtual's interim strategy is to simultaneously work around, or "patch," the current problems and to exert pressure for conformance on nonconforming service providers and application vendors.

C. Security and Administrative Issues

The importance of Internet site security is widely discussed and well understood. It is of particular importance, of course, in the operation of a commerce server, as such a server is an obvious prime target for would-be criminals. First Virtual began with the assumption that our success would invite ever more frequent and more serious criminal attacks.

There is no reason to doubt that assumption. Our monitoring software reveals regular break-in attempts from various sites, although none, to our knowledge, have succeeded. Anyone contemplating the implementation of an Internet commerce server should acquire significant in-house expertise on Internet security and also regularly hire outside teams to test that security and report any flaws. The same teams should not be used repeatedly, as they will exhaust their bags of tricks before long.

Unfortunately, the more secure you make your server, the more difficult it is to administer it, especially remotely. Even for a commerce system based on noncryptographic mechanisms, such as First Virtual's, cryptographic tools are essential for secure remote access to the server. (In fact, First Virtual commissioned the development of PGP-encrypted telnet for just this purpose.) Special attention should be paid to the issue of the lifetime of cryptographic keys, as discussed in the section on cryptography later in this chapter.

While this section is necessarily short on details, there is a very clear lesson that should be understood by anyone with sensitive information on an Internet-connected machine: there are many criminals out there, and they will try to break in, either for financial gain or for sport. You must inconvenience yourself to a considerable degree, and at considerable expense, if you want to thwart them.

D. Customer Service Issues

Beyond the previously discussed need for an Internet intermediary, running a commerce system on the Internet entails a host of customer service issues that may not be obvious at first glance, especially to those already extremely comfortable with life on-line.

It has been pointed out that, because the Internet population doubles every eleven to thirteen months or so, at any given moment more than half the user community has been on the Net for less than a year. In other words, "newbies" are the rule, not the exception. The reality is that an ever-increasing proportion of the Internet's population has only the barest, most rudimentary understanding of how anything on the Internet—or on their computer—actually works.

Compounding this is the ever-increasing number of Internet users whose command of the English language is quite limited. Although English is often described as the de facto language of computing and the Internet, this is neither a completely accurate description nor one that sits well with members of other linguistic communities. Internet commerce systems are inevitably international, and when a customer in Japan buys from a vendor in Japan, it is unreasonable to assume that both will be fluent in English if they need to discuss a problem with the transaction.

The combination of poor Internet understanding, questionable English skills, and real money on the line often creates a confrontational situation. While some problems occur because of actual bugs in the commerce system, the vast majority are some form of "pilot error" or are due to Internet problems outside the domain of the commerce system. It therefore seems likely that the customer service load is for the most part not a consequence of our server design and must be factored in to virtually any plan to provide Internet commerce services. (Indeed, cryptographically based schemes, which entail the provision of public key technology to naive users, are likely to carry an even heavier customer support load.)

Although we have tried very hard, First Virtual has not always been commended for the timeliness of its customer service. The application domain is very new, the questions very numerous, and the user base doubled every six weeks for most of the first year. On several occasions, the help department has become seriously backlogged. We would recommend that anyone contemplating a similar service should plan on excess capacity in their customer support department. On the positive side, however, is our observation that a sizable majority of all customer support interactions are with new customers in their first few interactions with the system or with the Internet. Once users are familiar with the system, they ask relatively few questions, and the questions asked by new users generally come down to a few common issues that are easily answered, often resolvable with further automation, and should become less common as the system's documentation continues to improve.

E. Cryptography: Myths and Realities

One of the most misunderstood aspects of Internet commerce is the role of cryptography. Some parties have claimed that safe commerce is impossible without cryptography. Others have (incorrectly) interpreted First Virtual's noncryptographic system as evidence that our company is philosophically opposed to the use of cryptography. Not surprisingly, we have given these issues a great deal of thought in recent months, and we have reached some tentative conclusions.

The major risk in cryptography is the compromise of the cryptographic keys. Sometimes a secret key will be stolen without the knowledge of the user with whom it is associated. Other times, a public key that is supposed to belong to a given user may be illicitly replaced by a public key belonging to a third party. Either of these events will completely undermine the utility of the cryptographic algorithms. Thus, a safe application of cryptographic technology will pay close attention to how public keys are associated with user identities, how stolen keys are detected and revoked, and how long a stolen key is useful to a criminal. Although it is beyond the scope of this paper to discuss the infrastructure and customer support requirements involved in providing and authenticating cryptographic keys for each of the world's credit cards, which number in the hundreds of millions, our operational experience leaves us skeptical that it can be done at all.

A major factor that can limit these risks is the notion of key lifetimes, in which a public/secret key pair is explicitly declared in advance to be useful only until a certain date. The longer-lived the keys, the more likely it is that an attack will undermine their value. This is an area with crucial security consequences that are often neglected by proponents of cryptographic solutions. People routinely ask, when comparing cryptographic solutions, "How many bits long are the keys?"—a question that refers to the difficulty of a direct computational attack to break the cryptography. A similarly simple question that can be asked about all cryptographic schemes is, "How long-lived are the keys?" For example, a 1024-bit key with a five-year lifetime is probably considerably more vulnerable to criminal attack than a 512-bit key with a one-month lifetime.

In assessing the importance of the various risks, it is important to distinguish between the two main applications of cryptographic technology: authentication (digital signatures) and encryption. These are often confused or conflated, because they both utilize the same underlying cryptographic algorithms, but they are very different and must be discussed separately for a clear understanding.

These two uses of cryptographic technology have radically different implications in commerce systems, at both legal and technical levels. Legally, nearly all of the problematic restrictions apply to encryption, not authentication, because governments are concerned about being able to detect spying and other criminal activity.

Technically, the differences between authentication and encryption are fundamental, and are crucial to commerce in the event that the cryptographic technology is ever compromised or "broken." A realistic analysis of any cryptographic commerce mechanism must include an analysis of the consequences that will occur if a malicious party manages to break the cryptography. (By "breaking" the cryptography, we refer to either defeating the basic cryptographic algorithms, stealing the secret keys involved, or finding a serious bug in a widely used software implementation.)

In the case of authentication, a criminal who has broken the cryptography can impersonate one or more users. On the Internet, it is fairly easy for the impersonator to make himself completely untraceable. This is obviously a problem, but it is a bounded problem, in that the possible damage caused by the impersonator can be limited. In particular, if someone explicitly claims, on the Net, to be Bill Gates, then this allows him only to take those actions that are permitted to Bill Gates. Merchants can limit risk by only allowing Bill Gates to have merchandise delivered to his own home, or they can use other methods (such as e-mail or telephone confirmation, for example) to confirm the cryptographically asserted identity, particularly in the event that the compromise of such authentication has become relatively common.

Encryption, on the other hand, is often more of an all-or-nothing technology. The key to assessing the value of compromising encryption technology is an assessment of the value of the information being encrypted. In the case where a criminal has broken an encryption mechanism, that criminal can read all the encrypted information. Again, the criminal can take steps to be essentially untraceable when he is reading the encrypted information via the Internet. The cost of such a criminal act is precisely proportional to the value of the encrypted information. The more valuable your information—and thus the more likely you are to want to encrypt it—the less acceptable is the risk of having it stolen by an anonymous malicious party on the Internet. To put it more simply: if information is so valuable that you need to encrypt it, it's possibly too dangerous for you to accept the risk of putting it on the Internet in encrypted form and having that encryption broken. (Note that such considerations apply exclusively to the use of encryption to protect economic value, as opposed to the use of encryption for privacy, which is a very different matter.)

In the case of credit card numbers, the information most commonly proposed for encryption on the Internet, the logic is simple. Imagine a world in which millions of credit card transactions travel over the Internet, encrypted, every day. If a malicious party finds a flaw that allows him or her to decrypt that traffic, he has now untraceably obtained a stream of credit card numbers that is, for all intents and purposes, infinite. While the credit card system has evolved to tolerate a certain rate of fraud, it is unlikely to prosper in a scenario where a single criminal can steal so many card numbers. (This is because credit card fraud today is often traced by a pattern of use and abuse, but a smart criminal who stole millions of cards would only use each once, and would thus be far harder to track down.) If the criminal was truly malicious, and was motivated more by vandalism than by raw greed, he could quite conceivably defraud a significant percentage of the world's credit cards in a single day, essentially destroying the integrity of the whole credit card system.

In assessing these risks, it should be understood that the credit card and ATM industries are based on closed networks. The Internet is the most open networking environment imaginable, was not designed with the kinds of safeguards that are taken for granted on closed networks, and allows anyone in the world to gain essentially anonymous access. This is an environment in which the bank card industry has virtually no experience or expertise. Cryptographic solutions are actually much more useful in closed networks than open ones because they constitute only a part of the overall security (notably, privacy protection against competitive financial institutions) rather than the sole defense against criminals.

A cryptographic system will only be as strong as its weakest link, and one rarely knows in advance what the weakest link will turn out to be. This means, for example, that it doesn't matter how strong your encryption algorithm might be if it is possible to steal the data before it ever gets encrypted, for example via a key management virus that attaches itself to the user's computer and monitors the user's raw keystrokes. Similarly, the best encryption in the world is useless if the data can be stolen after it is decrypted, for example by a conventional "break-in" attack on the machine of an Internet-connected merchant, processor, or bank.

An obvious but often-ignored corollary of this bottom line is that, in an Internet commerce system, cryptography should not be permitted to become a critical-path component with a catastrophic cost of failure. This strongly implies, for example, that a partial reliance on cryptographic authentication is far more defensible than a total reliance on cryptographic encryption. While there is undoubtedly a role for encryption technology, it is far better to keep the most valuable information—including credit card numbers and other sensitive financial instruments—entirely off the Internet.

Overall, First Virtual's experience with running a completely noncryptographic payment system has been highly positive, with fraud rates so low as to elicit the excited attention of banking partners. This does not imply that the First Virtual system will forever remain noncryptographic; indeed, the limited use of cryptographic authentication is being implemented for First Virtual's second system as of this writing. (And in answer to the questions that should always be asked about such systems: First Virtual will be using 1024-bit keys with one-month key lifetimes.) However, First Virtual's experience strongly suggests that cryptography is at most a single tool in the pursuit of security and is neither an absolute requirement nor the panacea that its proponents often suggest.

III. WHERE ARE WE GOING?

After one year of operation, First Virtual's biggest problem is clearly growth management. With a user base and transaction volume that double every six weeks, we face significant operational challenges. As of this writing, the growth had helped cause one significant operational outage (in August 1995), and that outage attracted wide publicity and concern. Naturally, First Virtual has been devoting a great deal of effort to trying to avoid any further such outages.

Beyond the struggle to simply provide good service in the face of such growth, however, the First Virtual system is being expanded in multiple directions. The system was recently upgraded to better permit the sale of physical goods and services, as opposed to the information products for which the system was originally designed. This upgrade will allow for enhancements such as the use of cryptographic authentication of certain critical messages sent from First Virtual to our merchants. Future enhancements will include internationalization (for languages and currencies), additional mechanisms for buyers to pay into the system and for sellers to receive payment, and better support for extremely small transactions, sometimes known as "micropayments." Another priority is to open the system to participation by multiple processors and acquirers in the banking world.

A brief mention should be made about why the initial First Virtual system was limited to information products, as opposed to physical goods. The answer is twofold. First, we were enamored with the unique aspects of information commerce, and the consideration of this uniqueness was what led to the initial design of our system. Second, although First Virtual is a pioneering company, it is also a conservative one, with conservative founders and backers. The risk involved in any loss is far higher for those selling physical goods, and it was appealing to "shake down" the system before encouraging anyone to depend on it for such applications. The lessons of that shakedown period, as presented in this chapter, have guided the development of additional mechanisms that we believe will make the system completely suitable for commerce in physical goods.

In the larger world of Internet commerce, we expect that there will be a gradual sorting out of the issues, as the nature of Internet commerce becomes clearer. We expect to see, at a minimum, a growing realization that there must be some kind of Internet-based intermediary to help facilitate the technical aspects of Internet commerce. As far as cryptography is concerned, there will probably be a continuing series of "scandals" as it becomes clear that no encryption software is unbreakable, and that Internet commerce cannot depend upon the existence of unbreakable encryption. One fear is that this may cause a backlash against cryptography, in which the baby is thrown out with the bathwater, and the many practical benefits of cryptographic technology would fall into disrepute. First Virtual will do what it can to make sure this does not happen.

IV. CONCLUSIONS

When First Virtual's system went live on October 15, 1994, there was still widespread skepticism that Internet commerce would ever really take off. A year later, such skepticism has largely vanished, in favor of wild speculation and press release fever about the mechanisms of such commerce. Meanwhile, a few pioneers have actually been doing business in cyberspace, making some money and encountering some unexpected problems and misconceptions.

The biggest unexpected problems center around customer service. The Internet is a complicated place, and it isn't getting any simpler. An Internet-savvy customer service department is an absolute prerequisite for anyone providing commerce services to the Net.

The biggest misconception is that the words "security" and "encryption" are synonymous, or even closely related. A more balanced perspective on discussions of Internet commerce can often be obtained by replacing "computer" and "encryption" with "automobile" and "door lock." The mere existence of a door lock does not imply that the ignition keys (or a wallet) should be left inside the car. In general, it is safest to lock your car and remove your valuables. Similarly, while encryption can provide a modicum of additional security on the Internet, it is far more important to consider what is being encrypted, and not to encrypt anything that is better kept off the Net in the first place.

Internet commerce is real, and it is growing at breakneck speed. Early speculations about it have often proven to be far from the mark. The history of the Internet suggests that those who want to play a role in its evolution should start with simple technologies that really work, and expand them from there as circumstances require. First Virtual's initial payment system is clearly only one step in a larger evolution. There are very exciting times ahead.

REFERENCES

The best source of basic information about First Virtual's Internet Payment System is the First Virtual Web site, at http://www.fv.com/. Most of the same information is also available via e-mail, starting with info@fv.com.

Technical details about the First Virtual payment protocols have been published as Internet Drafts, and will be published as Informational RFCs. They are available for anonymous file transfer from the machine ftp.fv.com, in the directory pub/docs.

Borenstein, N. S., and M. T. Rose. "The Application/Green-Commerce MIME Content-Type." First Virtual Holdings Incorporated, June 1995. File name: pub/docs/agc-spec.{txt,ps}

Rose, M. T., and N. S. Borenstein. "The Simple MIME eXchange Protocol (SMXP)." First Virtual Holdings Incorporated, June 1995. File name: pub/docs/smxp- spec.{txt,ps}

Stein, L. H., E. A. Stefferud, N. S. Borenstein, and M. T. Rose. "The Green Commerce Model." First Virtual Holdings Incorporated, June 1995. File name: pub/docs/green- model.{txt,ps}

Those without prior familiarity with the MIME protocol may find the MIME specification invaluable in understanding some of the preceding documents:

Borenstein, N., and N. Freed. "MIME (Multipurpose Internet Mail Extensions) Part One: Mechanisms for Specifying and Describing the Format of Internet Message Bodies." RFC 1521, Bellcore, Innosoft, September, 1993.

Chapter 8

Economic Issues in Electronic Commerce

Alok Gupta, Dale O. Stahl, and Andrew B. Whinston

ABSTRACT

Dramatic advances in networking technology and computing paradigms, coupled with significant advances in creation and management of standardized multimedia documents, has resulted in explosive growth of the Internet. A new business environment (electronic commerce) is rapidly developing where computer data networks are involved in more than just providing peripheral support to business transactions. However, traditional economic understanding of how markets operate and should be managed falls far short of providing enough economic and managerial understanding of this market. This chapter outlines a framework for electronic commerce, including the issues of pricing, accounting, and payment. We address the economic challenges in this market and present some simulation results from the point of view of social welfare and optimal resource management. We discuss the difficulties of sustaining the socially optimal behavior because of the private market competition and the lack of property rights. Finally, we present a model that we will use to explore and analyze the economic issues in electronic commerce, including the role of regulatory policies.

1.0 INTRODUCTION

In the last five years, growth of the Internet has been nothing short of phenomenal. There are already an estimated 25,000 merchants in 150 countries

This research was funded in part by National Science Foundation grant #IRI-9005969 and #IRI-9225010 but does not necessarily reflect the views of the NSF. Partial support was also provided by the Hewlett Packard Corporation and the Texas Advanced Technology Program.

selling or advertising their products on-line. It is estimated that nearly 20 million individuals will use the Internet for commercial purposes by the end of this millennium. The question we pose to the readers is: Have you bought anything on-line yet? The answer to this question is normally no. The fact remains that most people use the network for noncommercial purposes and the only flourishing business related to the Internet is providing the access to the network. Users (potential customers) of on-line services are either using the Internet out of curiosity, to gain access to vast amounts of free information, for other educational purposes, or for simple e-mail connectivity.

Still, the popular press is filled with stories about on-line payment systems (such as First Virtual Holdings™, Cybercash™, Netcash™, etc.), the variety of services available, and pictures of glorious futuristic scenarios. On the other hand, several researchers and experts are increasingly wondering aloud whether the future of public data networks will be limited to its present uses and it is time for stagnation. In our opinion there is exaggeration on both ends of the spectrum; the Internet will continue to grow, and value-added services will eventually be used with higher frequency than the traditional telemarketing or mail-order systems as the network starts providing real-time games, entertainment, and other information.

There is a considerable body of literature related to electronic commerce, and several prototype commercial services are being offered over the Internet. However, it is not clear how different pieces of this puzzle fit together, that is, how and where the different aspects of electronic commerce, such as access, products, prices, delivery of goods, payment, and accounting come together. In particular, little effort has been made to understand the economic dynamics and incentives of this market. In this chapter we attempt to define a framework for analyzing economic issues in electronic commerce. We critically discuss and analyze (1) infrastructure pricing, including a brief summary of several suggested pricing approaches; (2) service pricing, including the effect of infrastructure pricing, payment mechanisms, and accounting framework on the service pricing; and (3) competitive effects on service pricing and the potential need for regulatory policies for electronic commerce.

Economics can provide answers regarding the resource allocation problem by creating markets and letting prices allocate the scarce resources. However, the economic answer for the Internet is a bit more complicated. First, since most of the costs are sunk into infrastructure, the marginal cost of Internet data transport is essentially zero (so if Internet resources were private goods, prices should be zero). Note that we have separated the process of data transport from the process of producing the information content of the packet being transported. Second, Internet resources are public goods and consequently congestion is a potential negative externality. Marginal-cost pricing of public goods can lead to a "tragedy of the commons" in which the common resource is overutilized, causing avoidable losses for the whole society. When negative externalities are real possibilities, prices should exceed the marginal cost of production by the marginal social cost of the congestion, in which case a consumer uses the resource if and only if their private benefit from use exceeds the social cost[1] of that usage.

We look at the future of public data communication networks with optimism but with open eyes. Consequently, we refrain from arguing that excess infrastructure capacity will always be available. While it is true that on the national level (in the United States) there is a significant amount of (unlit) fiber-optical cable, we think the way data-intensive applications and number of users are growing it will not be true for long. Furthermore, bottlenecks will often be occurring at the access points. At present, the best analogy can be made with the airline industry; the space to fly planes in the sky is rarely a problem, although often there is congestion at the airports.

Thus, in our discussion of product and service pricing we will explicitly take a usage-based pricing for infrastructure into account. We discuss several of the suggested pricing approaches and analyze them critically. We then look at different facets of pricing and accounting under a layered architecture, where each component can be used independently in conjunction with different approaches. For example, we consider payment mechanism as a service that in itself adds cost to a commercial transaction, and thus it should be considered in the total cost of a service to the consumer. In other words, we isolate and analyze the different components of electronic transactions and then describe the mechanisms (glue) that will hold these components together.

In section 2 we discuss the future of data communication networks, the characteristics of the products, and the resulting need for different service qualities. In section 3 we discuss product and infrastructure pricing, and some suggested payment mechanisms. In section 4 we suggest a framework for electronic transactions and accounting that can accommodate various pricing and payment approaches for different kinds of users and different types of products. In section 5 we present economic challenges in electronic commerce along with some of our simulation results and discuss a framework to analyze a wide variety of economic factors that affect electronic commerce. Finally, in section 6 we conclude with suggestions for future research.

---

[1] Social cost is the collective delay cost of all the users of the network. Typically, the delays (and thus the social costs) in a network are an increasing function of volume of network traffic and they increase at a more rapid rate as the volume reaches the capacity.

2.0 THE FUTURE

To understand the nature of transactions for electronic commerce, it is necessary to understand the underlying nature of products and services that will be offered over the network. Furthermore, network communication protocols have to accommodate different service requirements. In this section we first introduce the different kinds of products that may be offered via the Internet and the related service requirements, and then we explain how different service requirements may be satisfied with the existing technology.

2.1 Products in the Electronic Marketplace

All kinds of products can be sold through the network, for example, cars, furniture, software, information, and movies. The important distinction among these products is that some can be delivered through the data network whereas others have to be shipped to the consumer via traditional channels. The payment mechanism for both kinds of services could be identical in spirit, but for informational products, perhaps, a wide array of challenging options will need to be designed and presented to the consumers; we will discuss some of these shortly. For now, we concentrate on the characteristics of the products and services that can be delivered through the network; in particular, we want to discuss the issue of data transmission requirements.

Some products, such as software and information, may not necessarily require a real-time data transfer (unless the consumer wants it), that is, a reasonable amount of delay in delivery is tolerable, which may be a result of delayed shipment or simply retransmission of dropped or corrupted data packets. On the other hand, some services such as teleconferencing, interactive games, and movies may require real-time data transfer with virtually no degradation in service quality in terms of retransmission. Also, as mentioned earlier, a consumer may have an urgent need for a service that does not otherwise need real-time transmission.

It is therefore necessary that these data transmission requirements be addressed by service providers or retailers. Clearly, this means that different levels of data transmission are required at the infrastructure level. Furthermore, it will be highly restrictive to tie a level of service to a type of service or product since consumers may have different needs.

Moreover, some products may be priced on the basis of usage. Consider the following examples:

1. A consumer downloads a software, which executes on the consumer's machine and monitors the usage (for example, a Java applet

that provides customized interface to a database); consumers are billed periodically according to their monitored usage.

2. A consumer sends a general query for details about a certain event; the service provider or the information broker sends all the information it can find, with different prices tagged to information from different sources; the consumer reads only selected sets of information and pays for only the information he or she actually uses.

In the latter case the consumer may have to pay high transmission costs; however, if the information is sought and retrieved piece by piece, there may be higher search-related transmission and processing costs. Clearly, in such cases the service providers and the consumers have to consider the trade-offs between volume transfer and selective search.

2.2 Service Levels and the Infrastructure

One possible way to provide different classes of services for electronic commerce is to provide different priority levels on demand. We do not favor coupling of services/applications to the priority classes such as suggested by Bohn, Braun, and Wolff (1994). They propose a voluntary precedence level choice for different applications dependent upon their delay requirements and loss sensitivity. In this scheme the consumers' traffic is monitored after some time interval (say monthly), and users may be penalized if they do not choose an appropriate precedence for their application. There is a clear lack of incentive to provide multiple precedence networks on the part of network providers under this scheme since it only adds to the overhead of managing multiple service classes and monitoring usage in those classes. Moreover, it will be a mistake to categorize the service requirements by just looking at the *appearance* or *title* of an application or service—we must look at the context in which an application is used. For example, consider e-mail-based real-time transaction systems that are being developed by some researchers (see Kalakota, Stallert, and Whinston, 1995) or e-mail-based EDI systems, clearly in such applications even e-mail cannot tolerate any delay. We believe only users can truly know what level of service is tolerable for their purposes, and service providers should play only a passive role in deciding the service quality. This can be ensured through a proper incentive mechanism, that is, by pricing the different service levels appropriately.

Another part of the problem arises from the fact that the Internet of the future will consist of several multi–service class data communication networks. Besides the technological issue of interoperability, one has to provide enough incentive for these individual networks to provide similar service class levels across the whole network. Specifically, why will a network provide a high service class to a request from another network without proper incentive, and if a price is quoted, how will a network requesting a service class know whether it is fair? We discuss pricing in more detail in the following sections.

3.0 PRICING

The total cost of any product, to the consumer, implicitly has three factors: search cost, price of the product, and delivery/acquisition cost. For products that have to be delivered via traditional channels, the delivery/acquisition cost is the cost of shipping via different available channels, for example, regular or overnight shipping or driving back with the product in a car; similarly, in a multiple service class network the delivery cost of a product or the service will be dependent upon the customer's required quality of service. Thus, it makes sense to price the network access according to a customer's required quality of service. There are several suggested approaches using discriminatory pricing for the network access to provide multiple service classes. We provide a brief summary and discussion of these approaches in the next subsection.

3.1 Infrastructure Pricing for Multiple Service Class Networks

First, let us consider why appropriate pricing of network infrastructure is important. As discussed earlier, electronic commerce will require multiple service class networks, which have to deliver appropriate performance. Appropriate pricing in these service classes can provide enhanced performance (in terms of response time and thus the quality of service)[2] and load distribution by managing the congestion. For example, consider the response time from a network node A to a network node B, which is a function of data volume traveling between the two nodes. Now, if there are users who can postpone requesting their services until noncongested times, the delay suffered by other users (or the deterioration in their service quality) can be reduced. Consider the case of free access, in which a user will submit a request if her incremental delay cost is smaller than her incremental benefits from requesting the services. However, from the point of view of the entire community, the total cost of submitting a request is the additional delay suffered by all the other users because of this request—social cost. Only those users whose

---

[2] We take a business point of view for the term *quality of service*. For the delay-sensitive applications and the users who require these services, any delay suffered in receiving the services can be perceived as a deterioration in quality of service.

incremental benefits from using the network during the congested times are higher than the incremental social cost should do so, while others should postpone their requests until uncongested periods.

Hence, if the access price is zero, too many users will use the network at congested times because they do not face the full social cost of their decision; in other words, they are not concerned with the service quality delivered by the network as long as their own service quality is adequate. The theoretical economic solution is to set the price of access during the congested period equal to the incremental social cost (less the private time cost or the deterioration in their own service quality); this is called the optimal congestion toll. Then, by comparing the incremental benefit of submitting a request with the total private cost (congestion toll + private time cost), each citizen will voluntarily make the socially optimal decision, including the choice of an appropriate service class in a multiple service class network.

In addition to achieving a socially optimal resource allocation for the network, socially optimal pricing provides correct signals for evaluating capital investment decisions. Without optimal pricing, there is a bias toward excess capacity. To see this, simply observe that, starting from a free access policy, social benefits can be increased by implementing optimal pricing without any additional capital investment, while under free access the same increase in gross social benefits would require costly capital investment. In other words, as compared with free access, socially optimal pricing can provide a higher level of performance without additional capital investment. We provide some gross estimates of these savings in section 5.

Several pricing schemes have been suggested for the usage of the network. These pricing schemes can be broadly divided into two categories: those suggested by the economists and those suggested by the practitioners. While the focus of the latter group is to suggest schemes that can readily be implemented and are relatively easy to understand, the former group often is worried about the economic implications such as social welfare, incentive compatibility, profit maximization, and so on. However, economic approaches seldom have addressed the issue of implementation and have rarely looked beyond analytically treatable models.

In our view, any infrastructure pricing scheme should satisfy the following five conditions:

1. It should have a theoretical basis to allow for analytical guidelines; however, the theoretical results should be based on appropriate abstraction of the real problem and not on oversimplified models.

2. It should be operational, since normative guidelines are of little use if an approach cannot be adapted for practical use.

3. It should adjust prices in real time to accommodate the dynamic

demand and the resulting dynamic state of the network; that is, it should consider the transient nature of the problem, since it is unlikely that the Internet will ever be in a steady state.

4. Overhead costs should be manageable. For example, some pricing schemes require networkwide information, while others require billing from each router in the path of information flow; this makes informational requirements in the former types of schemes and monetary requirements in the latter schemes unmanageable. Any potential gains from using a pricing scheme may be wiped out if the overhead costs of implementation are too high.

5. It should be adequately tested with reasonably scaled models.

We discuss some of the proposed pricing mechanisms in the following and discuss their merits and shortcomings with respect to the conditions specified above.

3.1.1 Dynamic Optimal Pricing

Stahl and Whinston (1991, 1992) and Gupta, Stahl, and Whinston [GSW] (1996a) developed this approach for network computing environments and investigated its practicality using simulation. Subsequently GSW (1995a, 1995b, 1996b) applied their network models to the Internet.

At the center of the GSW approach is a general mathematical representation of a computing network, a model of price- and time-sensitive user demand for services, and a stochastic model of traffic flows and buffers. It is shown that a socially optimal allocation of scarce network resources can be achieved by imposing optimal priority pricing at each site of potential congestion. The optimal prices depend on the traffic flow at the site, the size of the packets, the priority class, and the social cost of time. The latter can be econometrically estimated from the sensitivity of traffic to actual price and throughput time fluctuations at the site. The GSW approach distinguishes itself from other economic approaches (discussed later) by proposing a practical decentralized method of determining optimal prices in real time and constructing a simulation model to demonstrate the feasibility of this proposal.

In GSW (1995a, 1996b), the simulation model is calibrated to represent the Internet and to compare the historical free-access policy with the theoretical optimal pricing. This calibrated simulation suggests that without effective management of the Internet (as provided by efficient pricing), congestion and misallocation of resources could cost the economy hundreds of billions of dollars of lost benefits per year. This same simulation also demonstrates that the potential social gains of optimal pricing, if sought solely from capacity expansion, could have a capital investment cost exceeding the social gains. Thus, we argue that congestion is a very real concern and not just a theoretical fine point.

In the GSW vision a typical user deciding whether and when to access an Internet service would be presented with a menu of options, including the monetary cost and (when relevant) expected throughput time for each option. The options would specify a priority class and could also include a security/anonymity level, minimum guaranteed qualities, and contingency options such as "submit the service request when the cost falls below $b." The user would then select the most preferred option. A personalized smart agent could automate the user's decision process based on previously specified user preferences. Frequently updated price and time information would come from the user's access provider. Smart-agent software could serve this function also, gathering information from posted prices of transport providers and network congestion status reports.

The user would not receive a bill from each node and link of the network but would receive one bill from his or her access provider for the posted price of that access provider for the service requested.[3] In turn, the access provider would receive a bill from the transport providers to which it is connected based on posted prices and actual usage. Each network transport provider need keep accounts only for the adjacent providers to which it is connected, not the individual users. In the vertical direction, each telecommunication carrier (such as AT&T™, MCI™, Sprint™) need keep accounts only for the networks (such as PSI™, AlterNet™, ANS™, etc.) to which it provides Internet Protocol (IP) transport. This disaggregated pricing and billing approach mirrors the wholesale pricing practices in most industries. Ultimately it is the responsibility of the access providers to charge the user and to cover its costs vis-à-vis the transport providers.

Capital investment decisions can be greatly improved by the imposition of optimal priority pricing. First, as demonstrated in GSW (1996b), imposition of priority pricing alone may generate more benefits at a much lower cost than the cost of capacity expansion. Second, without priority pricing, since the physical resource allocation is inefficient, the observed congestion can be a bad signal regarding the parts of the infrastructure that should be expanded first. By imposing optimal pricing first, the distribution of network traffic can change significantly, revealing a different ranking of the

---

[3] Recall that we are dealing with network transport services only. The user might well receive bills for the content of the data transported from many independent content providers.

bottlenecks. Thus, with optimal pricing, capital investment can be focused on projects that will produce the greatest benefits.

This pricing scheme is quite consistent with all five of the conditions for infrastructure pricing. To further reduce the overhead and computational cost, this approach can be further approximated by a stepped-pricing scheme, as discussed in the next section.

3.1.2 Stepped Pricing by Facility

Optimal dynamic pricing specifies prices at each facility and for each moment in time, priority class, and job size. Potential administrative complexities of this ideal make it worthwhile to consider simple approximations to the ideal.

Congestion can be measured in terms of expected delays or the percentage of bandwidth capacity utilization. The optimal prices are a smoothly increasing function of bandwidth capacity utilization. One approach would be to approximate this smooth function by a step function, that is, a partition of bandwidth capacity utilization into exhaustive categories (such as 0–50 percent, 50–75 percent, 75–100 percent), and a price for each category. We will call this "stepped pricing."

Every such categorical scheme would have an "uncongested" category and one or more congested categories. In the uncongested category, the price would be set equal to zero, since the marginal social costs are essentially zero. In the congested categories the price would be an average of the optimal dynamic prices for the range of congestion in that category. In a two-category scheme, there would be just one nonzero price at each facility.

The best way to specify congestion categories and prices could be investigated theoretically and via simulation modeling. What would be the best way to improve the efficiency over that of a simple two-category stepped-pricing scheme? Would societal benefits be increased more by going to a three-category scheme or by introducing a two-priority system?

Edell, McKeown, and Varaiya (1994) present a specific system for metering traffic and billing users within TCP protocols. A test of this system based on the BayBridge gateway demonstrates that it is practical. Transport Control Protocol (TCP) traffic data from the University of California at Berkeley reveal that time-of-day usage pricing could decrease peak loads due to the shift of e-mail and bulletin-board traffic to off-peak times. More important, if prices were to vary dynamically in response to congestion, the efficiency of the network could be increased dramatically. Thus, a fairly good approximation to dynamic optimal pricing may be practical.

3.1.2 Static Priority Pricing

Cocchi, Shenker, Estrin, and Zhang [CSEZ] (1993) pose the general problem of designing a service discipline and a pricing scheme that maximize time-averaged user benefits. A service discipline is a mechanism implemented by the network operators to assign jobs to specific service classes (such as best effort, virtual connection, guaranteed minimum delay), and a pricing scheme associates a price (by bandwidth usage) to each service class (see also Shenker 1995). CSEZ specifically investigate a standard two-priority service discipline. Theoretically, there is an optimal allocation of user demands to each priority, and there are prices for each priority such that each user facing those prices will voluntarily select the socially optimal priority. Using a simulation model, CSEZ demonstrate that optimal priority prices can be found that significantly increase the benefits over single priority and discipline and the corresponding usage pricing. CSEZ require the revenue collected under the two alternatives to be the same. Since access charges can be adjusted to make up differences in usage-based revenues, this restriction is not necessary. If the optimal single-priority pricing scheme raises more (less) revenues than the system needs to cover fixed costs, then why should the two-priority scheme be constrained to generate the same surplus (deficit) of revenues? The preferred economic analysis would impose no revenue restrictions and would solve any resulting surplus/deficit problems separately. Any revenue restriction will muddy the comparison of the benefits of two priorities versus one priority, and will cause the prices to differ from the socially optimal level. Further, unlike GSW, CSEZ model the user demands as inelastic with respect to cost, that is, the demand is not affected by the cost; Shenker (1995) acknowledges the importance of elastic demand.

CSEZ do not present a computational algorithm for these prices, so we cannot assess the practical feasibility of that crucial task. From the mathematical model, it appears that a central authority would need vast amounts of proprietary information from the users about the value of each class of service, but the users have incentives to misreport that information.

These priority prices are "static" in the sense that they do not vary with the dynamic state of the network. There will be times when the network is badly congested and high-priority users will be paying too little. Moreover, in contrast with optimal dynamic pricing by facility, the CSEZ scheme effectively has a high-priority request paying a premium at every facility even if only some or none are congested.

While this approach has some theoretical base, its operationalization in a large network is quite infeasible. This approach also has a very high overhead cost component since it requires the information regarding the state of the whole network to compute prices. Furthermore, as discussed earlier, it is a static pricing approach that does not take the dynamic state of the system into account.

3.1.3 The "Smart-Market" Approach to Congestion Pricing

Parallel to the research described earlier, MacKie-Mason and Varian (1995) have proposed a different approach to implementing optimal congestion pricing. Rather than using econometric methods to estimate the social cost of congestion, they propose a continuous-time "Vickery" auction mechanism in which the users have incentives to state their true willingness to pay for faster service. This can be accomplished by an incentive-compatible auction (or "smart market").

To see the motivation of this approach, consider that there are a fixed number of jobs that users want processed in a given time interval and that everyone would like their job done sooner rather than later. In what order should the jobs be done? Let each person submit a monetary bid for the right to have his or her job processed. Submitted bids are ordered from the largest to the smallest, and the jobs are processed in this order. The price paid by every processed job is the bid of the first job not processed during the allotted time interval. If all jobs are processed, the price is zero. It is optimal for every user to bid the true value of the job no matter what the other users do. To see this, note that bidding more will increase your chances of having your job processed only in those cases where the price you pay turns out to be greater than the true value of your job, and bidding less will only decrease your chances of having your job processed without affecting the price you pay.

MacKie-Mason and Varian propose that the Internet operators run "smart markets" for packets at every potential site of congestion. Each user includes a bid in the header of every packet. The network gateways carry out the sorting at frequent periodic intervals. Under this scheme, every packet would suffer a one-period delay while packets are being queued and bids sorted, before proceeding to the normal routing and transmission function. Besides this deadweight loss of time, there are other theoretical and practical problems with this approach.

The efficiency properties of the smart market pertain to a static situation in which (1) all potential packets are present at the auction, and (2) the value of a packet should not depend upon the conditional passage of other packets through a node. Both of these assumptions are violated in a dynamic stochastic network. First, observe that to work in real time, bidding must be confined to fixed intervals of time; hence, packets that arrive later, even nanoseconds later, have no influence on the current price. In contrast, the fully optimal congestion prices depend on the extra delay imposed on all future arrivals. This "generational" bias will cause inefficiencies in resource allocation just as citizens in a republic may squander natural resources because the unborn cannot vote. Second, the value of having a packet transmitted is contingent on having other related packets transmitted also. No matter how a user allocates bids among the thousands of packets that constitute a single Internet transaction, ex post regret will be rampant. Sometimes almost all packets will get through without incurring any significant charge but the last crucial few will get dropped, so the user will wish the bid had been concentrated on the packets that encountered congestion. Other times a few crucial packets will get dropped first (but after all others have begun their journey), and the user will have wasted bids on the later, now worthless, packets. Of course, we could imagine an elaborate accounting system to ameliorate these problems, or we could imagine a dynamic bidding process in which each packet could communicate with the others so as to coordinate their bids as every packet proceeds through the network. Both of these solutions are clearly impractical in packet-switched computer networks.

3.1.4 Connection-Only and Flat-Rate Pricing

By far the predominant forms of pricing currently in practice are combinations of connection-only and flat-rate pricing. The connection-only fee is usually based on the bandwidth of the user's connection for a contracted period of time, with discounted rates for longer-term contracts. Recently, some frame relay networks have offered a Committed Information Rate (CIR) on top of a low maximum bandwidth connection fee. Users who stay within the CIR are guaranteed uninterrupted transport service, but if they exceed the CIR they receive best-effort service only. However, many customers, to the surprise of the providers, set the CIR to zero (Clark, 1995).[4] Moreover, since the users do not face the full social cost of their usage decisions, connection fees cannot induce the socially optimal reallocation of demands during congested times.

In addition to these fixed connection fees, many providers charge a variable fee based on active connection time (e.g., AOL and Prodigy). Since there is a positive correlation between connection time and bytes transmitted, one could view connection time fees as an indirect measure of bandwidth usage.

---

[4] Clark (1995) has proposed a pricing scheme similar to Committed Information Rates but more generally applicable beyond virtual circuit protocols. Presumably, as the Internet becomes more congested, users would begin to choose higher CIRs (or expected bandwidth) to ensure against interruptions during especially congested periods.

However, it is important to recognize that connection time is not an accurate measure of bandwidth usage, and it obviously does not discriminate between a real-time video session and an e-mail session. Hence it does not confront the user with the correct social cost of his or her specific usage.

Flat-rate pricing consists of a fee for bandwidth usage that does not vary with the level of bandwidth usage or the current state of congestion. Compuserve offers flat-rate pricing, and New Zealand and Chile have experimented with flat-rate pricing for their international link. The latter has had a bad experience primarily because of two disjointed competing networks, which raises the important issue of whether ideal socially optimal solutions can be implemented in privately owned competing networks; we will discuss this issue in more detail in section 5.

If Internet traffic were fairly uniform—characterized by an average flow with a relatively small variance and standard-sized noncontiguous packet streams—then a well-coordinated layered regional system of flat-rate pricing might achieve much of the maximum attainable efficiency. However, Internet traffic is anything but uniform. It is characterized by frequent irregular bursts of contiguous packets, and the variance in flow tends to increase more than proportional to the average flow. In such an environment there are huge potential efficiency gains from better resource allocation during and between bursty periods. These gains can only be realized by dynamic optimal pricing.

Wang, Peha, and Sirbu (1995) propose a two-part pricing scheme that consists of a flat rate for usage up to a guaranteed bandwidth and a surcharge for best-effort service beyond the guaranteed bandwidth. They solve for profit-maximizing prices rather than socially optimal prices. While they suggest an algorithm for computing their solution (a network-wide fixed point), whether it will work in practice is unclear. Using net user benefits rather than profits as the objective, one could solve for socially optimal two-part prices. However, since the price paid for bandwidth usage is independent of the state of congestion in the network, this scheme will not provide the necessary incentives for efficient usage.

3.2 Service/Product Pricing

As suggested by GSW (1995a, 1996a, 1996b) multiple service classes (and hence service qualities) can be provided by modeling the different service classes as different priorities and pricing the service according to the priority class it was acquired in. As discussed earlier, the cost of a product could be based on an outright sale or on the usage where the product will have usage monitoring and billing capability; throughout this chapter when we refer to

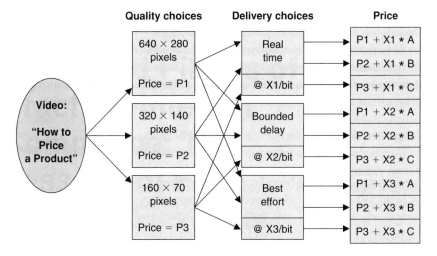

Figure 8.1   An Example of Consumer Choices and Prices

product prices, we include the possibility that this may be a pay-per-use price. In the context of electronic commerce the search costs may be modeled in the same way.

Thus, from our perspective the cost of a product, for on-line delivery, to the customer would be the cost of search, the price for the product, and the quality of service (infrastructure usage price in appropriate priority class) the customer desires. We will discuss the operationalization of this approach in the next section. Figure 8.1 provides an example of a possible pricing structure for a video clip, where A, B, and C are sizes of the video clip in full-screen, half-screen, and quarter-screen (quality choices) mode, respectively.

4.0 PAYMENT AND ACCOUNTING

We consider payment and accounting as separate network services that will be required along with any commercial service purchased or sold over the network. In this section we discuss some of the proposed payment mechanisms and suggest an accounting framework.

4.1 Payment Mechanisms

Several payment mechanisms have been suggested and implemented on the network in the last year, and several other proposals are being discussed.

Essentially, there are two schools of thought: develop electronic cash—which will facilitate anonymous transactions just as the traditional cash transactions do, and develop electronic credit cards—which will presumably provide more protection against fraud. Both types of systems have their challenges; for example, electronic cash is susceptible to possible duplication and other currency fraud, while electronic credit cards will sacrifice anonymity to a certain extent.

While several features such as illegitimate duplication, payment verification, and consumer protection against retailer fraud are the common threads in these payment mechanisms, there are several differences. Essentially, different consumer concerns are being addressed by different mechanisms. For example, while netbill (see Sirbu and Tygar 1995) focuses on smaller transaction costs, the netcash proposal (see Medvinsky and Neuman 1993) is more concerned with anonymity such as is provided by cash purchases, and global convertibility of electronic money or hard (electronic) currencies. However, as a practical matter, one feature has to be sacrificed to some extent to obtain another; for example, anonymity will increase the chances of fraud, and convertibility may add overhead processing, reducing the performance or quality of service.

One major shortcoming of these mechanisms is that they are looked at in isolation from consumer needs, accounting methods, and technological advances. For example, anonymity can be achieved via anonymous accounts, that is, it is not important that payment patterns of an account are identified as long as the person or organization owning that account remains anonymous. Furthermore, in the proposed mechanisms anonymity is actually partial in that the *bank* can still keep track of consumer payments if it wants to. The question that needs to be explored is whether the additional transaction cost inflicted in an effort to maintain this partial anonymity is justified.

The Netcash proposal claims that transaction costs may be as small as one cent for a ten-cent transaction (10 percent). However, in many instances even a cent per transaction is quite high, for example, if a broker wants regular stock updates and the payment verification takes place at every transaction. These costs can simply be avoided by alternative accounting approaches such as a credit or monetarily secured account where the customer is authorized to use the services up to a certain limit without verification. While the Netcash proposal does not exclude such possibilities, it does not consider them explicitly.

For example, if transaction costs are of primary concern, then we can propose yet another payment mechanism that stems from two main observations: (1) in most consumer transactions in the marketplace, users are generally satisfied with the level of anonymity traditional credit cards provide, and, perhaps more important, government regulations and laws may require that transactions be revealed to them; and (2) for electronic commerce, where many transactions will be time-sensitive, the number of messages that need to be processed should be minimized. We maintain some of the desired characteristics, such as protection of consumers and the vendors from refund or nonpayment, fraud protection against double spending and money duplication, and scalability. True scalability can be provided only when the same currency is used by all the "banks" or when convertibility agreements are in place among the different banks. We think that the latter approach is more practical and can easily be achieved by having a convertible relationship with traditional hard currencies.

Figure 8.2 illustrates necessary components of this electronic payment mechanism, which will facilitate a complete set of possible applications, including real-time applications such as movies or interactive games, with a minimal number of transactions. Under this scheme once a customer and a service provider agree upon the service quality and payment amount (we will elaborate on how this contract may be reached in the next section), the specified amount is verified to be in the customer's account by the provider and is reserved for the service provider by the customer (or its bank). At this moment the money is not transferred to the service provider and the service is not delivered; both the customer and the service provider have a key that needs to be submitted to the account in order to release the money either to the service provider or back to the customer (in case of failure to deliver required services). Once the customer receives the services, he or she releases the money to the service provider.

Note that in the case where the customer does not want to pay after receiving the services, the service provider can still prevent the money from being spent and can submit a claim directly to the bank, providing the proof

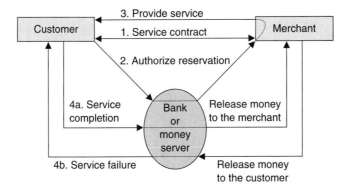

Figure 8.2 Necessary Components of an Electronic Payment Mechanism

of services rendered consistent with the contract. Similarly, the customer can get his or her money released if services are not provided and the service provider refuses to release the money.

Also, perhaps the most efficient way of maintaining an electronic money account will be by providing an account on which the entity issuing the money (the bank) has read and write permissions while a customer has only read and executable permissions (borrowing terms from the UNIX file system). Finally, a customer can provide read access and partial executable control to the service provider once the contract is agreed upon to facilitate the above-mentioned transaction. Such a system has a potential to be reasonably anonymous (barring the possibility that the bank monitors every transaction) since the bank needs to be involved only when more money needs to be added. Appropriate encryption can provide a bank's seal of money authentication to the service provider, who need not be given the information on whose account was actually accessed.

In our view, there will be several payment mechanisms operated by different "banks," and consumers will have a choice of a payment mechanism for their electronic product. For example, if some consumer wants to maintain a high level of anonymity while purchasing a product (e.g., a pornographic movie or a fascist book), he or she may choose a system that provides high anonymity. On the other hand, if for some other product the overriding concern is minimizing transaction costs (e.g., regular stock quotes) due to the number of messages that need to be processed, the same consumer may choose another payment mechanism for this type of transaction. In fact, a single payment mechanism may allow consumers to choose among the varying degrees of different attributes according to their needs. The vendors will have to subscribe to (or support) various mechanisms in order to be competitive. In the next section we discuss an accounting framework, which is the next layer on top of the products, pricing schemes, and payment mechanisms. A properly designed mechanism will have the potential to further reduce transaction costs and perhaps increase privacy.

Figure 8.3 provides a sketch of consumers' decision processes, the costs involved, and their total expected costs, including the costs due to payment servers. As the figure indicates, both consumers and service providers may subscribe to several payment mechanisms and may use the most suitable one for a particular transaction. Service providers may provide several service classes with different qualities of service in different classes, resulting in different prices for the same information. Note that, as indicated in Figure 8.1, the complicated process of computing prices for a given set of transactions will be transparent to the consumers, and they will just have a fixed set of choices from which to choose a service class. Furthermore, the choice of a service class will potentially be delegated to a smart agent working with a

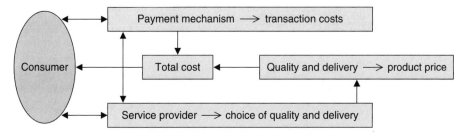

Figure 8.3 Consumer Decision Process and Costs

consumer's client software or to an information broker operating on a consumer's behalf. We believe arguments that criticize such pricing approaches on the grounds of being too complicated are naive; electronic commerce transactions will be aided by powerful workstations and, with appropriate software, these computers will provide unprecedented analytic sophistication to consumer decision processes. Even in the traditional markets such as airline ticket prices, or even gasoline prices, there are different prices for the same product, which may depend upon location, reputation, service, and product quality.

4.2 Accounting Framework

A proper accounting mechanism has the potential to further decrease transaction costs. For example, if a service provider is a regular customer, then an internal credit account can reduce the transaction costs associated with payment verification mechanisms by internalizing the process (electronic store cards). Furthermore, daily accounts can be created by obtaining credit verification once for a stipulated amount, if a consumer wants to access several pieces of information/services during a day or a given period. A proper accounting mechanism can be designed to suit the needs of a consumer from the perspective of minimizing transaction costs and delays.

Figure 8.4 illustrates an accounting framework and the process of reaching a contract between a vendor and a consumer. This figure is quite coarse in differentiating the consumer types; further granularity can be achieved by designing appropriate mechanisms for customers who are somewhere in the middle of the two extremes depicted in the figure. A contract requires three or four steps depending upon the consumer type.

The first step is the consumer's request for price quotes. The vendor then provides the price quotes, perhaps in several service classes; for example, an on-line video can be delivered in full-screen real time, half-screen real time,

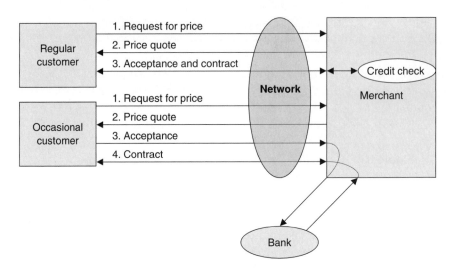

Figure 8.4   The Process of Contract Agreement for Different Types
of Customers

full-screen with bounded delay, half-screen with bounded delay, full-screen
with unbounded delay, and so on. The consumer then accepts a price and
service class or breaks off the communication. If a consumer accepts the service in a given class (and thus the price), the contract is established, pending
the payment verification. In the case of regular customers, this process is in-
ternalized and the consumer sends an account verification along with service acceptance. An occasional customer provides access to a bank account
for verification process. Finally, the transaction takes place as described in
Figure 8.2.

The vendors provide the cost of service in different classes by obtaining
the transmission-price information for different classes from their infrastructure providers. This process may be real-time, that is, they may have to obtain the price information every time a transaction takes place, or after a certain given interval of time, or it may be long-range time-based pricing such
as monthly prices with prices divided according to the time of day. Clearly
this makes the cost of a vendor's products dependent upon who they choose
as their infrastructure providers, whether their providers have interconnection agreements with other networks, and how open and fair the access to
different service classes is across the network.

If the price of a product depends upon the size of the product (full-screen
video versus half-screen), then there has to be a flow measurement mechanism in place. There have been successful implementations based on flow-
measured pricing (see, e.g., Brownlee 1994). However, there is always a

dilemma as to where the flow measurement should take place, that is, at the sender or the receiver. This is a complex problem, especially if there are no interconnection agreements among the networks over which the transaction is taking place. However, assuming that it is in the mutual interest of different service providers that they provide seemingly transparent connectivity, we favor the measurement at the sender's end. The reasons are multiple:

- Fewer billing and collection costs: If both sender and receiver are billed for traffic, for each transaction two entities need to be billed as opposed to only one.

- Since in a commercial setting most traffic will originate from the vendors, the measurement at the sender's end should be given highest priority.

- Consumers will have a more realistic idea of their costs since vendors can include the transmission costs in the price if the traffic is billed at the sender's end.

- Protection against junk mail: Consumers should not be charged for the material they did not solicit; imagine paying for all the junk mail one receives in traditional mail.

Until now we have discussed the desired properties of different components of electronic commerce. However, perhaps the single most important factor impeding electronic commerce is the lack of economic understanding about the interaction among the different entities of this market, that is, the consumers, the service providers, the infrastructure providers, and the regulatory policies. Service providers have to compete among themselves on several levels, for example, providing distinguishing features in terms of delivery options, usage options, and product features. On the other hand, service providers also have to ensure that their infrastructure connectivity and their own load management allow them to deliver the promised quality of service. In the next section we address the economic challenges in electronic commerce and provide a simulation framework to explore and analyze the economics of electronic commerce.

5.0 SIMULATING ELECTRONIC COMMERCE

In this section we report some of our results from simulations of a socially optimal per-transaction-based pricing scheme and discuss the competitive issues that will make it difficult to observe the socially optimal prices in practice. We then present a model for future research to analyze the impact of competition and regulation on electronic commerce.

In GSW (1996) an economic-based priority-pricing framework for transaction prices in computer networks is developed. In the context of electronic commerce the demand for services will be dynamic and somewhat unpredictable, making it difficult to compute optimal prices. Thus, we designed a simulation platform to use the transient system behavior and compute and implement the near-optimal transaction-based prices in real time. GSW (1995a, 1995b) present a simulation model of the Internet with transaction-based priority pricing as compared with free-access and fixed-access-fee approaches.

The theoretical model, used to develop the simulation model, is sufficiently general to include all kinds of transactions in electronic commerce, such as outright purchase of a product or service, usage-based purchase where computing takes place at the server's end, or usage-based purchase where computing takes place at the client's end. Of course, there has to be software development to facilitate these different types of transactions and the payment associated with them; nonetheless, from a conceptual point of view our transaction-based priority-pricing scheme has the potential to manage all these types of transactions. For example, in a usage-based purchase of a software where computing takes place at the server's end, the cost to the consumer includes processing costs at the server in the consumer's required service class, costs associated with facilitating payment, and transmission costs for final result in appropriate service class. On the other hand, if the computing takes place at the client's end, the cost to the consumer is the opportunity cost of using his or her cpu for other purposes, costs associated with facilitating payment, and part of the fixed costs attributed to this particular use, which arises for initial downloading of the software.

The results in these papers suggest that a real-time priority-pricing approach has the potential to effectively manage the network load when there is congestion, and since the prices are adaptive (with respect to load), pricing is never inferior to free access. As the congestion increases, the priority-pricing approach provides significantly higher benefits to both the service providers and the consumers. In the following we present some results indicating the cost savings and the inefficiency of simply increasing the capacity to deal with the congestion.[5]

---

[5] We direct readers to Gupta, Stahl, and Whinston (1995b) for the details of the simulation model and detailed comparative results.

5.1 Simulation Results

The results presented here involve two different information conditions. First, the results for the free-access policy are based on perfect information regarding the waiting times.[6] However, providing perfect information in a realistic situation is not practical because of the excessive cost involved in computing new information for every new request; furthermore, several requests can be submitted virtually at the same time, making this waiting time information invalid even if it was financially possible to provide perfect information.

In the more realistic condition of imperfect information, users would need to generate (or access) estimates of expected waiting times during the current period. Because stochastic queues have the property that the variance is at least as large as the mean, the task of generating accurate estimates from a finite amount of data in real time is nontrivial. We have experimented with many statistical methods and have had good results under the optimal pricing policy; however, the predictions under free access at higher loads are sufficiently poor to result in negative net benefits. Therefore, to provide a conservative estimate of the cost of congestion, the reported net benefits from a free-access policy are based on perfect information.

One of our significant contributions is the development of tools to predict the delays with sufficient accuracy while using our priority-pricing scheme. This allows us to compare the best-case (perfect information) results with free access to the imperfect information case with the optimal pricing. Thus, the results for the optimal pricing policy are based on predicted waiting times instead of perfect information. In this case both prices and predicted waiting times are updated at the same time, whereas in the former case only prices are updated after a fixed interval of time.

Table 8.1 displays net benefits and delay costs in dollars per month per server; these computations are based on calibrating the capacity cost according to the average cost of a T1 connection as follows. The current rental cost of a T1 line is about $1,500 per month, which implies that the cost of a 2.45 megabit-per-second capacity (the average capacity of servers in our simulation) is about $2,000 per month, or $0.00077 per second. The average job size in our simulation program was 2.4 megabytes, so an average server would handle one job per second. Thus, it is reasonable to assume that the mean value of a job is at least the cost of processing (i.e., $0.00077). In our simulation

---

[6] Note that the perfect waiting time information scenario case is the "best-case" scenario for our implementation of the free-access policy because users first check where they can get the fastest service and the information they get is exact.

Table 8.1 Estimated Dollar Benefits per Month with Perfect Information for Free Access and Periodic Updates for Pricing

Arrival Rate (X_o)	Benefits with Prices ($)	Benefits Free Access ($)	Delay Cost with Prices ($)	Delay Cost-Free access ($)	Internet Benefits ($)
50	1749.3276	1338.9921	123.9569	639.0016	103 million
100	2776.1812	630.6611	266.6029	1732.0273	536 million
250	3881.9087	515.7304	1629.5195	2041.7187	842 million
500	4401.1711	483.7473	3261.6245	2145.9051	979 million

the mean cost of delay was set to 0.008 times the mean value of a job (or only $0.022 per hour).[7] Table 8.1 compares the performance of a periodic update pricing case where delay information is not perfect with performance of free access with perfect information. This is an extremely conservative comparison; still pricing does significantly better than free access resulting in substantial gains. If we use the same information assumptions for free-access and optimal pricing, then the estimated Internet benefits of optimal pricing over free access double.

To scale these per-server estimates to the U.S. Internet (last column), we multiplied by 250,000, as a conservative estimate of the number of servers on the Internet having an average capacity of an average server in our simulation.[8] Thus, we arrive at a conservative estimate of the potential efficiency loss in the order of $10 billion annually. Given the historical annual growth rate of the Internet (100 percent), the potential loss will exceed $100 billion annually by the year 1999 or sooner.

The results presented here are suggestive of the benefits of applying a near-optimal pricing scheme on the Internet. Essentially, without a pricing mechanism users with zero or low delay cost have nothing to discourage them from overutilizing the services; however, with a pricing mechanism they are forced to obtain only the services for which their value is higher than the cost. In addition, they choose the appropriate service class dependent upon their service requirements. Service providers, on the other hand

---

[7] Note that this figure for delay cost is probably too low by an order of magnitude. However, recalibrating delay cost to 10 percent of the mean value of a job (or $0.277 per hour) leaves the net benefits reported in Table 8.1 essentially unchanged. On the other hand, a uniform rescaling of the value of a job and the delay cost would, of course, simply rescale all the numbers in Table 8.1 proportionally. Thus, Table 8.1 is conservative.

[8] Conservatively, as of October 1994 there were 2.5 million servers on the Internet (source: MATRIX News); it is safe to assume that collectively 10 percent of those servers have a capacity equivalent to our server capacity.

have incentives to provide multiple service classes because they can generate higher revenues and provide better service overall.

An alternative to optimal congestion tolls is to increase the capacity of the Internet so no one experiences congestion. We believe that the arguments in favor of simply overproviding the capacity on the Internet are in error. There are physical and cost limitations of providing capacity, whereas on the application level the desire for additional capacity seems boundless. Furthermore, future applications on the Internet will have inherently different qualities of service requirements. Thus, it is essential that appropriate resource management techniques be developed and tested for a multi–service class network.

To explore the cost of this capacity-expansion approach within our simulation model, we set $X_0 = 250$ and incrementally increased the capacity of every server in proportion to the aggregate delay costs experienced at that server until the aggregate net benefits rose to the level obtainable with optimal pricing and the original capacity. The required increase in capacity was 4.274 times the original capacity. The current monthly rental cost of this capacity expansion is $6,550, compared with a benefit increase of $3,184 per server. Thus, it would be uneconomical to increase capacity enough to achieve the same net benefits that could be obtained from optimal pricing.

5.2 Private Markets and Competition

In the presence of externalities (such as congestion), it is well known that noncooperative private market outcomes are not socially optimal, that is, the collective benefits of the buyers and sellers are not maximized. Further, given the interoperability requirements of the Internet, the number of network competitors will be finite and of nonnegligible size. In other words, the classic assumption of many small price-taking suppliers will be far from holding. Instead, the Internet market will be better described as a game with a small number of strategic players. Further, the game has some characteristics of a prisoner's dilemma, which implies that the tragedy of the commons[9] is not likely to be avoided by the noncooperative outcome.

We know very little about how a privately owned Internet might function from an economic point of view. The bulk of the theoretical results are confined to the unrealistic case of identical users, in which case two-part tariffs can support the social optimum. Intuitively, a monopolist who charges an access fee and a usage fee, since he can extract all the user surplus with

---

[9] Tragedy of the commons refers to the reduction in value of a "public good" because of overuse.

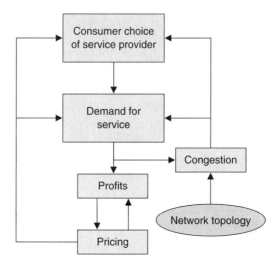

Figure 8.5   Complexity of Private Markets

the access fee, has the incentive to maximize that surplus by charging a usage fee equal to the optimal congestion toll (Oi 1971). Further, even if there are several (identical) network providers (and identical consumers), they will choose a usage fee equal to the optimal congestion toll (Scotchmer 1985b).

Unfortunately, these results vanish in the realistic case with heterogeneous users. For example, if users differ in how they value delays, then the social optimum will involve segregation of users by delay cost into subnetworks, but some of the subnetwork owners have incentives to upset this optimal segregation. It is not hard to construct simple examples for which there does not exist a "pure-strategy" noncooperative equilibrium.[10]

To understand the complexity of this game, consider what is involved in forecasting the network outcome given some fixed pricing structure. Taking a hypothetical assignment of users to various components of the network, what are the expected waiting times throughout the network? The expected waiting times are a function of the demand for services, which in turn depend on the expected waiting times. Thus, forecasting the expected waiting times involves the solution of a fixed-point problem (recursive in nature) for each component of the network. But then given these expected waiting times, the users will choose the least-cost alternative, so the tentatively assumed assignment of users is likely to be inconsistent with cost

---

[10] Witness the phone company wars.

minimization. We need to solve another fixed-point problem, with the waiting time fixed-point problem nested within it, just to solve for the network outcome at some fixed pricing structure. Figure 8.5 graphically represents this challenge.

Now the owners of the components need to consider alternative pricing structures, and for each alternative they need to solve the above two-level nested fixed-point problem. A noncooperative pricing equilibrium entails solving a higher-level fixed-point problem. Recognizing the rapidly changing nature of the Internet, it is not clear that the players will converge to an equilibrium of the game before the game itself changes.

On top of these problems, the organizational structure of the private Internet is complex. At the ground level are phone lines, fiber-optic cable, routers, and servers. At the next level are service providers (databases, shopping services, finances, etc.), and above this level are information brokers (such as AOL, Prodigy, and Microsoft). It is likely that the higher-level brokerages will severely limit the ability of network entities to use access fees to extract surplus, in which case they will lack effective incentives to charge optimal congestion tolls.

In this environment we may need an active public policy involving price regulation or Pigouvian taxes to avoid a tragedy of the commons. In the

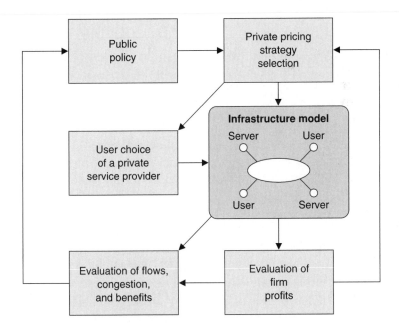

Figure 8.6 A Comprehensive Model to Analyze Electronic Commerce

classic common resource situation, the imposition of a public fee (or tax) equaling the marginal social cost of use will prevent the tragedy. Such a fee is equivalent to optimal congestion tolls. The simulation results of GSW strongly suggest that the computation of optimal taxes is feasible.

However, since the environment is so complex, the optimal policy is not obvious. We need to develop a model of the Internet that contains the essential and important characteristics, and can serve as a test bed for conducting policy studies. Figure 8.6 graphically presents this model and depicts the interaction among different entities involved in facilitating (debilitating) electronic commerce.

We will use this model to analyze several key questions, for example: How will alternative regulations or taxes affect the industry structure, the pricing schemes, the pattern of use across service and user classes, congestion, social benefits, and investment incentives? Will the Internet become dominated by a few powerful players, and if so will that favor efficiency? Will there be incentives for or against interconnection agreements? How desirable is a multi–service class, platform-independent, interoperable network, as compared to specialized networks for specialized services? What impact will competition have on potential service quality?

6.0 SUMMARY

The evolution of the Internet and the new paradigm of commerce (especially for informational/computing products), that is, electronic commerce have stirred unprecedented excitement and opportunities. However, we still have to overcome significant technological and managerial obstacles. Moreover, it seems that the technology is evolving at a far greater rate than the ability to manage it. In this chapter we have presented a comprehensive view of electronic commerce and have discussed the following issues: (1) pricing based on service class, quality, and usage; (2) framework for payment/accounting; (3) economic challenges; and (4) tools to analyze the impact of different entities involved in electronic commerce.

We believe that consumers will have to be provided with a variety of service classes and usage options, where the associated prices will give them incentives to choose appropriate service class and usage level for their needs. Several payment mechanisms will coexist, providing differentiated services. For example, some may provide higher security, whereas others may provide a higher degree of anonymity and convertibility. Since every attribute of a payment mechanism increases overhead or reduces performance, consumers will perhaps choose different mechanisms at different times.

The challenge of pricing digital information goes beyond the "already complex" problem of pricing information—a common good—because of the simplicity of duplicating, reselling, and altering the information. Furthermore, the delivery mechanism, that is, a public data network, involves several entities that may be different for different users and different for the same users at different times; compensating each entity requires complex and efficient accounting mechanisms and interconnection agreements. Since the lack of property rights may not allow socially optimal congestion tolls and competition may not necessarily provide incentives for large service providers to make interconnection agreements, which may drive the prices down, it is not clear what kind of pricing strategy will evolve and sustain the market. We present a comprehensive simulation model (under development) to study the competitive issues and the effect of regulatory policies.

While a rich set of buyer options will perhaps enhance consumers' value from product/service usage, there are also potential economic traps for consumers. For example, in pay-per-use cases, service providers can start maintaining consumer profiles and can potentially extract all the consumer surplus by perfect discrimination in consumer prices, especially if the market is dominated by few large players. In other words, service providers can customize prices for each individual consumer based on their usage and spending patterns, setting the prices as the maximum amount of money a consumer is willing to pay. This is quite a strong argument in favor of anonymity and privacy; however, there are practical limitations in providing privacy—in a public network "someone" can always monitor your transactions, and thus no truly private transaction can take place. Then, it is imperative that we analyze the economic trade-off of providing "partial" privacy with the potential efficiency of pay-per-use transaction and study the confounding economic implication of perfect price discrimination.

A better understanding of the economic issues is necessary before electronic commerce can make a significant impact in the market for informational and traditional products. Significant advances in standardization of communication protocols, software, documentation, storage and retrieval of information, and cheaper hardware will keep on tantalizing us with the dreams and opportunities. Unless, however, we can direct a concerted effort at understanding the economic, managerial, and business implications and impact of this new market, electronic commerce will remain a dream.

REFERENCES

Abreu, D. (1988). "Towards a Theory of Discounted Repeated Games." *Econometrica* 56: 383-396.

Bohn, R., H-W Braun, and S. Wolff (1994). "Mitigating the Coming Internet Crunch: Multiple Service Levels via Precedence." Technical report, San Diego Supercomputer Center, University of California at San Diego, ftp: //ftp.sdsc.edu/pub/sdsc/anr/papers/precedence.ps.z.

Brownlee, N. (1994). "New Zealand Experiences with Network Traffic Charging." *Journal of Electronic Publishing*, http://www.press.umich.edu:80/jep/.

Clark, D. (1995). "A Model for Cost Allocation and Pricing in the Internet." *Journal of Electronic Publishing*, http://www.press.umich.edu:80/jep/.

Cocchi, R., S. Shenker, D. Estrin, and L. Zhang (1991). "Pricing in Computer Networks: Motivation, Formulation, and Example." *IEEE/ACM Transactions on Networking* 1, no. 6: 614–627.

Edell, R., N. McKeown, and P. Varaiya (1994). "Billing Users and Pricing for TCP." Department of Electrical Engineering and Computer Sciences, University of California at Berkeley.

Friedman, J. (1971). "A Non-cooperative Equilibrium for Supergames." *Review of Economic Studies* 38: 1–12.

Fudenberg, D., and E. Maskin (1986). "The Folk Theorem in Repeated Games with Discounting or with Incomplete Information." *Econometrica* 54: 533–556.

Gupta, A., D. O. Stahl, and A. B. Whinston (1996a). "An Economic Approach to Network Computing with Priority Classes." *Journal of Organizational Computing and Electronic Commerce* 6:71–95.

———— (1996b). "Pricing of Services on the Internet." In *IMPACT: How IC2 Research Affects Public Policy and Business Markets*, ed. W. W. Cooper, D. Gibson, F. Phillips, and S. Thore. Westport, CT: Quorum Books.

———— (1995). "A Priority Pricing Approach to Manage Multi-Service Class Networks in Real-Time." *Journal of Electronic Publishing*, http://www.press.umich.edu:80/jep/.

Kalakota, R., J. Stallert, and A. B. Whinston (1995). "Solving Operations Research Problems Using a Global Client/Server Architecture." Working paper, *Center for Information Systems Management*, University of Texas at Austin.

MacKie-Mason, J., and H. Varian (1995). "Pricing the Internet." In *Public Access to the Internet*, ed. B. Kahin and J. Keller. Englewood Cliffs, NJ: Prentice-Hall.

Mailath, G. (1992). "Introduction: Symposium on Evolutionary Game Theory." *Journal of Economic Theory* 57: 259–277.

Maskin, E., and J. Tirole (1988). "A Theory of Dynamic Oligopolgy, II: Price Competition, Kinked Demand Curves, and Edgeworth Cycles." *Econometrica* 56: 571–599.

Medvinsky, G., and B. C. Neuman (1993). "Netcash: A Design for Practical Currency on the Internet." *Proceedings of the First ACM Conference on*

Computer and Communication Security, November 1993. http://nii-server.-isi.edu/gost-group/products/netcheque/documentation.html.

Oi, W. (1971). "A Disneyland Dilemma: Two-Part Tariffs for a Mickey Mouse Monopoly." *Quarterly Journal of Economics* 85: 79–96.

Scotchmer, (1985a). "Profit-Maximizing Clubs." *Journal of Public Economics* 27: 25–45.

———— (1985b). "Two-tier Pricing of Shared Facilities in a Free-Entry Equilibrium." *Rand Journal of Economics* 16: 456–472.

Shenker, S. (1995). "Service Models and Pricing Policies for an Integrated Services Internet." In *Public Access to the Internet*, ed. B. Kahin and J. Keller. Englewood Cliffs, NJ: Prentice-Hall.

Sirbu, M., and J. D. Tygar (1995). "Netbill: An Internet Commerce System Optimized for Network Delivered Services." http://www.ini.cmu.edu/NETBILL/publications/publications.html.

Stahl, D., and A. Whinston (1991). "A General Equilibrium Model of Distributed Computing." Center for Economic Research Working Paper 91-09, Department of Economics, University of Texas; also in *New Directions in Computational Economics*, ed. W. W. Cooper and A. B. Whinston. Dordrecht, Netherlands: Kluwer Academic Publishers, 1994, 175–189.

———— (1992). "An Economic Approach to Client-Server Computing with Priority Classes." Technical report, Center for Information Systems Research, University of Texas at Austin.

Wang, Q., J. Peha, and M. Sirbu (1995). "The Design of an Optimal Pricing Scheme for ATM Integrated-Services Networks." *Journal of Electronic Publishing*, http://www.press.umich.edu:80/jep/.

Chapter 9

A Flexible Framework for Network Payment

B. Clifford Neuman

ABSTRACT

This chapter discusses the design of a flexible framework for network payment. The problem is approached from the perspective of merchants, customers, and providers of financial services. The principal role of a financial service provider as a risk manager is described. Several payment models are presented and their characteristics discussed. The NetCheque®[1] and NetCash systems are described. These systems, developed at the University of Southern California, show how the design of a payment system can influence its flexibility by minimizing system-imposed constraints on the policies implemented by servers. In these systems, certain aspects of the relationships between the customer, merchant, and payment service provider are left unspecified by the payment mechanism; when the system is used in different settings, these aspects are determined according to the contractual relationship between the parties.

PAYMENT FROM THREE PERSPECTIVES

This section discusses the concerns of the three parties to a payment: the customer, the merchant, and the financial service provider. It identifies the characteristics of a payment mechanism that are important to each party.

---

[1] NetCheque is a registered service mark of the University of Southern California. All other product or service names are trademarks or service marks of their respective owners.

The Merchant

Merchants want to sell products and services. To that end, it is important that customers feel comfortable using the payment methods the merchants accept, and it should be easy for potential customers to make impulse purchases. The potential customer base is of particular importance to a merchant and is limited in part by the number of customers able to use a particular payment method.

Merchants are also concerned with the transaction fees that are incurred to clear payments, the time required to complete a transaction, and the exposure to risk from counterfeit or stolen payment instruments or customers with insufficient funds to complete payment. Some of these characteristics may be affected by the payment model used or the payment method selected, while other characteristics are established in the contractual relationship between the merchant and the financial service provider.

The Customer

Customers want to feel that the money in their accounts is safe and want to use that money to make purchases with as many merchants as possible. Customers do not want to invest time learning how to use new payment systems, and they usually don't want to maintain separate accounts for different merchants. They don't like paying transaction fees, and they don't like waiting for their payment to be processed or for an account to be established; they want instant gratification. As was the case with merchants, some of these desires are affected by the technical choice of payment method, but many are established in the contractual relationship between the customer and the financial service provider.

The Financial Service Provider

Financial service providers want to make a profit for the services they provide. One way to increase profits is to have more customers, and the ideal situation for a financial service provider is to be the only game in town, with all transactions processed by their server or servers. Customers and merchants, on the other hand, want a choice and are distrustful of payment mechanisms that force payments through a single financial service provider.

Competition between providers is encouraged by mechanisms that support multiple servers and allow payments to clear between providers. Such systems allow customers and merchants to independently select financial service providers, and financial service providers are forced to compete on the basis of price, performance, reliability, and value-added services. In such a system, financial service providers are compensated less for the processing function but more for their true contribution, that of managing risk.

The Financial Service Provider as a Risk Manager

Risk management is one of the principal services provided by financial service providers. Merchants want to make sure they get paid for the services and products they provide to customers. Customers want to be sure that merchants provide the products and services for which they are paid. Customers and merchants want to be sure their funds are safe when in the custody of the financial service provider, and the financial service provider wants to be sure that it will be paid by customers for the charges it honors from merchants, and that merchants will return the funds collected on disputed charges.

For financial service providers, risk management has two aspects: contractual and technical. Risk is allocated across parties through the contractual aspect. For example, merchants may agree to accept the risk of returned payment instruments for some kinds of purchases. Alternatively, the risk may be borne by the financial service provider, who collects a greater percentage of the transaction for accepting the risk.

Financial service providers might require customers to place funds on deposit before charges are authorized; alternatively, the financial service provider can extend credit to the customer and assume the risk of nonpayment. The customer who places funds on deposit in advance assumes risk from a failed financial service provider. If the provider extends credit, it assumes the risk of making payment on behalf of dishonest or insolvent (deadbeat) customers. Credit checks and third-party endorsements can reduce, but not eliminate, these risks, and interest charges and other fees can compensate parties for incurring this risk.

PAYMENT MODELS

Because concerns are different for different parties to a transaction, the situations within which payments are made will vary, and because of the diversity of payment requirements for different applications, no single payment model is suited to all situations. In society today we use cash, checks, credit cards, and wire transfers in different situations. The same will apply to payment on the Internet.

Most recently proposed, announced, and implemented Internet payment mechanisms can be grouped into several broad models [NM95]: secure presentation, electronic currency, credit-debit systems, and, to a lesser extent, direct transfer and collection agents. This section describes these models and discusses some of the situations for which each is best suited. Because different models are suited for different situations, whatever system finally evolves must support the exchange of value across different payment models.

Secure Presentation

Secure presentation of payment information is presently the most widely deployed means for network payment. In this model of payment, the customer's payment information, usually a credit card number, is sent to the merchant encrypted so that it can be read only by the merchant, or in some approaches by a third-party payment-processing service. The payment is then processed using the existing banking infrastructure. Purchases using forms submitted through NetScape's SSL [SSL96] or SHTTP [RS94] are examples of secure presentation. Mastercard and Visa's SET [SET96], and the initial payment system provided by CyberCash [CC96], also fall into this category.

From the perspective of the merchant, the biggest advantage of secure presentation is that the customer does not need to be registered with a network payment service; all that is needed is a credit card number. This provides a much larger customer base and supports impulse purchases; the customer doesn't have to wait for a new account to be set up before making a purchase. For the customer, using the secure presentation model for payment is easy, and the customer's exposure to risk is familiar (e.g., the same as for using a credit card). The secure presentation model for payment is well suited for purchasing the kinds of products and services over the network that customers might otherwise purchase in person or by telephone.

There are two main drawbacks to the secure presentation model. The first is the exposure of account information on machines that can be accessed from the Internet, including the customer's PC or workstation, and the merchant's system. This risk will vary depending on the implementation and on the service provider. If disclosed, such information can be used for fraudulent purposes, but for customers in the United States this is usually only an inconvenience since consumer protection laws limit the customer's liability. Fraud is a serious issue, however, to the financial service providers who incur the loss. The second drawback is that the cost of clearing credit card payments through the existing financial infrastructure makes this model of payment ill suited for micropayments (payments of a penny or two) where the transaction cost would be many times the payment amount.

Electronic Currency

In electronic currency systems, customers purchase electronic currency certificates from a currency server, paying for the certificates through an account established with the currency server in advance or through other forms of payment. Electronic currency represents value and may be transferred to merchants in exchange for goods and services. Once accepted, the merchant can deposit the currency or spend it elsewhere. Electronic currency systems must prevent double spending, the use of the same currency certificate with multiple merchants. Some systems prevent double spending through the tamper resistance of the devices used to store the currency, while others depend on post-fact or on-line verification through a database of currency certificates, and some use a combination of the two approaches. DigiCash [Cha92], Mondex [Mon96], and USC's NetCash [MN93] are examples of electronic currency systems.

The main advantage of electronic currency is its potential for anonymity. This anonymity can take several forms. In DigiCash's unconditional anonymity, one cannot identify the client to which a currency certificate was issued even if all parties collude, but a client who attempts to spend the same certificate twice discloses enough information to determine his or her identity. Other forms of anonymity are weaker, providing simply that currency servers don't maintain the information needed to identify the customer to whom a certificate was issued, or that collusion between many parties would be needed to make such a determination. This level of anonymity, combined with the client's ability to choose a currency server, is often sufficient for practical purposes.

A second advantage of electronic currency systems, though one that is often debated, is the ability for some systems to support off-line operation, that is, the ability to make payment while completely disconnected from the clearing infrastructure. This is possible in systems that rely on tamper-resistant devices, but the tamper resistance of such devices is open to debate. In particular, it is difficult to know for sure how resistant a device will be to tampering a few years down the road. As technology changes, such a compromise could breach the integrity of the entire system.

The principal disadvantage of the electronic currency model is the need to maintain a large database of past transactions to prevent double spending.

Electronic currency is suited to applications that require anonymity. Where greater accountability is required, one would be better off using one of the other models of payment.

Credit Debit

When using a payment mechanism that follows the credit-debit model, customers are registered with accounts on payment servers and authorize charges against those accounts. These accounts may have positive or negative balances, and as charges are posted to the customer's account, positive balances are reduced or negative balances become further negative. Customers either deposit funds with the provider in advance or pay negative balances after charges are posted. The timing of such payments, and whether the system is run in credit or debit mode, will be different from system to system. USC's NetCheque system [NM95], CMU's NetBill [ST95], and Fist Virtual's InfoCommerce system [FV96] are all examples of systems that follow the credit-debit model.

Flexibility is one of the principal potential advantages for systems supporting the credit-debit model of payment. Differences in the placement of payment servers and the policies governing the timing of payments allow a single mechanism to be used in a variety of settings.

Auditability is another advantage of the credit-debit model. The owner of the debited account can determine who authorized payment and how the instrument was presented. For this reason, the credit-debit model is particularly suited for business payments. The model does not typically provide anonymity, though it may be extended to do so.

The principal disadvantage of systems supporting the credit-debit model is that a separate account must be established for use of the payment system before the customer can make a purchase. Thus, this model is not particularly suited for onetime impulse purchases.

Direct Transfer

Direct transfer is less common than other forms of payment on the Internet. Using direct transfer, the customer and merchant are registered with accounts on a payment server, and the customer directs the payment server to transfer funds to the merchant's account. The merchant provides the goods or services after verifying that the transfer has occurred. The trade-offs for this model are similar to those for the credit-debit model.

Collection Agent

While not a separate payment model on their own, collection agents can be established that accept payment on behalf of third-party merchants. The agents accept the other forms of payment described in this section. When using a collection agent, the customer contacts the merchant and is provided with purchase information that is then presented to a collection agent who collects payment and provides the customer with a receipt. Upon presenting the receipt to the merchant, the customer receives the contracted product or service. The OpenMarket payment switch [GPST95] is an example of a collection agent.

CHARACTERISTICS OF PAYMENT SYSTEMS

When comparing network payment systems it is important to consider several characteristics, including security, reliability, scalability, anonymity, acceptability, customer base, flexibility, convertibility, efficiency, and ease of use [NM95]. Some characteristics will be more important than others at different times. A payment method should not be judged on an absolute basis but instead in terms of how well it meets the needs of the kinds of transactions for which it is to be used.

Security

One expects payment systems to be the target of criminals since breaching the security of a payment system can provide immediate financial benefit to an attacker. For this reason the payment system must be hardened against all forms of attack, and the vulnerability of the system to attacks through the Internet should be considered. These attacks will take the form of passive eavesdropping, active modification of messages, impersonation, and attacks against the computers involved in the transaction, including the customer's PC or workstation, the merchant's computer system, and the system of the financial service provider.

Reliability

If electronic commerce becomes widespread, businesses will come to depend on the proper functioning of the network payment infrastructure. For this reason the payment system must not be prone to failure, whether the result of failed computers, software bugs, or intentional attack by vandals. The best way to improve the reliability of a system is through redundancy. A payment system should not present a single point of vulnerability whose failure will bring down the entire system.

Scalability

Many new services perform well when first introduced. As new users join, the performance will often degrade because of growth in the number of operations performed by servers, and because of the growth of the databases maintained and searched. This can increase the time needed to perform each operation. If a service has been designed correctly, it should be possible to compensate for this growth through the addition of new servers, but for some systems the coordination between servers becomes difficult. To be scalable, the payment infrastructure must support growth in the number of servers, the servers should be distributed across the network, and the systems should avoid the use of central servers through which all transactions are processed.

Anonymity

If appropriate for a transaction, a payment system should prevent disclosure of the identity of the parties to the transaction, and it should not be possible to monitor an individual's spending patterns. The level of anonymity that is needed must be balanced with the costs in terms of other characteristics, and with the need for accountability. If anonymity is desired, the strength of the anonymity guarantees should be sufficient so that the cost of tracking a transaction outweighs the value of the information obtained by doing so.

Acceptability

Customers don't want to keep track of more than a couple of accounts. For this reason they would like a payment method to be accepted widely. The more widely accepted a payment method is, the more worthwhile it is for a customer to maintain an account, and ultimately use the method. One way to improve acceptability is to make it possible to clear payments through multiple financial service providers, allowing customers registered with one provider to make payment to merchants registered with different providers.

Customer Base

From the merchant's perspective, customer base is the flip side to acceptability. Merchants want to sell products, and without a large enough base of customers using a payment mechanism, it is often not worth the extra effort for a merchant to accept the mechanism. Once critical mass for a payment method is reached, more customers will adopt the method, which will in turn encourage more merchants to accept it, bringing in even more customers.

Flexibility

Different situations dictate different relationships with respect to the timing of payment and risk management. They also call for different characteristics in terms of anonymity, accountability, and the other characteristics described in this section. With slight changes, some payment systems support a range of characteristics. By using such an adaptable payment system, the infrastructure supporting the mechanism can be reused, saving the cost of reimplementing it for other payment mechanisms.

Convertibility

In some cases the differences in characteristics that are needed may be so great that different payment methods are required. In such cases users of the Internet will select financial instruments that best suit their needs for a given transaction. To be useful in combination with other payment methods, funds represented by one mechanism should be easily convertible into funds represented by others.

Performance Efficiency

Merchants want business, and customers don't like waiting in line. If a merchant has a popular product, the merchant will want to take orders as quickly as possible. For a given number of computers accepting orders, the performance of the payment system will affect the rate at which orders can be accepted. Additionally, some applications will make multiple purchases on behalf of a user, and the longer it takes for each purchase, the longer the user has to wait. For this reason the performance of a payment system is important.

Economic Efficiency

Some payments will be a couple of pennies, for example, paying for the result of a database query or similar operation. For applications that require such payments, the cost per transaction of using the infrastructure should be small enough that it is not noticeable.

Ease of Use

Merchants want customers to make impulse purchases, and many customers want instant gratification. For many situations the ease of use of a payment method must be considered. Users don't want to be interrupted to provide payment information for each page they browse, so the integration of a payment system should allow the specification of situations for which payment should be automatic. However, users still want to have some say in what is charged and will be concerned if an error in the rule set can cause them to spend more than they intend. For this reason, payments beyond a threshold should require explicit approval. Users should be able to monitor their spending easily.

TWO SYSTEMS: NETCHEQUE AND NETCASH

We have developed the NetCheque and NetCash systems at the University of Southern California as part of a flexible framework for network payment. Reliability and scalability are provided through the use of multiple accounting and currency servers. These servers can be maintained by different financial service providers, and the system supports the clearing of payments between providers. The NetCheque system is a distributed payment system based on the credit-debit model. Both credit-style accounts and debit-style accounts are supported on a single server; the account is configured based on the contractual relationship between the customer and the financial service provider. The NetCash system supports the electronic currency model of payment and uses the NetCheque system to tie together independent currency servers and back the currency issued by such servers. When NetCash is used in combination with NetCheque, service providers and their users are able to select payment mechanisms based on the level of anonymity desired, ranging from nonanonymous and weakly anonymous instruments that are scalable to unconditionally anonymous instruments that require more resources on the currency server. This section briefly describes the NetCheque and NetCash systems.

The NetCheque System

A NetCheque account works in much the same way as a traditional credit card or checking account. A customer registers with a network payment provider and deposits funds into a NetCheque account or establishes a credit limit. The customer can then write an electronic document that authorizes the transfer of balances from the account. This payment authorization, a NetCheque payment instrument, includes the name of the payer, the name of the network payment provider, the payer's account identifier, the name of the payee, and the amount of the payment. Like a paper check or charge slip, a NetCheque payment instrument bears an electronic signature and must be endorsed by the payee, using another electronic signature, before it will be paid.

The NetCheque system was designed to support small payments needed for some kinds of electronic commerce. This requirement for handling micropayments dictates high performance, which is obtained through the use of conventional, instead of public-key, cryptography. Security for the NetCheque systems is based on the Kerberos system [NT94]. A valid payment instrument is authenticated by verifying an attached checksum (similar to a digital signature), which is embedded in a Kerberos proxy [Neu93]. This proxy authorizes the payment described in the instrument, and the authenticity of the proxy is verified by the customer's accounting server during processing of the payment.

For performance, the Kerberos proxy used for authentication is based on conventional cryptography, but it may be replaced by a signature using public-key cryptography with a corresponding loss of performance. The main operational disadvantage in using conventional cryptography is that the authenticity of the payment instrument can be determined only by the customer's accounting server. The impact of this is minor since the customer's accounting server would otherwise need to be contacted anyway to check the account balance. A second limitation is that conventional cryptography provides a lower level of nonrepudiation since the customer's payment provider has the information necessary to issue payment instruments on behalf of the customer.

The NetCheque system is a distributed accounting service, and payment instruments are exchanged between accounting servers to settle accounts through a hierarchy. When an instrument is deposited, if the payee and the payer both use the same accounting server, the response will indicate whether the instrument cleared. If different accounting servers are used, the payee's accounting server places a hold on the funds in the payee's account and indicates to the payee that the instrument was accepted for collection. If an instrument that was accepted for collection is later rejected, it is returned to the depositor, who can take action at that time.

As instruments are cleared through multiple accounting servers, each server attaches its own endorsement, similar to the endorsement attached by the payee. If the customer's accounting server is trusted to properly settle accounts, the payee's and payer's accounting servers can settle the payment directly, bypassing higher levels of the hierarchy. Such trust might be based on certificates of insurance representing endorsement of the accounting server [LMN94].

The NetCash System

The NetCash system provides a framework within which electronic currency protocols can be integrated with the scalable, but nonanonymous, NetCheque service that was described in the previous section. It supports the issuance and exchange of currency from multiple issuers, and the purchase and sale of currency with the proceeds taken from or deposited to NetCheque accounts. NetCash strikes a balance between unconditionally anonymous electronic currency and signed instruments similar to checks that are more scalable but identify the principals in a transaction.

Currency is backed by account balances that have been deposited by the currency issuers through the NetCheque system. When currency is exchanged between issuers, the NetCheque system is used to transfer the balances backing the currency to the account of the new issuer. The NetCheque system is also used to convert electronic currency into debits and credits against customer and merchant accounts. Trust in the currency issued depends in part on the procedures followed to track the amount of currency in circulation, and the adequacy of the account balances that back the currency. Such assurance is provided through assertions by insurance providers and other licensing agencies, with the assertions represented on-line through assurance credentials [LMN94].

In general, the issuers of currency in the NetCash system provide weaker guarantees of anonymity than are provided by Chaum's DigiCash system [Cha92]. In particular, when using NetCash, the customer's identity may be available to the currency server when the currency is first issued, and the merchant's identity is available when the currency is deposited into the merchant's account. One expects that customers and merchants will choose to use currency servers that don't record such information, and such policies may be specified contractually. Further, once currency has been purchased, it can be exchanged anonymously for new coins, or it can circulate without identifying successive possessors. The longer the chain of custody, the harder it is for anyone to identify the party making payment.

The representation of the currency issued by NetCash currency servers can vary from server to server. The NetCash framework provides for the exchange of currency between servers. As such, it is possible to provide different classes of currency with different levels of anonymity. Though the majority of transactions on the Internet will not require anonymity, and most that do can get by with the level of anonymity provided by NetCash, where unconditional anonymity is required, the NetCash framework can be extended to integrate exchanges from Chaum's protocol or from other electronic currency mechanisms. Such exchanges would be applied to those transactions that require them, perhaps with an additional transaction fee, while still providing scalability, acceptability, and interoperability across the payment system as a whole.

Placement of NetCheque and NetCash Servers

Because of the flexibility of the NetCheque and NetCash systems, servers can be placed in organizations that at first might not seem trusted to provide their own payment systems. Constraints on the relationships between servers protect other parts of the system from inappropriate behavior by a malfunctioning or dishonest server.

For example, anyone is allowed to issue currency using the NetCash system. The only difference between currency issued by one provider and that from another is the amount of trust users place in the currency. In the NetCash system, one's confidence is derived from the combination of the funds backing the currency in the NetCheque account of the currency server, together with the presence or absence of an assurance credential.

Similarly, any organization can establish its own NetCheque server to maintain accounts internally. Such organizations must keep funds on deposit with better-established NetCheque servers with a sufficient balance to cover the total of all checks that are to be written against internal accounts. Users can be authorized to write checks against internal accounts. When these checks are spent with merchants outside of the organization in which they originate, they clear first through external NetCheque servers where the funds of the organization have been deposited. When such a check clears, the organization's "correspondent" account is debited, and the check is transmitted to the internal NetCheque server and posted against the appropriate budget line in the local accounting system.

CONCLUSION

When designing a network payment system, it may often seem best to base the design on a single familiar model from the paper world, but it is possible to find similarities across methods that allow a common implementation, leaving to policy the final determination of how the system is to be used. When selecting a system for network payment, there are many characteristics that must be considered. Because payments are used for many purposes, some characteristics will be more important in some situations, while other characteristics will be more important in other situations.

To provide the best integration of a payment system into as many applications as possible, a framework is needed within which these diverse needs can be accommodated. Such a framework should support the convertibility of payment from one form to another and must provide for the clearing of payments across independent financial service providers. When such a framework is in place, financial service providers will be able to compete on the basis of value-added services and fees, providing for better service and a more efficient system as a whole.

REFERENCES

[Cha92] David Chaum. "Achieving Electronic Privacy." *Scientific American* 267 (August 1992): 96–101. http://www.digicash.com

[CC96] CyberCash Web site: http://www.cybercash.com

[FV96] See Chapter 7 of this book, Borenstein et al., "Perils and Pitfalls of Practical Internet Commerce." http://www.fv.com

[GPST95] D. Gifford, A. Payne, L. Stewart, and W. Treese. "Payment Switches for Open Networks." In *Proceedings of IEEE Compcon '95,* March 1995. http://www.openmarket.com

[LMN94] Charlie Lai, Gennady Medvinsky, and B. Clifford Neuman. "Endorsements, Licensing, and Insurance for Distributed System Services." In *Proceedings of the Second ACM Conference on Computer and Communications Security,* ACM Press, November 1994.

[LMP94] Steven H. Low, Nicholas F. Maxemchuk, and Sanjoy Paul. "Anonymous Credit Cards." In *Proceedings of the Second ACM Conference on Computer and Communications Security,* ACM Press, pp. 108–117, November 1994.

[MN93] Gennady Medvinsky and B. Clifford Neuman. "NetCash: A Design for Practical Electronic Currency on the Internet." In *Proceedings of the First ACM Conference on Computer and Communications Security,* ACM Press, November 1993.

[Mon96] Mondex Web site. Reach through http://www.mondex.com

[Neu93] B. Clifford Neuman. "Proxy-Based Authorization and Accounting for Distributed Systems." In *Proceedings of the 13th International Conference on Distributed Computing Systems,* pp. 283–291, May 1993.

[NM95] B. Clifford Neuman and Gennady Medvinsky. "Requirements for Network Payment: The NetCheque Perspective." *In Proceedings of IEEE Compcon '95,* March 1995. http://www.netcheque.org

[NT94] B. Clifford Neuman and Theodore Ts'o. "Kerberos: An Authentication Service for Computer Networks." *IEEE Communications* 32, no. 9, September 1994.

[RS94] E. Rescorla and A. Schiffman. "The Secure Hypertext Transfer Protocol." Available from http://www.eit.com

[SET96] "Secure Electronic Transaction (SET) Specification." Available from the site http://www.visa.com

[SSL96] Specification available from http://www.netscape.com

[ST95] Marvin Sirbu and J. Douglas Tygar. "NetBill: An Electronic Commerce System Optimized for Network Delivered Information and Services." In *Proceedings of IEEE Compcon '95,* March 1995.

PART 4

Document Management and Digital Libraries

Part Four consists of papers that explore the areas of document management and digital libraries. Chapter 10, by Larry Masinter, explains the role of document management in business processes within an organization as well as in interorganizational applications. The first part of his essay reviews tools for managing corporate documents, such as those for storage and retrieval, and creation and auditing. In his opinion, the new developments will be utilized in managing documents on a global basis. Security, providing for encryption, and authentication will have to be incorporated into such a framework. On-line implementations of intellectual property rights and payment systems will be needed to facilitate electronic commerce in documents.

In Chapter 11 on smart catalogs and virtual catalogs, Arthur M. Keller outlines an approach to developing consumer-oriented electronic catalogs using knowledge representation tools developed in the artificial intelligence field. The goal is to employ the powerful knowledge representation tools that will enable consumers to search for products that optimally satisfy their criteria. Another aim is to provide the consumer with a virtual catalog that contains information derived from actual catalogs of different companies that collectively meet his or her needs.

Chapter 10

Document Management and Electronic Commerce

Larry Masinter

ABSTRACT

The global network is changing the way every business works. In particular, new networked applications will affect the way in which organizations work with documents. Currently, electronic document management systems are used to facilitate document-centered work on networks inside single organizations. These kinds of applications will expand to include groups outside the enterprise.

This chapter contains three parts: (1) a brief overview of electronic document management; (2) a review of the assumptions for future networking capabilities and electronic commerce; and (3) an overview of four kinds of document management applications and an exploration of the ways in which the network will change the nature of document management for each of those applications.

1. DOCUMENT MANAGEMENT: OVERVIEW

Document management systems are designed to help individuals, work groups, and large enterprises manage their documents stored in electronic form. Document management systems provide a means to store, easily locate and retrieve, and exercise control over document-based information through the document's life cycle within the context of a group or large organization.

The field of electronic document management can be confusing because different terms are used, referring either to specialized applications, to technical components, or to particular types of media the systems are used to manage. For example, some systems are described as *publication management* systems because they are geared toward aiding in the publication process. Some systems are marketed as *information retrieval* products, as information retrieval is an important component of document management. Systems that are oriented primarily toward the management of scanned images are described as *image management*. However, each of these can be considered a type of document management systems, and all will change because of the changes in networking technology that are sweeping the world.

Document Management Components

Document management systems combine a number of functional components. *Authoring* components integrate the user's desktop creation tools with the document management system to simplify the entry of the user's work into the management system. *Acquisition* components aid in the bulk import of documents that originate outside the system, for example, by allowing entry of paper documents using scanners, fax, or conversion from externally acquired electronic media.

A variety of *information retrieval* methods are employed to find relevant or correct documents within large repositories, either by full-text retrieval, semantic analysis, or probabilistic methods. Document management systems usually feature searching in repositories of documents both by context and by content. Contextual information for a document is derived from outside the document itself: for example, who wrote it, when it was written, the work group that produced it. Content search uses the words in the document itself, or the document's structure, for retrieval.

User interface components interact with the information retrieval facilities in the server to support *search*. *Information visualization* is a method of using advanced graphic capabilities to help users visualize larger information spaces and structures. *Workspace management* is a method of using two- or three-dimensional images to help users organize the state of their work. These components interact with the document management components through a network interface.

Document *library services* keep track of the attributes of documents as they are being worked on in various parts of the organization. For example, a user can *check out* a document, reserving it so that no one else can edit it at the same time. When the revision is complete, the user *checks in* the document, letting others access and revise the new version. These kinds of control mechanisms are important for keeping consistency in the creation/review cycle when many people are engaged in working on a common corpus.

Document management systems are *distributed*. Users at PCs on a network access a common repository of documents on one or several servers. For large networks, or for users with laptop computers that may operate without being connected to the network, distributed system transaction technology is used to keep updates and additions consistent.

While document libraries and repositories keep track of documents and their attributes, *workflow* components keep track of users, tasks, work queues, audit trails, and the like. That is, they model the work of the organization in which the documents participate.

2. GLOBAL NETWORKING TRENDS: OVERVIEW

This section lays out some of the assumptions about the future direction of the global information infrastructure that will support new document management applications.

The Internet is growing at an enormous rate, and on-line services and corporate networks are interconnecting. The conclusion of this evolution will be a system in which there is *one network* for connecting computers, services, and people. As with the Internet today, the future network will be a federation of independently operated networks; some components of those networks will have special services, but interactive services will be available across the entire network.

Two fundamental capabilities are being developed that allow for secure communication across the global network. First is the ability to *authenticate* the source of a message or network connection so that the identity of a (potential) user can be assured. Second is the ability to have *secure communication* with that user, without anyone else being able to eavesdrop or modify the conversation. These capabilities require not only the deployment of cryptographic software but also the development of a worldwide infrastructure for determining identity and associating network presence with individuals.

Several developments in technology and infrastructure for managing *copyright* and intellectual property are also important for some sectors. This includes both systems and institutions, and a legal framework for describing, tracking, and credibly accounting for use of intellectual property. These developments are accompanied by changes in the legal and regulatory environment.

Finally, *distributed payment* methods are being promulgated by consortia of banks and credit agencies, network providers, and others offering accounting and billing services. These services allow for secure transactions and reliable settlement of accounts between buyers and sellers.

These elements of electronic infrastructure are enabling a very large variety of new systems for electronic commerce: the ability to trade in services and goods across the world. The word *trade* is perhaps too narrow, as the commerce that it engenders is not only commercial but also intellectual and social.

One particular kind of trade that is more affected than any others is trade in documents. That is because, of all the goods and services that might be traded, documents can be transmitted across a network, and document services can reasonably be performed by others remotely, while most other goods and services require additional transportation of physical material in order to complete.

3. DOCUMENT MANAGEMENT AND ELECTRONIC COMMERCE

The combination of electronic commerce and document management technologies will give rise to new market segments and opportunities. The opportunities will differ according to the kind of use they are intended to support. The following describes four broad categories of document management, along with the opportunities for applying electronic commerce in those domains.

3.1. Document as Memory: Knowledge Workers

For knowledge workers, document management systems are used to organize and keep track of the state of the organization and the communication between individuals.

Office automation systems are used to create memos, letters, and status reports. However, repositories of these documents contain the state and interconnection of an organization. Work groups and enterprises invest in document management systems as a way to help them keep track of the work that they have done and are in the process of doing, in order to avoid redundancy and duplication of effort.

In addition, work group document management systems offer library services for preserving update consistency, similar to check-out and check-in capabilities of software source code control systems. When a user checks out a document, the system locks the document from other users' changes. When the document is checked back in, the document management system makes it available for others to revise. Along with maintaining update consistency, the document management application tracks revisions in a multi-author/editor setting.

Some current applications of document management in this context include the following:

Product organizations keep track of customer complaints and suggestions received by phone, mail, or fax, and maintain them in a common database for review by developers.

Law firms keep copies of contracts, depositions, and previous correspondence with clients. For example, a large multinational firm believes it has an obligation to offer similar legal advice to all clients in similar situations; the company wants the system to keep track of all material as it is produced in each of its offices.

A marketing department might manage competitive profiles, references to magazine and newspaper articles, and product information on-line for quick reference.

Opportunities for Electronic Commerce in Work Group Document Management

The trend to reengineer organizational practices using document management is spreading. Meanwhile, the boundaries of organizations are blurring, to the point where traditional document management systems are inadequate. Although currently most work groups are connected on a LAN or enterprise network, there are many situations where the need to share state crosses those boundaries. It is for this reason that many groupware products are adding Internet capabilities so that ordinary users with a forms-capable Web browser might participate. Some current examples of network-based distributed document systems include the following:

Company and consumer feedback. More and more organizations are receiving customer correspondence from the network, containing feedback from their customers. These electronic support forums are an important technical base of descriptions of problems and solutions for the company and its customers. While product support groups for computer products have long been found on on-line services such as CompuServe and Prodigy, the trend is spreading to other industries and to the Internet.

Distributed work groups. Increasingly, conferencing systems are being used for managing the distributed job of cross-organizational document-intensive collaboration. For example, the program committee of the Fourth World Wide Web conference used the Internet to manage the entire process of paper submission, review, reviewer comments, updates, and responses to authors. Similarly, the National Information Infrastructure Awards committee program used a "virtual judging environment" suite of software for allowing reviewers to rate, evaluate, and publish their ratings of sites.

The mechanisms of electronic commerce will allow the impromptu creation of geographically distributed organizations that form for a common purpose. Thus, trade associations, consortia, and professional organizations might employ work group document management technology and groupware to coordinate their efforts.

3.2 Document as Process: Insurance, Financial Service, Government

Some organizations have well-defined work processes to deal with a flow of paperwork. Workflow software is used to manage the organizational process and to route documents along the steps of the process. The workflow software tracks the progress of documents as they are routed through an organization and processed by individuals fulfilling process roles. While document repositories are often organized around the documents, their attributes, and repositories of them, workflow systems are centrally focused on users, roles, tasks, work queues, and processes:

Insurance companies use workflow to handle claims adjustment.

Financial services companies use workflow in order to regularize the handling of loan approvals.

Government offices use workflow to handle the routing of filing, approvals, and other processes that involve a large number of applications, a large clerical staff, and a need for fair and equitable handling of all involved.

Commercial organizations might use workflow to handle order entry, delivery, and collection.

In general, organizations use workflow to minimize the delays in their work processes. The primary opportunity for electronic commerce in workflow systems is the ability to include those outside the organization in the work it-self. Some current examples include the following:

Order entry. Many manufacturing and sales organizations are integrating their workflow systems for processing orders and delivery with network interfaces. Whether a customer orders pizza, a hotel room, or computer parts, the process automation becomes much more valuable when there is not a company employee in the way between the customer and the product.

Fulfillment tracking. The next step beyond order entry is to allow customers to track their orders directly on the network. FedEx has both custom soft-ware and an interface using the World Wide Web to allow customers to find out the status of their package delivery.

In each of these cases, the challenge is to merge the external user inter-face over the public Internet with the internal workflow processing steps of the organization.

As companies outsource work to independent contractors, the workflow might extend to include tasks performed by those contractors. The bound-aries of enterprises are blurring, and this will require the transition of enter-prise workflow to be able to deal with participants beyond the enterprise.

3.3 Document for Product: Manufacturing and Service

Organizations that produce products also produce documents that accom-pany those products. While many of the steps of document production are the same, there is an essential difference: for these organizations, the docu-ments are critical auxiliaries to the actual product that customers purchase from them. In these situations, the documents are still part of a production scenario, but the organization and management of the document construc-tion are subsidiary to some other work process.

Electronic commerce will enhance the manufacturing and service seg-ments in a large number of ways. However, in particular, it will have a pro-found impact on the way in which documents are managed within them.

CALS (Continuous Acquisition and Life-Cycle Support) is a Department of Defense (DoD) strategy for achieving effective creation, exchange, and use of digital data for weapon systems and equipment. Originally, it was in-tended that industry selling equipment to the government, whether missiles or tents, would provide all of the specifications, repair manuals, and so on in electronic form. As a part of this effort, a large number of specification stan-dards were created. Document management systems and databases were deployed to help vendors keep track of their documentation as it was being produced. This initiative was originally conceived as delivering its documentation in physical media (tape, disk). CALS created standard descriptions for CAD drawings, images of text, SGML marked-up text, and reports.

In one large aerospace company, almost every plane off the assembly line has a different configuration. The documentation for the repair and maintenance of the plane needs to match the configuration shipped. The document management system allows the configuration of the shipped documentation to match the product. As more and more manufacturers move into custom product delivery and just-in-time manufacturing, it has become increasingly important to have a system that can allow documentation to track the changes in the products. The documents produced are field service procedures and parts diagrams.

Pharmaceutical companies are required to submit documentation for proposed new drugs, including data on clinical trials and other evidence. The New Drug Application process is time-consuming, and shortening the time for submission is critically important in shortening the approval process. The creation of document itself is linked to the process of testing.

Financial services firms produce data about their products, fact sheets about investments, reports on mutual funds, and so on. This information is a critical part of their service.

Opportunities for Electronic Commerce in Product Documentation

Direct electronic communication with consumers will greatly improve the quality and responsiveness of the organizations in supporting their customers, especially with highly technical products. It improves customer satisfaction by making sure the right information gets to customers when and where they need it.

In addition, manufacturers can obtain and reuse documentation components from their suppliers and can feed back requests for changes, greatly enhancing the communication path. In today's business climate, more and more companies are outsourcing critical components of their organizations' design or manufacturing work, and the ability to interact at will with suppliers is a critical capability. For example, chip companies can make their data sheets on the Web. This trend is not restricted to the electronics or computer industry. For example, GE Plastics makes its data sheets available on the Web.

In the building industry, a large number of vendors are making three-dimensional renderings of their products available as AutoCad plug-ins, enabling contractors, architects, and planners to understand how their products will fit in the projects they are building. These "documents" are candidates for electronic document management in the future.

These efforts are critical to fulfilling the promise of electronic commerce. Companies with a wide range of products need to integrate the document management of on-line product information with the external network availability of that information to fulfill the promise. Electronic commerce mechanisms of digital signatures, time-stamping services, and the like are necessary to make this information secure and useful.

While document management systems have been used for the assembly, production, and printing of catalogs, now catalogs can be delivered on-line. The ability to deliver catalogs over the network means that it is possible to give consumers far more information than was previously available, in more detail, and in a more timely fashion. This is a positive move, but it will also require more diligence, as it is not acceptable to deliver out-of-date prices or specifications of discontinued items.

3.4 Document as Product: Publishers and Education

For publishers, documents are their product. Whether newspapers, magazines, book publishers, academic presses, or entertainment organizations distributing film, video, records, CDs or tapes, publishers produce and distribute documents in the same way that manufacturers produce and distribute physical goods. Of all the industries empowered by electronic commerce, publishers are privileged in that it is possible to deliver samples and actual product completely over the network without transmission of physical objects.

Publishers currently use document management systems for document assembly, reuse, and quality control. However, the opportunities to extend their document management system to include authors and creators (as the source of their material) and consumers (using the network for distribution) is enormous.

Many publishers use document management today to aid in the production of their material. For example, textbook manufacturers produce varying versions of their material based on the market requirements in different regions; however, they reuse the same text. Document management systems help in keeping track of all the components.

Opportunities for Electronic Commerce in Publishing

Publishers are extending their business to use the global network in a variety of ways:

Ready availability of promotional material. It is possible over the network to deliver samples and excerpts, and to offer search, storage, and backlist material in a way that is unprecedented. Bookstores, publishers, and academic presses are all promoting their products over the network.

Order entry. The next step beyond cataloging the products is to actually take orders over the network. Thus, many bookstores on the Web allow ordering of documents.

Distribution of product. For those materials that are delivered to the ultimate consumer in physical form, it is still possible to use the worldwide network to deliver the product information to the point of manufacturing at time of need.

Product delivery. A number of trials for actual delivery of content are being undertaken. More progress in the areas of copyright management, usage monitoring, and copy protection will be necessary before publishers will be willing to move more aggressively in this way. Either access is restricted to subscribers (clients), usage is controlled and restricted by copyright, or the reproduction of the material is directed toward ensuring that the integrity of the message is preserved, as in advertising.

Insofar as the document management systems used to aid in production can be extended to interconnect directly with end users and recipients, the reach of publishers will be enhanced. However, publishers are limited in their ability to market final product on the network because of limitations in the technology, infrastructure, and legal protection afforded to intellectual property owners. A number of technology trends may help, though:

Copy detection. The ability to either mark individual network copies of documents to detect an illicit copy or the source of an infringing one may help with auditing and copy management.

Copyright management. The development of an infrastructure to allow payment of copyright fees to rights owners will help satisfy many of the worries of publishers. Mechanisms for recording, paying, and limiting the recipient's access to copyrighted material are being deployed.

CONCLUSIONS

In each area of electronic document management, there are two ways to look at the growth opportunity. From the point of view of Internet development and electronic commerce, document management facilities add a source of "back-end" technologies. From the point of view of document management providers, the Internet and electronic commerce provide new ways to extend their products to reach beyond the work group and enterprise to the collaborator, customer, or supplier. In each of these cases, the emerging network infrastructure will change the way in which organizations interact with others in ways that are both a challenge and an opportunity.

REFERENCES

CALS Standard Repository. <http://navysgml.dt.navy.mil/cals.html>

The Document Management Guide. Waltham, Mass: Interleaf, Inc., 1994. <http://www.ileaf.com/docman.html>

Frappaolo, Carl. "The CW Guide to Document Management." *Computer-World*, April 10, 1995, p. 92.

Garris, J. "Digging through Your Data." *PC Magazine*, November 8, 1994, p.NE1(4).

Nadile, Lisa. "Document-Management Standards Pave 'Open' Path." *PC Week*, July 18, 1994, p. 8.

Rooney, Paula. "PC Document Management Catches Eye of Big Business." *PC Week*, May 18, 1992, p. 45.

Chapter 11

Smart Catalogs
and Virtual Catalogs

Arthur M. Keller

ABSTRACT

This chapter presents an architecture for electronic catalogs, called smart catalogs and virtual catalogs. Smart catalogs are searchable, annotated combinations of machine-readable (i.e., minimally processable) and machine-sensible (i.e., actually understood by the computer) product data. Virtual catalogs dynamically retrieve information from multiple smart catalogs and present these product data in a unified manner with their own look and feel, not that of the source smart catalogs. These virtual catalogs do not store product data from smart catalogs directly (except when caching for performance); instead, virtual catalogs obtain current product data from smart catalogs to satisfy specific customer queries. Customers interact with

This chapter has benefited from feedback of numerous people who have heard presentations, read earlier drafts, or participated in discussions. In particular, Michael Genesereth designed the overall intelligent agent communication architecture used by smart catalogs and virtual catalogs and implemented the facilitator, Narinder Singh implemented an early version of the facilitator, and Mustafa Syed programmed some of the other components in our initial prototypes. Note that an earlier version of this paper, coauthored by them, appeared at the Workshop on Electronic Commerce following CIKM in December 1994. A subsequent version of this paper appeared in the USENIX Workshop on Electronic Commerce in July 1995. Infomaster, a virtual information system representing our second-generation smart catalog technology, was developed by Donald Geddis. Several other people have worked on the development of smart catalogs. These include Felix Chow, Rohan Aranha, Bob Engelmore, Wanda Pratt, and Rupert Brauch.

This work was funded through a subcontract from the CommerceNet Consortium, which in turn derived its funding from a cooperative agreement with the U.S. Technology Reinvestment Program, as well as over 150 companies and organizations. In addition, several companies have provided funding of this project toward the construction of pilot smart catalogs. Some of the base technology used in this effort was funded by the DARPA Knowledge Sharing Initiative and the Intelligent Integration of Information program.

smart catalogs and virtual catalogs through the World Wide Web (WWW) or other interfaces.

1. INTRODUCTION

Electronic catalogs are a key component of electronic commerce. The procurement process extends from product selection to source selection to negotiation of price and other terms and conditions to ordering to order fulfillment to payment. Electronic catalogs are the reference for product selection and can assist with source selection and description of terms and conditions. Other electronic commerce components, such as Electronic Data Interchange (EDI), handle the other aspects of the procurement process.

Electronic catalogs can be organized as individual company catalogs or they can participate in a multicatalog framework. Currently, companies that have electronic catalogs organize them uniquely. Companies perceive that there is a competitive advantage to how they organize their catalogs. Furthermore, each company has to base its electronic catalog at least in part on legacy systems or legacy organizational structure, and these influence the nature of the electronic catalog produced.

The challenge is to enable companies to have their catalogs to participate in a multicatalog framework while still retaining their individual uniqueness. That is, these catalogs are highly heterogeneous. Often they are organized as a collection of static HyperText Markup Language (HTML) documents for the WWW. Sometimes these catalogs are stored in databases.

Electronic catalogs organized as a collection of static HTML documents typically use ordinary WWW protocols and WWW clients, such as Netscape™. Each HTML document, called a page, is stored in a separate file, and these documents can link to other documents somewhere on the Internet. You can think of the WWW as a giant menu system, where each document contains content as well as links to other documents. Typically there are no road maps to the WWW, so the user navigates from document to document, hopefully getting closer to the information desired.

Each vendor maintains its own (collection of) catalogs. There may not be uniformity even among multiple divisions of the same company, let alone among multiple companies manufacturing or selling comparable products. Because of the difficulty of locating documents within a catalog, some vendors provide search interfaces for their own catalogs. Typically, these search interfaces are for keyword or text search, although some sites support structured searches of databases.

There are a variety of limitations of this typical approach to electronic catalogs. It is hard to find what you are looking for. You have to figure out where to start. For example, in order to find information about a particular product, you must first determine which companies make that product and then separately visit each company's catalog, and then navigate through each of those catalogs separately to find the desired product. The fact that each vendor organizes its catalogs differently makes such navigation more difficult.

Few catalogs have the ability to search by content (i.e., reverse-search). Those that support reverse-search typically use keyword- or text-based searches. Keyword searching techniques, such as Wide Arch Information Service (WAIS), are of only limited help, as they require that the user phrase the query using the terminology of each data source, and vendors tend to use differing terminology from each other to describe products. For example, consider a search for VCRs with editing capability. Different manufacturers use their own proprietary names to describe editing capability. The user may not know the distinctive name used by each manufacturer. Also, keyword searches typically cannot be used to answer such queries as VCRs without editing capability.

Some electronic catalog systems, such as Step Search by Saqqara Systems, support structured search. However, this approach currently only works for a single catalog at a time. PartNet is experimenting with structured cross-catalog search. However, PartNet requires that the catalogs be stored in relational databases and has only limited support for heterogeneity. PartNet supports different database systems, different field and table names, and some unit conversion, but not more complex translations among heterogeneous catalogs.

In contrast, the smart catalog approach supports reverse-search (i.e., search by content) of multiple vendor catalogs based on a deeper understanding of the contents of these catalogs, so it supports an extensive framework for heterogeneity.

Section 2 describes the goals and principles of smart catalogs. Section 3 describes the overall architecture of a smart catalog. Section 4 describes the concept of a virtual catalog. Section 5 contains a usage scenario of smart catalogs and virtual catalogs. Section 6 describes the current status and future work of this project. Section 7 gives our conclusions.

2. GOALS AND PRINCIPLES

The primary goal of the smart catalog approach is to enable the creation of single-company catalogs with powerful search mechanisms that facilitate the transition to multicompany cross-catalog search mechanisms. A secondary goal is to enable the reuse of catalog information for other purposes than originally intended.

In May 1994 the CommerceNet Catalog Working Group developed a list of about thirty requirements for electronic catalogs, which can be summarized as follows. The system should be scalable and support distributed search (not centralized). Heterogeneous information sources should be supported (not one format or one structure forced on all catalogs). The system should provide up-to-date information (printed catalogs and CD-ROMs are obsolete as soon as they are produced). The system should have an open architecture (allow connection of new information sources, adhere to standards, and allow integration of other approaches and legacy systems). A variety of search techniques should be supported (e.g., menus, keyword, text-based, parameterized, structured "reverse-search"). Cross-search of multiple catalogs for comparable products should also be supported by each catalog.

The requirement for an open architecture supporting a variety of search engines led to several design decisions. First, we separate the query processing core from the data sources and the user interfaces. Thus, multiple user interfaces can access the remainder of the system. Also, a variety of data sources can be connected, including various search engines. Second, we use an intelligent agent–based architecture. This architecture supports such functions as translation, routing, and notification. Third, internally we use a very powerful query and data description language that is capable of encoding practically any data source or query capability. This language, known as Knowledge Interchange Format (KIF), was developed as part of the ARPA Knowledge Sharing Initiative and is currently undergoing standardization by ANSI. We also use Knowledge Query and Manipulation Language (KQML) in order to communicate KIF among the agents in our architecture. KQML was also developed for the ARPA Knowledge Sharing Initiative. We use ontologies to formally describe the structure and the terms of each catalog as well as the relationships among these terms.

3. ARCHITECTURE

Our architecture is illustrated in Figure 11.1. It consists of intelligent agents communicating with facilitators, plus other components, such as data sources and user interfaces, that interact with the collection of intelligent agents and facilitators.

The communication language used by the intelligent agents in our architecture is Agent Communication Language (ACL). ACL consists of the KQML, KIF, and a set of ontologies. KQML consists of performatives, such as "ask-one," "ask-all," and "tell," that describe the nature of the action to be taken. KQML has the role of the communication language in CORBA. KIF is based on First-Order Predicate Calculus and is the content language we use

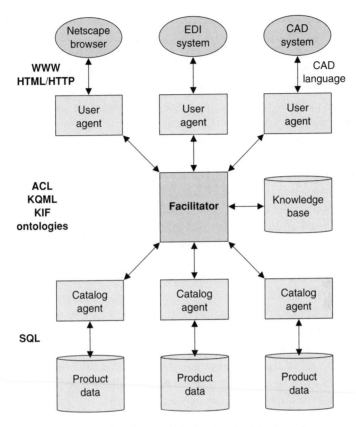

Figure 11.1   Smart Catalog and Brokering Architecture for
Electronic Commerce

with KQML. KIF is powerful enough to contain or to encapsulate any other
first-order or simpler content language, so that any information may be obtained from the information source, translated to the desired format, and
transmitted to the requester, assuming the necessary components exist. Each
product database is described by an ontology (another term for ontology is
"controlled vocabulary"), which defines the database, its structure, the terms
used in it, and how they relate to each other. One can think of KIF as the content language, KQML as the transport protocol, and ontologies as the terminology used within the KIF language for interoperating intelligent agents in
our architecture.

Each facilitator in our architecture acts as a broker. Facilitators perform
routing and translation. Each facilitator stores agent-provided advertisements of coverage in a knowledge base along with relevant ontologies. For
example, an agent may advertise that it can respond to queries for VCRs.

The facilitator uses these advertisements to determine which agents can support a particular request. For example, a request for Super-VHS VCRs with editing capability will be given to the above VCR agent, among others. The facilitator translates requests into the language and terminology used by each responding agent and also translates responses into the language and terminology used by the requesting agent. For example, one manufacturer refers to editing capability as "random assemble editing," while another manufacturer uses the terms "Control L" and "Control S" for its editing systems. A facilitator will decompose requests requiring action by multiple agents and then compose the responses for the requester. For example, a request for reliable used cars that cost less than $5,000 and get more than thirty miles per gallon will be decomposed into a request to a classified advertisement service for used car listings, a request to a car-rating service for the ratings of those cars, and a request to a car specification service for gas mileage for the reliable cars for sale.

Product data are stored in databases, for easy search and maintenance. Such data include structured information, parameters, text, pictures, sound, video, and so on. Each product database communicates with a catalog agent using its native language, such as SQL. The catalog agent performs three roles: it advertises the coverage of a product database; it understands queries and translates them into the language of the product database; and it packages answers from the product database into ACL, our standard format for communicating among intelligent agents.

Consider the query for Super-VHS VCRs with editing capability. Suppose that there is a catalog agent that advertises to facilitators that it can respond to requests for VCRs. Its ontology defines the concept as "random assemble editing." Its database specifies which of the company's Super-VHS VCRs have random assemble editing. The relevant facilitator has a taxonomy that indicates that Super-VHS VCR is a subclass of VHS VCR, which in turn is a subclass of VCR. The facilitator's knowledge base has a rule that random assemble editing is a form of editing capability. Our query for Super-VHS VCRs with editing capability is translated by the rule to random assemble editing. Because VCR is a superclass of Super-VHS VCR, our VCR agent is given the request for Super-VHS VCRs with random assemble editing. The agent converts this ACL query into an SQL query against the catalog database. The result is packaged by the agent into ACL. Depending on the request of the user interface agent, the facilitator will return the resulting information about Super-VHS VCRs with random assemble editing, or will translate these reponses into Super-VHS VCRs with editing capability.

Someone using a WWW client, such as Mosaic or Netscape, will connect to a user agent using the ordinary WWW protocols HTTP and HTML. The user agent will present the user with an HTML form, either statically or dynamically created. The user will describe the desired object using an HTML form. When responses come back from the facilitator, the user agent will prepare dynamically created HTML documents with those responses.

We define four types of ontologies. *Base ontologies* are used to define common terms, such as engineering math, legal terminology, and standard terms and conditions. Base ontologies are shared among all users of this approach and are created by universities and research laboratories. For example, a common business term for payment timing is "2 10 net 30," which means that a 2 percent discount may be taken for payment within ten days and full payment must be received within thirty days. It is unreasonable for each catalog using our approach to have to separately define this term; rather, such definitions should exist for all to use. *Domain ontologies* contain terms common to all or most vendors in an area, such as CPU speed, RAM size, or disk storage capacity. Typically, domain ontologies are created by standards bodies and trade associations. *Product ontologies* contain company-specific terminology and refer to domain ontologies, such as NuBus cards for the Apple Macintosh. Individual companies create product ontologies, although other companies may refer to them. *Translation ontologies* are used to translate specific terms used in one ontology or information source to related terms used in another ontology or information source.[1] For example, a translation ontology may explain that random assemble editing is a form of editing capability for VCRs. Individual companies create translation ontologies to enable them to compete in other markets. We expect there to be service organizations that create and maintain product ontologies and translation ontologies on behalf of other organizations.

4. VIRTUAL CATALOGS

One important problem with using the WWW for product catalogs is the interaction between manufacturers and distributors or retailers. Consider a retailer that sells products from multiple manufacturers. The retailer will want to include product information from each manufacturer in its product catalog. Replicating all this product information in the retailer's catalog would incur a considerable storage and maintenance cost. The typical current approach using the WWW is for the retailer to hyperlink to each manufacturer's catalog so that the customer may obtain detailed product specifications.

---

[1] The term "articulation axiom" is sometimes used to refer to entries in a translation ontology. Translation ontologies may be used to create an ontology algebra supporting translation across multiple ontologies.

There are several problems with the hyperlink approach. First, the customer may get "lost" within the manufacturer's Web space and not know how to get back to the retailer. Second, the manufacturer does not know the context of the customer's interactions with the retailer. Third, the customer may stumble upon a how-to-order page provided by the manufacturer and wind up ordering from someone other than the original retailer. Fourth, if the customer does make it back to the original retailer by using the "back" button, no information determined at the manufacturer's site is carried along with the customer, such as the desired product configuration. Fifth, if the customer gets back to the retailer through the manufacturer's how-to-order page, the retailer does not know the original context of the interaction with the customer (e.g., other products selected for order in this same session).

One approach to multivendor catalogs is the integrated approach, where all the catalogs are stored on one site using one implementation; a notable example of this approach is produced by Open Market. An alternative is to provide some mechanism for manufacturers to respond to specific queries by retailers to satisfy customer requests for product information. This latter approach, which can be based on a business relationship between the retailer and the manufacturer, is the one we take in a virtual catalog.

Virtual catalogs allow retrieval of product data using a distributor's catalog by combining information from multiple manufacturers' catalogs. This retrieval is performed dynamically, upon the user's request, based on the user's search criteria, using the terminology of the distributor or any connected vendor, and it will retrieve data from any relevant connected vendor. Therefore, the distributor's virtual catalog is always kept up-to-date and in synchrony with each manufacturer's smart catalog. The distributor can choose to display all of a manufacturer's products or only a subset of those products. Also, a manufacturer's catalog information may be cached at the virtual catalog site and updated as it changes. Translation of terminology and concepts may occur when information is retrieved to be cached or when information is retrieved from the cache, or a combination of these times.

With virtual catalogs, the distributor maintains control over the interaction with the user. The user never interacts directly with the manufacturer's catalog. Instead, the manufacturer's information is retrieved on demand and is presented to the user with the distributor's look and feel, not the specific look and feel of each manufacturer. The relationship between the user, virtual catalog, and smart catalogs is shown in Figure 11.2.

There are two key business relationships in the virtual catalog world, as well as many supporting business relationships. The two key business relationships are between the customer and the retailer (the virtual catalog), and between the retailer and the manufacturer (the smart catalog). Processes

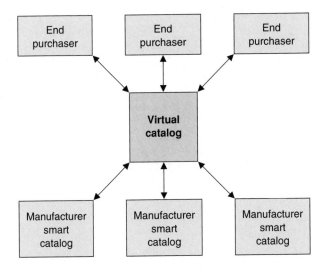

Figure 11.2   Virtual Catalogs

may exist in the virtual catalog to bridge these relationships. For example, orders from customers may trigger resupply EDI transactions to the manufacturer, or the order may be forwarded to the manufacturer for drop shipment of the product directly to the customer. In addition, there are supporting business relationships. For example, if credit cards are used for payment, the customer has a relationship with the issuing bank, the retailer has a relationship with the acquiring bank, and the two banks have a relationship for clearing the credit card charge. Similarly, there are relationships for order fulfillment, shipment, and so on.

Virtual catalogs are appropriate for retailers and distributions as well as in-house procurement catalogs, but they also enable new business models. A virtual distributor may operate using a virtual catalog and a variety of business relationships for order fulfillment, shipment, and other business functions. The virtual distributor may not even have any inventory, warehouse, and so on. The virtual distributor could be a completely computerized setup, automatically providing product information using manufacturers' catalogs, taking orders, and arranging for order fulfillment and payment.

5. SCENARIOS

Consider a customer's request for color PostScript inkjet printers for the Macintosh costing under $1,000. The user agent will translate the query into KIF and submit it to a facilitator. The facilitator handling the query will consult its knowledge base for the facilitators or agents that can handle this request. For example, the facilitator may transmit the request to the catalog agents for Apple and for Hewlett-Packard. The catalog agent will then interrogate the product database and translate the answer into KIF. For example, the Hewlett-Packard catalog agent may respond with the description of the HP DeskWriter 660C printer. The Apple catalog agent may respond with the Apple Color StyleWriter Pro. The facilitator will then collect these responses for the user agent, which will package the responses in HTML for the Mosaic client. The user agent and facilitator are provided by the virtual catalog company. The catalog agents and product databases are provided by the manufacturers as part of their smart catalogs.

A customer may instead be interested in color PostScript laser printers for the Macintosh for under $3,000. As of this publication, such printers cost around $5,000, but prices are dropping, so the customer may request notification when any such printer is newly announced or is lowered in price. This request will be stored in the relevant facilitator's knowledge base. When a manufacturer announces a new product, it will have a catalog agent send a message with the announcement and any changes to the advertisement of the agent to the facilitator. The facilitator will then send appropriate notifications to those parties who have expressed interest in this news.

Notice that the facilitator notification scheme is symmetrical. Catalog agents express interest in being given product data queries. User agents express interest in being given product data announcements. The same notification scheme is used for both types of activities.

Operators of virtual catalogs have several alternative models for paying for their operation. The operator may take and process orders and use the markup on the transaction. Alternatively, the operator may make money merely by providing information. (When information is free, search is valuable.) The operator may charge manufacturers, either a fixed fee or per referral. The operator may charge customers, either by subscription or per search. The operator may sell demographic information on customers or on searches to market research firms, manufacturers, retailers, or trade associations. Of course, an operator may obtain revenues from several of these approaches.

6. CURRENT STATUS

The architecture of smart catalogs and virtual catalogs is an application of the facilitator architecture long in use in the Logic Group of Stanford University's Department of Computer Science. The facilitator architecture has been demonstrated in the domains of software interoperability and concurrent engineering. It is now being applied to the domain of electronic commerce as part of Stanford's Center for Information Technology's (CIT) efforts on CommerceNet.

Several smart catalogs have been built in collaboration with several companies in the domains of workstations, test and measurement equipment, and semiconductors. We have also created smart catalogs for several manufacturers and a virtual catalog that can search these smart catalogs. We are working on creating additional smart catalogs for a larger scale trial. Please contact Arthur Keller by e-mail at ark@cs.stanford.edu or by WWW at http://logic.stanford.edu/commercenet.html for more information.

7. RESEARCH ISSUES

While the basic architecture for smart and virtual catalogs for electronic commerce now exists, a variety of research and development problems remain. Ontologies are now created largely through a manual process. Although some tools exist (such as the Ontology Editor of Stanford University's Knowledge Systems Laboratory), these tools merely facilitate the manual creation of ontologies. Tools are needed that use existing descriptions of data to create initial ontologies that may need manual elaboration. For example, data dictionaries could be used to populate part of an ontology for the corresponding database.

A significant effort will be required in creating the base, domain, and product ontologies needed by our architecture. This effort must be decentralized and scalable for it to succeed. Existing and emerging standards must be used whenever possible to create ontologies that will be adopted widely. An important consideration regarding the smart catalog approach is that it will enable a much greater degree of data reuse than is possible today, and much of this benefit is obtained through the creation of the ontologies. We have yet to create a large collection of ontologies, so the scalability of ontologies is still an issue.

An important feature of our smart catalog approach is the support for heterogeneity. While our approach to heterogeneity has been demonstrated in test cases, the scalability of our approach has not yet been demonstrated. It is critical that the approach to dealing with heterogeneous information sources approximate a linear cost model rather than a quadratic cost model or worse. Only through a larger deployment can we effectively demonstrate that a linear cost model is appropriate.

Security is an important consideration. Some information about products should be disseminated only to certain parties. Assertions made by agents must be verified to ensure that they do not interfere with assertions made by other agents. Both authentication and authorization need to be added to our agent model for widespread deployment to occur.

There are costs associated with responding to inquiries. While some catalog access is free, other access may require payment. Incorporating a payment model into a catalog query mechanism remains to be done.

When there are alternative information sources that can respond to an inquiry, there must be some objective and fair criteria to determine which of these sources is chosen. Differences in quality of information sources, experiences in using the various sources, and parameters of the request, such as willingness to pay and response time required, need to be considered in determining which information source to utilize. These issues are still open problems.

8. CONCLUSION

This chapter has described an architecture for electronic catalogs for multiple companies that interoperate. Companies create smart catalogs of searchable, machine-sensible product information. Retailers and distributors create virtual catalogs that provide customers with product information dynamically requested from manufacturers' smart catalogs. Virtual catalogs provide a new degree of interaction between manufacturers and retailers or distributors. Virtual catalogs enable new business relations and new business models.

REFERENCES

ANSI X3T2. "Knowledge Interchange Format Reference Manual," ed. Michael R. Genesereth. March 1995. Available from URL http://logic stanford.edu/papers/kif.html

DARPA Knowledge Sharing Initiative External Interfaces Working Group. "Specification of the KQML Agent-Communication Language," eds. Tim Finin and Jay Weber. February 9, 1994. Available from URL http://logic.stanford.edu/papers/kqml.html

Genesereth, Michael R., and Steven P. Ketchpel. "Software Agents." *Communications of the ACM* 37, no. 7 (July 1994): 48–53.

Gruber, Thomas R. "Toward Principles for the Design of Ontologies Used for Knowledge Sharing." In International Workshop on Formal Ontology, Padova, Italy, 1992.

Open Market's URL is http://www.openmarket.com

Saqqara Systems' StepSearch can be seen at URL http://www. saqqara.com

Wong, William T., and Arthur M. Keller. "Developing an Internet Presence with On-line Electronic Catalogs." Workshop on Electronic Commerce, December 1994. Available from the URL http://www-db.stanford.edu/pub/keller/1994/cnet-online-cat.ps

PART 5

Business Applications

The final section includes papers covering a wide range of business applications. In Chapter 12, Aimo Hinkkanen, Ravi Kalakota, Porama Saengcharoenrat, Jan Stallaert, and Andrew B. Whinston show how to integrate supply chain management into the framework of electronic commerce. Given the faster pace of decision making in an electronic commerce environment, there is a need to think of supply chain management in a comparable real-time setting. This chapter introduces an aggregation of smart software agents that roam computer networks linking suppliers, manufacturers, shippers, warehouses, and customers to sense changes in the environment and, in collaboration with other agents, respond with suitable actions. Distributed real-time agent-based software systems that manage large-scale systems such as in supply chain management will become more prominent in the future.

Chapter 13, by R. Preston McAfee and John McMillan, introduces electronic markets as being a stage in the evolution toward market-based resource allocation. The authors summarize the advantages of moving from bureaucratic resource allocation to a market-based approach and present several interesting examples. A highlight of the chapter is a summary of what is probably the most significant electronic market, namely, the allocation of the spectral frequency, in whose development the authors played an important role. The chapter reviews the advantages of using a computer-based market in conducting the auction from the perspectives of both the buyer and the seller.

In Chapter 14, on Intranets, Ramnath Chellappa, Anitesh Barua, and Andrew B. Whinston outline the distinction between traditional local area networks and the potential for creating a private worldwide network based on Intranet technology. Their concept of a corporate Intranet computing environment is a secure global network that supports corporate-wide applications for internal supply chain management as well as human resources management. The authors define a "true" Intranet, a concept that expands the scope of Intranets from simple corporate Web servers to a functional network.

Chapter 15, by Ramnath Chellappa, Anitesh Barua, Jennifer Oetzel, and Andrew B. Whinston, describes *EC World,* an electronic journal on the Internet that was developed by the staff at the Center for Information Systems Management at the University of Texas, Austin, for publishing papers related to electronic commerce. *EC World* supports on-line discussion of published papers so that publication is viewed as a dynamic process with continued interaction between authors and commentators. The software system will be used as an experimental environment for exploring new directions in electronic publishing and its role in electronic commerce. This chapter presents a reengineered view of electronic publishing that centers around user involvement and new knowledge creation.

Chapter 12

Distributed Decision Support Systems for Real-Time Supply Chain Management Using Agent Technologies

Aimo Hinkkanen, Ravi Kalakota,
Porama Saengcharoenrat, Jan Stallaert,
and Andrew B. Whinston

ABSTRACT

The concepts and tools of electronic commerce will impact the operations of companies producing physical commodities. This chapter introduces the idea of real-time management of the entire operational process from manufacturing to delivery to the consumer. A software agent organization is responsible for directing the physical flows and is coordinated by a bidding mechanism supported by an electronic payment system. The agents are geographically dispersed in a computer network reflecting the geographical network of the physical system. This chapter provides a broad overview of how the software system will operate to control the physical supply chain environment.

This research has been partially supported by the Office of Naval Research under grant N00014-95-1-1206.

1. INTRODUCTION

In today's global competitive market, first-class products no longer guarantee success in the aggressive battle for market share. Today's successful manufacturing companies face ever-increasing productivity combined with overall cost cutting. Companies that survive in the present global competitive environment show a heightened awareness of customers' needs. They see product flexibility and mass customization as a necessary means for survival.

Manufacturing companies in the West have mainly reached the preceding objectives through technological advances and investments in order to be able to compete with lower labor cost companies in other parts of the world. Downsizing and reengineering efforts have restored companies to their "lean-and-mean" model.

During the eighties, companies started to emphasize their logistical functions, while becoming aware that such functions permeate all other functional areas of a manufacturing company. Other functional areas, such as marketing and finance, are driven by the operations and productions function. It has become clear that marketing decisions have a serious impact on logistical functions and vice versa. For example, a marketing promotion campaign should be coordinated with production planning, since a higher demand may be expected. On the other hand, when raw materials are cheap, or when the factory temporarily shows an overcapacity, the marketing department may decide to cut price and/or start other promotion campaigns to increase demand.

Also financial decisions are driven by production and logistical decisions. Production of new products requires the investment in raw materials and consumes financial funds as the result of machine set-up costs. Financial managers have to be aware of the increased demand for capital to finance the production plan. Likewise, the delivery of finished products generates financial income, and so the forecast demand can be used to calculate the accounts payable and receivable in the future. Thus, production, finance, and marketing decisions cannot be made independently; all these decisions are driven by the activities in the supply chain of a manufacturing company. In order to keep its market share and increase profits, a company needs to make integrated decisions and consider the consequences in all other functional domains. Since this is a complex task, successful companies will keep on relying on information technology to help in making integrated decisions. Consequently, technological advances are necessary to keep a competitive advantage.

Today's information systems are characterized by an increased availability of on-line and real-time information. Optical and radio frequency bar codes, for example, are being used to monitor inventories and to locate parts and products within the plant. At any time of the day, it is possible to know what and how much inventory is available at the plant. Through the Internet and the World Wide Web, external real-time information has become abundant: real-time financial information, as well as commodity prices, can be accessed immediately. The successful manufacturer of the future will exploit this new opportunity for cutting costs and raising productivity. Companies that miss this opportunity will hardly be remembered in the near future.

The availability of real-time worldwide information creates the following new opportunities to build a competitive advantage. On-line information makes it possible to quickly react to changing conditions. For example, when finished goods inventories are continuously monitored, the depletion rate may be used to predict potential problems such as overstocking or product stock-out before such events actually occur. At this point, the event can be prevented by reactive decisions, for example, by producing extra units of the product in question. The on-line information makes it possible to react to real-time changing (unanticipated) conditions in a timely manner. Next, the on-line information can be directly fed to software, programmed to take appropriate action in most of the situations. For example, when inventories of raw materials are monitored, a decision can be automated to start an electronic negotiation with the raw material's supplier and to calculate the "optimal" order quantity, based on requirements, availability, and price. This results in higher productivity for the decision maker (in this case the inventory manager) because, in the example just mentioned, most of the inventory management functions have been automated.

The purpose of this chapter is to describe an information system to be used in this real-time environment. This information system tracks and monitors on-line real-time information that is being captured by most present systems, but it uses this information to manage and control all activities in the supply chain and to relieve human decision makers of most of their task. This system will rely heavily on quantitative models to generate "optimal" solutions to the real-time problems that occur. In addition, it will store information that was relevant (e.g., about the occurrence of certain events), so that it can later be used by other software or human decision makers for detailed analysis. Moreover, the software will assist the end user in making decisions outside its area of responsibility (e.g., when certain events occur where human intervention is needed) by providing suggestions and presenting information in a way that assists in making quick decisions. The structure of this software system will closely resemble the structure of a human organization; we call it an *agent organization*. This system and its operation are described in the rest of the chapter.

The next section describes the supply chain management process and the typical decisions involved. It will outline how this evolution toward real-time models seriously affects the way of managing the activities in the supply chain. In the third section, we will take a close look at the information technology that is presently available and how the present technology can be expected to evolve. We describe our agent organization technology and how it can be used to implement distributed decision support systems. Then, in the fourth section, we apply this distributed decision support system to supply chain management problems. The system architecture is presented, and theoretical issues of agent resource allocation and coordination are given.

2. SUPPLY CHAIN MANAGEMENT

The last decade has seen the rise of a plethora of acronyms that are used in conjunction with production and operations management and control. To name just a few, we have had JIT (Just-in-Time), TQM (Total Quality Management), ZI (Zero Inventory), ECR (Efficient Consumer Response), and VMI (Vendor Managed Inventory). All of these methods can be seen as focusing on one particular problem that may occur in the supply chain. For example, JIT would require a factory to keep inventories (raw materials, work-in-process, finished goods) low and to produce and distribute goods in a timely manner. There is, of course, nothing wrong with this mentality, and the last thing we would argue for is to maintain maximal inventories and be just too late. However, the JIT rule of thumb ignores many other aspects that cannot be seen independently; for example, if the availability of input materials is uncertain and irregular, the factory may need to store a higher inventory to ensure smooth and continuous production. So, whereas all of the preceding acronyms make intuitive sense, we argue here that the supply chain problem has to be tackled as one integrated problem. We need a production planning and control model that focuses on all aspects of the operations and distribution activities and that links with other functional domains such as finance and marketing. Of course, such a model in its entirety becomes very complex and cannot be used without a sufficient computational infrastructure. It is not humanly possible to carry out this task without the use of a distributed decision support system.

Starting in the seventies, many companies paid a lot of attention to logistical functions and how they could be improved to lower total production and distribution costs. The emphasis was on how to make *internal* operations more efficient by addressing a number of questions: What is the optimal order quantity? Which production plan is better? What is our best distribution system, and how would we dispatch our trucks? The company's operations were seen as isolated from the outside world, and no attempt was made to coordinate these operations with the activities at the supplier's and customer's end. When companies such as Procter and Gamble realized that many cost savings were possible if they could have at least some control over the customer's orders, the concept of supply chain management was born. By monitoring the customer's inventories, one can predict the earliest time a stock-out would occur and when the customer would be ready for a new shipment. This flexibility for inventory replenishment makes it possible to smooth out production and distribution peaks, eliminating either overtime labor or excess inventories of finished goods to accommodate those peak demands. So, supply chain management not only involves the management of the logistics functions as was done in the past (striving for *internal* efficiency of operations) but includes managing and coordinating activities upstream and downstream in the supply chain. In this respect, supply chain management eliminates non–value adding activities, such as overtime labor and excess inventories. Nowadays, it is common for manufacturing companies to make their production and/or materials requirements plan available to their suppliers, who, in turn, can use this information to drive their production and distribution plan. Also, continuous replenishment (CR) programs have become commonplace, in which a company virtually takes over the inventory management function of the customer by committing to replenish their inventories without occurring stock-outs, in a way that reduces the customer's total inventory costs.

In general, the following questions have to be answered for an effective supply chain management:

- How much of each raw material or intermediate or finished product should be procured or converted at each facility?

- Which supply sources should be chosen, and what are target inventory levels?

- What constitute the best production schedule, the optimal batch size, and the optimal production sequence?

- What should the target levels of finished goods be, and how can we forecast demand most accurately for each individual customer?

- What is the best mode of transportation, and which mode should be used for which shipments?

- What are the optimal warehouse locations and sizes?

- Which financial resources will we use to finance our production plan?

- How will our current material ordering policy and the customer's payment policy influence the cash flow, and how do we hedge against price fluctuations of finished goods and/or commodities?

- Which products should be manufactured in which countries, and what are the global implications in terms of duties, duty drawbacks, tariffs, and taxes?

Again, it should be stressed that all of these issues are interrelated. The only reason these questions have been answered separately in the past is because it was impossible to solve integrated problems of such complexity. However, over the past decade, many companies have solved these problems in a (more or less) integrated fashion. The advent of cheaper computational power and better mathematical solution algorithms has made it possible to solve the complete supply chain problem. These models are generally solved as some variant of linear programming problems containing tens of millions of variables. The output of these systems is a *master production plan*, specifying the daily supply chain decisions over the next few weeks. Needless to say, these models make heavy use of forecast data, such as demand, cost, price, and material and labor availability. Actual daily operations are guided by heuristic rules and ad hoc adjustments to this plan. Our proposed decision support system will allow these adjustments to be automated. Moreover, the reoptimization will be done in such a manner as to converge to a global optimum of the system as a whole.

Nowadays, with the on-line real-time availability of both internal and external information, making ad hoc manual adjustments to the production plan is not sufficient. First of all, the abundance of this information makes it impossible for any decision maker to control and reoptimize the production plan, since they will be overwhelmed with information. Not only is it impossible to sift through and filter out the relevant information in a sufficiently short amount of time, but the question remains of what to do with the data just gathered. Therefore, in order to optimally adjust the production plan, some optimization or analytic software will have to be used to come up with the best corrective actions.

The proposed system will not only filter out relevant information but take corrective action as well. The system will relieve the human decision maker of most of his or her routine adjustments, yielding higher productivity and higher quality in terms of the decision-making process. For example, suppose that an optimal distribution plan has been calculated for the coming week. This plan, of course, is based on such details as forecast demand, truck availability, and so on. Now, in light of updated demand figures (calculated, for example, by a marketing agent that projects the recent rate of depletion of the retailer's stock into the future), the distribution plan may have to be slightly modified. In addition, major (unanticipated) disruptions also occur in real time. For example, a snowstorm may immobilize certain trucks in the region, while at the same time shipments to retailers in the affected region become impossible. In this case the distribution plan will have to be modified in a major way to find the new optimal plan.

In the next section, we will closely examine the status of current information technology as it is relates to the context of supply chain management. Then, in section 4 we will apply the information technology concepts to supply chain management.

3. INFORMATION TECHNOLOGY

At present, most business information systems can be characterized as distributed, on-line systems. The appearance of cheap personal computers and workstations forced a distributed architecture, moving away from the more centralized, mainframe-oriented systems of the past. These client/server systems have the following features: graphic user interface that allows for on-line real-time retrieval and update of information and data stored on different servers throughout the company; that is, rather than a centralized database, current business information systems rely on distributed ones. Such an architecture has vast computational power, and the overall system can be seen as a parallel computing system whose utilization is not even nearly used up to capacity.

Moreover, the company's system is now connected worldwide via the Internet or World Wide Web (WWW). Most companies now make information available on that medium, and, if not, they almost all can access information from outside. Real-time information pertinent to the company's operations can be accessed in real time: stock quotes, commodity prices, and so on. On the other hand, electronic commerce allows for even more automation and less clerical work. Ordering can be automated via EDI (electronic data interchange) messages, and the entire shipment notification procedure, from billing up to and including payments (via electronic funds transfer or other payment systems now available on the WWW), can be done electronically and automatically, if so desired.

With this real-time on-line information and network connectivity (both inter- and intra-organizational), the use of software agents (or intelligent agents) becomes very natural. Software agents are personal assistants that relieve their end user from most routine tasks. For the end user (or some other human agent), it is almost impossible to distinguish whether the software agent's actions have been performed by a human or a machine. For example, software agents exist that find documents on the Internet which are of interest to the end user. An agent constructs a prioritized list of documents, and it is hard to distinguish whether this list has been constructed by software or by, say, the user's secretary. Software agents also exhibit the ability to "learn" or to express "rational" behavior. Software agents are implemented just like viruses: they continuously execute in the background of the machine, and—without the user being aware—monitor real-time information as it changes.

Software agents are an ideal technology for real-time supply chain management. Since almost all information is being captured directly in real time (such as inventory depletion via barcodes), a software agent can be easily implemented to monitor these specialized situations. When inventory falls below a certain level, it calculates an optimal order quantity (based on prices, availabilities, and future depletion of the product) and initiates the ordering process by sending EDI messages to the supplier. The supplier will not be able to distinguish between the orders of a software agent or a manual order placed by a human decision maker. The agent displays rationality in its decision-making process; consequently, there does not seem to be anything "artificial" about the actions it performed. Moreover, the agent carries out the same task as would its end user, thereby significantly increasing the latter's productivity by unburdening him or her from the routine (programmable) tasks.

Recently, a new programming language known as Java has appeared, which is especially suited to develop applications on a network. The Java language can be used for agent programming as well and runs on top of the WWW, providing the end user with multimedia interface. Peer-to-peer process communication on the WWW, which has been proven to be very difficult to implement with previous technology, now becomes rather easy with the Java language. This feature allows us to develop a multiagent system with suitable interagent communication by using Java. From the previous section, it is clear that all aspects in the supply chain are interrelated and that decisions made at one point in the supply chain ripple through and impact all other decisions downstream as well as upstream. So, in order to drive the whole supply chain to an optimal state, interagent communication and coordination is necessary. Such a multiagent system, which needs explicit coordination rules between agents and where the overall system itself has an objective, is called an agent organization (Hinkkanen, Stallaert, and Whinston 1995). In an agent organization, agents must obey certain rules and their behavior is driven by incentives so as to achieve the overall system's goal, just as in an organization of humans. So, whereas the individual agents perform highly specialized tasks, their behavior is not myopic by means of the organizational rules. The incentives the organization provides for the individual agents (such as goals, and other criteria to be maximized), together with the authority of some agents (the hierarchically "superior" agents) to change "inferior" agents' behavior, guarantee that the state of the overall system is being optimized, that is, that the supply chain operates under minimum cost conditions while respecting constraints on customer service levels, product quality, as well as other physical constraints (such as plant capacity or truck capacity).

The agent organization executes in parallel on the company's distributed computer system. Individual agents perform tasks that can be identified with one or a few human decision makers. For example, the agent that was monitoring inventory and reordering new products could be the inventory manager's agent. So, for the end user this agent acts as his or her personal decision support system, carrying out most decisions automatically and alerting the user when something unexpected happens. When viewed globally, the whole agent organization can be seen as a distributed decision support system. Each agent has the responsibility for one specific task (which it does in parallel with the other agents), but the organization as a whole (through communication and coordination) accomplishes a higher objective: optimal integrated supply chain management.

In the next section, we will describe the implementation and operation of this agent organization in full detail. We will also give the links of the system with other parts in the company, such as accounting, finance, and marketing. As such, our software organization can be seen as the mirror of the human organization, where every individual agent supports the decision-making process for one or a few human end users, and if it were possible to create "perfect" agents (i.e., agents who are prepared and programmed to react to every possible situation that can occur, and behave in an optimal manner), there would no longer be a need for any human decision maker. The factory would be completely managed and driven by software agents. Unfortunately, while this situation seems to be an ultimate goal, it cannot be expected to be realized practically. We will be content to implement agents that can accommodate as many situations as possible, thereby relieving its end user from most of the burden of making routine decisions and increasing his or her decision-making efficiency and quality.

4. DISTRIBUTED DECISION SUPPORT SYSTEM FOR SUPPLY CHAIN MANAGEMENT

4.1. System Architecture

In the previous two sections, we looked at the business processes and the relevant areas where supply chain decisions have to be made, and then examined the present relevant information technology. In this section we apply this technology to develop the real-time decision support system that will optimize the supply chain decisions. As will be seen, there is a tight fit

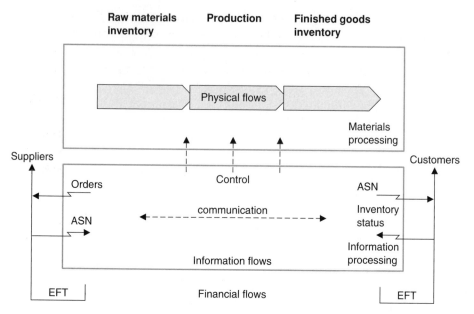

Figure 12.1   Relationship between Physical, Information, and
Financial System

between the information system that we propose (the distributed decision
support system) and the business processes it supports.

The overall system and its interactions are presented in Figure 12.1. The
physical, information, and financial flows are completely integrated. The information flows, though, drive both as physical and financial flows. The information system is composed of our agent organization as described in the
previous section, together with the other (traditional) components of the
business information system, such as databases, accounting applications,
and so on. The agent organization will automatically feed information to
those components (e.g., when it sent an order to a supplier, a copy of the
message is kept in the database) and uses it for its internal operation (e.g.,
before sending out an order, the database is consulted to get information
about suppliers). The agent organization monitors and controls the activities
in the supply chain, shown by the dotted arrows in the figure. They monitor
and gather data through the following means:

- EDI messages. This channel is used to get information about what is going on upstream and downstream in the supply chain and records information about the *external* world.

- Scanners (bar codes, radio frequency bar codes, optical scanners). This information channel is used to monitor the raw physical flows, in order to be able to update inventories, production rates, and so on, and is used to get information about the *internal* state of operations.

- Interagent communication. Through messages sent to other agents, the state of the overall supply chain can be tracked and the relevant information to make certain decisions can be accessed.

Control and reoptimization of the supply chain is the other responsibility of the agent organization. Access to all relevant information is guaranteed, and the individual agent takes corrective action to optimize supply chain operations. It does so by applying quantitative models and analytical tools to get "optimal" decisions. These decisions can be implemented automatically, for example, in a computer integrated manufacturing (CIM) or robotics environment, or the decisions can be reported to the human decision maker who then (maybe after his or her approval and scrutiny) will implement the decision. As mentioned earlier, these decisions are not limited to the area of operations and production: they span all functional domains up to and including financial decisions, via electronic funds transfer (EFT) and other means of electronic payments, marketing, and accounting as well.

It is important to mention that there is complete symmetry between the physical and the information system. Where transformation, assembly, input, or output takes place in the physical system, a software agent performs information processing to monitor, control, and reoptimize this physical operation. Materials transfers correspond to information flows between the agents. This guarantees the tight fit between the information morphology and the physical system. In that respect, the organization of software agents closely resembles a human organization, where the members' tasks and the organizational structure are built according to the business processes that are to be performed to reach the organization's overall goal. Over time, through external and environmental changes and technological advances, the business processes change and, consequently, so does the organizational design. The software agent organization is very similar in that respect, and the fact that each agent is maximally autonomous and independent allows for the necessary flexibility to dynamically change the agent organization.

Figure 12.2 gives an example of our decision support system for a manufacturer of cookies and candy bars. For simplicity, the operations involve only one processor (an oven), and we have inventories of raw material and finished products. Our small company is managed by three persons: the raw materials inventory manager, the production manager, and the finished goods/distribution manager. Each one has his or her own computer, and

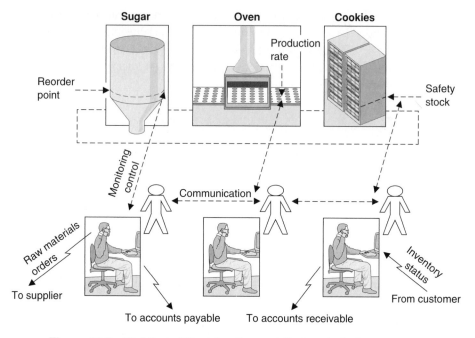

Figure 12.2 Distributed Decision Support System in Action

the humanlike figures at the back end of the computer are the software agents.

The raw materials inventory agent monitors the depletion of sugar. When the reordering point has been reached, it sends an EDI message to the sugar supplier, with the quantity ordered and the order price. The supplier can be selected from any of the suppliers in the (distributed) database that the agent can access, and the price can be negotiated electronically by the agent. The optimal order amount is calculated based upon past usage and future demand for sugar. This demand can be derived from the production *plan*, which is generated once a week, say, for the whole company. Of course, in light of changing, real-time conditions, this production plan may not be applicable anymore, and the agent can send a message to the production agent to query the latter about its future production plans or its latest adjustments to the plan. Then it can select a supplier and an order quantity to generate the minimum cost acquisition, while maintaining feasibility of the (adjusted) production plan. When an order is to be placed, the inventory agent asks permission from the financial agent to inquire whether enough funds are available to finance the acquisition. When an order has been sent, it alerts the "accounts payable" agent to update the latter on the financial implications of the order.

The production agent mainly monitors and controls the production rate of the two products: cookies and candy bars. It should be able to detect when the production process needs (automatic or human) intervention. For example, production rates fluctuate within a certain margin, but when the rate falls outside this margin, intervention is necessary. The production agent calculates optimal batch sizes, when a trade-off is to be made between inventory holding costs (high with large batch sizes) and changeover costs (high with small batch sizes). It adjusts the production plan, which was calculated on the basis of forecast demand but may—in real time—prove to be no longer relevant. So, upon receiving messages from the finished goods inventory agent, which is the one that both monitors the finished goods inventory and forecasts short-term demand based on EDI messages about inventories at the customers' sites, the production agent continuously updates the "optimal" batch sizes in order to produce the correct product quantities.

Besides the tasks just mentioned, the finished goods inventory agent is also responsible for calculating an optimal distribution plan. It knows the retailer's inventories and uses this information to calculate the optimal time for replenishment, in case the company has a continuous replenishment program with the retailer. In case an electronic order arrives via EDI from a retailer, the agent may want to find out the credit status of the customer before acknowledging delivery of the order. It asks the "accounts receivable" agent about the balance of the customer's account; when it gets approval, it sends an EDI message to the customer to confirm the delivery. After it calculates the optimal distribution plan, it sends an advance shipment notification (ASN) to the customer to signal the delivery date and time. When the customer sends back a "shipment received" message, the inventory agent sends a message to the "accounts receivable" agent, who then sends an electronic bill and updates the financial situation to reflect this future income.

It is important to note that every agent is really the assistant of a human decision maker and is specialized for one particular problem area. This makes the decision support system easy to adapt, modify, and extend. Rather than having one large (centralized) software system, ours uses a distributed system where the agents are as autonomous and independent as possible. They communicate by messages (e-mail, for example), which allow for the agents to run on different platforms, even programmed with different software tools. When an agent's decision logic has to be modified in light of new business processes or environments, this change only affects the one agent, which gives enormous flexibility from a software development point of view. Also, it allows for a modular implementation of the whole system: only one part can be automated at one time (e.g., the production and inventory agents), and future agents can be plugged in to automate other aspects or functional domains (e.g., the financial agents). The only issue that has to be taken into account is the *message space*. What are the different types of messages that agents can interchange and that are sufficient to control and reoptimize the whole supply chain activity? This question is related to the problem of agent coordination, which is addressed in the next subsection.

4.2. Agent Coordination and Resource Allocation

In the previous subsection, the basic operation of the agent organization was described. However, for reasons of exposition, the situation was kept very simple. The agent as described there was highly independent, and the supply chain situation as painted there could be solved by solving three separate unconnected subproblems: one for the raw materials agent, one for the production agent, and one for the finished goods agent. Now, however, assume that we have a production agent for cookies and a production agent for candy bars. Each production agent has its own goals, that is, to replenish the finished goods inventory at a rate ordered by the inventory agent.

Now suppose the following situation arises. It appears that the demand for cookies is higher than expected, and so the cookie production agent gets a message for increased production from the finished goods inventory agent. However, the production of the desired amount of cookies, combined with the required amount of candy bars, is not feasible because not enough sugar is available. So, the "sugar agent" gets messages from both production agents asking for their respective amounts, which would result in a negative inventory. Now, the question becomes: Who gets what and in what amount?

This issue is one of *resource allocation*. When scarce resources (such as machine time, trucks, labor, budgets, and so on) are shared between different agents and used for different purposes, how does this resource agent decide the "optimal" allocation? This issue is a critical one, and an agent organization is built around the premise that the solution of the resource allocation problem is crucial to induce the optimal behavior of the system as a whole. With a centralized approach, the solution to this problem is obvious, since the central authority has all information to calculate an optimal allocation. However, in our distributed environment no such central information is available, and we do not want to burden the resource agent with the collection of all the data and solution of this centralized (large-scale) problem as this would be infeasible in a real-time situation. Therefore, a mechanism has been designed that induces an optimal state for the system as a whole, while not requiring the massive exchange of information and solution of a large-scale problem (Hinkkanen et al. 1996).

Without going into too much technical detail, it is possible to describe the mechanism of resource allocation as very similar to a simultaneous auction,

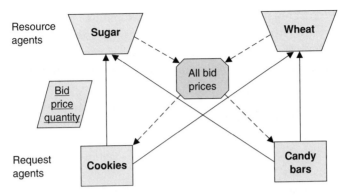

Figure 12.3   The Bidding Process for Resource Allocation

as depicted in Figure 12.3. When an agent requests the use of a resource (for now, we will call this agent a "request agent"), it submits a bid to the agent responsible for that resource (for now, we will call this agent a "resource agent"), containing the "price" it is willing to pay and the amount requested. Then, in contrast to a usual auction, the resource agent selects winning bids but does not allocate the resources at this time. Rather, it makes all bids public to the requesting agents, who can then adjust their bids. This process is repeated for a number of rounds, and then the actual resource allocation is performed. The resources are not allocated at once because a request agent may need different resources in order to function, and only access to all resources results in feasibility. For example, when the cookie production agent sends a bid for sugar to the sugar agent, it also sends a bid for flour to the flour agent. Of course, we would like to avoid the situation where the cookie agent is allocated the requested amount of flour without being granted any amount of sugar. (Cookies would taste really peculiar, and it is hard to imagine any demand for them at all!) So, when the bid for flour is selected, but not the bid for sugar, the agent can increase its bid price for sugar to get the desired amount.

Now the question becomes: How does the agent decide what price to bid? The answer is that an agent is programmed to maximize its revenue for the production of cookies, that is, it is given a unit revenue and calculates the optimal production quantity. Now the agent can only bid in a manner such that the "cost" of the resources does not exceed the revenues from the finished products. So, the resource will be used where its use is valued highest. In the preceding example, where the demand for cookies was underestimated, the finished goods agent sent a message to the production agent because the inventory of cookies fell below a certain level. The inventory agent, in order to induce the cookie production agent to produce, sends a higher unit price for a cookie (this price can be calculated as a decreasing function of inventory, for example), so that the cookie agent can bid a higher price for the use of the resources, and, if the inventory of candy bars is "sufficient," the sugar will be used for production of cookies rather than for production of candy bars. The coordination mechanism is somewhat more complicated than is described here, but the informal description more or less captures the process. It can be proven that this coordination mechanism—under very mild conditions—induces the optimal behavior of the agents, "optimal" in the sense that it drives the state of the overall system to its optimum. In our discussion we used the concept of "price" and "auction," as this was the best analogy we could think of. "Prices" may also be seen as "priorities," and the auctions are nothing else than the process of prioritizing the uses of the resources. Also, we used "request" agents and "resource" agents in our description, but it should be made clear that an agent can be a request agent for several resources while at the same time being a resource agent for another set of resources. The coordination mechanism specifies the rules the agents must obey to be members of the organization. These rules prevent myopic behavior of the agents and act as standards as well for the implementation of new agents, yielding a distributed system that permits "plug and team-play" agents to build a software system.

4.3. Extensions of the Agent Organization

In the preceding subsections, we emphasized the use of the production agents, that is, the agents mainly monitoring and controlling the physical flows. Of course, we could have outlined how the financial subsystem would work. There the financial agents get messages about incoming and outgoing money streams. They then plan the cash flows so as to minimize financial costs, such as interest to be paid for short-term loans, exchange risks, and so on.

Actually, the financial subsystem is an important system by itself. We have only briefly pointed out the relationship between the physical flows and the financial flows, but controlling and optimizing financial flows is important for a large manufacturing company. Good financial planning can result in tremendous cost savings. Just think about all factors a global company has to take into account when doing financial planning:

- Currency exchange risks
- Uncertain commodity prices
- Fluctuating interest rates

- Duties, tariffs, and different international tax rates

- Different international labor laws

- Uncertain customer payments

Those problems are also real-time problems, as the data used for the financial optimization change in real time. Again, these data (interest rates, exchange rates, and so on) are available on the Internet or World Wide Web, and this information can be accessed by the financial agents to control and optimize the financial transactions (e.g., which banks should be dealt with, how one would convert one currency into another). For a more detailed description of an application of financial optimization problems using real-time data, the reader is referred to Kalakota, Stallaert, and Whinston (1996).

5. CONCLUSION

This chapter has described the reasons why manufacturing companies in the future need real-time, adaptable decision support systems if they want to remain competitive. We presented the current information technology and how it can be used to implement these real-time systems. The global interconnectivity was an important feature of the present and future computational environment. We introduced the concept of agent organizations for developing the distributed decision support systems that control and optimize supply chain activities. Effective supply chain management is *integrated* supply chain management. The physical (material) flows drive all other functional areas in a manufacturing company, and we specifically outlined the interface between the physical flows and the financial flows that are generated by it. The distributed system is flexible and adaptable: new business processes can easily be automated without a major revision of the agent organization.

REFERENCES

Kalakota, R., J. Stallaert, and A. B. Whinston. "World Wide Real Time Decision Support Systems for Electronic Commerce Applications," *Journal of Organizational Computing and Electronic Commerce* 6 (1996):11–32.

Kalakota, R., and A. B. Whinston. *Frontiers of Electronic Commerce.* Reading, MA: Addison-Wesley Publishing Company, Inc., 1996.

Chapter 13

Electronic Markets

R. Preston McAfee and John McMillan

ABSTRACT

Electronic markets introduce new forms of exchange, permitting decentralization of markets that were previously administered in a bureaucratic fashion. This chapter considers the design of such emerging markets, describing existing and future applications.

The introduction of high-speed computers, together with new understanding by economists of how complex markets function, has made possible a new kind of market, an electronic market. These new markets permit decentralized decision making in situations where, previously, decisions were necessarily made centrally, and inefficiently.

Traditional markets, as understood by economists beginning with Adam Smith in 1776, involve many buyers and many sellers transacting at a price determined by supply and demand. This competitive model of traditional markets continues to serve as the basis for understanding market transactions for many goods and services. The key assumptions underlying the competitive model are that (1) there are many buyers and sellers, and none of these buyers and sellers represents a significant fraction of total demand or supply; (2) the good or service to be transacted is homogeneous or standardized, that is, does not have idiosyncratic or differentiated features across distinct units; and (3) buyers and sellers are well informed about the quality and characteristics of the good, as well as the transaction price.

There are numerous examples of competitive markets. The stock market is an excellent example, as well as commodities markets that transact a diverse set of standardized goods such as platinum, plywood, and pork bellies. In addition, many other markets function as reasonably competitive

We thank Lynn Hunnicutt for comments.

markets, such as restaurants in urban areas, groceries, automobiles, computers, videotape rentals, and recorded music. All of these feature some degree of product differentiation—for example, a Toyota is not the same as a Ford, and a French restaurant not the same as an Italian restaurant—but nevertheless, there exist sufficiently good substitutes to any one producer's product that no producer can extract significant profits from the buyers by exerting monopoly power. The unfettered free market is the best way of allocating such goods and services. By seeking an advantage over competitors, producers offer higher quality and lower prices, thereby serving the consumer well and increasing the standard of living.

There are other goods and services for which the competitive assumptions fail in a dramatic way. For example, a competitive market would not produce much in the way of national defense. Suppose that the fifty states had to undertake their own defense independently and without coordination. Some of the benefits of the defense of the coastal states would accrue to the interior states; the interior states might be willing to pay for some of the coastal defense, but in the absence of a national government there would be no mechanism to compel the interior states to make such payments. Economists call this failure to pay for benefits received "the *free-rider* problem." Furthermore, defense of neighboring states would be poorly coordinated or not coordinated at all, requiring extra expenditures relative to a coordinated defense. Overall, a decentralized approach to national defense would serve the states poorly; for this reason, national defense is considered by the Constitution to be one of the jobs of the federal government.

It was Adam Smith's remarkable insight that the price system can serve to coordinate buyers and sellers. The traditional market achieves a high degree of coordination in the production of some goods and services. Millions of specialized inputs are used in the production of goods, and firms have come into being to serve the demand for these inputs. The production of something as simple as a pencil requires many specialized inputs, which are often produced by distinct firms. Coordination is achieved through the price system—if one input is in short supply, the price rises, encouraging further production of that input.

The price system is not always able to solve the coordination problem, however, as the example of national defense shows. Consider a new microcomputer operating system. Consumers won't value the operating system unless there is software to run on it. Similarly, consumers won't value software for the operating system unless they own the operating system. Thus, to get the market started, a firm producing a new operating system often pays other firms to adapt their software to run on the new system, and the introducer of the operating system may write a substantial amount of software itself, creating a base of software to encourage consumer adoption of the new operating system. The solution to the coordination problem has taken place partly within the firm, rather than through external markets. Such internal solutions to coordination problems, which are common in market-based economies, are one of the reasons we see very large corporations, with tens of thousands of employees.

The first recognition by the U.S. court system of the failure of competition in the provision of goods and services involved the desire by the state of Illinois to regulate the maximum price charged for warehousing grain. In the 1877 decision in *Munn v. Illinois*, the U.S. Supreme court ruled, "When private property is devoted to a public use, it is subject to public regulation." The *Munn* decision served as the precedent that permitted Congress to establish the Interstate Commerce Commission in 1887, with the purpose of regulating railroads. Three years later, the Sherman Antitrust Act permitted the federal government to prevent cartels (or trusts, as they were known) and monopolization of industry. Later, the Clayton Act extended antitrust authority to such diverse behaviors as resale price maintenance, tying, exclusive dealing, and price discrimination.

Traditional markets fail to deliver efficient levels of goods and services for a variety of reasons. We have already considered the problem of introducing a new operating system, which is valueless unless software exists to run on it, while the software is valueless unless consumers adopt the new operating system. This reason for a failure of the marketplace is known as a *coordination failure*, and can sometimes be solved by the existence of a very large firm, without government intervention. The standard reason for market failure is that of *natural monopoly*, where a single provider of a good has lower costs than two or more independent providers. Natural monopoly is a consequence of *scale economies*, where average cost is declining in the quantity produced. In a natural monopoly the efficient scale of operation is close to the size of the market. Natural monopolies have been thought to occur in electricity generation and distribution, railroads, telephone networks, and the distribution of natural gas. Historically, governments have responded to the problem of natural monopoly through two methods: regulation and government-owned production. In the United States, regulation has been the primary tool, and has been applied to telephones, electricity, trucking, airlines, natural gas, railroads, and recently to cable TV. Elsewhere, the government-owned firm has been a more significant policy tool; for example, Canada owns Air Canada, the Canadian National Railroad, and even the major oil company, PetroCanada. In the United States, about the only significant government ownership in private industry is the government's participation in Intelsat, the telecommunications satellite system, and historically in its participation in RCA.

Problems associated with market failures are not only solved by governments; firms such as railroads, telephone companies, or airlines may grow large in order to provide efficient services in the presence of network externalities.[1] For example, consumers desire convenient and inexpensive airline connections, and airlines respond by creating a hub-and-spoke system, which allows relatively low-cost connections throughout the network. In order to function efficiently, however, a hub-and-spoke system requires a large network, so only a few producers can compete in the national market. Similarly, the complexity of building cars, and of achieving an efficient scale of production using assembly lines, necessitated large car companies. In all cases, these solutions to market failures are administrative in nature; decisions about production and distribution are made by authority, either government authority or managers in a firm.

A variety of problems are associated with administrative solutions to market failures, and these problems arise whether the administrators are government officials or firm managers. With respect to government officials, Nobel laureate George Stigler's *capture theory* indicates that regulated firms have a great incentive to induce government officials to bend regulations to suit the firms, primarily to inhibit competition. This theory has been applied to railroad, trucking, and airline regulation, where in many cases the regulations seemed designed to inhibit competition and lead to high prices. The state of Texas licenses lawn sprinkler installers, which appears to be a way of limiting entry into the lawn sprinkler installation business, rather than protecting ill-informed consumers from shoddy lawn sprinkler installations. Similarly, within firms, Paul Milgrom's *influence cost theory* indicates that firm employees have an incentive to lobby upper-level management for changes that suit the employees rather than increasing the profitability of firms. This theory holds that large firms will be inefficient in some respects unless strong market forces require them to behave efficiently in order to exist.

Both the influence cost theory and the capture theory are manifestations of the difficulty in providing incentives in the absence of market forces. When the profit incentive is muted or absent, either firms or government have little incentive to serve the consumer and a great incentive to lead a comfortable life. An extreme example on the government side is the Food and Drug Administration's hesitancy to license drugs aimed at alleviating fatal illnesses; an act of Congress was required to force the FDA to expedite the licensing of such drugs.

---

[1] Network externalities arise when individual consumers are made better off by greater participation in the network. This benefit of increased use might arise directly, as in a telephone network, where an increased use permits a user to call more people, or indirectly, e.g. increased use of an operating system causes more compatible software to be written.

In some of the examples we will visit, the government is replacing administrative procedures with bidding mechanisms. These mechanisms have the advantage of applying market forces to the allocation problem at hand, but they have the second advantage of raising revenue for the government. For example, the Federal Communications Commission has historically allocated licenses to use the radio and TV spectrum to the firms making applications that best served the public interest, as judged by FCC administrators. Recently, the FCC was authorized to use auctions. Not only do auctions eliminate the incentive of firms to expend resources lobbying the FCC, which is ultimately a socially wasteful activity, but the auctions themselves have raised approximately $9 billion for the federal government!

In many instances, it is not immediately obvious how to decentralize the allocation of some good or service. Many of the regulations were imposed in response to problems in the market allocation. For example, the inability of consumers to easily verify the quality of meat sold in the marketplace led directly to the regulation of meat quality. Similarly, privatizing a state-owned railroad replaces a state-run monopoly with a privately run monopoly, and it is not immediately apparent that the consumer is better served by the latter than the former. In some circumstances, however, a market solution is possible, but the market solution requires a more complex market arrangement than the traditional supply and demand marketplace. The new markets created by deregulation often require complex allocation mechanisms. Selling electricity contracts or spectrum licenses, for example, means matching the demand and supply of a large number of interlinked items, and the market mechanism must be well designed to function efficiently.

The new electronic markets are neither simple supply and demand markets, nor administratively operated hierarchical decision-making processes. Electronic markets combine features of administrative decision making with market pricing. For example, they may use contingent or combinational bidding, where one's bid for a given item is contingent on the purchase of other items, as in the proposal to decentralize Sweden's railway system described later. Alternatively, the electronic market may permit iterated bidding on multiple items, as in the FCC simultaneous ascending auction described later in the chapter. The virtue of electronic markets is that allocation mechanisms may be implemented that are much more complex than the traditional marketplace yet that retain market forces through competition.

Electronic markets may function in creating allocations of goods and services where traditional supply and demand work poorly. The failure of traditional competition may result from idiosyncratic and differentiated goods, ill-behaved preferences (e.g., buyers need to acquire several units for any to be valuable; an extreme example is the airport landing and takeoff right allocation, for the right to take off from one airport is of little value without the right to land at another airport at the right time), or matching problems, such as arise with matching students to colleges or doctors to hospitals.

FUNCTIONING ELECTRONIC MARKETS

There are several examples of functioning electronic markets involving complex algorithms. This section discusses some of the more visible and significant examples.

1. National Resident Matching Program (NRMP)

The matching of residents to hospitals is a difficult economic problem to solve. There are tens of thousands of residents and thousands of hospitals in the United States. Unlike traditional markets, the "goods" (residents) are differentiated in skills, and worse, have preferences over the hospitals that might employ them. Thus, the assignment of residents to hospitals creates a two-sided matching problem. That traditional markets don't operate effectively in such an environment can be seen by example. Suppose a potential resident x would like to work in hospital A but will take B if necessary. Meanwhile, B offers x its position, while A offers its position to resident y, with x as the fallback offer. Then x will wait to see what y does. Such considerations can create a gridlock in the system.

The response of hospitals to such gridlock is to "jump the gun" and try to lock in the best candidate prior to the optimal time for the market to operate, that is, when the best information is available about the hospital's needs and the candidate's skills (as described in Roth and Xing 1994). Consequently, the market will tend to "unravel," in the sense of operating much too early, in particular, with resident matching occurring in the first or second year of medical school.[2] Starting in the late 1940s, in both the United States and Britain, the medical community responded with attempts to centralize the matching process. Only some of these attempts were successful, and the reader is referred to Roth and Sotomayor (1984) for details. The successful attempts involved the use of a matching algorithm that respected the preferences of the participants. In this algorithm, known as the National Residents Matching Program (NRMP), the hospitals rank the candidates who have

---

[2] Roth and Xing (1994) show that this phenomenon is widespread and includes football bowls, jobs for new lawyers, court clerkships, jobs for Japanese university graduates, and even fraternities and sororities, where the name "rush" arises from the unraveling of the matching process of female undergraduates to sororities. Many sororities use an algorithm to allocate candidates, although currently these algorithms are implemented by hand rather than by computer.

applied to them, and the candidates rank the hospitals to which they've applied. The algorithm first executes "1:1" matches, that is, executes the matches where the hospital ranked the candidate first and vice versa. The elimination of these matches then requires reordering the remaining rankings; for example, a hospital that ranked candidate x first and candidate y second would now rank candidate y first if candidate x has already been matched. The procedure then attempts to execute the "2:1" matches, where the candidate ranks the hospital second but the hospital ranks the candidate first. The process continues, executing matches that the hospital ranks first, until no new such matches are possible, while consistently reconfiguring the rankings to reflect individuals and positions removed from the system. (For further details, see Roth and Sotomayor 1990.)

We wish to stress two key features about the NRMP. First, the mechanism is quite complicated, relative to a traditional market. In the United States, 20,000 residents are matched annually through the NRMP. This market, then, does not resemble a traditional supply and demand market, and it is difficult to envision the functioning of the market absent the use of computers to keep track of the rankings, although the early use of the system, implemented in the 1950s, was without computers.

The second important feature of the NRMP is that the system is entirely *voluntary*. Neither hospitals nor potential residents are compelled to use the system, yet 85 to 90 percent of them do use the system. Thus, unlike administrative solutions to market allocation problems, the NRMP is a market-based solution. However, the market algorithm is substantially more complicated than that of determining a price for a homogeneous good.

In many ways the NRMP is perhaps the best example of a functioning electronic market. However, the program's functionality has recently been encountering problems associated with couples. The NRMP did not originally respect the preferences of couples, and early attempts to incorporate the desire of couples to locate in the same city were failures, for the initial attempt only respected the preferences of one member of the couple. While the theory of "many-to-one" matching (for example, hospitals desire many residents, while potential residents desire at most one hospital) is well understood, there is little theory to guide one in the choice of an algorithm to deal with couples, which remains a topic of continuing research. Nevertheless, the NRMP demonstrates viability of complex electronic markets with significant economic activity.

2. Electricity Generation

Britain has decentralized the production of electricity by splitting the national electric utility into three firms (one nuclear and two fossil fuel companies), and then permitting those firms, along with other domestic producers or co-generators (who produce electricity as a by-product of other operations) and foreign nations, to bid for the right to supply electricity. As a practical matter, what appeared good in theory has worked out relatively poorly in practice, mainly because the design produced inadequate competition (see Green and Newbery 1992). Effectively, the nuclear company, co-generators, and France, the main foreign supplier, all offer fixed quantities. As a consequence, the price is set by the two fossil fuel companies, which can manipulate prices by curtailing supply.

Possible solutions to the failure of competition to guarantee good prices include offering a bonus to the low bidder—for example, favoring the low bidder with the lion's share of the production—as a way to encourage more vigorous price competition, and lengthening the terms of the contract, so that the ability of the firms to achieve a cooperative solution is tempered by the desire to grab a large share of the sales for a long period of time. Ultimately, it may be necessary to break the industry into smaller components to ensure more vigorous competition.

As the United States and other countries follow Britain's lead in breaking up electricity monopolies and connecting regional suppliers, there is a need for innovative market designs that induce effective competition among electricity suppliers, while respecting both the physics of electricity transmission and the economics of volatile demand and inflexible supply. The most advanced thinking on the design of electricity markets is outlined in Chao and Wilson (1995).

3. Electronic Treasury Bill Auction

The U.S. government annually auctions around a trillion dollars worth of Treasury bills. Traditionally, these have been sold to roughly forty qualified dealers via a "discriminatory" auction in which the dealers submit bids for various quantities of the Treasury bills. Given the amount of debt to be sold, the high bidders win the auction and pay prices equal to their bids. The auction is referred to as discriminatory because different bidders may pay different prices; indeed, a single bidder may pay different prices for various quantities. For example, a bidder might request $100 million at 5.1 percent, $50 million at 5 percent, and $100 million at 4.9 percent (low interest rates correspond to high prices), and if the market price is 5 percent, the bidder would get the first $100 million at 4.9 percent and the remaining $50 million at 5 percent.

Recently, the Federal Reserve, which conducts the auctions, has begun experimenting with both electronic bidding and uniform price auctions.

Rather than have the bids occur on pieces of paper dropped into a box, they may now be submitted via the Internet. This makes bidding easier and, it is hoped, will attract more potential bidders to the auction. In addition, the government is experimenting with uniform price auctions, in which the price is established by the highest price that will permit sales of all the Treasury bills.

At first glance it would appear that a uniform price auction merely reduces the government's revenue. However, this reasoning fails to account for the changes in bidder behavior. The uniform price auction reduces the risk that a bidder will pay too much for the Treasury bills; the only way a given bidder can pay too much is if a substantial portion of the bidders overestimated the value of the Treasury bills. In contrast, in a discriminatory auction, a given bidder can pay too much by overestimating the value unilaterally. This reduction in risk associated with the uniform price auction results in much more aggressive bidding behavior, a fact confirmed by recent research on the subject. Indeed, the uniform price auction may result in *higher* prices, once the effect on bidder strategies is accounted for, since bidders pay less than their bids.

Uniform price auctions are not much more complicated than traditional supply and demand markets. The distinction is mostly in the electronic submission and calculation of bids, freeing the bidders from the necessity of being physically present in the market.

4. Federal Communication Commission's PCS Auctions

Starting in 1994, the Federal Communications Commission auctioned spectrum for Personal Communication Services (PCS) using a novel auction designed by economic theorists. PCS represents additional spectrum to provide services such as paging, cellular telephony, and perhaps even the provision of movies and other entertainment without wires. The licenses were divided up both in frequency and in geography, resulting in a total of over 2,500 licenses to be offered.

There are two traditional ways of selling such a variety of licenses. The licenses might be sold through a sequence of oral auctions. In such a sale, the licenses might be ordered from largest to smallest, and then sold off one by one in that order using a traditional oral auction. Alternatively, the licenses might be sold simultaneously through sealed-bid auctions. This is the way that offshore oil is sold by the U.S. Department of the Interior.

Both selling methods would present formidable problems for bidders. In general, it is difficult to bid sensibly on any one license without knowing the prices of other licenses, in order to evaluate the possibility of substituting low-priced licenses for expensive licenses. Thus, sequential auctions will tend to make bidding on early licenses difficult and fraught with the possibility of error. Simultaneous sealed-bid designs exacerbate this problem, for one bids on every license "blind," without knowing whether one will win adjacent licenses or not. In both cases the auction is likely to misallocate licenses.

Even in the case of identical licenses, a sequential design can create problems. Perhaps the best example of these problems arose in the 1981 RCA transponder auction, in which seven virtually identical items were auctioned sequentially. As shown in Table 13.1, the prices varied dramatically, with the highest price over 34 percent in excess of the lowest price. The results were ultimately nullified by the FCC, and it took more than a year for the ensuing legal tangles to be sorted out.

Economic theorists designed an alternative auction to eliminate these problems. Called the simultaneous ascending auction, it proceeds in rounds, and the prices are successively raised until no one wants to bid on additional licenses. The effect of these repeated rounds of bidding is that, toward the end of the auction, bidders know the approximate prices of other licenses and therefore can make sensible bidding decisions (early on, it is less important that the decisions reflect precise information about the final prices because the early prices are low).

At the time of writing, the FCC has run three simultaneous ascending auctions. The first involved the sale of ten nationwide paging (or *narrowband*) licenses, with the data from this auction presented in Table 13.2. The first five licenses are identical; the next three are identical to each other but different from the first five; finally, the last two are identical to each other.

Table 13.1 RCA Transponder Auction, November 1981: A Sequential Auction of Similar Items

Order	Winning Bidder	Price Obtained
1	TLC	$14,400,000
2	Billy H. Batts	$14,100,000
3	Warner Amex	$13,700,000
4	RCTV	$13,500,000
5	HBO	$12,500,000
6	Inner City	$10,700,000
7	UTV	$11,200,000
Total		$90,100,000

Table 13.2 Nationwide Narrowband Licenses: Auction Results

Name	Type	Final Bid	Minority Credit	Winner	Round
N-1	50-50	80,000,000	0	Pagenet	37
N-2	50-50	80,000,000	0	Pagenet	37
N-3	50-50	80,000,000	0	McCaw	33
N-4	50-50	80,000,000	0	McCaw	33
N-5	50-50	80,000,000	25%	MTel	37
N-6	50-12	47,001,001	0	AirTouch	24
N-7	50-12	47,505,673	0	BellSouth	25
N-8	50-12	47,500,000	25%	MTel	24
N-10	50-0	37,000,000	0	Pagenet	45
N-11	50-0	38,000,000	25%	Pagemart	46
Total		$671,006,674			

The simultaneous ascending auction did an excellent job in four respects. First, similar items sold for similar prices, with the striking result that the five largest licenses all sold for exactly the same price. Second, bidders were able to aggregate licenses efficiently. There is some advantage to a bidder winning two licenses to win adjoining licenses; when this was possible, it occurred. Third, the auction appeared to be relatively immune to "gaming." Some dramatic "jump bids" were made during the auction, but these bids did not affect final prices with the one exception of Pagemart's jump to $38 million on N-11, which probably resulted in Pagemart paying $1 million more than necessary. That is, insofar as jump bidding affected prices, the jump bids hurt the firms that made them. Thus, the simple strategy of bidding on the licenses you would like to win, until these licenses become too expensive, seemed to work well in the auction. Finally, the prices in the auction were approximately ten times the industry estimates, which probably reflects more on industry estimates than on the realized auction prices.

The second simultaneous ascending auction held by the FCC involved regional licenses. The nation was divided into five regions, and six licenses were offered on each region; these data are summarized in Tables 13.3 and 13.4. Once again, the auction did a terrific job of permitting the aggregation of licenses. In particular, four bidders were able to assemble nationwide coverage through the auction, although this occurred at slightly greater expense than occurred in the nationwide sales. Moreover, attempts at gaming the system apparently failed in a spectacular way. Pagemart's apparent "punishment strategy" involved bidding against anyone who bid on license 1. Consequently, Lisa-Gaye Shearing induced Pagemart to bid against her on the

Table 13.3 Winning Bidders by Region and Spectrum Block

Size (KHz):	50-50	50-50	50-12	50-12	50-12	50-12
Region/ Block	1	2*	3	4	5	6*
Northeast	Pagemart	PCSD	Mobile Media	Advanced Wireless	AirTouch	Lisa-Gaye Shearing
South	"	"	"	"	Insta-Check	"
Midwest	"	"	"	"	Ameritech	"
Central	"	"	"	"	AirTouch	Benbow
West	"	"	"	"	"	"

South license number 5 by bidding on license 1; in the end, Pagemart paid several million dollars to withdraw its bid on the South license 5.

The third simultaneous ascending auction run by the FCC involved much more valuable licenses, with almost fifty times as much spectrum for sale (divided into two equal-sized licenses), divided geographically into fifty-one "major trading areas." Three of these licenses had been allocated already, so that ninety-nine licenses were put up for auction, two in each major trading area except one in New York, Los Angeles, and Washington. The auction raised $7.7 billion dollars for the federal government.

Unlike the paging licenses, it is difficult to assess the efficiency of the large auction. Three bidders were able to produce nearly nationwide coverage by combining their PCS purchases with existing cellular operations. The

Table 13.4 Discounted Final Prices ($ millions) by Region and Spectrum Block

Size (KHz):	50-50	50-50	50-12	50-12	50-12	50-12
Region/License	1	2*	3	4	5	6*
Northeast	17.500	14.850	9.471	8.950	8.675	10.251
South	18.400	18.780	11.800	11.543	8.000	11.262
Midwest	16.810	17.360	9.291	10.057	9.500	10.251
Central	17.340	17.136	8.250	8.791	8.262	10.488
West	22.549	22.800	14.857	14.281	14.281	10.921
Total	92.599	90.931	53.669	53.622	48.718	53.173
Nationwide	80.000	80.000	47.336	47.336	47.336	47.336

bidding is described in more detail in McAfee and McMillan (1996). It will be many years before we know with any degree of certainty whether the auction did a good job of permitting sensible bidding, but at this point the bidders themselves have not complained, no resales have occurred, and the prices were nearly double the amount expected by the government.

FUTURE APPLICATIONS OF ELECTRONIC MARKETS

We consider that decentralized markets, operated via bidding through a computer network, will determine allocations in a significant and growing fraction of economic activity. In this section we explore just a few of the potential future decentralized markets that may be created with new technology.

1. Cable TV Provision

Currently, cable television signals are distributed by companies that own the wires connecting households to the central distribution point. Running wires to houses is almost certainly a natural monopoly, and it would be expensive to create competition by running two sets of cables to every household.

However, it is unnecessary to actually run multiple wires to each household in order to create competition. An alternative is to separate the provision of cable signals from the ownership of the wires. The wires might be owned by a town or city or even at the neighborhood or street block level, which takes bids on the provision of signals. Such a mechanism could allow competition in the provision of cable services, while minimizing the natural monopoly problem.

It may be that competition from satellite-based or terrestrially based wireless services will inject serious competition into the cable TV market, rendering complex bidding schemes unnecessary.

2. Railroad Operation

A fascinating study of Sweden's railroad operation has been conducted by Charles Plott of the California Institute of Technology. The goal of this study is to decentralize the operation of Sweden's railroad system. Decentralization of railways presents formidable problems, and heretofore railways have been run only in an administrative fashion. Some of these problems include the avoidance of crashes, both head-on collisions and faster trains overtaking slower ones, and the efficient routing and timing of train departures. Plott envisions decentralizing the railways using a bidding scheme, where firms can bid for the right to use tracks at various times of the day or night. The bidding scheme permits bundling of bids (or bidding on bundles), so that one can request the use of the track from *A* to *B* bundled with the use of the track from *B* to *C* (for details, see Brewer and Plott 1995). Like the FCC's auction design, Plott's bidding scheme permits revision of bids, which continues until no one wishes to change their bid. As in our discussion of cable TV, Sweden would continue to own the railroad tracks themselves; the right to use the tracks would be decentralized. Plott's study represents the most ambitious attempt to use electronic bidding to decentralize a market that traditionally resisted decentralization.

3. Airline Landing/Takeoff Slots

The rights to use airport gates and runways are valuable at most airports. Currently four U.S. airports auction these rights. A problem with the auctioning of such rights, however, is that the value of the right to take off is highly tied to the right to land somewhere else at a particular time. Thus, if one wins the right to take off from Chicago's O'Hare Airport, one had better win the right to land at an appropriate time at another airport!

Bidding schemes that permit one to bid on the elements of a package, such as that used by the FCC or in Plott's study of Sweden's railways, are essential to the decentralized allocation of airport landing slots. The increasingly high value associated with landing rights and the increased density at major airports make efficient allocation of these rights increasingly important. (Bidding mechanisms for airport landing rights have been investigated by Grether, Issac, and Plott 1989.)

4. Computer Bidders

The ultimate in electronic markets involves computers as the buyers and sellers. Computer scientists at the Xerox Corporation have designed a system in which computers bid against other computers for the use of still other computers' capacity (see Huberman and Hogg 1995). In large computer networks, linking thousands of computers of different types, the assignment of computing tasks to individual computers is highly complex. A good allocation of jobs requires a huge amount of knowledge about the relative urgency of the different jobs and the capacities of the various computers. As a substitute for the expensive and time-consuming process of gathering all this information centrally in order to make an optimal decision, the Xerox team has introduced a scheme in which each computer is given a "budget" and is programmed to bid for time on other computers. Willingness to pay signals a user-computer's urgency of need; and willingness to sell signals how much capacity a computer has available. As a result of this "market," the computer network operates with improved efficiency.

CONCLUSION

An important conclusion to be drawn from the experience with electronic markets is that *details matter*. A striking example occurred in the auction of satellite cable licenses in Australia. The Australians used sealed-bid auctions, in which the high bidder wins and pays his or her bid. In this case there were two licenses, and the opening high bids were $212 and $177 million Australian dollars. No penalty for withdrawals was imposed. Both of the winning bidders withdrew their bids, and the licenses were then allocated to the next-highest bidders, who turned out to be the same firms, with bids of $5 million less! These bidders once again withdrew their bids, and the licenses were awarded to the third-highest bidders, again the same firms. This process continued for the better part of a year, resulting in final prices around $100 million less than the original winning bids. Such a minor detail as the size of the withdrawal penalty ultimately had major significance in the auction outcome.

Details matter, and, as a consequence, a great deal of thought and experimentation will be necessary to decentralize the allocations of goods and services that were previously allocated by administrative procedure. Both economic theory and laboratory experiments using paid participants will play a central role in devising electronic decentralized markets. The value of decentralizing such allocations, and bringing market forces to bear on such goods and services, is probably in the trillions of dollars in efficiency gains, quality improvements, and lowered costs to consumers.

Table 13.5 Australian Auction Outcomes

Initial Winning Bid	Final Price after Withdrawals
A $212,000,000	A $117,000,000
A $177,000,000	A $77,000,000

A desirable feature of decentralized market design is the simplicity of participants' strategies. Although the market design may be complex, the simpler the participants' optimal strategies, the better the market may be expected to function. One of the major flaws of a sequential auction of related items is that, to bid on early items, bidders must forecast the prices of later items. This forecasting is much more complicated, and much more prone to error, than simply observing the prices of other items in the simultaneous ascending auction. Good design of a market should not rely on participants figuring out complex strategies. The best design makes participation simple, which both encourages wide participation and minimizes the likelihood of participant error.

Modern economic theory offers exciting prospects for further innovations in market design. The FCC's spectrum auction was designed using ideas from economic theory. According to *Fortune*, it was "the most dramatic example of game theory's new power. . . . It was a triumph, not only for the FCC and taxpayers, but also for game theory (and game theorists)." As noted in *Forbes*, "Game theory, long an intellectual pastime, came into its own as a business tool." Electronic markets of the sort implemented by the FCC have a wide range of potential private-sector applications.[3] One possible use is by a firm buying interrelated inputs from other firms. Conventional procurement specifies the level of assembly at which components are to be purchased. If instead an electronic market were used, the procuring firm could define the components finely, and have the potential suppliers bid component by component, with the possibility of winning several contracts and so supplying a bundle of components. By the set of components it bid for, each supplier would reveal its economies of scope (a lowered cost of doing two or more activities together rather than separately). Another possible application is in the sale of a multidivisional corporation. An electronic market could allow buyers to bid division by division. The bidders could thereby express their ideas on which parts of the firm fit together and which should be spun off as separate companies or closed down. The uses of electronic markets have just begun.

---

[3] Some applications are currently being explored by Market Design, Inc. (whose principals are Paul Milgrom and Robert Wilson of Stanford University, Peter Cramton of the University of Maryland, together with the authors of this article).

REFERENCES

Brewer, Paul, and Charles R. Plott. "A Binary Conflict Ascending Price (BICAP) Mechanism for the Decentralized Allocation of the Right to Use Railroad Tracks." Mimeo, California Institute of Technology, February 1995.

Chao, Hung-Po, and Robert Wilson. "Multiple-Unit Auctions." Unpublished manuscript, Stanford University, November 1995.

Green, Richard, and David Newbery. "Competition in the British Electricity Spot Market." *Journal of Political Economy* 100 (1992): 929–953.

Grether, David M., Mark R. Issac, and Charles R. Plott. *The Allocation of Scarce Resources: Experimental Economics and the Problem of Allocating Airport Slots.* Boulder, CO: Westview Press, 1989.

Huberman, Bernardo A., and Tad Hogg. "Distributed Computation as an Economic System." *Journal of Economic Perspectives* 9 (1995): 141–152.

McAfee, R. Preston, and John McMillan. "Analyzing the Airwaves Auction." *Journal of Economic Perspectives* 10 (Winter 1996): 159–175.

McMillan, John. "Selling Spectrum Rights." *Journal of Economic Perspectives* 8 (Summer 1994): 145–162.

Milgrom, Paul. "Employment Contracts, Influence Activities, and Efficient Organizational Design." *Journal of Political Economy* 96 (1988): 42–60.

Roth, Alvin E., and Marilda A. Oliveira Sotomayor. "The Evolution of the Labor Market for Medical Interns and Residents: A Case Study in Game Theory." *Journal of Political Economy* 92 (1984): 991–1016.

———. *Two-Sided Matching: A Study in Game-Theoretic Modelling and Analysis.* Cambridge: Cambridge University Press, 1990.

Roth, Alvin E., and Xiaolin Xing. "Jumping the Gun: Imperfections and Institutions Related to the Timing of Market Transactions." *American Economic Review* 84 (September 1994): 992–1044.

Smith, Adam. *An Enquiry into the Nature and Causes of the Wealth of Nations.* Chicago: University of Chicago Press, 1976.

Chapter 14

Intranets: Looking beyond Internal Corporate Web Servers

*Ramnath Chellappa, Anitesh Barua,
and Andrew B. Whinston*

ABSTRACT

In the business world, the popularity of the Internet has been overshadowed by the Intranet phenomenon. A true Intranet should be conceptualized as a secure and reliable enterprise-wide network and associated applications which use Internet technologies and standards. However, this chapter shows that this vision is yet to be realized. Most Intranet implementations today focus primarily on internal corporate World Wide Web servers (Intrawebs) for the purpose of simple document distribution. The full potential of Intranets can be realized only if the diverse management capabilities and functionality available in a Local Area Network (LAN) environment can be replicated at an enterprise-wide level using the Internet platform.

1. INTRODUCTION

While media attention has been focused on the growing popularity of, first, global e-mail communication and then the multimedia World Wide Web (WWW), the use of the Internet has been growing "behind the scenes" at an even greater rate through the spread of "Intranets." We are not referring to thousands of organizations that have registered Internet domain names, Internet Protocol (IP) addresses and Web sites. While these are visible outposts of enterprise networks, millions of other machines on intraorganizational networks are linked via the Internet, but are shielded from the view of unauthorized users from outside. These machines comprise the many Intranets that have been established to serve as enterprise-wide networks. The open platform and the Transmission Control Protocol/Internet Protocol (TCP/IP) of the Internet that connects the machines allow them to function as a cohesive whole despite widely differing hardware platforms, operating systems, and functional uses. An Intranet can be defined as a secure corporate network with rich functional features of Local Area Networks interconnected by the Internet and/or its technologies and applications.

A functional analysis of Intranets reveals that they are predominantly used to implement a company's business protocols. Applications may fulfill a simple mail-routing function or may be part of a complex groupware environment. No matter what their function or degree of sophistication, all enterprise-wide networks must take into account the organization's paramount need to secure its business protocols from outside threats. Far more than with the relatively isolated WWW outposts, Intranets require a high level of security.

Although most so-called Intranets today actually resemble internal Web servers, the shape of things to come is already clear. While LANs enriched stand-alone computers by linking them together, Wide Area Networks (WANs) expanded the potential geographic scope of the LANs. The Internet and its WWW have since elevated the concept of a WAN to new heights. And, in a way, Intranets have brought us full circle, since they are sometimes also referred to as virtual LANs on the Internet and attempt to merge the best of both worlds. As the following brief overview highlights, each stage of the progression in network technology has opened up new opportunities for organizations, which along the way have also had to cope with the technology's limitations.

2. LOCAL AREA NETWORKS

LANs refer to a group of computers physically connected by a cabling medium that enables communication among the machines. Since their introduction only over a decade ago, networks have become virtually indispensable to all but the smallest businesses. Their popularity has been spawned by rapid advances in networking technologies and protocols, as well as the increasing expectation of and need for connectivity.

The backbone of a traditional LAN is its network operating system (NOS), which provides powerful functionality to the computers that have been networked. By using an NOS such as Novell's Netware® or IBM's LAN Manager®, it became possible to allocate resources on the physical network and bring teams of colleagues closer together than ever. For example, a single printer or fax could be used by an entire network of machines located throughout the building, and team members located all over the network could share files from a single machine.

Further development in networks led to the client/server technology that enabled specialized servers, such as database and mail servers, to be accessed by multiple machines on the network. This resulted in even greater efficiency in resource allocation. For instance, instead of maintaining multiple databases within a company, a powerful database server can be set up that will centralize the data. By processing the data on the server, the various client machines throughout the company no longer need to be equipped to handle massive database processing but can instead be used for purely client-side functions with a graphical user interface.

By virtue of their very limited geographic scope, LANs also meet a key requirement for organizational computing—security. And if a company is housed in a single building, a LAN, with its easy management of resources and client/server functionality, would offer an ideal solution to its need for shared resources and applications without any threat of intrusion from the outside. The significance of these advantages are clearly reflected in the popularity of new applications based on networking such as Microsoft's Office. There is no threat of security in using Microsoft Office or, for that matter, most applications based on LANs.

But today's companies are rarely as hermetically sealed off from the world—and the competition it represents—as they once were. Mergers and the need for economies of scale have forced even small businesses to link offices from coast to coast. The need to break down the geographic barriers of LANs is undeniable—hence the spread of WANs in the business world.

3. WIDE AREA NETWORKS

Most WANs used by organizations are proprietary networks specially developed at high cost for specific and often limited purposes. An example of a WAN is the SABRE reservation system's network used by American Airlines. Companies typically lease lines from the phone company to use as the dedicated means of communication between departments that may be on opposite coasts. In addition to making their own organization more cohesive, many large companies use Electronic Data Interchange (EDI) networks to communicate with key suppliers. However, the cost of developing, setting up, and maintaining proprietary WANs is a significant limiting factor. More than the cost of hardware, the inflexibility of these technologies is severely limiting.

As the world turned global in the late eighties, computer networks rushed to keep up. Granted, a company's LAN allows the accounting department to use the marketing department's color printer, while its WAN allows the production department to input its cost-accounting data directly from the plant in Waco to headquarters in Minneapolis through its leased line. But what happens if manufacturing moves to Malaysia? What if the company wants to open a branch in Budapest? Setting up a proprietary WAN based on satellite communication to handle this would be cost-prohibitive for even most large multinational corporations. This is where the Internet—the ultimate WAN—finds its niche in the corporate world.

4. THE INTERNET AND THE WORLD WIDE WEB

While LANs are restricted by their need for physical cabling, the Internet's routers and gateways provide communication from literally anywhere to anywhere else in the world. The Internet consists of interconnected computers, each of which possesses a unique IP number and communicates using TCP/IP suite. At the top level of TCP/IP, numerous other protocols enable specific applications. For a long time, Simple Mail Transfer Protocol (SMTP) remained the predominant protocol for communication, and applications such as list-servers and multiuser mailing lists that required public or private communication were centered around this protocol. Telnet, on the other hand, is used to invoke remote interactive sessions, although it is text-based and lacks the ability to support multimedia.

A new protocol known as HyperText Transfer Protocol (HTTP) serves as the basis for the Internet's multimedia arm—the World Wide Web. Many companies have latched onto the WWW as their shop window to the world, publishing corporate and product information for potential customers surfing the Net to access. These companies are clearly motivated by more than just the wide range of multimedia features and applications the Internet has to offer; the attraction also lies in the sheer number of potential Net customers.

Estimates put the number of Internet users—and hence potential customers—at anywhere from 8 to 10 million. The number of Web servers rose from 130 in June 1992 to 120,000 as of the end of 1995! The Altavista search engine from Digital, on the other hand, claims to index 30 million Web pages from 225,000 servers, a significant number of them in corporations.

Whatever numbers come closer to current reality, it is clear that the Web has already transformed the Internet into a powerful marketing tool. Its multi-media documents with voice, video, images, and text are used both to adver-tise and to inform. It seems like everyone from Hollywood stars to lawyers to staid Fortune 100 companies have established home pages to get their names and faces in front of potential customers. Companies such as Hewlett-Packard, for example, also use the Web to distribute information on the patches to their operating systems. Microsoft allows users to download ex-tensions and updates to their applications and operating system off the Web. And other companies have put working models of products on the Web for users to download and test.

These applications are certainly a welcome sign of the boom in user-driven electronic commerce, but they represent only a fraction of the poten-tial that the Internet and the Web have to offer. Despite the initial difficulties and risks they have had to overcome, there is a far greater "silent majority" who are already using these electronic media for intraorganizational elec-tronic commerce—what we call Intranets or enterprise-wide networks.

5. LINKING THE ENTERPRISE AND THE INTERNET: THE CHALLENGE OF INTEGRATION

Within a single generation of managers, computers and computer networks have changed the way business is conducted. Probably within the next decade Intranets will once again spark fundamental changes. Almost every single business process in an enterprise today involves computing. From ac-counting databases to marketing to manufacturing, every division of a firm is dependent on a wide variety of computers and networks for sharing re-sources and disseminating information. The very persuasiveness, indispens-ability, and diversity of these computers make the implementation of radical changes such as linking disparate networks over the Internet into Intranets a distinct challenge.

Organizational networks today bring to mind the concept of the melting pot. Their heterogeneous architecture is made up of different platforms, op-erating systems, communication protocols, security requirements, and appli-cations accumulated over time—yet they must be forged into a cohesive whole that functions efficiently and seamlessly. This heterogeneity has typi-cally been driven by the applications that different divisions choose for dif-ferent functionality. A company's marketing and sales division, which is concerned with product documentation, would quite naturally prefer a well-established desktop publishing suite. Since suites such as Microsoft Office and Lotus Notes are predominantly available on desktop computers and do not require the computing power of UNIX workstations or mainframes, the marketing and sales departments are likely to adopt PCs as their computing platform. The engineering division, on the other hand, might well require the power of a more expensive UNIX workstation to run VLSI applications or high-performance CAD/CAM applications.

The choice of a particular computing platform also usually influences the LAN operating system and protocols. Typically, machines were interconnected using proprietary network operating systems that also required use of their own proprietary communication protocols. For example, the administrative department of a firm might have a network of PCs connected by Novell's Netware, which uses the communication protocol IPX/SPX. A network of Apple Macintosh computers would use AppleTalk as its communication protocol, while Microsoft networks might use Microsoft DLC or Net-BUI.

Integrating such disparate systems with the Internet started at a very simple level—communication in the form of e-mail. Through a "patchwork" solution, a network interface card (NIC) that was "bound" to Netware's IPX/SPX protocol, for example, was allowed to communicate with the Internet's IP addressing scheme and the TCP/IP suite. Gradually, through new patchwork add-ons, networks were able to access an increasing number of Internet-based applications. Along with this expanded access, however, came a very real threat to an organization's security.

Since e-mail was not a potentially insecure application, particularly given its initial inability to send binary data, few organizations placed much emphasis on implementing firewalls or other security measures. As companies began to expand their use of the Internet to include ftp, Telnet, and most recently the World Wide Web, the dangers were brought home quickly. These applications involved using files on remote machines. This more intimate access could allow a hacker to upload a virus or to breach secure files during the process. There is also a concern that the additional passwords needed to use ftp or Telnet, for example, could be sniffed. The potential security threat posed by Web applications is no different from what ftp and Telnet kind of applications might offer since the packets travel in exactly the same way.

Despite these concerns, the lure of the vast resources and global reach of the Internet has spurred the development of security schemes based on sophisticated encryption techniques that allow companies to safely link up. With this advancement, companies are now moving beyond the simple establishment of Web servers to dispense information to the general public and are setting up Intranets that are able to share documents and data through secure intraorganizational transactions over the Internet. The enterprise-wide network may itself be composed of many LANs. For example, the California division of a company could house three LANs, one for its R&D division, one for its marketing department, and one for its administrative section, while the Malaysian plant may have its own LAN. Regardless of this, if each machine possesses an IP number and can communicate using the TCP/IP suite, effective firewall and encryption configuration can produce a secure Intranet.

6. INTRAWEBS

Taming the Internet for enterprise-wide usage is no simple task. The process of capturing and yet channeling its power is analogous to domesticating a wild animal to suit one's purpose. In moving toward an Intranet, the first step a company often takes is to set up an internal Web site. It is able to use the same technology for internal workgroup collaboration and transactions as for its "external" Web site that advertises to and interfaces with customers, augmented by measures that protect the integrity of private, company-specific information. A comfortable level of security can be achieved by building firewalls around the firm's organizational networks and encrypting data that travels over public gateways and routers. In this way, access is limited to only those machines from within the enterprise-wide network.

As is typical of evolving technologies in general, most aspects of Intranets today are quick-and-dirty solutions rather than well-thought-out, complete implementations. Intranets, or Intrawebs, are today still at the stage where they have adopted Internet capabilities rather than adapting them. A careful analysis of these early-stage Intranets shows that the predominant focus is on the application of Web-associated technologies, with Web browsers being the accepted front ends to information and applications.

Standard Intranet Capabilities Available Today

While there is a lot of excitement about Intranets, most implementations today provide a rather narrow range of capabilities, including e-mail, on-line publishing, on-line searching, and application distribution.

E-mail. Internal electronic mail to employees throughout the enterprise is a very common feature of Intranets. Rather than using proprietary e-mail applications, more and more organizations are adopting standard SMTP-based e-mail systems. These systems do double duty as mail handlers for messages to and from the outside world as well.

On-line publishing. Publishing of corporate and organizational documents is the most common use of Web—and Intraweb—technology today. Corporate documents such as pension plans, annual reports, standard announcements, and newsletters can be accessed, obviating the need to distribute this information in the traditional manner.

On-line searches. Searching for corporate documents, external linkages, and other typical text-based systems such as catalogs, price lists, and product lists fall into this category.

Application distribution. Applications common to a firm such as, say, an Excel macro that would be useful to a group, can be easily downloaded from this central Intraweb site. Updates and version control are easily handled because of central maintenance.

Further Intranet Developments

As barebones Intranets become increasingly popular, new applications are being developed that incorporate even more of the features users enjoy in their LAN technologies. Although they are still rough and require a great amount of tweaking, the following abilities are currently being introduced to Intranet technology:

Groupware-like tools. The WWW, augmented with efficient scripting and development, offers a groupware-like environment that allows for interaction among users. One such tool is the MIS Forum of the University of Texas at Austin's Center for Information Systems Management. In fact, the Web itself has often been popularly referred to as the "poor man's Lotus Notes."

Common user interfaces. Intrawebs can be used as a common interface to many applications. It is predominantly the convergence of technology that is driving users in this direction. For example, it may be more efficient to run a POP Mail service and an NNTP-based news service using one front-end browser for both applications, reducing the number of applications that a user needs to learn.

Wide area database access. The Web and associated technologies offer an excellent and viable front end for wide area database access. This is immediately applicable to Intrawebs as well, which need to access databases distributed across the enterprise network. Using sophisticated security implementations and CGI and Database Interface (DBI) scripting, organizational users can safely access these databases using a Web client.

Platform-independent applications. Tremendous growth and development in the area of new, dynamic programming languages like Java offer a wide range of possibilities for the Intranet setting. In a heterogeneous operating system environment, Java largely eliminates vendor dependence. A single accounting package written in a platform-independent language can be employed throughout the organization whether it is to be run on a UNIX workstation, a PC running Windows 95™, or a Macintosh.

7. MOVING BEYOND THE INTRAWEB: TRUE INTRANETS

As mentioned at the beginning of this chapter, a true Intranet should merge the advantages of the Internet with those of LANs. As we have seen, in may ways this has been accomplished by adopting the functionality of the WWW and applying it to an internal corporate setting. It is now time, however, to move beyond this Intraweb stage. True Intranets should have *all* the functionality of LANs, including the following that Intrawebs do not currently accommodate:

File management. File management simply refers to the ability to add, delete, view, or modify files on different systems. In UNIX environments this is typically accomplished by the use of Network File System (NFS), which allows authenticated users to access file systems on different machines to be mounted on other systems in a transparent fashion. In a Novell–Netware based LAN, clients communicate to the server and set up network "drives." In this way, by using a file manager on any machine on the LAN, a user can manipulate files on any other system. By associating file types with certain applications, files can even be edited seamlessly.

Although the underlying method would need to differ in an Internet setting, the ability to accommodate similar file management function would make Intranets far more robust. If a branch in Malaysia could *safely* browse through and edit files on a computer at company headquarters in California as though it were next door, the geographic barriers to global business interactions would indeed be broken down. Today, such a process is feasible only with a certain amount of complexity. It may involve "ftp"-ing the document, editing it, and possibly uploading it to the original server again.

Print services. Printing is one of the resources that most commonly needs to be shared among network users. In a LAN, printers can be connected to print servers that can be accessed by any client machine on the network. At this point there is still no easy way for a company's vice president in Kuala Lumpur to send his presentation slides to the printer in the company's San Jose office.

Application sharing. This is one of the key aspects of the LANs. Today, most networks use a network version of an application rather than a standalone; that is, the application is installed on a server and thus clients do not need to posses a copy. This setup has significant advantages not only in licensing but also in centralized management and version control. Since the setup is centralized, it is possible for organizations to keep track of specialized macros, additions, and so on, that are made to its applications. This involves installing applications such as a Microsoft Office suite on a machine designated as the application server; all client machines would invoke the application of the server, and thus individual client-side installations would not be required.

Today there is really no safe way of sharing applications on the Internet. For example, you cannot have an application installed in San Jose that can be invoked by a machine in Malaysia in a *secure* fashion.

While these are just three examples of missing components in an Intranet suite, there are many more functions and features that are needed before Intrawebs can truly be called Intranets. Companies such as Netscape have been moving in the right direction in their vision of an open network. Web browsers that can act as effective front ends to many applications that earlier required individual tools are proof of this. Applications such as those involving file transfer, document browsing, e-mail, and news reading can all be accomplished today by Netscape's Navigator.

A network today is defined not by its hardware but by the range of applications it offers and its NOS. For example, a network is more commonly referred to as a Netware network or Microsoft network rather than as a token ring or ethernet. Similarly, the popularity of Intranets would be reflected in the suite of applications they offer. In developing future tools, it may be wise to think carefully about how many features to bundle into any one tool. While it is advantageous to use a Web client for multiple purposes, it may not be prudent to overburden one application to handle all functionality. It may also be more prudent not to bundle security with file servers but rather to maintain a separate security server that authenticates requests to and from the file server and other servers on the Intranet. In this way clients such as the browers will have the minimum required knowledge of security.

8. CONCLUSION

The movement of organizational networks toward Internet-based technologies has clearly reached the point where it is unstoppable. It has also reached the point where it has become necessary to rethink the meaning and technology of Intranets. While it is certainly a welcome move on the part of organizations to use Intrawebs as an efficient means of information dissemination, it is also necessary for them to rethink their entire networking strategy if they want to move away from vendor dependence. This is the distinct trend of the future, and tools are already being developed to make this possible.

Chapter 15

Electronic Publishing versus Publishing Electronically

Ramnath Chellappa, Anitesh Barua, Jennifer Oetzel, and Andrew B. Whinston

ABSTRACT

The Internet offers an unlimited potential for electronic publishing. Publishing houses have seized this opportunity with numerous on-line magazines and journals. This chapter shows that electronic publishing has focused on the Internet primarily as a medium of distribution, and has not reengineered the publishing process itself. To take full advantage of the capabilities that the Internet provides, publishers must rethink the roles of readers and contributors. The power of incentives and reward systems must also be harnessed to achieve more dynamic interaction between readers, authors, and editors than in paper-based publications. Further, the credibility and standing of an on-line journal and its publications can be enhanced through dynamic feedback regarding the reputation and status of its readership. Internet applications must be developed to allow publishers to incorporate these factors into the electronic publishing process. *EC World*, an on-line journal in the field of electronic commerce, is an example of a publishing process that incorpates some of these ideas.

INTRODUCTION

Over the past few years, the Internet and its associated technologies have proliferated exponentially. While there is ongoing debate about the Internet's impact and role in business and society at large, it has not prevented firms and individual users alike from using the Internet, particularly the World Wide Web, to fulfill a variety of objectives. One such usage has been in the area of electronic publishing. It has been argued that rather than the telephone, cable or broadcast TV is the best model for the Web publishing. However, most models of publishing today on the Web do not fully exploit the potential of the medium.

In this chapter, we emphasize the need to reengineer the model of publishing in traditional media to suit the Web. The concept of publishing is evolving rapidly with the advent of digital media and has taken a new turn in the form of on-line electronic journals. Journals and magazines on the Internet (although they could be on private networks as well) that offer their content on-line to readers are referred to as *electronic journals*. At the least, the multimedia potential of the Web allows for printing of pictures and graphics as in the case of printing on paper. In addition, many of these on-line journals also contain "live objects," for example, a live link to another document, an audio clip, or maybe even digital video. Some journals also offer interactivity in the form of on-line forums, while a few allow for their readers to customize the content and its presentation. However, many of these appear to simply use the paradigm of publishing in the traditional sense and to transfer it to the Web. The issues that arise in a reengineered electronic publishing environment could be vastly different, and could potentially alter the way we think about publishing today.

PUBLISHING ON THE WEB

Why are so many firms rushing to publish on the Web? There are many obvious incentives for publishers to use the Web as the medium of distribution. Simply put, by virtue of its ease of creation and the span of distribution, the digital medium is a low-cost and potentially high-revenue system. The cost of establishing on-line journals is extremely low, particularly if the firm maintaining it is also a traditional publisher. This means there is no need for a separate information-gathering staff; since most publishing is digital to begin with, the cost of conversion to a Web format is also extremely low. Also, there is literally no limit to the size or amount of content that can be offered. Therefore, a myriad of traditional publishing houses can be seen offering their fare on the Web today.

The potential for generating revenues through advertising on the Web is lucrative. For example, Time Warner charges an average of $30,000 for three months of advertising on its electronic versions of *Time, Life, Sports*

Illustrated, People, and *Entertainment Weekly.* Some companies also charge users a fee to browse through their site.

The other aspects of the Web that are appealing to on-line publishers are its flexibility, ease of use, interactivity, archival capabilities, and global scope. On-line publishers have also discovered interesting aspects about their readers. For example, when *Elle* (a magazine whose print readership consists primarily of young women) brought its fashion pages on the Web, it found that the on-line version of *Elle* was attracting a predominantly male readership. While this was not the intended target to begin with, *Elle* refocused its advertising to target men by supplementing cosmetic and dress-shop advertising with ads for car dealerships. Apparently male readers were interested in downloading pictures of models! Whatever the reason, this reflects a possibility of change in the target readership and therefore a change in associated business practice.

BusinessWeek has taken advantage of the electronic format to publish stories that did not make it to print publication for one reason or another. The electronic format offers publishers a forum for all types of articles, not just those that target the widest audience or generate the largest profits. The fact that there is virtually a zero print cost associated with on-line publishing and potentially unlimited space enables magazines to offer content and cater to a variety of readership.

A survey of available electronic publishing activity shows a dramatic change in the profile of the publishers. The large publishing houses are not the only ones offering electronic magazines; in fact, it is the small and new publishing houses that have been creating ripples by offering very selective information. Just like a newsgroup for nearly every subject on the face of the planet, today there is "something-line" for every area. As of February 25, 1996, there were reported to be 162 newspapers with electronic pages on the Web, triple the number in 1994 (Interactive Newspapers '96 Conference, February 25, 1996), and self-dubbed E-zine archivist John Labovitz calculates that there are at least 1,000 homemade publications on-line. In fact, surveys suggest that half of the busiest sites on the Web are from magazine publishers.

WHY DO READERS NEED THE ELECTRONIC FORMAT?

The obvious question from the perspective of a reader of a newspaper or magazine is "So, why would I want to read something off a computer?" After all, one cannot snuggle up in bed with the computer (yet!) or read an E-zine on one's bus or train ride to work (although this is nearing reality).

Despite these limitations, readers are seeing a great many advantages of subscribing to electronic publications. One of the key reasons appears to be the fascinating format of the hypertext document along with the interactivity of the Web. For example, a reader browsing through the election results in Russia could follow a hyperlink to read about each candidate and possibly even view a speech by the candidate. While it is possible to include most of the information even in a printed form, it would be a futile effort to convert a weekly or monthly magazine to an encyclopedia. Some information is time-independent and may need to be referenced while the reader browses through time-dependent articles. The archival capability of the Web comes out an obvious winner in this area.

Another direction in which E-zines are moving is toward customization of news and information for the reader. Today, with sophisticated programs and software, users can customize what they wish to see. By capturing user profiles, publishers are able to channel information to users according to their requirements. For example, there are many who never read the sports section of a newspaper but may be very interested in financial markets. So a filtered/customized edition of the *New York Times* or the *Austin-American Statesman* can be created on the fly to serve this reader without even a mention of baseball or basketball. However, there may be many who will claim that such focused presentation leads to the loss of serendipity, that is, the possibility of a reader "chancing" on certain information items.

A REENGINEERED VIEW OF PUBLISHING

While the preceding scenarios describe the status of on-line publishing today, they tend to reflect only the power of the medium in terms of its archival and distribution capabilities. Publishing electronically is not the same as electronic publishing. Electronic publishing should reflect not only the electronic version of the material to be published but also a redesigned process of publishing. Reengineered publishing should help enhance the roles of readers and contributors, facilitate the dynamic creation and refinement of knowledge, and enable the integration of information and ideas from diverse but complementary fields. In order to achieve these objectives, electronic publishing must harness the power of incentives and reputation effects. For example, reward mechanisms explicitly aimed at stimulating readers and contributors to provide high-quality inputs need to be incorporated in the electronic publishing model. This incentive-enriched publishing process is enabled by technologies that support a higher level of interaction among various participants.

To illustrate these issues in some detail, we focus on publishing in scientific disciplines. Electronic publishing can not only lead to improved knowledge dissemination but can also be used to create new knowledge. Such knowledge can be made valuable through successive refinement and longitudinal argument based interactions between authors, readers, and other experts. To better understand this paradigm, it might be helpful to analyze the targeted readership or electronic communities for which these on-line magazines are published.

How do we rethink communities in an electronic world? The primary objective of a reader in a scientific discipline is sharing and acquiring knowledge in his or her field of interest. Therefore, the role of a learner/contributor could switch often, depending upon the context. These communities are typically created around products, companies, and general areas of interest. For example, there are many on-line magazines on the Web today that focus specifically on Microsoft's products. While magazines catering to these special interest groups can follow the traditional mode of collecting, editing, and publishing information, they can also make use of the fact that they can actually receive information from their readers, some of whom may be experts in the said area.

However, in trying to obtain such information or, in effect, to create new knowledge, many new factors need to be taken into account. For example, consider the incentive for people to contribute. Is there any financial incentive for contributing, or is there a certain prestige associated with publishing or contributing to a particular journal? A fresh approach to designing electronic publishing processes would require that some kind of incentive mechanism be built into the system to encourage readers to become active participants. Micropayments constitute one possible reward scheme that is relatively simple to support with existing technologies.

Micropayments usually refer to small monetary transactions on the network. For example, as an incentive to an individual to contribute to a discussion, an electronic journal could offer a small sum (e.g., one dollar) per contribution along with subsequent payments contingent on the extent to which it stimulates further interactions. The notion of micropayments in this case is not to send a check for one dollar to the contributor; rather, it can be seen as a point system, where the system keeps track of each person's points and the user possibly can redeem them later for free subscriptions or products. Incentives need not be all financial; in fact, social rewards in the form of recognizing contribution (e.g., "contributor of the month") can be equally effective in stimulating quality participation.

Traditional publishing models usually do not take into account the overlap of communities and coalitions between communities they serve. Usually a journal addresses a particular readership domain, while there may be many communities whose interests span more than one common domain. It is certainly not practical to print a customized version for each of these domains; however, electronic publishing can allow for the convergence of these communities. Therefore, the system should allow for a greater knowledge of the users and their profiles to mass-customize for such communities.

Since the role of a reader would be significantly empowered in our vision of an electronic publishing environment, the need to add new features and functions such as on-line voting may assume greater relevance. Such capabilities not only allow for the users to influence the nature of material published but also shed light on the views and opinions of peers and experts in their domain. It is not difficult to conjecture how such a process might lead to a higher stature for a journal via reputation effects. For example, if a certain reader or expert holds a reputation in a certain field, and if he or she endorses a certain article, the piece is likely to enjoy greater credibility. Similarly, by validating certain articles or pieces of information through voting and other processes, the authors will be able to improve their standing within the electronic community.

Electronic publishing technologies also have the potential to get prominent personalities in a readership base more involved in the knowledge creation process. Highlighting the stature of its readership, an electronic journal can differentiate itself by adding to the reputation its contributors and its readers.

While the preceding constitute some factors that need to be rethought for a new model of publishing, it is still necessary to incorporate them in a systematic manner. One way of accomplishing this involves the adoption of a business approach to publishing. Such a perspective recognizes that electronic publishing can be described as a set of processes similar to electronic commerce activities in a networked organization. It calls for a shift of focus by traditional publishing houses from the mode of distribution to reshaping interactions among various constituents of the process. The next section describes the case of *EC World*, an on-line electronic journal that attempts to capture some of the processes.

EC WORLD—A FORUM FOR THE 21ST CENTURY

*EC World - A Forum for the 21st Century** is the first on-line electronic journal established exclusively for the domain of electronic commerce. *EC World* is an entirely Web-based journal built on Internet protocols and relational database management systems (RDBMS) technology. While the primary objective of *EC World* is to provide a platform for dissemination and creation

* Please see URL:http://ecworld.utexas.edu/.

of knowledge in the area of electronic commerce, from an administrative perspective it has been structured along the model of a networked organization. There are two main facets to *EC World*, one based on informal collaboration between the relevant actors (readers, authors, and reviewers) and the other a completely formal process for article submission and review. The former takes place within the public Internet domain, while the latter is modeled as a workflow and supported over an Intranet setting to satisfy confidentiality requirements.

The informal collaboration is an example of a special interest group forum where readers post questions, comments, counterarguments about specific issues in electronic commerce such as Electronic Data Interchange (EDI), on-line security, payment systems, and so on. All users are required to register, while there is a guest account for users who just wish to browse the journal contents. The formal aspect of *EC World* is the article submission process, where a prospective author creates a preformatted file in HyperText Markup Language (HTML) and submits it on-line to the journal. During submission the author is required to indicate areas of interest that closely match the thrust of the article. Based on the author's selection, a subset of reviewers (who are members of the advisory board and have preregistered themselves as having expertise in certain areas within electronic commerce) are automatically chosen and notified of the submission. Upon receipt of notification, the reviewers are expected to connect on-line to a private repository of the journal (which represents an Intranet setting) in order to review the article.

For increased efficiency of article handling, the system automatically appends the reviewer's comments and recommendations to the submitted article. Based on the perceived need to avoid a situation where one reviewer is influenced and biased a priori by other reviewer's comments, the system hides the latter from a reviewer's view. In some circumstances, however, the review process may require changes in its workflow, and the technology base of *EC World* is well equipped to accommodate variations in the workflow components. Once three reviewers have reviewed an article, the system notifies the administrators of *EC World* of the result, and the article is either accepted, sent to the author for suggested revisions, or rejected.

CONCLUSIONS

While electronic journals abound in the Web today, in order to harness the full potential of electronic publishing we need to rethink the model of publishing itself. We suggest that a reengineered publishing model would involve a greater role of users and contributors in the publishing process. To implement such a model, many issues such as the changing roles of the reader and contributor, dynamic and new knowledge creation, and the integration of time-dependent and time-independent information need to be addressed.

Further, incentives and reputation effects can play a major role as enablers of these new objectives. Thus, to benefit significantly from this reengineered view, a business analysis of processes and subprocesses involved in electronic publishing is required. One way of conducting such an analysis is to model the electronic publishing process as a set of electronic commerce activities similar to those in a networked organization. Through this approach it is possible to capture various aspects of this reengineered publishing process and thus employ means and create incentive schemes to make them more efficient.

Index